Understanding, Nurturing and Working Effectively with Vulnerable Children in Schools

In times of increasing pressure on schools and teachers, it is essential that teachers are equipped to understand the emotional and relational factors in learning and teaching. Vulnerable and disaffected children need understanding and nurturing rather than reactive management, which can easily exacerbate their difficulties, leaving them unheard and defensive, and even undermine teacher confidence and effectiveness.

Understanding, Nurturing and Working Effectively with Vulnerable Children in Schools offers a comprehensive and accessible exploration of the difficulties faced by teachers and schools from at-risk and disaffected children, including repeated trauma and insecure attachment patterns. The book describes how a thoughtful 'relationship-based' approach can both alleviate such difficulties and offer a second-chance attachment experience, enabling students to discover that it might be safe to let down their all-consuming defences a little; thus freeing them to begin to learn. It offers:

- practical suggestions in note form – making them easy to use, refer to and assimilate;
- numerous case examples and teacher-friendly theoretical background material;
- a wealth of ideas for ways forward, including differentiated responses to children in the light of their particular patterns, developmental stages and unmet needs.

Written from extensive professional experience, this is an essential handbook and resource book for trainers, schools, teachers and school staff, and also for educational psychologists and those in children's services working with vulnerable children in pre- and primary schools, as well as those in special schools and units.

Angela Greenwood is an educational psychotherapist with many years' experience training and supervising staff and working therapeutically with children in domestic abuse, pupil referral units, mainstream settings and in private practice. She co-facilitated the local Nurture Network, and the Safe to Learn course for school staff.

'This book is timely! Positive relationships are at the heart of all good teaching and learning; they allow us to reach out to our learners, to understand them, form strong connections and create the learning environment they need to flourish. Angela draws on her professional expertise and extensive experience to give clear explanations, examples and pertinent case studies, all grounded in relevant theory, which enlighten those who have important work to do in supporting our most vulnerable learners; children who require especially fine and considered attunement from the adults who work with them. As a teacher educator I consider this to be an important book to deepen understanding of the issues in relation to attachment while providing a wealth of material to use with our student teachers.'
　　　　　　　　– Rosie Moore, senior lecturer, School of Education, University of Brighton

'In light of the ongoing debate around exclusions and the increase in mental health issues, the release of this book is extremely timely. It will help professionals to reframe their understanding of behaviour and what children and young people might be communicating through it. The book is grounded in accessible theory with illustrative examples showing how these relate to practice. In addition, Angela Greenwood provides readers with realistic and effective strategies to help them engage with and support the children and young people in their care.'
　　　　　　　　– Michael Surr, education development officer and editor of *nasen Connect*,
　　　　　　　　nasen (National Association of Special Educational Needs)

'Angela Greenwood has captured here, in one volume, all the most compelling and salient psycho-dynamically informed approaches and strategies for supporting children and young people in education settings. This work is replete with examples of how attachment theory and associated perspectives may inform how teachers, learning support assistants and other educational professionals can provide the optimal conditions for children to feel safe to learn, and to flourish. This book will, no doubt, make a significant impact on school staff, school systems, organisational structures within education, and, most vitally, on the children and families they serve.'
　　　　　　　　– Nicole Schnackenberg, educational psychologist and author of *False Bodies, True Selves: Moving Beyond Appearance-Focused Identity Struggles and Returning to the True Self*

'This book is a summary of what all teachers should understand and practice if we are to help all children to learn. It describes the implications of early social and emotional childhood experience for later behaviour and responses in the classroom and relates this to teaching practice and delivery. An essential read for all education staff.'
　　　　　　　　– Heather Geddes, educational psychotherapist and author of
　　　　　　　　Attachment in the Classroom

Understanding, Nurturing and Working Effectively with Vulnerable Children in Schools

'Why Can't You Hear Me?'

ANGELA GREENWOOD

Routledge
Taylor & Francis Group

LONDON AND NEW YORK

First published 2020
by Routledge
2 Park Square, Milton Park, Abingdon, Oxon OX14 4RN

and by Routledge
52 Vanderbilt Avenue, New York, NY 10017

Routledge is an imprint of the Taylor & Francis Group, an informa business

British Library Cataloguing-in-Publication Data
A catalogue record for this book is available from the British Library

Library of Congress Cataloging-in-Publication Data
A catalog record has been requested for this book

ISBN: 978-0-367-02544-1 (hbk)
ISBN: 978-0-367-02546-5 (pbk)
ISBN: 978-0-429-02525-9 (ebk)

Typeset in Dante and Avenir
by Swales & Willis Ltd, Exeter, Devon, UK

Visit the eResources: www.routledge.com/9780367025465

MIX
Paper from
responsible sources
FSC
www.fsc.org
FSC™ C013985

Printed in the United Kingdom
by Henry Ling Limited

I would like to dedicate this book to all the children I have worked with over the years and from whom I have learnt such a lot and gained such valuable experience.

Thank you.

More than 20 years have passed now and I have lost touch with you all; but as the years go on I realise more and more what you have given me – including the memories enclosed in your anonymised stories and artwork, some of which I have included in these pages to bring the text alive and 'ground the thinking'. If I haven't been able to contact you about this I thank you now, and wish you well.

I will always remember you.

Angela

Contents

Boxes

Case studies

Acknowledgements

So many people have contributed to this book, sometimes in ways they are not even aware of, and I want to acknowledge and thank them all. Some are more obvious, like through case discussions and verbal contributions, photography and editing suggestions, and some much more foundational like facilitating my career path and learning, to the point where I feel I have something important to give and share from experience.

Steve Decker set me on the path many years ago by alerting me to the discipline of educational therapy, which was exactly right for my journey ahead. By chance I met him again recently and he made some very helpful editing suggestions. Thank you Steve.

The Caspari Foundation (educational psychotherapy professional and training body – www.caspari.org.uk) gave me a solid and very relevant training and supervisory support for which I am profoundly grateful. Educational psychotherapists Gill Morton, my first supervisor, and Heather Geddes, my more recent supervisor and mentor, are but two from a long line of professionals from whom I have learned so much. Thanks also to the current staff and psychotherapists from Caspari like Luke and Lynsey, who continue to enhance my understanding through engaging cutting-edge speakers and conversations.

And thank you Heather for your introductions to Rosie Moore (inclusion lead on the University of Brighton's teacher training course) and also Anna Brookes (head of East Sussex Virtual School for children in care), which came at precisely the right time to support my proposal! And Helen – thank you for all your productive networking!

Heather's book *Attachment and the School Child*, which many readers may know, has been particularly influential. Richard Bowlby's talks and DVDs on attachment also contributed to my knowledge and trainings. Thank you both.

A special thank you to Professor Ron Best, and to author and educational psychologist Nicole Schnackenberg who so very warmly and enthusiastically encouraged me to 'go for publication' because as Nicole said, 'This book is so important. It needs to be "out there".' I'll help you get a publisher.'

Tina Axup has also been a very significant influence, both in facilitating wonderful career opportunities and in our joint (and often voluntary) support group and training work – leading inadvertently to the experiences that have culminated in the book. Thank you Tina. And thanks also to all the Safe to Learn (STL) team, especially Dr Louise Marshall and Sorcha Ennis who enhanced my knowledge of neuroscience. Long may STL thrive in its various manifestations!

On the technical side I am hugely grateful to Andrew J. Haines and Abbie Greenwood for their photography and Photoshop skills, time and ever-available willingness. Thank you both.

Bella I can't thank enough. Her capacity to really 'live and talk the talk' and her generosity in sharing are unrivalled. She knows how grateful I am, and I think it is mutual. Thank you Bella.

Pauline, Sally, Richard, Sarah, Phil, Diana, Jensine and Helen deserve special thanks for their generous sharing, which led to the vivid and evocative case studies.

And finally all the friends and colleagues who so kindly gave their time, knowledge and skill in editorial support and recommendations, including Nicole, Steve, Ron and Heather, as well as Mary, Diana, Chrissie, Chris, Margarete and Sonja.

Last but not least I want to thank my ever-encouraging family, especially my husband Dave who has patiently endured and supported my busy preoccupations at times over the past year and my daughter Zoe who has been so helpful with the PowerPoints. Thank you with all my heart.

Foreword

Children carry with them into school a wide range of responses to learning, from excitement and engagement to total rejection of any new information and knowledge, and even of teachers. Schools can be severely challenged by the hard to teach pupil, affecting measured outcomes as well as the well-being of teaching staff.

This book seeks to address the difficulties that such children present in the classroom in terms of their learning and behaviour by enhancing the awareness and understanding of school staff.

Learning presents challenges for everyone. In the early years these include significant separation from the home environment, engagement with unfamiliar adults, tolerating not knowing and engagement with a peer group. These experiences can be exciting but also challenging for those with limited capacities to face uncertainties. They can trigger responses in the child affecting their behaviour and their capacity to engage in learning.

The author seeks to inform our understanding of the issues affecting children in school who fail to learn, and those who have puzzling and disturbing behaviours and disrupt lessons for others. She brings extensive experience of work with individual children, parents, teachers and whole school staff. It is informed by her training (with the Caspari Foundation – www.caspari.org) in educational psychotherapy, and so deals with the unconscious as well as the overt issues affecting children's behaviour and learning in school. Such issues can undermine both vulnerable children and their teachers; but if understood and responded to thoughtfully, they can become an avenue for change and growth.

Achieving in school is a significant aspect of our development in terms of acquiring knowledge, social interaction and engagement with others and later involvement in work and the community. Failure to achieve in the school system has implications for the well-being of individuals and for society as a whole. It can reflect poor or even abusive home environments and lead to mental health issues affecting behaviour, employability and social interaction later on. Mental health is a critical issue for every society today. Broken relationships and families, self-harm, aggressive responses and offending are just the tip of the iceberg. Children struggle with a wide spectrum of difficulties. Society responds with psychological treatments and medication but it can also often be punitive and exacerbate the problems.

However in terms of intervention, in my experience as a teacher and an educational psychotherapist, the place where vulnerability can be most easily identified and nurtured is in the early school years. All children in our society pass through the education system from around age 4, and in this setting they are involved on a daily basis with education staff, teachers and support workers. The relationships and the secure base that early years staff create with their children can make a real difference to learning, as well as playing a significant part in their later engagement in work and society.

The vulnerability of children in terms of behaviour and learning is explored and discussed, including within the well-researched framework of attachment theory – which presents the early social and emotional development of children within the context of relationships with parents – and thence with other significant adults in school. This has implications for the child's capacity to cope with challenges and uncertainties, implications for resilience and implications for engagement and involvement with the learning task and with others. The three insecure attachment patterns (identified by attachment theory research) in relation to pupil responses to the teacher and to the learning task are described in detail, along with interventions that can support children's learning in each case.

A particularly strong aspect of the content is the way understanding is directly linked to intervention throughout the book, by reflecting on what is happening rather than just reacting to a behaviour. Thus the particular response of teaching staff to a child's behaviour is linked to thinking and understanding their attachment pattern and the child in detail, and to talking it through with others.

The content relates to children, to teachers and to the whole school, so it supports practice across the system of education, making a valuable contribution to our understanding, and to our maximising of the school system within society. It also emphasises the importance of attachment-based training and support for teachers and for school staff, which is essential in providing appropriate responses and interventions for the children who are so hard to teach and reach. I recommend this book to all involved in education practice.

Dr Heather Geddes
Teachers Cert, MA, PhD, educational psychotherapist
Author of *Attachment in the Classroom* (2006)

Preface

Understanding and Working More Effectively with Vulnerable Children in Schools is intended as a handbook for trainers, schools, teachers and school staff and also for educational psychologists and those in children's services working with vulnerable children. This is because it is intended to be both:

- an aid to understanding children and relationships, including the sometimes puzzling and difficult dynamics that can develop between staff and vulnerable children/students, or even between staff in relation to such children;
- as well as a handbook and reference book for staff, and a resource for training.

The book is particularly oriented towards primary schools and staff, although early years and secondary staff and other child workers may also find the thinking helpful with their vulnerable young people. Some of the thinking may also be helpful for those working with autistic children, although it does not specifically address their needs and difficulties, which are often rather different.

In these times of increasing pressure and stress many classes, especially in inner-city schools, have a small number of students who just can't learn and respond to good teaching. They can cause huge anxieties for staff. Their behaviour disrupts relationships and the learning of others – sometimes stretching the capacities of the whole school.

All teachers need to know how to understand and work with their more vulnerable and learning-resistant children. Such understanding, and the timely and conscious use of the significant relationships that occur naturally in school, will benefit everyone. Empathy and thoughtfulness will be evoked in all children when they see the more vulnerable ones being cared for and responded to in a firm and thoughtful way. Teachers will benefit too, as the description of a 'nurturing school' illustrates so vividly in the final chapter.

The book will be particularly useful for those working with children with attachment and behavioural difficulties, children in pupil referral units, nurture bases and special schools for children with emotional and behavioural difficulties. It may also be helpful for social care staff working with children, children's homes staff and foster and adoptive parents and agencies.

It will also be useful for educational psychologists, SENCOs and other professionals writing reports in relation to their work with very vulnerable children.

It has many suggestions based on detailed understanding of children's particular difficulties, which may be useful for recommendations.

It is also intended to support those delivering courses on the subject matter. The book includes course notes and practical suggestions in note form – making them easy to use, refer to and assimilate, as well as plenty of teacher-friendly theoretical background material and many case examples. Although the content of all the chapters are interrelated and there is much cross-referencing, in many ways the chapters are designed to 'stand alone' and could be used as complete trainings on their own. This does lead, however, to some repetition in order to facilitate sense and coherence in the chapters.

I hope that the book will become part of initial teacher training as well as 'in-service training' courses. I feel that to include such understanding, thinking and collaborative working in teacher training is imperative in these pressured times, and I welcome the work of the Consortium for Emotional Well-Being in Schools (CEWBS), whose House of Commons Paper 1515 – 'Attracting, Training and Retaining the Best Teachers', speaks to this end.

Learning from experience

This book arose out of my experience:

- offering training and clinical supervision in schools and privately – including at a pupil referral unit;
- working with teachers, school staff, foster and adoptive agencies and parents, around issues and concerns relating to their most troubled pupils and children;
- working as an educational psychotherapist with the most vulnerable and disturbed children in a Women's Aid setting, privately, and in schools; and
- facilitating and sharing in a local nurture staff support group.

In my work at the pupil referral unit I operated from a psychodynamic, attachment and a developmentally nurturing perspective – a theoretical orientation that everyone and particularly the leadership at the unit overtly subscribed to.

Such a theoretical orientation involved understanding behaviour as communication and the provision of an emotionally containing and secure base for both the very vulnerable and damaged students, and for the staff who worked there. It involved understanding the role of attachment in behaviour and learning, and enabling staff to realise their significant opportunity to offer the students in their care a second-chance experience of a secure attachment relationship. Our experience was that as the students began to be able to trust the staff and the reliable resilient setting, they could start to develop a 'secure base' in school. They could start to discover it was safe to let down their all-consuming defences a little, which slowly freed them to begin to learn.

For the younger and most damaged children we operated a classical nurture base with opportunities for regression and a family-type atmosphere, which enabled them to risk dependent relationships and move slowly towards internalising their *own* capacities for learning and managing. Empathically and tentatively putting their apparent feelings into words (in small doses – as they were open to it) moved them slowly in the direction of being able first to *know* what they were feeling, and gradually to become able to *name* the feelings themselves and even to *notice* feelings in *others*.

In the whole unit we observed at first hand how this attuned predictable relationship-based approach eased their anxieties, reduced their outbursts and enabled them to relax enough to begin to learn. The frequency with which children needed 'holding', for example, and also their exclusions from school, reduced considerably.

So from this and other mainstream school experiences, it became clear to me that this psychodynamic and attachment-based way of thinking, understanding and responding could bear fruit with children and classes, with teachers too and more recently with whole schools. I became increasingly aware that school staff in all settings need this knowledge.

The opportunity for teachers and school staff

The good news for teachers and schools is that whatever has developed already in a child or young person, if they are given a secure nurturing environment, and significant, attuned, thoughtful and consistent attachment relationships, even vulnerable or 'disturbed' children can change and grow, and already formed dysfunctional patterns can be eased and replaced, or at least overlaid, with functional ones. It may not be easy and it will take time; but it's possible.

In 2008 I started offering training in this understanding and thinking to teachers, teaching assistants (TAs),[1] managers and other childcare workers: trainings that included case discussion and reflection exercises, as well as helpful ways of thinking and responding.

A recent training experience was to write and present (together with two other professionals) a nine session Safe to Learn course for teachers in the borough, which was repeated every term for three years (until the funding ran out).[2] It was very well received and attended, and when it ended I felt strongly that it was important to share the thinking more generally – so schools and training institutions could have access to it. Hence the book!

Of course teachers are not social workers, but the relationships they form with their students make all the difference. Teaching and learning relationships will happen anyway and enhance the child's wish to learn – or interfere with it; and indeed enhance or interfere with the teacher's capacity to teach both particular students and sometimes the whole class. We all know from experience how we learn best from people we like and admire. Teaching and learning relationships matter. Research also shows that teacher–pupil relationships make a difference to academic success.[3]

An important aim of the book then is to help school staff develop a deeper and more detailed understanding of these children and the dynamics they can precipitate around them, in order to foster their thinking and nurturing capacity and facilitate their thoughtful empathic responsiveness in tough situations. Through looking more deeply into their difficulties, I hope to show that it is possible to understand that in a profound sense and in the heat of the moment some children *just can't help* the way they react. They need help – a *first-hand experience* of a different kind. This is where the amazing opportunity of schools and school staff comes in. School staff who see the children every day of the school year necessarily make significant relationships with their students – 'for better or worse'. What I am really describing is a *relationship-based approach* to both understanding and working successfully with vulnerable children.

Although all teachers need and hope to develop good working relationships with their students as a foundation for teaching and learning, this more conscious relationship-based way of thinking and working is rather different. My aim is to give teachers and school staff involved with the more vulnerable and 'damaged' children in our society a more nurturing way of working and added understanding and thinking capacities, including the ability to draw on their innate caring capacities as and when children need it.

The book ends with a chapter on a very successful nurturing school, where this thoughtful and relationship-based way of working is integrated into the whole school, developing both the knowledge, reflectiveness and confidence of teachers and staff, and the thoughtful leadership of managers (including their choice of staff) in relation to vulnerable and disturbing children.

Notes

1 TAs (teacher assistants), also sometimes called LSAs (learning-support assistants), both support individuals and groups of children in school.
2 Appendix 5 gives the course outline, and a version of Safe to Learn is available via the eResources for the book at www.routledge.com/9780367025465.
3 J. L. Spilt, H. M. Y. Koomen, J. T. Thijs and A. van der Leij, 'Supporting Teachers' Relationships with Disruptive Children: The Potential of Relationship-Focused Reflection', *Attachment and Human Development* 14, no. 3, 305–318; Jessica Toste, 'Reconceptualizing Teacher–Student Relationships to Foster School Success: Working Alliance Within Classroom Contexts' (30 May 2012), www.edcan.ca/experts/jessica-r-toste.

Part I

Part I introduces some helpful theoretical and background knowledge to give a framework for thinking about and understanding what might be going on under the surface for those children in school who trouble or 'get' to us. Understanding something of attachment theory, neuroscience, unconscious processes and the effects of trauma can make a real difference to how we respond and work with such children, and enable them to learn and develop. Out of the theory, practical responses and suggestions naturally arise and some are included here, while Part II goes on to emphasise and describe the practical, nurturing and relationship-based ways of working, drawing on the theory described in Part I.

Introduction to attachment theory

LSOphoto

Figure 1

The chapter begins with attachment – the quality of our 'affectional bonds'.[1] You could even say we are born with a history. Of course we all have a genetic inheritance, but we also come into this world with unique foetal experiences – of being in our particular mother's womb for nine months with the sounds and hormonal flows of our particular parental environment, which even before our first breath, can prime us to expect calmness or fear stress, for example. What a difference there is between the infant who has regularly heard Mozart and enjoyed a relaxed calm foetal time, and an infant who has been subjected to shouting and screaming and frequent doses of stress hormones through the umbilical cord.

You could say we are born unfinished. Infants are born helpless and they won't thrive either physically or emotionally without a closely attentive mother who engages with them, thinks about them and cares for them well enough. Sometimes, however, their experience is very different. In extreme cases like the severely neglected Romanian orphans, babies can even die without care. Whatever our early experience, it makes a difference. It makes a difference to our capacity for empathy and resilience, for example, to our need for defences and to our openness (or not) to curiosity and learning.

Secure healthy attachment makes all the difference. Through cries, reaching out and similar behaviours, babies are programmed to seek attachment with their mother or primary caregiver, who (ideally) responds to their needs and cries, providing not only for their physical needs of food, warmth and protection but also and increasingly meeting their emotional needs, through thoughtful reflection and understanding responses. This relationship is interactive. Even at birth the baby actively roots for the nipple. Baby and mother[2] are, and need to be, part of a dyadic interrelationship (described by many parent/infant psychologists[3]), which ideally enhances the emotional health and growth of both of them and leads to a secure base from which the baby can begin to explore the world.

This secure relationship enables the baby to look around and go away from mum for short periods, and slowly to experience being a separate self. This is a gradual process and it is puzzling for a baby to discover 'what is me and what is not me'. Even in the first few months we can observe a secure baby with mother close by begin to look around, or crawl or toddle away and start to explore the outside world with all their senses. Then after a while, or when something unexpected momentarily rocks their security, they look or go back to mum for reassurance, before beginning to explore again and of course continuing to learn from experience that mum will be there when needed and that exploration is fun and interesting. This experience of feeling 'inside' the mother's mind and of knowing that his needs with be taken seriously and eased and responded to is one of 'emotional containment', which we will explore, and link in to a child's experience in school, in Chapter 5.

As Bowlby (often referred to as the 'father of attachment theory') said, 'All of us, from the cradle to the grave, are happiest when life is organised as a series of excursions, long or short, from the secure base provided by our attachment figures.'[4] Children with warm satisfying early relationships are likely to have similar relationships in the future. They are likely to be available, responsive and helpful. They are likely to have an image of themselves as potentially loveable and loved. They are likely to be confident and open.

Bowlby talks of each of us as having an 'internal working model'[5] – an internalised model of how the world is, how people will respond to us and how we are or should be, derived from our earliest attachment experiences. A secure internal working model facilitates the development of mental and emotional health.

Ambivalence

As the healthy young child's attachment matures they can increasingly integrate the 'bad mummy' who tells them off and isn't there just when they need her, with the 'good mummy' who returns as expected and hugs them after bad times into an experience of integrating these opposites, and into ambivalence:

> *Sometimes things and people are OK and sometimes they are not so OK, but that's OK because I am really loved and remembered. And even if I make mistakes it's not the end of the world. Mummy might be cross – but she will always love me. I can apologise, and anyway we can always talk things through.*

This is resilience.

Separation

Attachment also derives from a child's experiences (and understanding responses during experiences) of separation and loss. Experiences of separation and loss can evoke feelings of anxiety, fear and anger, but if these experiences are talked through and processed, they can lead to emotional growth and learning. *Without* comforting support, however, such experiences can be difficult or even damaging, as we shall see in Chapter 3.

This process is both experiential, fostering emotional capacity and security, and also neurological, fostering connections and hormonal flows in the brain relating to (particularly intense) experiences (see Chapters 2 and 3).

Joy and delight

Crucially, secure attachment and emotional health relates also to experiences of interactive joy and delight as mother and baby engage playfully together, enhancing dopamine and opioid production (Margot Sunderland calls these hormones 'joy juice'[6]), fostering enjoyment of learning and relationships and developing personality. Frequent experiences of joy and fun are wonderful and lead to high levels of aliveness, enthusiasm and energy for life. But babies also need help to 'come down' from these heightened states. Sunderland continues:

> Intense feelings of joy produce lovely chemicals in the brain, but also high levels of arousal including activation of stress chemicals, so an essential parenting function is to help your child handle 'the stress of joy' so that she does not feel overwhelmed by it.[7]

Secure parents do this naturally of course, but TAs in school, adoptive and foster parents and other significant adults may need alerting to this crucial function with children when they engage with them in (essential) moments of delight, excitement and attachment-based play.

This early attachment-based play progresses on to 'play in the space between' the mother and the toddler (also called 'potential space'[8]). Gradually the secure base allows the toddler to disengage from the relationship for a while and become interested in the objects and activities themselves, introduced initially by the mother. Through repeated experiences like these a child begins to become a separate person with the capacity to engage with play, creativity and learning, and to relate naturally and confidently with others.

Language

From the very start parents put child-friendly words to their musings and understandings, and even babies pick up on tone of voice and gestures. But as the infant becomes a toddler and then a child, so language begins to play a more conscious role in the understanding and processing of experiences. As parents communicate their understanding and empathic support as well as their delight through language, tone of voice and actions, slowly children begin to make sense of their feelings, and take in their parents' timely words. Through talking through and processing their experiences children learn to think about and differentiate feelings, and to label and integrate their affective experiences. This leads to empathy.

The reason that I have gone into such detail about the secure child's good-enough attachment and their emotionally nurturing and containing experiences, is that through understanding in some detail the importance of healthy supportive attachment relationships, and of a facilitating environment for emotional security and exploration, we can begin to have some idea of what is missing in some children as well as gaining a clearer picture of what a second-chance attachment experience (see Chapter 7, pp. 138–155) might look like.

Difficult, insecure and traumatic beginnings

The aim of attachment behaviour is to seek comfort, proximity and contact with a strong attachment figure, especially at distressing times.

With insecure vulnerable children we are thinking about children who very often have not only *not* had a secure nurturing beginning, but have very often had all sorts of hurts and parental projections dumped on to and into them, which they have no capacity to cope with or process. Their inner world is so very different from that of the secure children described above.

In the classroom, for example, a child who has *not* learned to expect his difficulties to be supported and tolerated or his anxieties to be understood, will find it hard or even impossible to tolerate the uncertainty of not knowing or the fear of not managing something. The fear of no support, or worse still of humiliation when things go wrong, can easily lead to overwhelming anxiety and 'stuckness'. As well as the possibility of becoming stuck in early developmental stages (see Chapter 7), such feelings can be unbearable and need to be expelled immediately – through defensive 'projecting out' into someone else, which can be easily misunderstood, 'punished' and lead to a very negative self-image – a secondary problem, which again gets acted out! This acting out is particularly triggered when fear, stress or insecurity looms.

For most children the principal attachment figure in their life is their mother, so the mother's mental health and availability to bear and manage these inevitable projections is crucial.

Without effective support *attachment patterns can tend to cycle through generations*.

The earlier these experiences happen the more they are likely to become hard wired into the child's developing brain, as we shall see in Chapter 2.

Although each child's attachment behaviours are unique and vary in severity, it can be helpful to think of three different categories of insecure attachment, each of which have a very different cause and differently affect both relationships and learning, requiring differing responses and ways of working to ease and manage them.[9] In Chapter 6 we will look in detail at these patterns and how to respond helpfully to each of them.

Notes

1 John Bowlby, *The Making and Breaking of Affectional Bonds* (London: Tavistock, 1979).
2 Throughout the book, for 'mother' or 'mum' read 'mother or father or carer', although the mother is usually the most significant.
3 Beatrice Beebe, 'My Journey in Infant Research and Psychoanalysis: Microanalysis, a Social Microscope', *Psychoanalytic Psychology* 31, no. 1 (2014), 4–25.
4 John Bowlby, *A Secure Base* (New York: Basic Books, 1988), 62.
5 John Bowlby, *Attachment and Loss* (New York: Basic Books, 1969), 12.
6 Margot Sunderland, *What Every Parent Needs to Know* (London: Dorling Kindersley, 2006), 90.
7 Ibid., 26.
8 D. W. Winnicott, *Playing and Reality* (Abingdon, UK: Routledge, 1991), 41, 47.
9 See Heather Geddes, *Attachment in the Classroom* (London: Worth, 2006).

Useful neuroscience

2

A simple introduction for school staff and child workers

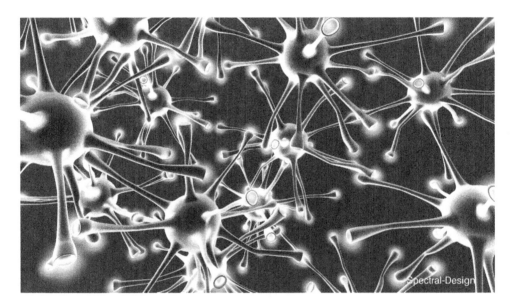

Figure 2

In accordance with the scope of the book this mostly focuses on preadolescent neuroscience. Neuroscience is the study of our brains. This includes the structure of the brain, the neurons (electrically excitable cells that transmit information to other neurons through the transfer of chemicals), and the hormonal (chemical) flows between parts of the brain and between the brain and the body (evoking tension, freezing up or excitability, for example).[1] Brain development is linked to both experience and relationships. Understanding how experience affects brain development, and how hormonal tendencies affect behaviour, for example, can be another way of making sense of children's development and inhibitions.

The first thing to understand is that the brain is use dependent. Children need healthy experiences and healthy relationships to forge healthy links. The chapter begins with some simple biology and then interweaves this with facilitating and inhibiting factors, developmental stages and the effects of trauma on the developing brain.

Three brains

You could say we have three brains – three brains that work together, developing and growing in response to our inner and outer experiences throughout life. Our brains are particularly affected by powerful and significant experiences like trauma, loss, sudden realisations and immense joy. All of this begins in the womb. Thus the brain of the foetus can be affected by beautiful music, for example, and by calmness and joy in the mother, stimulating the release of 'happy' hormones like dopamine and serotonin. Conversely, shouting, stress, drugs and alcohol, for example, stimulate the release of cortisol and adrenaline (stress hormones) in the brain and body.

Infant brain development is dyadic. That is we (including our brain structure and hormonal flows) develop in relation to our early attachment experiences – initially and usually with mum, dad and family members. We are born as 'work in progress' and that is both a risky and an amazing opportunity.

The reptilian brain

All vertebrates have an 'old primitive' brain (dating back to an earlier evolutionary stage), which activates instinctive behaviour related to *survival*. It also controls our bodily functions like hunger and our digestive system, breathing and circulation, movement, posture and balance. Our fight, flight or freeze response to danger is energised from our 'reptilian brain'. Reptilian responses are automatic and often outside conscious awareness.

Autonomic nervous system

The reptilian brain goes right down into the brain stem and connects to the vagus nerve, which travels down the spinal cord and out to many bodily organs, activating the parasympathetic nervous system. The parasympathetic nervous system and the sympathetic nervous system are the two parts of the body's autonomic nervous system, which regulate and energise the body as needed. The sympathetic nervous system, also travelling down and around the spinal cord, arouses and energises our bodies, includes priming us to fight or flee, while the parasympathetic nervous system helps us calm down after arousal, and activates the rest and digest systems in the body.

In her chapter entitled 'The Science of Comforting', Margot Sunderland writes how '[c]omforting a screaming child activates her vagus nerve . . . restoring order to her bodily systems'.[2] Sunderland describes how the ongoing availability of parental love and comfort is an invaluable gift for a baby, fostering good 'vagal tone', bearing much fruit in the future in terms of a calm, resilient, balanced and clear-thinking quality of heart and mind, and even benefitting the immune system. School staff working with vulnerable little ones may need to offer similar calm and comfort – including safe holding, as their vagal tone will likely need much support.

The mammalian brain

The 'mammalian brain' is found in all mammals. It contains the limbic system, which is the home of strong emotions like fear, separation anxiety, rage, playfulness, our explorative urge and the sexual urge in adults. These can be powerful and they need the thoughtful and regulatory capacities of the higher rational brain to be managed. Infants cannot do this for themselves, as the higher rational brain does not come fully 'online' until around 2 years of age. So caring parents, and later thoughtful school staff, who can talk with children about their 'big feelings' and help them regulate, are part of this process, helping to foster the crucial links between the different parts of the brain within the child.

Within the mammalian brain is the amygdala, which is involved in the formation, perception and memory of emotions. Acknowledging and talking about feelings with children is obviously crucial for healthy brain connections. The amygdala is also involved, through repeated experience and brain stimulation, in expectations deriving from what has happened to us, leading, for example, to fear conditioning and to positive conditioning too.

At stressful times the amygdala also communicates with the hypothalamus – which releases stress hormones in preparation for fight or flight. Sometimes strong emotions and bubbling stress hormones can overpower our higher rational brain and we need help to calm down. If traumatised children have repeatedly not had support when strong fearful emotions become triggered they cannot learn to regulate their outbursts. They need help. Sometimes the only option is to wait for the stress hormones to dissipate.

Deep within the mammalian brain is the hippocampus, which is involved in memory. Brain scans show that the hippocampus is significantly reduced in children who have suffered severe early trauma, leading some researchers to conclude: 'We don't know how much this cell death affects a child's working memory. However adults with a shrunken hippocampus score lower on memory and verbal reasoning tasks.'[3] This is obviously concerning.

The higher rational brain

The higher rational brain contains the neo-cortex (sometimes called the frontal lobes), and in evolutionary terms, it is the newest part of the brain. It wraps around the mammalian brain and is mostly located at the front of the head. Its capacity for thinking, creativity, problem-solving, reasoning and reflection makes us superior to other animals and it is greatly influenced by our experiences. It is the part of the brain that can be most affected by nurturing thoughtful parenting (or the lack thereof).

The frontal lobes consist of a left and a right side, each of which have different and complementary functions. As well as visual and spatial processing, the right side registers feelings and can sense emotional atmospheres. Jill Bolte Taylor's experience highlights how the right side also opens us up to our more 'spiritual' capacities for oneness and openness to unconditional love and to the unknown[4] (when conditions are right). It has connections with the limbic system and the fight or flight system, so it can sense how the body is responding. The left side includes our verbal centres. It is good at speech and language processing and putting feelings into words. It is the more rational 'thinking' side. The left side is usually dominant in our rational, competitive target-oriented culture and education system. It can even inhibit and belittle our right-side capacities, which can be thought to be 'soft' and imprecise.

The corpus callosum is a complex of fibres linking the right and left sides, enabling them to work together to modulate and process experiences by putting words and rational reflection to feelings, experiences and emotional states. The corpus callosum slowly develops its functionality during baby- and toddlerhood, with a growth spurt at around 2 years of age. So whereas babies and toddlers can shift rapidly between positive and negative states, needing parents to help them manage their 'big feelings', after two years, through parental encouragement to think and talk about their feelings and experiences, children begin to develop self-awareness and self-regulation. This process continues throughout life, and is facilitated by attuned reflective conversations with others, especially significant adults in school. Normally the corpus callosum slowly increases in size with age up to adulthood, but in children without attuned, thoughtful (parental) support, its capacity can be inhibited.

In *What Every Parent Needs to Know*, Margot Sunderland says that, 'Some scientists believe that a key factor in why a person lacks compassion and concern for another is that their corpus callosum is not passing emotional information effectively between the two sides of the brain'.[5] One could say that healthy experiences forge healthy brain connections – leading to healthy behaviour.

The higher rational brain then enables us to reason and solve problems, and to learn and achieve – notably through education. Through reflecting on experience, and openness to others and the world, it can also facilitate creativity and imagination.

The links between the different systems in the brain both aid our capacity for self-regulation and help us grow into emotionally rounded human beings. The role of parents and teachers in helping us to engage with and reflect on our inner lives and that of others helps build these crucial links. Nurturing children's caring emotions experienced through the right brain to right brain communications and the limbic system, for example, leads to the capacity for empathy, kindness and concern. Similarly, learning, curiosity and love of learning is more than just getting information and taking it in. The deeper and more enduring connections are 'right brain' to 'right brain'. The empathy we are talking about here is really heartfelt. Secure parents naturally have these connections with their children and the children can *feel* the empathy, which affects them in a tangible kind of way.

Our own aliveness and brain connections also affect our passion for learning and for a subject or task in hand. We can see this passion for exploration and learning in a healthy classroom with an inspiring teacher. At the other extreme, however, when the links to the mammalian brain's emotional and social systems, and the connecting capacity of the corpus callosum have been severely damaged or not developed, the higher rational brain can be responsible for awful cruelties.

The links we are talking about here are both *structural* and *chemical*. Hormones (chemical signals) pass along the synapses (a synapse is the structure that enables neurons to link with each other), and are expressed as emotions and behaviours via the limbic system.

In our brains we have 100 billion nerve cells called neurons, which become connected to each other through developing axons (the 'arms' that grow out of the cell wall). Super-fast messages in the form of chemical impulses (hormones or neurotransmitters) travel between neurons by 'leaping' a small gap (synapse) on to the axon of the nearby neuron.

Connections between neurons (see Figure 4) form through experience. If neurons did not communicate our bodies would do nothing. Repetition of experiences leads to a web of connections – in other words, practice makes perfect.

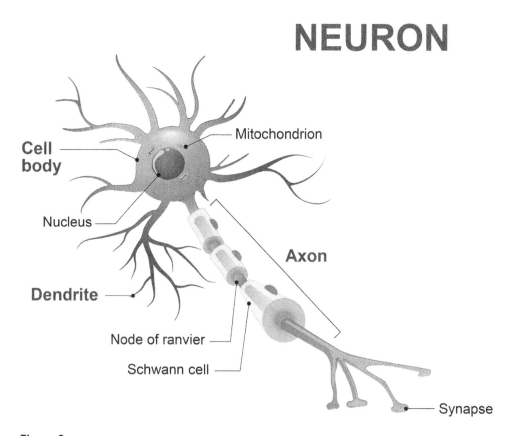

NEURON

Cell body

Mitochondrion

Nucleus

Axon

Dendrite

Node of ranvier

Schwann cell

Synapse

Figure 3

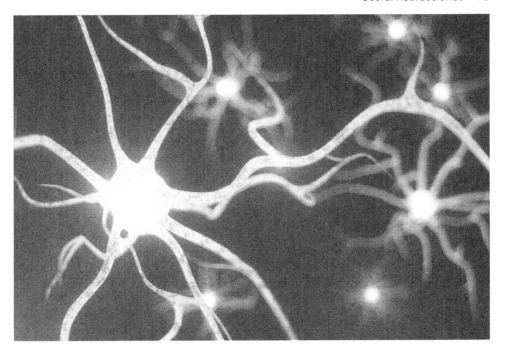

Figure 4

Early brain development

Babies are born with 200 billion brain cells, which are mostly unconnected. The first few years of life are critical periods for brain growth, offering the best chance for healthy connections in response to the parents' nurturing and attuned availability. In ideal circumstances, comforting and nurturing words, tactile and olfactory experiences and experiences of being held combine to strengthen an infant's brain pathways and induce emotional and social intelligence – or not! Neuronal connections – when two neurons fire simultaneously or in quick succession – are made in response to experience, leading to a memory or an association – 'cells that fire together wire together'.[6] Thus cell connections are formed, unformed, reformed and strengthened in direct relation to experience. Many connections are lost. As Allan Shore says, 'If you don't use it you lose it',[7] referring to 'synaptic pruning', when frequently used connections are strengthened and those infrequently used are eliminated. This may sound negative but actually 'pruning' is important for both brain organisation and avoiding overload.

If we look at brain development in *attachment terms* we can see that the mother's and infant's brains are intimately connected. 'Primary maternal preoccupation' (a phrase coined by Winnicott in 1956[8] to describe how mothers are hormonally programmed to be totally preoccupied with their infants for the first few months) is indeed necessary for healthy brain development as well as for secure attachment. Hormones, as well as cell connections are important. The infant's reptilian and mammalian brains are 'designed' to be intimately connected to that of the mother. Parts of the prefrontal cortex don't 'come online' until well into the first year of life, so the first relationship between mother and baby is limbic to limbic system, or right brain to right brain. Intuition and non-verbal communication including practical, rhythmic and tactile communication and nurture are key here. Rocking, singing, laughing, soothing and engaging words and intonation all contribute to bonding, a natural and necessary process.

The primitive impulses of infants can be overwhelming. 'Urgent' needs and hurts can elicit rage and distress – releasing stress hormones, which babies and children need help to regulate. Present, attuned parents naturally want to calm and sooth their babies when they are distressed. This cycle, *need – evoking strong emotions – attuned mother noticing and calming – baby becoming soothed and relaxed – mother and baby both happy – eye contact and smiles*, produces happy hormones (opiates and oxytocin) within both mother and baby.

But it's not just calming and soothing and practical care that a baby needs. As Allan Schore says in Richard Bowlby's attachment DVD:

> In the first year of life *joy* is the key affect. By joining with the child in making this dyadic system, what they (parents) are doing is they are interactively co-regulating very high levels of positive emotion. So essentially what the attachment system is – is an interactive mechanism for generating and regulating very high levels of positive affect – enjoyment, joy, interest and excitement, through tickles and movement, etc. – facilitating laughter and bonding . . . It's the amplification of positive states that really allows for growth. Dopamine is trophic allowing synapses to bind together.[9]

Thus the dyadic regulation capacity is born and practised and bears fruit. It arises out of connection and is facilitated through joy, interest and excitement, followed by calming and comfort. The support to calm down is particularly important for vulnerable children. A nurture teacher I knew practised this cycle with her group – through upward or energetic movements followed by sinking down to the ground; and through louder and louder percussion music followed by quieter and quieter sounds – ending with a moment of silence. I have tried a similar process with a parachute. Such 'practice' can be very useful for regulating both positive and negative emotional states. This is important knowledge for school staff working with the most deprived and disturbed children. In their capacity for giving their 'special pupils' a second-chance attachment and nurture experience, and freeing them to learn, *putting effort into* creating this sort of relationship – through joy, laughter, light safe touch and little moments of fun, followed by help to calm down, is essential. Repeated experiences of fun, laughter and interest within significant relationships prime children's brains to be open to such hormones and their minds and bodies to enjoy relationships. It wakes up their 'aliveness', their capacity for joy and their confidence. It also facilitates dependent attachment relationships, whereby children can (ask for and) use significant adults to help them cope with strong (both positive and negative) emotions and calm down (dependence precedes independence).

Sunderland (2006)[10] calls these fun experiences 'high intensity relational moments'. They include singing, rhythm and physical play together, stimulating what Sunderland calls 'happy hormones'.

Psychiatrist and neuroscientist Bruce Perry teaches the value and use of rhythmic-patterned activities for traumatised children. When they get stressed, self-regulation can be quite impossible for them, because both their (thinking) higher rational brain and their (emotional) mammalian brain can shut down. Repeated rhythmical activities can aid 'repatterning', as he explains: 'To change any neural network in the brain, we need to provide patterned, repetitive input to reach poorly organized neural networks involved in the stress response. Any neural network that is activated in a repetitive way will change,'[11] thereby reinforcing the value of poems, songs, dance and action rhymes in early years education.[12]

Moving on

As they move into toddlerhood higher brain functions continue to develop. Parental attentiveness, thoughtful responsiveness, empathic engaging language and the provision of stimulating experiences all aid this development, providing it is not inhibited.

> *My daughter had many weeks in hospital during her toddlerhood and childhood including three major operations, and for a while her growth was inhibited. I always remember a friend who was a nurse saying, 'Children can't grow and develop while they are preoccupied with pain and illness'.*

Some 90 per cent of the growth in brain connections occurs in the first five years – leading to a proliferation of synapses (connections) within a short time. This then is a crucial time for learning, making early years education and provision crucial. There is another brain growth surge in adolescence (see below), offering crucial opportunities for schools and school staff.

By age 7 brain 'sculpting' has slowed somewhat; although the good news is that brain plasticity (the capacity of the brain to adapt to experience) allows our brains to continue to develop and grow in response to experience throughout life. Teachers and significant school staff will have daily opportunities to facilitate new healthy brain connections through attuned caring and nurture, and through understanding words and actions.

Trauma and the brain

When the foetus is in the womb it gets chemical messages through the umbilical cord from the mother. Ideally these are positive and nurturing. But if the mother is frequently stressed the baby can receive relatively large doses of the stress hormone cortisol, which 'washes over the developing brain like acid',[13] and programmes the brain to be more receptive to cortisol. This will affect the limbic system and cortex areas of the brain linked to emotion and attachment, resulting in these areas of the brain becoming '20 to 30 per cent smaller'[14] in children who have experienced trauma.

Although this tendency can later be eased with the help of attuned significant others, enabling such children to internalise the capacity to self-regulate is much more difficult for them compared to those children without such a history.

Trauma inhibits and disturbs brain development. During a traumatic event a child will experience a surge in stress hormones, which will activate their fight or flight system.

Where such experiences occur early in life and persist or happen on a regular basis without caring, containing support, long-term problems can result. Thus in many ways children can't help their reactions. A surge in stress hormones will also become triggered at the slightest *similar* stress, leading to triggered behaviours and outbursts, which the child can't help, and can't manage without help. This tendency will need sustained, relationship-based help to shift.

Severe neglect can also have devastating consequences. Brain scans of Romanian orphans showed very reduced activity in the temporal lobes (which regulate emotions) because of their very limited emotional experience in the orphanage – inhibiting their capacity to manage their emotions.[15]

So, as well as being related to present experiences, children's behaviour problems in school could be triggered by re-activated stress hormones – linked to raised levels of cortisol during the first three years of life.

This increases the activity in the brain structures linked to vigilance and arousal, creating a brain *wired* to be hyper alert to stress (post-traumatic stress syndrome; PTSD). This can look like ADHD, and children can sometimes be wrongly diagnosed and medicated. The effect of such experiences on learning are described in more detail in the section on children with chaotic/disorganised attachment patterns in Chapter 6.

A few words about the adolescent brain may be helpful for readers involved with older students. Adolescence heralds a second wave of development affecting the higher rational brain, partly influenced by surging sex hormones at around age 12 in boys and age 11 in girls. Adolescence brings in a period of brain reorganisation and growth. The number of connections in the frontal cortex increases, leading to more synapses than we need. As in the early years there is an increase in synaptic pruning – leaving fewer but stronger branches.

Myelination, a covering sheath around the axons (see Figure 3) enables the branches that remain to become thicker and stronger. The corpus callosum grows stronger allowing for more connections between thought, feelings and experience. These changes bring many benefits, both at the time and in the future. For example, stronger links develop between the hippocampus and the frontal areas – leading to an increased capacity to integrate memory and experience with decision-making.

The frontal cortex areas develop richer connections – enabling adolescents to hold and think about more information.

The neural connections between the amygdala (sometimes called the brain's emotional processor) and the cortex become denser, leading (hopefully) to emotional maturity – with dips along the way!

Thus the brain prepares itself for the important and complex tasks of adulthood:

- developing social skills and managing new relationships;
- developing a sense of identity, including sensitivity to social rejection and distress;
- making decisions for the future;
- learning to regulate emotions effectively;
- getting used to a new body;
- refining the transition from dependence to independence;
- achieving a manageable separation from the family.

This is not easy though, and sometimes their turbulent hormones and brain changes can lead to teenagers becoming argumentative, overreactive and inappropriate. They can become impatient and resist advice, and be very sensitive to hints of rejection. A healthy urge towards risk-taking stretches their capacities and their openness, but it can also lead to a loss of ability to plan ahead or imagine the consequences of an action. Vulnerable young people are much more at risk in adolescence. Unsupported vulnerability can lead to 'acting in' through self-harm, depression, eating and body dysmorphic disorders, and 'acting out' through antisocial behaviour, gangs, promiscuity and (comforting) addictive behaviours. Adolescents can *need* more defences – making them more difficult to support. But with thoughtful attuned support, from staff who have the sort of knowledge and understanding described throughout the book, hopefully this turbulent time will be managed well enough. School counsellors can be very helpful especially in secure secondary schools, but catching the deterioration early or waiting till they are 'ready', as well as the availability of (separate) support for parents, will be crucial. With a reliable secure base adolescence is a real opportunity for change and growth.

As this chapter comes to an end, you may be wondering whether school staff really need all this detail on brain development. I have included it because it enables us to understand that many children's outbursts, 'overreactions' and many behaviours (including positive and empathic behaviours), are conditioned and in a sense automatic – wired into our brain structures that we each develop in relation to our early and cumulative experiences. If vulnerable children's experiences and their resulting brain structures and hormonal flow tendencies have sadly been and become dysfunctional, it doesn't mean that their patterns can't change, but they do need help. They need new and *repeated* healthy patterns to 'overwrite' the old ones. School staff can make a real difference here, which as mentioned already, has a direct effect on children's openness to and capacities for learning.

Notes

1 For a simple, vivid and illustrated introduction to the brain in relation to early development I recommend the chapter entitled 'Your Child's Brain', in Margot Sunderland, *What Every Parent Needs to Know* (London: Dorling Kindersley, 2006). I am also indebted to Sorcha Ennis, Louise Marshall and Tina Axup for their PowerPoint presentation on neuroscience for the Safe to Learn training course, which has also informed this chapter.

2 Sunderland, *What Every Parent Needs to Know*, 44

3 N. S. Neki, R. K. Singh and S. Rastogi, 'How the Brain Influences Neuro-Cardiovascular Dysfunction', *Journal of the Association of Physicians of India* 52 (2004), 233–230, cited in Sunderland, *What Every Parent Needs to Know*, 42.

4 For readers who would like to know more about this I recommend neuroscientist Jill Bolte Taylor's account of the amazing insight she gained from her severe stroke, which completely removed her left-brain capacities for a period while her right brain gloried in uninhibited bliss – leading her to wonder if we are not out of balance as a civilisation. Jill Bolte Taylor, *My Stroke of Insight* (New York: Viking, 2008).

5 Sunderland, *What Every Parent Needs to Know*, 232 (referring to the work of Martin Teicher, 'Scars That Won't Heal: The Neurobiology of Child Abuse', *Scientific American* 268, no. 3 (2002), 68–75).

6 Often referred to as 'Hebb's Law'; the exact quote from Siegrid Löwel is 'neurons wire together if they fire together'. S. Löwel and W. Singer, 'Intrinsic Horizontal Connections in the Visual Cortex by Correlated Neuronal Activity', *Science* 255, no. 5041 (1992), 209–212.

7 Allan Schore interview clip on Richard Bowlby's *Attachment* DVD (1996).

8 D. W. Winnicott, 'Primary Maternal Preoccupation', in *Through Pediatrics to Psycho-Analysis* (London: Tavistock, 1956), ch. 24.

9 Richard Bowlby private *Attachment* DVD, freely available from him.

10 Sunderland, *What Every Parent Needs to Know*, 193–199.

11 B. D. Perry and E. Hambrick, 'The Neurosequential Model of Therapeutics (NMT)', *Reclaiming Children and Youth* 17, no. 3 (2008), 38–43.

12 For a fuller description of the benefits of patterned repetitive rhythmic activity for aiding regulation see attachmentdisorderhealing.com.

13 Rita DeMaria, Gerald R. Weeks and Larry Hof, *Focused Geneograms: International Assessment of Individuals, Couples and Families* (New York: Brunner-Routledge, 2013), 89.

14 Ibid.

15 See scans on Richard Bowlby's *Attachment* DVD (1996).

The effects of unsupported trauma

3

Oleksil Spesyvtsev

Figure 5

The chapter begins by describing a healthy response to difficulties and trauma. A 'good-enough' mother (a term coined by Winnicott[1]) tunes into her baby's feelings, thinks about them, tries a response, maybe tries again, until she understands what her baby is communicating. Then she responds helpfully with nurturing actions, soothing sounds and words, resulting in an experience of containment[2] for the baby, who can then return to a calm state.

Over time, and as children have enough good experiences of *containment*, babies and children begin to develop their own capacity for emotional containment. They develop resilience. They also move towards feeling safe enough to separate for a while and explore, play and learn.

Similarly when experiences that are disturbing and even devastating occur to a secure child, the parents will know immediately, stop what they are doing and attend to the child with words and soothing actions until he calms down. With older children this may entail lots of listening and talking through in different ways. In the case of more traumatic experiences like death, accidents, losses and hurts, memories or hints will inevitably come up again and again to be talked through 'in small doses',[3] as the child indicates he is open and needs to talk about them. Young children will frequently find ways to 'play through' their new and exciting experiences, their hurts, their painful and frightening experiences and their worries. Talking and playing, and dreams and stories are all ways we naturally use to process what has happened to us, enabling us to *integrate* painful experiences, which although they still evoke sadness and pain, can nevertheless be thought about, talked about, learned from and shared with others. This could be called 'learning from experience',[4] which as we grow older, includes internal reflection and making links with other experiences, observations and knowledge, leading to personal growth and maturity.

The quality of emotional support, hurting or anxious babies and children receive from their primary caregivers during and following traumatic experiences makes all the difference.

Responses to trauma

When traumatic pain threatens *without support and containment*, however, it is devastating. Without immediate empathic support and comfort, and without the ongoing availability of an attuned listener and attachment figure the trauma remains unintegrated and unthinkable, and may be repressed from conscious memory. Or sometimes (in the case of adults and adolescents) they may want to talk about their (version of) experiences over and over again but in a muddled way.

Unprocessed unintegrated pain is unbearable. It can't be thought about or talked about, although anxieties relating to feeling memories may be triggered by even the slightest hint of the trauma. Triggers can evoke reactions that are out of proportion and more suited to the original unprocessed trauma. Barbara Dockar-Drysdale talks of panic as being the 'hallmark of unintegration'.[5] Triggers can also evoke dissociation, psychosomatic manifestations or dangerous and even puzzling behaviour outbursts. The unbearableness of their experience can get right inside us – so vividly portrayed in Figure 5 at the beginning of this chapter, in Figure 6 and also in Case Study 1.

The baddies are coming. Get back now. Aaaaah! No No No No

Figure 6

Case Study 1   The effects of abuse: a TA shares her experience

I once worked with this poor little girl. It was so sad. She had been sexually abused quite badly when she was about 6 or 7. When she first came she was quite terrified. You couldn't really get near her. I worked quite closely with her and started to build a bit of a relationship with her. It was all on her terms though. She would only engage with me when she chose to. I couldn't try to engage her. I couldn't take initiatives with her. But if she wanted something she would engage with me to get the thing she wanted. I guess I could understand that having grown-ups take initiatives with her would have been terrifying and she couldn't bear that. I imagine there was a feeling that she might become hurt or unsafe, or something might happen that she didn't like. So she needed to be the one to be in charge. Because I understood something of that, at first I would engage with her when she wanted me to – as that was the only opportunity I had to do anything with her. There was just no way in, other than to go along with her pushiness. I felt that what she actually wanted was contact, but she wasn't aware of that of course. What she would want was just to have a conversation about something.

Sometimes she was quite violent and her behaviour could get really out of control. She would hurt us sometimes, but she could really go for other children, so we would have to stop her. But it was difficult. Sometimes we would be able to get her out of the room without actually touching her, but on occasions we just had to hold her, because she was in danger of hurting other children. We were always very wary of holding her, because we knew about the traumatic abuse from her uncle, and we sensed that holding her could exacerbate her state. When we did need to move her she would sometimes just go limp and crumple. It made us feel absolutely horrific – like we were further damaging a damaged child. We were very mindful about that and we often talked to each other about it.

When I think about it now I realise she must have had a big fear of being held. But strangely she would keep putting us in the situation where we needed to physically move her away from someone. Maybe unconsciously she only knew (and needed but hated) a sort of scary but uncomfortable contact (because we all need contact), as if unconsciously she was forcing us to give her what she wanted or needed but also feared, making us fear the contact too!

Early trauma before language tends to get repeatedly acted out – with awareness of the current hurt – often magnified out of proportion by the trigger, but without understanding of the links to past hurts. The *earlier and the more frequent* the hurt, the more difficult it is to shift the pattern (see Chapter 2 on neuroscience). In *The Body Keeps the Score* psychiatrist and researcher Bessel van der Kolk talks about the impact of child abuse and neglect on the developing brain. Through his study of abused children, he concludes that 'for abused children, the whole world is filled with triggers'.[6]

The most extreme response to trauma, and the only response of frequently neglected or abused and helpless babies, is to freeze. Freezing means dissociation – no feeling, no reaction, no brain activity (see Case Study 11, p. 49). Repeated traumatic abuse, neglect or loss can occasionally lead to dissociation becoming the default response for older children when anxiety is triggered. The little girl's 'crumpling' in Case Study 1 is an example of dissociated behaviour.

Sometimes these dissociated, regressed and dysfunctional effects are very obvious and painful to see. They can get right into their *bodies* like little S and his brother G in Case Study 2, while R's anxious bullying was perhaps his way of making sure things didn't fall apart.

Case Study 2   The effects of acute neglect

S, G and R had suffered acute neglect from their addicted parents since they were born. They lived in a state of squalor, frequently being tied to their high chairs. S and G were 'cared for' and bullied by R, their 5-year-old brother and 'carer'. When they were adopted, 3-year-old S was permanently frozen up and couldn't speak or make eye contact at all, while 4-year-old G had acute speech and language difficulties and was doubly incontinent.

More often as children get older and they *can* fight and run, it is these active responses that are more likely to be triggered. Sometimes an outburst may have no *observable* cause because the trigger may be a slight hint of the original trauma – pushing them 'over the top'. Others may have been regularly scared into submission. This can sometimes become imprinted into a compulsive need to please, appease, help, apologise or become like a doormat. These children tend to become bullied and victimised again and again and to have little or no confidence or energy to resist or assert themselves. Thus the automatic defences – fight, flight and freeze – often includes 'appease', or as Walker[7] calls it 'fawn'.

Such difficulties can be both brain based and relate to repressed memories, which bubble up like a volcano. Until children find a relationship that can bear and survive the pain and fear, a relationship that can become real and usable, trauma will be repeatedly acted out with both (usually significant) adults and with peers.

In extreme cases, not only can the pain not be thought about, but thinking as a separate person, thinking and reflecting as such, having interests they can think and talk about, making connections and wondering, etc. cannot become activated in their minds. Not only is there no internalised capacity to manage their feelings (including of course asking for help), but in these cases there is no inner world. Likewise they cannot play creatively. The risk of opening up to possibilities is too scary. I remember in the early days of my work at the pupil referral unit, thinking that some of the children there were just like a bag of reactions. They found it extremely difficult to have a conversation about anything. They could only be provocative, boastful or flippant. I remember observing their interactions with each other, which (to myself) I used to call 'banter'. It seemed to solely consist of making either physical or verbal digs at a peer who then reacted, precipitating a cycle of vicious reactions, until someone got hurt or it was stopped by a firm 'containing' adult, or perhaps it fizzled out. Sometimes, especially with abused boys and older children their violent and aggressive 'acting out' is because they feel they have to 'stay on top', to alleviate the fear of being hurt or humiliated or going into unbearable vulnerability.

I have also seen, however, how the development of real usable and significant committed relationships, available in the here and now, can enable children and young people to both calm down and relate when triggered hurts are contained as illustrated in Case Study 3.

Case Study 3   Containing triggered hurts

G could be very challenging. His teacher just didn't want him in the classroom. He was thrown out of the classroom all the time. So the learning mentor worked with him a lot. On one particularly bad day he was sent to her. He stood by her office door with his sleeves rolled up and his fists out and a scowl on his face and screamed, 'I'm going to run and punch you!' to which she replied, 'Mmmmmm . . . Shall we just sit down? How about we have a cup of tea first?' and they sat down. Maybe he was a bit stunned by her reaction. Her containing, familiar presence was like a positive trigger perhaps – and he shifted into a different state.

Younger children and girls often find themselves 'pushed' into the victim or the rescuer role.

With sexually abused children the acting out can be both aggressive and sexual, and they can swing between perpetrator and victim roles.

ADHD-type behaviours like fidgeting, hyperactivity and provocation can actually be unconscious ways of blocking awareness and not getting anywhere near the unprocessed pain. The problem is that some ADHD (attention deficit hyperactivity disorder) or ODD (oppositional defiant disorder) diagnoses can just be seen as observable conditions and be 'drugged away', too easily preventing understanding and offering therapeutic and/or body-based trauma support.

Bessel Van der Kolk calls child abuse '[t]he nation's [USA's] largest public health problem'.[8] He advocated for and lost the battle to have the diagnosis of 'developmental trauma disorder' replace most childhood behavioural diagnoses – like ADHD and ODD, etc. In other words, he was advocating treating the causes rather than managing the symptoms. He talks about developmental trauma as the 'hidden epidemic'. For those interested I highly recommend his surprisingly readable, detailed research-based book, *The Body Keeps Score* (2014), which addresses both causes and therapies.

Intergenerational transmission

An exacerbating factor frequently found in cases of complex or ongoing trauma is parents 'dumping' their own unprocessed pain on to their babies and children – when for some reason they (the parent) get 'near the edge'. Their needy children sense that and react, provoking the parent to react back or ignore them. Young children have no capacity to contain their parents' pain (let alone their own) – leading to fear, guilt and anxiety or even inhibition, as well as 'doubling' the trauma. Gianna Williams coined the term 'receptacle' for the projective use such parents make of their children – when they blame, shout, take out or 'dump' their bad feelings on to them.[9]

Thus children become scapegoats for the family. Teachers and others, like S's teacher (see Case Study 18, p. 99) who didn't want him in her classroom, can become driven to re-enact the pattern.

This evacuation (shouting and blaming) on to their children can vary with the parent's *own* stress and pain levels (e.g. premenstrual tension), making it unpredictable and very anxiety provoking for the child.

So a mother's mental health problems are risk factors for her children, and for the unborn child too, which need to be taken seriously. Breaking these cycles is crucial.

Skilled attachment-based (not short-term) counselling for mothers may be helpful, when they are open to it.

Shame

When a parent takes his or her feelings out on the child in a critical or hostile way it provokes unbearable pain and pervasive *shame*. Shame is different from guilt. Guilt can be acknowledged. When we feel guilty we are aware that we have done something hurtful and we wish we hadn't done it. We can almost be *driven* to want to make it better. Shame is unthinkable. It has to be hidden and vigorously denied if it threatens to come to the surface, for fear of unbearable humiliation and embarrassment. Trainers may like to use Exercise 1 with school staff.

Exercise 1   Understanding shame from the inside

If you feel comfortable close your eyes.

Gently bring to mind something that is hard to talk about (I am not going to ask you to talk about it, but just think about it for a second).

Now imagine *I asked you to talk about it.*

(After a second or two) Open your eyes.

What do you feel? What does it make you want to do? Invite a few comments from the floor.

Unlike guilt, shame can't be processed without very sensitive help. It has to be acted out – either mildly or hurtfully (see section below). The task of significant adults is to slowly move a child from shame towards guilt so the underlying hurt and ongoing dysfunctional pattern can be eased. Good, attuned and trusted relationships will make a big difference here, in slowly enabling 'shameful' hurts and behaviours to be acknowledged and talked about – usually in the context of understanding that a child's tendencies are not their fault. Very regressed 5-year-old R drew the picture shown in Figure 7 of both of us with our eyes covered up – vividly illustrating how we mustn't see the scary hurting things.

Figure 7

Healing stuck emotional hurts requires processing the unprocessed (emotional) pain, and enabling it to become sufficiently integrated, so that the anxiety it evokes can be bearable and talked about, when it comes into consciousness. For young children this often means *playing and symbolising* those hurts and anxieties over and over again. Some children need this in the concentrated contained form of play therapy, educational or child psychotherapy.

In school, talking it through slowly and in small doses with trusted adults when it comes up, can also enable it to be integrated – so it no longer preoccupies them or triggers unbearable states. My experience as an educational psychotherapist was often that the (younger) children would *play* or work through scenarios in the metaphor (safely, once removed from real memories and experience) with me, and then take opportunities to *talk* their worries and hurts through with their parents, carers or a trusted adult in school. Our roles were complementary – mine working at the unconscious level, and the trusted adult in the conscious realm.

More severely and regularly traumatised children often end up with (or come from families with) chaotic/disorganised attachment patterns. So many of the features and suggestions for schools from Chapter 6 (p. 110–119) will be relevant here.

Severely neglected and abused children can end up in the care system as 'looked-after' children. All schools these days are required to have LAC (looked-after children) coordinators who take a particular and proactive interest in looked-after children and their families, so a section on their particular needs and difficulties is included here.

Looked-after children[10]

Looked-after children may need to be suddenly removed from their homes because they are in danger, or their families may have had lots of professional support, which in the end was found not to be keeping them safe. They may have been in and out of foster care or living with family members for varying periods of time, leading to conflict-ridden and feared removals.

Some will end up in long-term foster families or become adopted, which may bring relief, but adjustment and loss is never easy. They may feel the need to put on a brave face to keep their new parents happy and committed to them. They may bury their hurts for fear of 'rocking the boat'. But especially around *big transitions* they can start to feel very anxious (although they may not show it openly) They may become triggered back into the horrors of their previous traumatic losses – which may have been successfully buried for most of the time. Parents and school staff can be completely *thrown* and undermined by a sudden and drastic change in a child. At such times the children can be very difficult to parent and to teach.

This can even happen with lots of transition visits between schools and very supportive parents. The problem, I think, is that sometimes the child has been so well settled with their (no longer new) and trusted parents, and so settled in their familiar primary school with trusted teachers and friendly staff, that everyone quite forgets that as an adopted child such a significant loss and new beginning can trigger long-buried fears *big time*.

Usually, however, as staff come to care about their looked-after children, real empathy and connectedness is evoked, and with lots of empathy and thoughtful support such difficulties can be understood, accepted and talked through – leading to emotional growth and learning.

The problem is when triggered fears come up, such children can panic and project out, or 'project in' (with self-harm or eating disorders, for example). They can even feel 'bad' or 'mad' – leading to shame.

The legacy of shame, which is unthinkable and therefore has to be acted out, can be particularly important here. Shame can even be provoked by *fear* of humiliation. School staff as well as foster and adoptive parents can unconsciously get caught up in these hurtful 'dramas' and react to the child's hurtful projections – exacerbating the problem.

As well as setting firm boundaries and consequences, it is important to avoid any hints of humiliation or judgement when talking to them. Demonstrating that their feelings are understandable and that they will be helped when things get difficult will slowly enable a child to move from shame to guilt. Each helpful talking through will enable them to move a little way forward.

Until this happens children can be stuck in 'pervasive shame' and need help to rebuild their 'broken' relationships and move towards guilt, talking through and reparation.

Guilt, which *can* be felt and thought about, and therefore 'processed', is achieved when a child has had enough experiences of empathic 'restitution after shame' with a trusted adult, to be able to bear to think about such sensitive issues – leading to their wanting and being able to mend their *own* hurts and 'broken relationships' (repairing breaks in a relationship is discussed on pp. 115, 130 and 169).

This is where understanding and trusted school staff who put effort into their relationship with a foster child (for example) and who can bear but not collude with their hurtful comments and behaviours, are so important. Adults who can think *about* them and *with* them and slowly disentangle their feelings and find ways to talk things through, can make all the difference. But it takes time, and support from management may be crucial.

Interestingly research shows that while looked-after children's education is affected by their experiences and status, it is the children in short-term care who fare worst educationally,[11] which is perhaps understandable given the uncertainty and changeableness of their status, and their lack of a long-term 'curative' secure home attachment experience.

An important point discussed in some detail by Caroline Archer and Alan Burnell, is that looked-after children can develop and show different attachment styles in different relationships and situations[12] (Archer and Burnell talk about these different patterns in terms of a *hierarchy* of 'internal working models' of attachment – see pp. 4 and 53).[13] Thus looked-after children can have an *underlying* and very disturbed attachment pattern and 'internal working model' of expectations from their earliest relationships and experiences, which is hidden underneath their more secure pattern with their adoptive or long-term foster parents. These underlying reactive patterns can sometimes become triggered quite unexpectedly in school or at home – causing big and puzzling problems, especially if this dynamic is not understood. Such triggers can include changes, endings and especially big transitions like moving schools.

Similarly there can be a difference between home and school patterns. This can sometimes cause big problems between home and school (see Case Study 8, p. 46).

The task of long-term foster and adoptive parents is to offer the child a second-chance attachment relationship through a first-hand experience of being emotionally contained and loved anyway. Significant adults in school need to offer a school-based experience of this too, not only to reinforce the healthy pattern they are hopefully getting at home, but because insecure reactive children can't learn, concentrate or relate without a trusted adult and environment to facilitate a secure base – from which they can be open to exploration and learning (see Chapter 10 on creating a secure base).

Domestic abuse

The trauma of many children arises out of ongoing and sometimes violent family conflicts in which they are at best helpless observers, or at worst frightened for themselves or their parent. Parents can be frightened and cling to their children too, as an inclusion manager describes in Case Study 4.

Case Study 4   Clinging to each other for safety

When B started he had difficulties coming into school. This is quite normal for new children, but not for mums too. B's mum didn't want to leave him, and in the first week she herself couldn't leave the building. So she came and sat in my office.

I had several conversations with her and she told me quite a lot about B's background and about the severe domestic abuse she had experienced with his dad. That was why they had moved boroughs. Social care had been involved for a while, but they had dropped the case when she went into a refuge. So she hadn't had any recent support. Mum said she felt she could never leave B, because she worried too much about him. She had always had to protect him from his dad and she still felt very protective (I wondered if she needed him to 'protect' her too).

Meanwhile, in class B was starting to act out in such a way that he seemed to be pushing to be sent home. Then we found out that that was what had happened in his last school. So we made a timetable for him, which included time in the school nurture base and some time in class. Mum was sometimes invited into the nurture base too, which seemed helpful for her. We also did attachment-based work with both B and his mother. For some months in the classroom he could still be very disruptive. It took several months (for both of them) to really trust us.

Family conflicts and violence can be very complicated and entangled. Both the parents' and the child's inner and outer worlds affect each other. Children can be victims as well as helpless observers. Often they are unable to talk about what is happening and ease the pain. When their carers are also their abusers, or at least unavailable to help them through their traumatic experiences, children can become *emotionally damaged*.

The *younger a child is* (even beginning in the womb) when the violence, shouting and rows occur around him, the more entrenched and unprocessed will be the emotional damage they sustain, because their immature brains are not yet able to process experiences without the practical and empathic response of an attuned caregiver.

Early experiences of neglect or abuse, or of domestic abuse, in the absence of a containing mother figure, will affect both the 'hard wiring' and the hormonal systems of a developing baby's brain (see Chapter 2). For example their brain chemistry and the hard wiring of their brains can be 'stretched' like a worn elastic band, by their (need for) massive adrenaline rushes and 'fight, flight, freeze' reactions just to feel 'alive'. This could contribute to a child getting diagnosed with ADHD.

It feels important therefore to include a section on domestic abuse, a particular form of trauma, which sadly is not uncommon. It can be helpful to understand something of the dynamics that affect and inhibit such children and their learning, dynamics they can internalise and act out. For five years I worked as an educational psychotherapist in a Women's Aid setting offering psychotherapy to children affected by domestic abuse, alongside their parents having their own counselling and other support. Below are my notes for an INSET (in-service training) about domestic abuse for school staff.

Some links between inner and outer worlds in children who have experienced domestic abuse

Traumatic reactions

1. The most severely affected children and those still in, or recently from abusive settings can be suffering from PTSD, affecting sleep, night terrors, reactivity and dissociation, etc.
2. Long-term domestic abuse can cause a family to become preoccupied with fear, terror and helplessness, leading to a mother having little or no space in her mind for her children or using her children for her own comfort and support, rather than being available emotionally for them.
3. For a baby or a child in such a situation, the feeling of not being contained is very painful – like being dropped or chucked into the black hole between their desperate need, and not having their need met.
4. The experience of not being able to rely on mum to be able to contain them – and therefore not being able to rely on anyone – can lead to the following:

    (a) Reaction patterns and brain patterns being affected long term.
    (b) The need to defend against all reminders or triggers: through constant or sudden movements (ADHD type) or behaviours such as fight / flight reactions, which can get them into further trouble and make parents and teachers react without thought.
    (c) A vicious cycle of reactivity between the child and mum or child and teacher.

5. *Shame* can be the reason why children can't talk about their worries and hurts and work through them in the normal way with supportive adults or friends. Or they may just sense, or be told explicitly, that you don't talk about family problems at school. It can be a huge and inappropriate burden for a child to have to carry family secrets. This can affect both their learning and their behaviour, as the pressing and shameful worries and hurts leak out in various ways. The need to keep the hurtful memories safely buried may make any sort of thinking or remembering difficult or even impossible, for fear that the thinking may bring up unbearable thoughts. This may cause difficulties with learning to read or spell, as well as with remembering what they have been taught or asked to do. It may make particular areas of the curriculum too uncomfortable to take part in – like listening to particular stories or a topic on 'my family', etc.

The shame of having violence at home which cannot be talked about, and which feels so different and 'bad' compared to other 'normal' families can be hard to contain, and erupt out in strange ways, for example:

(a) making noises or doing things that embarrass others – so *others* feel the shame not them, or because the hurting feelings can't be held inside any longer and just 'bubble out' (I worked with a child like this once and school staff found him very irritating);

(b) being particularly sensitive to any hints of humiliation, (especially any negative comments about their mum or dad) and defending against them vigorously in any way they can, like running away and hiding or anti-social behaviour;

(c) refusing to have a go at things that may expose their difficulties or weaknesses (as weaknesses have been ridiculed in the past).

6. Feeling utterly and painfully helpless to prevent scary and hurtful violence at home can be hard to bear, particularly for oldest children and boys. Sometimes the *unconscious guilt* and pain of failure and helplessness can be alleviated by children being *driven* to get involved in and try to 'sort out' other children's conflicts in the school playground or classroom – particularly those involving 'friends', relatives or siblings. This can lead to 'double trouble' at school, especially if it is not understood, and even escalate into notorious repeated patterns and reputations.

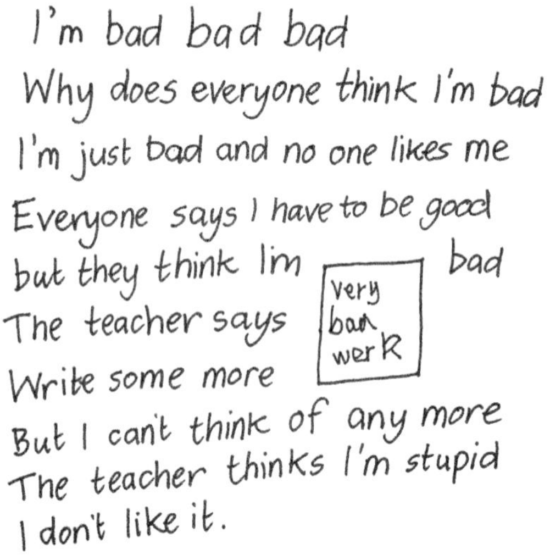

I'm bad bad bad

Why does everyone think I'm bad

I'm just bad and no one likes me

Everyone says I have to be good

but they think I'm bad

The teacher says [very bad werk]

Write some more

But I can't think of any more

The teacher thinks I'm stupid

I don't like it.

Figure 8

7. Memories of times when they misbehaved and didn't manage to contain their feelings, or times when, for example, their untidiness resulted in big rows or accusations that their behaviour is making things worse, can lead to children carrying *huge and inappropriate guilt feelings*. These can be hard to bear and lead to children feeling loved only if they are 'good'. They may then feel driven to need to please significant adults like teachers all the time, or to unconsciously test out whether they will *still* be loved when the adults *really* see what they are like, while underneath they feel not good enough or even 'bad' (see Figure 8).

This needing to be good can even 'leak' into therapy and counselling relationships, interfering with opening up to the real issues.

8. Some girls may need to be extra 'good' or helpful, or be rescuers of others and get over involved. Or they may be very passive and quiet, even becoming quite withdrawn or dissociated, leading to what can look like autistic spectrum behaviours. The fact that they do not cause so much trouble for their teachers can mean that their hurts and needs don't get noticed and they are not referred for help nearly as often as acting-out boys. It takes a perceptive teacher to see under the surface and recognise the hidden hurts within, which without help could fester into serious problems later on.

9. A child's capacity to process little hurts could be inhibited, because they have lost or never had the experience of someone being there to understand and support them and carry them through.

Effect on attachment patterns

Such children can have (possibly severe) attachment difficulties as well, when their mothers are prevented through fear, depression or terror, from bonding with their infants in the normal way. These attachment difficulties can manifest in many ways:

1. The most damaged children and families will be *chaotic/disorganised* (see Chapter 6). Such children may find it difficult to sleep at night, because of memories, dreams or flashbacks of night-time trauma. They may find it impossible to sleep without their mum's protection. Others may need to sleep with their mums because that is the only time they can get close to her, as during the day they are driven to act out their anger towards her and end up feeling rejected. Their learning can be affected too as the disorganisation gets into their fingers, bodies and minds causing dyspraxia and dyslexia, as well as forgetting and losing things.
2. An insecure attachment pattern often seen in children affected by domestic abuse is the *resistant/ambivalent* pattern (see Chapter 6), rooted in the variability and unpredictability of their parent's availability and empathy. Mum is sometimes warm and sensitive and sometimes anxious and preoccupied, or even frightened or frightening. Dad is sometimes loving and sometimes terrifying.

    'When I am most scared mum is too caught up in hurt and anger to comfort me.'

3. *Inverted attachments* occur when the child feels the need to 'parent' the mum (sometimes called the 'parentified child'), leading to a need to become very controlling.
4. A *merged attachment* can arise when separation has been experienced as traumatic abandonment or rejection, leading to unbearable aloneness. Where the father has been a terrifying figure, traumatised children can 'need to' cling exclusively to the mother to feel 'safe'. Traumatised mothers may also cling to their child, leading to stuck and fraught preoccupations between them both with no room for anything else. Such an anxious adhesive attachment can become entrenched, inhibiting the ability to explore outside the mother and to learn, and to school absence and refusal. It can also lead to difficulties managing all endings and transitions. Case Study 5 illustrates this being acted out in the sand, and how talking this through and slowly weaning the merged play helped.

Case Study 5   Weaning a 'merged' relationship

With a history of severe domestic abuse and a mother with variable mental health, 7-year-old T was understandably chaotic/disorganised but with many resistant/ambivalent features. When I first knew him, for example, he was very merged with his mother – sleeping with her and finding it extremely difficult to go to school (she needed him for her own comfort too). Mum started and engaged well with counselling and he had parallel therapy. In his therapy he repeatedly wanted to race cars in the sand and he always needed me to accompany him – so our two cars would drive round and round together in parallel. After a while I realised that we were 'acting out' a merged relationship in the sand, and I slowly weaned him into short and gradually longer periods of 'zooming' the cars round on his own, while I watched. At first he found this very difficult and would try to resist. It was clearly difficult for him to feel thought about when I wasn't actively 'zooming' with him, but with lots of talking through, and explaining that I was watching and wondering about him and the cars as they raced, gradually he shifted. He started to enjoy talking together about the play and the races. Our relationship began to feel more secure and his painful stories showed more resolution. In school his attendance improved and his writing and learning 'took off'.

These *anxious attachment patterns* will unconsciously become transferred into relationships and ways of relating with teachers and TAs in school, pushing them unconsciously to collude with the child's inappropriate expectations (e.g. merging too much). It is helpful for teachers to be aware of these dynamics, and try to find ways to respond differently.

Internalised aspects

The *internalisation* of both a desperately needy baby part, and an angry dangerous baby part, anxious about the damage it can do to its mother, but *unable to stop projecting*, can cause hurtful inner conflicts.

1. Sometimes anger may be *internalised* and 'acted in' against the self, in self-harm, eating disorders or various other manifestations of negative self-image, probably because expressing the anger openly would feel too risky, although they will not be aware of the link. Girls are particularly prone to this – usually when they are slightly older, and it can be very hard to shift, particularly if it becomes entrenched.

Leaking out of overwhelming hurting feelings that evoke punishment and blame, can lead to *bad* or even *mad* self-images, leading to more acting out or underlying *depression* and even suicidal feelings. These are very painful feelings and children can be driven to cover them up with distraction and bravado. This inner world of fear and badness is like a terrifying black hole to be avoided and defended against at all costs.

Unremediated trauma can lead to a cycle of getting into trouble and school exclusions,

Figure 9

because of the 'panic and disrupt' behaviours so vividly illustrated in W's 'black hole' drawing in Figure 9. The trouble is, these rubbishy feelings can easily be triggered in the school situation where learning tasks provide so many opportunities for failure and fear of failure.

2. For some children (and families) symptoms tend to be expressed *psychosomatically* – through headaches, tummy-aches, skin complaints, etc. These can then lead to *secondary problems* of school absence and rounds of hospital investigations, etc.

3. Domestic abuse can affect a child's inner life and *identifications*. The experience of being a victim is so engrained that they tend to become the victim in all relationships. Or they are so terrified of becoming a victim that they have to be a perpetrator to stay 'on top'. Sometimes they can flow between the two identifications.

4. Some children can grow up thinking and experiencing that the dysfunctional patterns they observed and experienced are what close relationships are. They may only know, for example, a sexualised version of getting close to others. They may experience that *conflict is inextricably linked with 'love'*. They may feel and fear that when you get close to someone they will end up hurting you or letting you down – so you are *better off avoiding closeness* and trust altogether – by always keeping your distance, or by provoking *them* first so *your* vulnerable bit doesn't get hurt. This is why in school such children will often hurt the teachers or TAs or the peers they feel closest to. *Sometimes just when the relationship seems to be going well they (are driven to) sabotage it.* It is very helpful for schools to be aware of this (potential) dynamic, and not immediately react by replacing a (very suitable, secure and empathic) one-to-one worker who has been hurt or rejected. Understanding and 'working with' the problem is helpful for everyone (see Case Study 42, p. 303). Understanding and supportive managers are crucial. Professional advice and clinical supervision may also be helpful with these more subtle links.

5. Such children may *come over as tough* even though underneath they may be *terrified* of their own *rage*, and of their inability to control themselves in these situations. They desperately need someone else to *control them and keep them safe*, and help them calm down in a safe way, as well as therapeutic help to heal their damaged inner worlds. If they do not find this containment on a consistent enough basis they may be unconsciously driven to 'push for it' until they find it *inappropriately* – in the last resort this may be 'in the shape of a prison cell'.[14]

Anger and acting out

Children can be angry with both their father and their mother, because of what has happened, or what has *been allowed to happen*, but this may need to be repressed for fear of further hurt, or of adding to their mother's hurt. Buried anger may then be *acted out* in different ways and other places:

1. The repressed anger may come out at school, or be transferred on to peers or siblings. Sibling rivalry is more than just acting out role modelling. It may be safer to take out angry feelings in school, or on a sibling rather than on a parent. In school similar rivalry can be acted out with 'friends' or 'enemies' – usually *not* just any child, but those with whom the child has a significant but ambivalent relationship.

2. Sometimes anger is 'projected' into others through winding them up either physically or emotionally – to make them into the angry one. It can then feel justified to complain of feeling hurt or badly treated, whereas getting in touch with the original or deeper hurts of not being properly loved and nurtured by our parents, or being scared by them, could be unbearable – especially when we need superficially to hang on to our image of a good idealised mum (or dad), because we depend on them. Such behaviours can lead already troubled children to become labelled or friendless at school.

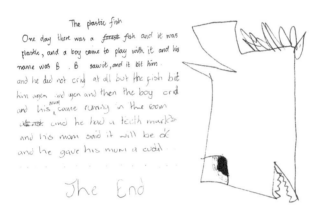

The plastic fish

One day there was a ~~forest~~ fish and it was plastic, and a boy came to play with it and his name was B . B saw it, and it bit him and he did not cry at all but the fish bit him agen and gen and then the boy cried and his mum came running in the room and he had a teeth marks and his mom said it will be ok and he gave his mum a cudil

The End

Figure 10

3. Anger is often a *secondary emotion* hiding deeper more painful feelings like fear, sadness and hurt relating to trauma, abuse, loss and neglect. Boys particularly are more likely to cover up their more vulnerable parts and feelings with toughness, bravado and anger.

4. Some children could become so preoccupied with anxiety that their needs aren't being met now, that they can only act or *react* to get them met, or *panic*.[15] They can be triggered into primitive aggressive behaviours to defend themselves in a 'dangerous world'. Such defensive and aggressive ways of relating and reacting will go directly into the child's (automatic) procedural memory, and lead to ongoing brittle, easily triggered *action–reaction* patterns, and long-term emotional difficulties. Triggered out-of-control episodes and behaviours may get children into 'double trouble' both at home and at school –often leading to *exclusions* and a 'bad' self-image.

5. *Out-of-control* outbursts can feel like helplessness, panic and 'spilling out' – not knowing how, when or whether the process might stop (like a toddler tantrum with no mum). These experiences can be very hard for carers and teachers to manage – evoking anger, helplessness and reactivity. It can be helpful to understand these feelings as those that the children themselves couldn't manage when they were helpless, traumatised infants and to seek help and have strategies in place.

6. Outbursts can sometimes be provoked by just observing vulnerability or helplessness in another child – which is so unbearable that it *has* to be attacked and annihilated (see Case Study 10).

Inhibitions and links to learning

1. The *capacity to process pain will be inhibited* – because they have lost, or never had, the experience of someone being there to understand and support them and carry them through, leading to poor resilience, poor toleration of frustration and learning difficulties.

2. *Frustration* may be impossible to bear, because it triggers the fear of unbearable pain – leading to *destructive attacks* on whoever (or whatever) has frustrated them. Having no

capacity to tolerate frustration inhibits learning, risk taking and thinking (which could actually relieve some of the frustration).

3. Paradoxically, *praise* can also evoke rubbishy feelings when a child's underlying feelings of being no good and bad are thrown into sharp relief. It can sometimes be hard for teachers to appreciate that some children are just too damaged to cope with praise (see p. 71–73).

4. Domestic abuse can *inhibit*:

   (a) *The capacity to mourn losses and endings* – because of unprocessed and perhaps repeated traumatic losses that can't be thought about – making school transitions very problematic.

   (b) *The capacity to symbolise.* Symbolic expression – through art, play or words – involves living with an unknown outcome. Unprocessed trauma brings the fear threshold so near the surface that fear of what may 'come up' is unbearable. This can have a direct effect on children's capacity to learn, try new things, play and create, and thus on their capacity to reach their potential.

   (c) *Memory.* Trauma can inhibit the capacity to remember, *think about* and talk through and thus *integrate* unbearable pain, because thinking might bring up unbearable pain. This also inhibits learning and remembering.

   (d) *Concentration* – getting in the way of starting or completing tasks.

Family aspects and complications

Children are *not just individuals.* They are also parts of *families* on which they depend, in which they are caught up and through which they learn about and experience close relationships and their own hurts and worries.

1. A child can play a *role* in and for the family, not just for themselves, but for others too. We all tend to slip into roles and patterns of relating in our families (like being the joker, the tough one or the helper). In broken, violent or dysfunctional families these can become *unhelpfully entrenched.* A 'good' sibling can be relieved of having to act out their own anger, when the 'baddie' in the family does it so effectively for them, while at the same time enabling them to continue to wear the 'halo'. Sisters often slip into this role in relation to brothers, because girls tend by nature to 'act in' rather than act out, but it can happen in many ways. It can also happen, that such roles can become reversed later on in life, or when the 'baddie' has had help to work through his difficulties and no longer needs to continue to act them out in the same way.

2. A child can sometimes act out in ways that *resonate with feelings mum (or dad) can't bear to acknowledge in themselves,* evoking particular irritation or ridicule. Sibling rivalry can be two children acting out the massive conflicts which they see/saw between their parents, but were unable to sort out.

3. *Sibling rivalry* can also continue to play a role for the mother or the separated parents, by giving them a more bearable form of family conflict to focus on and struggle with, rather than their own guilt ridden and still painful conflict.

4. Children can *unconsciously* develop problems or difficulties, which (perversely) keep a fractured family together (see Case Study 6).

Case Study 6   A learning difficulty communicates

When I was a SENCO (special educational needs coordinator) I worked with T, a bright girl who had very resistant/dyslexic difficulties, and who was also stuck in between her parents' very antagonistic relationship. Despite their fractured relationship, both parents were very worried about T's lack of progress and we had regular review meetings with them all together, thinking about her with lots of concern, which she rather revelled in. Meanwhile all the usual daily dyslexic-type support was having little effect. The stories we wrote together were all very sad and helpless – about drowning, needing help and needing to tie things together – clearly metaphorical; as were the particular letters she continually got stuck on – M and W – one facing up and the other down. She described her 'M' picture as a messy mole's house – which needed the two sides tying together, while her 'W' picture had water in the two halves, both of which were very wobbly, causing the children to fall down and drown. Sad and even traumatic, but not unhelpful as a communication, as she clearly communicated wanting her parents to stay together and not wobble – an impossible dream in the circumstances. I arranged a separate meeting with the parents and we looked at the pictures and stories together and thought about how they might talk about the realities of their separation with her – something they had been reluctant to do until then. They had feared upsetting her – and themselves, but they knew they had to talk about things as the conflicts were getting worse and Dad was moving out imminently. They said they would try to talk to her, perhaps with a supportive neighbour. For a while after that things deteriorated in our learning time. We were containing a lot of resistance and anger, but in class T's teacher noted an improvement! It felt as if the containment and the honesty was bearing fruit as a few weeks later her reading and writing slowly became easier and we could even talk about Dad's new house.

> We all need to matter and be noticed and held in mind by those closest to us, and to know enough of the truth so we can sort things out in our minds with the help of supportive adults or friends – even if it's painful. Out of desperation children can develop anti-social or even dangerous ways of being noticed and thought about – which is better than nothing when your mum is too often preoccupied with her own hurts and worries.

5. An entrenched pattern may develop or continue within some families, and thus within the child, that *one always looks on the bright side*, and avoids even thinking about uncomfortable things – leading to difficulties taking any risks in learning, and the uncomfortable things erupting out inappropriately (see Case Study 7).

Case Study 7   Avoidant looking on the bright side

Interestingly the one child I struggled to help through psychotherapy and parent consultations when I worked at Women's Aid was a child from just such a family, where hidden addictions were not acknowledged, while very educated mum continually looked on the bright side. Interestingly in his therapy the child seemed to become so 'addicted' to games and to winning that his therapy became very stuck, and I felt the need to remove the games for a period. He was not happy. Talking this through with him afterwards seemed to shift something.

6. When a mother at last manages to extricate herself and her children from a dangerous, overcontrolling or violent partner, the children's pent-up emotions can at last feel free to come out into the open. This can be a particularly difficult time for the mother, when her own trauma is still raw. Her momentary sense of relief, and of at last being free, can be shattered by having to cope with children and behaviour she is not used to having to control. Maybe the scary dad did all the discipline, leaving her deskilled or lacking in strength or confidence, or maybe the children were not (able to be) like this before. Maybe she herself is scared by such strong emotions from her growing children (much like she was of their father). Maybe their *rivalry* is just too much to bear, painfully reminding her of the conflicts she has only recently escaped. Maybe there has been a pattern of weak, dependent women and strong overbearing men in her extended family or history.

7. Mother–child relationships can deteriorate drastically at this time and become a serious secondary problem for both the mother and the child. It can happen that a boy can become labelled as being 'just like his father' – an accusation that hurts deeply, but that he can't help 'acting out'.

8. In extreme cases, *a child may start abusing the mother*. Sometimes one child in particular will slip into the role of expressing these powerful emotions *for* their siblings, or sometimes siblings will act out in different ways. This can lead to entrenched patterns both for the children themselves and for their carers and teachers, of feeling, for example, that *one is the goodie and one is the baddie* in the family – with consequent feelings of favouritism, rejection and resentment. Teachers can be struck by how children from the same family can be so different, and even exacerbate the labelling, leading to long-term self-esteem difficulties.

9. Where a mother just hasn't the *energy, resources or confidence* to cope with a particularly rebellious younger child, it can be both convenient for her and helpful for the family at large when an older (usually a) daughter can take over the role of managing the difficult one. The younger child may act out dangerous behaviours in an effort to get mum's attention, requiring his sister to be ever more vigilant, and his mum to be ever more 'depressed' and despairing. This may be the cause of children missing school or being continually late, and can lead to secondary problems, such as their mother being taken to court, or as they get behind with their school work, they lose their confidence and get into more trouble at school.

10. As they grow older it can be particularly difficult for a child who is the *same sex as the violent perpetrator* to grow up without those tendencies. In addition to having negative and violent role modelling, they may be or feel rejected, especially when their father has a new family who take precedence. But still somehow in the back of their minds they *want to be loved by their fathers*, or to have a father who loves them. In extreme circumstances they may feel that the only way they can feel close to or accepted by their father is to *be* like him – even like him in rejecting and abusing mum. They may rationalise that it's best to be a tough man (thus preserving their sadly needed image of a *good* tough dad – because the opposite is unbearable). They can even 'delight in' their tough self-image, and gain peer kudos for their toughness (sometimes called: 'identification with the aggressor'[16]). They can become disaffected from what parents and teachers think. This pattern can also happen with violent mothers and daughters, although statistically it is less common.

11. Another child in the family may evoke *sympathy* by being the helpless victim.

12. 'Splits' can develop in the (extended) family between those 'on the father's side' and those 'on the mother's side', which can be exacerbated by children being on the receiving end of *ongoing resentments between their parents*, even when they have separated. Splits can be projected into staff teams, and unconsciously and unhelpfully re-enacted by workers.

13. Children can feel painfully *stuck in the middle* of their parents, even after they have separated. Conflict-ridden contact experiences can continue for months or even years and may need help to shift. Their learning and behaviour can both deteriorate around contact times, especially when they are unreliable.

14. Domestic abuse is sometimes intertwined with or related to *parental mental health problems*. Any lapse in mum's mental health or capacities will tend to cause a child to relapse into anxious fears and acting-out behaviours, as well as exacerbating their insecure attachment, leading to more anxious behaviours. These behaviours and anxieties may then manifest in other settings, and inhibit learning and concentration.

With therapeutic and practical help for children and parents[17] such children and families *can change* (see Case Study 5, p. 31). But it is not easy. Even the journey towards change can evoke anxiety, relating to the scary loss of one's only known sense of 'how life is' and identity (perhaps as the tough one who gets into trouble or the helpless one that everyone 'rescues'?)

From the teachers' and the school's point of view, however, it is important to emphasise that any particular behaviour or symptom, including all these described above, does *not mean* that a child has experienced domestic abuse. These behaviours and symptoms will always mean something, but they could be linked to other traumas. As with suggestive artwork or stories, it is not helpful to draw any definite conclusions. They are, however, indications that something is troubling the child, and this needs to be taken seriously, and shared and discussed with selected colleagues, and with parents.

Understanding and responding helpfully to children who have experienced domestic abuse in school

Supporting each other and working together is crucial because:

- Children from such families will expect adults who care for them to have conflicts or be unable to cooperate; so it is helpful for them to experience adults overtly cooperating and supporting each other around their care and management.
- Managing boundaries securely (and with empathy) is very important for the parent–child and teacher–child relationships, and for the inner security of the child. It is never easy to change patterns of course, and such children might understandably have become programmed into needing to be in control. Supporting each other, and supporting (especially single) parents with this may be very important. The previous section on family aspects and complications illustrates why this might be difficult both for the mother on her own, and for the child. Parent work and support will need to include setting boundaries. Reversing a trend to give in to them (for an easy life) is not easy, but the longer you leave it the more difficult it can be to change.[18]

- Such children will inevitably tend to project and leak out their angry, worrying and hurting feelings on to both adults and peers – especially on to those closest to them. Understanding that we are sometimes 'pushed into' strong reactions by the child's projections, and stopping to think or talk with a colleague can help prevent unhelpful collusions and reactions.
- As they come to trust significant adults, such children may also either overtly or subtly disclose something worrying. Significant adults need to keep an eye open for such disclosures or indicators and always follow child protection procedures.
- Individual or group supervision and work discussion groups (see much discussion and examples of this in Chapter 16) can help alert us to their tendencies and offer a thinking space where alternative and more helpful responses can be discussed and reviewed.
- Ultimately we teach what we are. Developing our own self-awareness and emotional maturity enhances our capacity to contain the children's projections and communications, as well as fostering the atmosphere and containing capacity of the school.
- All the patterns and possibilities discussed above may be unhelpfully transferred into other significant situations and relationships, sadly evidenced by the story of D in Case Study 21, p. 106). Developing our understanding and knowledge is always helpful. This does not mean loosening boundaries. Empathic responses plus firm boundaries and supportive colleagues are all important. Sometimes patterns of intense conflict and control dynamics in families can be unhelpfully transferred on to staff groups or networks. Watch out for destructive splits and hurts within staff groups. Making opportunities to talk such dynamics through in an understanding way may help to ease and solve differences without blaming.

Some practical suggestions for school staff

Please see 'suggestions for teachers' for the 'chaotic/disorganised child' in Chapter 6, pp. 110–119, and if the child is displaying resistant/ambivalent behaviour, see pp. 100–106.

General points specific to children who have experienced or witnessed domestic abuse

1. It may be necessary to allocate a key worker who can build trust, in case the child needs to disclose anything.
2. Therapy that includes a concentrated and safely contained use of metaphor can be helpful when they are secure enough.
3. Parent work may be needed.
4. Parallel work with the parent and child can be helpful – addressing the outer and inner world.

Good school-based preparation

1. Allocate someone in the school to investigate domestic abuse resources in the area, to go on any relevant training and share findings with the staff.

2. Have posters about domestic abuse, and about domestic abuse services in the area on the parents' noticeboard. Domestic abuse awareness programmes are usually available for schools.
3. Have a selection of leaflets from the various agencies available both to give to parents, and in a public place where they can pick them up anonymously.
4. Having a 'crisis support' person in the school can be helpful, both for particular children, and for a busy teacher to know there is someone she can send a troubled child to. There may need to be rules as to when it is OK for children to go and when not.

Responding to individual children and families where you suspect, or where there is, domestic abuse

1. Share your concerns with selected others, either on a 'need-to-know' basis, or to check if they have similar concerns.
2. If they do have similar concerns, it is usually helpful to have a meeting with mum, to talk things through in a general way to begin with, but also to give mum an opportunity to share with you anything that could be getting in the way of their child's happiness, progress, ability to concentrate, make friends, take risks, etc. Comments like these may open up possibilities without judgement:

    'I'm just wondering whether there might be anything on her mind at the moment, anything that could be getting in the way of her . . .'

    'I don't know if this is relevant, but there is help available for children and families where there have been episodes of domestic abuse.'

3. Make an ongoing relationship with mum/carer. If you suspect domestic abuse in the current family set-up, but it doesn't feel comfortable to bring up the subject, it may be helpful for someone in the school to have a reason to try to develop a trusting relationship with mum. Meet regularly. Share information with staff (including TAs) who work closely with the child. A family support worker would be helpful.
4. Where children are showing quite worrying symptoms, it may be helpful to allocate a key worker to them – who can keep an ear open for child protection concerns.
5. Watch out for changes in types and levels of difficulty:

    (a) *Emergent* difficulties, such as recent changes in behaviour and circumstances, in children and families where there have not been significant problems before. It is helpful in these cases to assess whether the parents can empathise with their child's difficulty or not. Those who can may respond well to quite short-term interventions. Sudden changes can also indicate child protection concerns. If you are ever unsure about a child's safety then the safeguarding coordinator is the person to talk to.

    (b) *Entrenched* long-term and complex problems, which are likely to need more skilled or long-term therapeutic help.

6. You may want to read the child's file in detail and check out any involvement from other agencies.
7. Keeping a diary of things that have come up or been noticed about the child or family may be helpful.

8. Some children may need or benefit from a short individual or small-group time on a weekly basis – as may some mums, if resources are available.
9. If you discover that there is real cause for concern about a child or family you may need to think carefully about the best way to respond. Having a consultation with a specialist professional may be helpful. There are various levels of response:

   (a) Safeguarding procedures may be needed.
   (b) Short-term crisis support followed by a meeting with mum.
   (c) One-to-one support in school from a key worker or someone with experience of and empathy for such children.
   (d) Home-school link worker/key worker support for mums and families.
   (e) Multi-agency cluster involvement, where a mum agrees to this, will facilitate multi-agency support.
   (f) One-to-one talking and drawing with a student counsellor. Secondary pupils and some older juniors can often use a talking-based opportunity well. Younger children may need to communicate through art, play and stories.

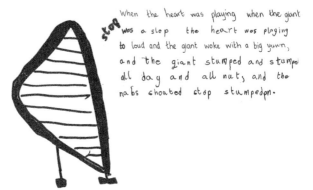

   (g) Psychotherapy, play therapy, or counselling for older children.

Figure 11

   So many aspects of domestic abuse may need to 'come up' to be processed, like anxiety about what the neighbours might hear, as we can sense in Figure 11, for example.
   (h) Counselling for mums.
   (i) Referral to an outside agency.

   – Domestic abuse services often offer individual and group therapeutic services for children and women.
   – Domestic abuse projects and centres often offer legal and housing advice as well as a 'drop-in' service, and the refuge is available for families who need a safe place to stay.
   – The NSPCC (National Society for the Prevention of Cruelty to Children) works with children who have been sexually abused.
   – CAMHS (Child and Adolescent Mental Health) is appropriate for the most complex cases involving self-harm, suicide, child and adult mental health, multiple family and sexual abuse problems. Family therapy may also be available.
   – Social care supports families with disabilities, children in need and where there are child protection concerns.

Because domestic abuse is a family problem, parallel work with parents or mothers can be crucial in order to make a difference. However with older teenagers, a counsellor's confidential relationship with a student may prevent this (at least for the time being).

Something all traumatised children need is emotional containment (this is the subject of Chapter 5).

Notes

1 D. W. Winnicott, *Playing and Reality* (Abingdon, UK: Routledge, 1991), 10.
2 Emotional containment is the subject of Chapter 6.
3 D. W. Winnicott, *The Child, the Family and the Outside World* (London: Pelican Books, 1992), 69–74.
4 W. R. Bion, *Learning from Experience* (London: Heinemann, 1962).
5 Barbara Dockar-Drysdale, *Consultation in Child Care* (London: Free Association Books, 1993), 34, 54.
6 Bessel van der Kolk, *The Body Keeps the Score* (New York: Viking, 2014), 108.
7 Described in Peter Walker, 'The 4Fs: A Trauma Typology in Complex PTSD', http://pete-walker.com/fourFs_TraumaTypologyComplexPTSD.htm.
8 Kolk, *The Body Keeps the Score*, 32.
9 Gianna Williams, *Internal Landscapes and Foreign Bodies* (Abingdon, UK: Routledge, 1998), 26–27.
10 See also the section on long-term foster and adoptive parents in Chapter 15, p. 293–296.
11 Rees Centre, *Educational Progress of Looked-After Children in England: Linking Care and Educational Data* (2015), http://reescentre.education.ox.ac.uk/research/educational-progress-of-looked-after-children.
12 Caroline Archer and Alan Burnell, eds, *Trauma, Attachment and Family Permanence* (London: Jessica Kingsley, 2003).
13 Ibid., 65.
14 D. W. Winnicott, 'Aspects of Juvenile Delinquency', in *The Child, the Family and the Outside World* (London: Penguin, 1954), 231.
15 Dockar-Drysdale, *Consultation in Child Care*, 34, 54.
16 M. Lanyando, 'Traumatisation in Children', in *Child and Adolescent Psychotherapy*, eds M. Lanyando and A. Horne (London: Routledge, 1999), 386.
17 For a number of years I worked as an educational psychotherapist at Women's Aid, where we offered psychotherapy to children affected by domestic violence, in parallel with their mothers receiving their own counselling and support.
18 Two handbooks by Caroline Archer that may be very helpful for parent workers are: *First Steps in Parenting the Child Who Hurts: Tiddlers and Toddlers* (London: Jessica Kingsley, 1999) and *Next Steps in Parenting the Child Who Hurts: Tiddlers and Toddlers* (London: Jessica Kingsley, 2000).

Understanding unconscious processes 4

Steve Debenport

Figure 12

This chapter is about familiarising school staff with the unconscious processes that go on all the time within all of us, and within relationships and dynamics in the classroom and the school.

In secure adults and children much of these dynamics are helpful and supportive, for example:

> *'Everything will work out, even if at times things are a bit difficult.'*
>
> *'Teachers will help me if I need it.'*
>
> *'Teachers will always listen to me even if I have to wait a bit.'*
>
> *'Learning something new is usually interesting,'*
>
> *'Talking things through is helpful.'*
>
> *'I am loved anyway even when my parents get cross with me.'*

But with very vulnerable and disturbed pupils and in stressful school settings the opposite can be true, and staff too can get hurt and anxious and their confidence can even become undermined. Negative dynamics can sap our energy and enthusiasm, and our effectiveness as school staff. This is not about teachers 'becoming social workers' or about needing lots of time – which they don't have – but about giving them enough understanding to enable them to step back a little, reflect internally on a situation or a puzzling child before responding, or maybe talk things through with trusted colleagues and come to see such processes in a clearer and more objective light. Thinking and talking things through can enable a more thoughtful response to difficult situations with children, and to possible misunderstandings with staff. Developing the capacity and skill to take opportunities to offer the odd thoughtful comment or response in a tricky situation – rather than ignoring or exacerbating it can open up possibilities for growth. This is not about solutions or knowing, it may be just acknowledging that we 'wonder about' something.

Let us think first about some of the processes we might observe.

Acting out

Anything that can't be thought about gets acted out: 'Freud alleged that acting out is in place of remembering . . . The forgetting that has had to take place . . . is of incidents in earlier life which have been extremely painful'[1] – incidents that were distressing and unsupported and that have therefore needed to be hidden. They remain, however, in the back of the unconscious mind as painful unprocessed 'bits', which need to be avoided for fear of the unbearable terror that even hints of them might evoke.

Acting out is triggered automatically and unavoidably when unbearable anxieties, shame or humiliation even *threatens* to arise. Anything that can't be thought about gets acted out. Conversely, even painful things that *can* be thought about are not acted out. Usually they are talked about and acknowledged so they don't need to be acted out. They are safely contained and OK in the mind, or made bearable by being tentatively shared with trusted others: *'I'm a bit nervous, will you come with me?'* leads to feeling supported, affirmed and cared for (see Case Study 24).

When it can't be contained, however, anxiety becomes unbearable and 'spills' or erupts out on to others or into hurting or rubbishing ourselves – leading to 'behaviour difficulties'.

Acting out is not just naughtiness. Of course it often has to be stopped and there may be consequences, but understanding something of the underlying causes can make all the difference when setting firm boundaries with vulnerable children. Understanding a behaviour's relationship to *particular* anxieties relating to a child's early history, perhaps (see Case Study 22, p. 126), or in more extreme cases to ongoing fears of humiliation, will make all the difference to our response.

Acting out could be to do with needing to ensure they are held in mind – when their resistant/ambivalent attachment needs are activated (see Chapter 6 for more on the resistant/ ambivalent attachment pattern and also Case Study 19, p. 100). Or it could be to do with needing to keep a *safe enough distance* – because closeness is threatening (see Chapter 6 for more on the avoidant attachment pattern and also Case Study 17, p. 92).

All these processes are unconscious of course. They are often called *defences* because they defend the child (or the adult) against threatened psychological pain. One could say that defences are needed until they are no longer necessary, The current and previous chapters explain in many ways why such defences are needed, especially by the more traumatised, 'damaged' and hurting members of society, and the essence of this book is to explain how we can play our part in alleviating that need. The child's behaviour could be seen to be acting out what can't be thought about. But sensitive, thoughtful, aware others might observe it.

The opportunity revealed through the acting out is that a sympathetic teacher or significant adult might be able to 'hear' the pain being defended against, wonder about it and find a way to gently acknowledge it so that it can slowly be owned and the need to repetitively act out such anxieties can be eased, little by little, or no longer necessary.

Some unconscious defences against anxiety (sometimes called defence mechanisms)

- A vulnerable child may develop a tough and *invincible 'false self'*,[2] displaying an attitude of bravado in his relationships and behaviours. This often covers up a feeling of helplessness and a fear of vulnerability. Maybe he was helplessly exposed to domestic abuse when he was too little to defend the victim or himself, or when to express his anger would be dangerous. For such children, experiencing or even observing unbearable vulnerability, hurt or injustices, can quickly evoke a need to display toughness. They need to eradicate it, even to bully the vulnerable victim – to cover up any burgeoning fears or feelings of vulnerability (see Case Study 10, p. 48).
- A child who has been repeatedly ridiculed or criticised may need to become *omniscient* (knowing everything already) because the experience of not knowing is felt to be too uncomfortable or humiliating. This can lead to difficulty accepting help, making learning and attempting tasks very difficult, or to work refusal or distractive behaviours, because trying and getting stuck or getting things wrong is unbearable.
- *Omnipotence* is about needing to be all-powerful, originating in early life perhaps when a child felt unbearably helpless observing hurtful things going on around or

to him. It can lead to controlling behaviour with both adults and peers. Not being in control – therefore not knowing what is going to happen – is just too risky.

- Vulnerable children may sometimes be driven to *deny* or *lie*, in order to avoid having to 'lose face' and experience unbearable humiliation. The problem is that this can easily lead to big 'double trouble' and punishment of the symptom – and to even more denying and lying. This can in turn damage the child's self-image (which can also get acted out). I once knew of an adoption that irreparably broke down because this was not understood, and it could not be talked through thoughtfully because the parents were so appalled and disapproving of the behaviour.
- At the other extreme there is the *compliant child*, who fears and avoids conflict, aggression and competition – and therefore avoids taking risks, having opinions and developing higher learning skills. For good reasons they may frequently feel the need to apologise or rescue others. As adolescents or adults they may only feel comfortable in enmeshed, distressing helping relationships, mirroring perhaps the role they slipped into in the family as a child.
- Some children may need to *evoke sympathy by becoming a victim* – through crying, grumbling, resentment, tale-telling, blaming and engaging others in 'dramas'. Maybe being hurt and sharing hurts is the only way they can feel heard and attended to at home. If we don't recognise their underlying tendency and need in school they may unfortunately hook us into colluding with their problems and dramas. We can also react the other way, by ignoring them or becoming negative about them.
- *Splitting* is a dynamic in which one person or group is seen as all good, while the other is seen as all bad. Others (including teachers) can sometimes become drawn into these dynamics and even 'enjoy' the putting down or 'terribilising' of the other, vicariously feeling better themselves in the process. Splitting can also occur within and between organisations, groups and families, and between home and school, as shown in Case Study 8.

Case Study 8   Triggered regressed patterns causing splits between home and school

Two of the most neglected children (3 and 5 years) I have come across, were adopted by a very secure and caring professional couple. One particularly dysfunctional pattern in the birth family was that, in the absence of practical care, F, the older one, would feed and 'manage' the younger one (within a 'sea' of rubbish, neglect and shouting); and he developed a consequent need to control and manage things, which persisted even years after the adoption. He had also learnt how to manage and 'split' adults to avoid getting into trouble. This resulted in him 'holding himself together' in school and appearing to be a good pupil, and then when he came out of school at the end of the day full of pent-up stress, he would take it out on (and need to control) his younger sister, which had a devastating and potentially dangerous effect on her, which his parents, despite all their wonderful commitment and skill, struggled to manage and to keep his sister safe. At parent consultations school staff would be full of compliments about how well F was managing, apart from the occasional incident where something would go missing – something that the parents would assure the school had been included in his bag – only to discover it days later on someone else's peg! When the parents tried to share their concerns about his controlling behaviour and their problems at home, school staff reacted with, 'Well, he's fine in school', leaving the parents feeling undermined and blamed, as if the difficulties were due to their poor parenting. Although there were some staff who could hear and understand their situation and provide their son with the attuned support he needed, this misunderstanding and split between home and school, which was at least partly unconsciously manipulated by the mixed up and very controlling little boy, continued for nearly a year.

We can all get caught up in splitting because idealisation can be difficult to resist; or we can become the painfully denigrated one that no one really understands and listens to. I remember my supervisor once pointing out how a child I was working with had idealised me. She wondered when I was going to fall! Splits can change!

- *Projection* is when we unconsciously push painful feelings out on to someone (or something) else – to make *them* feel the pain, not us. This can give us some temporary relief – so we don't have to feel bad and we don't have to apologise or suffer the consequences. It could happen in response to a behavioural trigger, or in response to a learning task that feels a bit too challenging. Rubbishing the task can sometimes feel easier than risking humiliation or having to ask for help. The other person will feel the projection in varying ways of course. They may even go along with it and take the blame. They may placate the child for 'an easy life', or they may react back and a big drama may grow around it involving teachers and an 'incident'.

At stressful times vulnerable children can sometimes project into those they work closely with. If this painful process is not recognised for what it is, teachers or TAs can carry around unnecessary stress, anger, guilt and helplessness, making teaching and supporting them difficult. This can also become 'acted out' within staff and staff teams leading to scapegoating, as R's teacher describes in Case Study 9.

Case Study 9   The power of projection: a new SENCO is amazed by the staff's resistance to R

We have this child in school called R. He comes from a big deprived family of five boys, many of whom have been through the school, and he joined the school just as I arrived. I remember coming into the staffroom one day and all the teachers were going, 'Oh that family, they're the worst,' and 'Oh yes, do you remember when . . .' They all had their horrific stories. Teachers just didn't want him in the classroom. He was thrown out all the time. Talk about scapegoating. No one thought to wonder why he might be like that.

Thus vicious cycles are born. The secret is to recognise and not 'buy into it'. We need to talk about it openly and support each other, and think *together* how we might best respond and ease children's dysfunctional but very 'real' needs.

Of course we can also project out parts of *our* personalities – making the *other* the sensitive one, or the lazy one or the clever one – thus denying those qualities in ourselves. Projection may be done with body language or with actions – like turning away, attacking others or putting others down; or with words, e.g. *'he's stupid'*, *'he's weird'*; or by putting ourselves down, e.g. *'I'm useless'*, *'I'm rubbish'*. It can also include attacking vulnerability, because one's own vulnerability is unbearable as it was never supported, and possibly ridiculed or even abused (see Case Study 10).

Case Study 10   The unbearableness of vulnerability

I remember hearing from a TA how P, a very disturbed and needy child I had just started to work with, was walking down the corridor with her after an incident in class one day and there was a rather quiet little girl just sitting on a chair with her head down outside the office. P took one look at her and for no apparent reason just kicked the chair from under her!

- *Repression* is when ideas, experiences and impulses are automatically pushed into the unconscious and therefore 'not known' and not remembered. Traumatic, violent or abusive sexual experiences are frequently repressed, as a way of coping with trauma and somehow carrying on. It can sometimes, as Bessel van der Kolk describes, be 'pushed into' the body or into psychosomatic symptoms.[3] The problem is that such experiences are buried somewhere, causing puzzling sensitivities that can be triggered; or phobias or obsessions that arise later on and can be difficult to shift for no obvious reason.
- Sometimes repression can be related to family secrets; or things can be more consciously buried – often related to *'knowing' what one is not supposed to know, and feeling what one is not supposed to feel*.[4] These can lead to learning inhibitions that are unconsciously linked to fearing 'learning what one is not supposed to learn' when 'sensitive' subject matter comes up. It can also relate to fear of retribution if one tells of 'secrets', making necessary disclosures and trauma work difficult.
- *Manic busyness or hyperactivity* can be a way of masking anxieties and uncomfortable feelings that might surface if we were still. In some more disturbed children, anxieties can threaten all the time and this defence can be around semi-permanently and get confused with ADHD and therefore be medicated, when really it originates from PTSD, developmental trauma or reactive attachment disorder (an American category similar to chaotic/disorganised attachment; see note 3 and also p. 107). The point is that medication may work (or not) but the underlying cause will remain, and side effects of the medication may complicate the problem. Later on it may come to the surface to be properly processed, with help of course.
- *Distraction* is a way of not thinking about uncomfortable or painful things by changing the subject.
- *Psychosomatic symptoms* (see above) may arise automatically out of anxiety or stress – usually in older adolescents or adults. It can be helpful to wonder what the body is communicating.
- Younger children may *wet or soil themselves, or cry* when stress arises – as if their anxieties are 'leaking out' (like G in Case Study 2, p. 23).

- *Freezing, withdrawal,* going numb or absenting themselves can be another way for helpless toddlers to avoid facing feared pain. Frequent *dissociation* in older children, however, can be a concern, as shown in Case Study 11.

Case Study 11   Dissociation relating to trauma and trauma triggers

A primary teacher told me about a 9-year-old looked-after child (L), who was fostered by her grandparents. She was removed from her parents when she was 2 years old because they both had severe drug and alcohol problems. There had also been domestic abuse and both parents were currently in prison. The grandparents were elderly and found L and her little brother quite exhausting and difficult to manage, although they were very committed to them. The teacher described how L had a tendency to dissociate and go blank when she was faced with a piece of work she felt she couldn't do, even though the teacher knew it was well within her capabilities. She also shared how more recently while her parents were in prison, L had noticeably settled and the dissociation had eased somewhat. Then her mother came out of prison and went to live with her partner who, after a few days 'threw her out' and mum had come back to L's grandparents to sleep on the couch. Mum was apparently in and out of the house and quickly back on the drugs and drink, with little time for her children. Predictably L regressed and the dissociation came back. We agreed that this was related to her preoccupied neglectful mother's reappearance. We also discussed how dissociation is often related to very early trauma, before children have words, or when to act out their anger and hurt could lead to children being shouted at or worse – leaving 'freezing' or switching off the only option.

In mild cases, dissociation can be regarded as a defence mechanism in order to master, minimise or tolerate stress; while more pathological and frequent dissociation could lead to dissociative disorders later on and should be investigated. Petit mal can sometimes be confused with dissociation and may need to be checked out.

- *Delinquency.* Adolescents may engage in *delinquent acting out* or turn to drink or drugs – to cover up unbearable feelings anxieties.

Defences can interfere with learning (see Chapter 7). Any of the above defence mechanisms could be triggered by a learning task that feels too challenging, that threatens to touch on a sensitive issue or just the task of learning itself – because learning requires us to:

- be able to tolerate frustration;
- be able to tolerate need and dependence;
- be able to bear not knowing;
- feel OK with someone else knowing more than you and helping you.

So if, defences are needed until they are no longer necessary, the question is how do we move children in the direction of their defences no longer being necessary? This is the subject of the remaining chapters (and of all the practical suggestions too).

Transference and countertransference

Transference

Transference is a particular form of projection, when patterns of relating, expectations and 'relationship dynamics' from an earlier (usually parental) relationship become transferred into new significant relationships. Children naturally bring expectations into school with them, influencing how they expect to be treated, and how they have 'learnt' to behave in relationships with significant others and in response to little challenges. All this happens unconsciously and naturally and in most cases it is not a problem. Secure children evoke positive transference. They expect teachers to like them and treat them kindly. They expect to be listened to and supported when they have a little problem. They are confident to ask for help when they need it, and to say if they can't manage something. They expect people to be reliable, and if someone is late or absent they imagine there is a good reason that they can talk about. This makes teaching them easy and enjoyable.

Other more negative transference, however, can cause problems for teaching and learning:

- Children who have been the recipients of too much destructive criticism in their early years, for example, may push us to (need to) criticise them.
- Children whose parents could not bear to see them struggle may push us to do things for them, as their frustration is so hard to see and to hear.
- Children who have needed to be perfect for their parents may imagine the teacher's absence is related to their bad behaviour, which has got the teacher down, leading to guilt and anxious acting out.
- Rejected children may behave in such a way as to make us want to get rid of them. Case Study 18 on p. 99 vividly illustrates how a child with acute separation anxieties pushed unaware and stressed staff into giving up on him.

Through transference a child's powerful feelings and expectations can get right inside us, pushing us to respond in unhelpful ways (unconsciously colluding with their expectations), and then afterwards we can feel bad or angry. In Case Study 12 a TA describes getting 'hooked into' a child's challenging transference, and the powerful learning experience this later became, as she thought more deeply about it and realised what had happened.

Case Study 12 The unhelpfulness of getting hooked: a learning experience

One day when I worked at the pupil referral unit I was in the timeout room with a child for a very long time (about four hours!) and still he was swearing and yelling at me and trying to kick me. I was trying to stay calm – which I'm normally very good at, but I guess I got to the point where it started to get to me. He had been swearing at me for about an hour and I just felt helpless to stop him. So I found myself saying 'Every time you swear that will be two more minutes that we are staying in this room. I counted: 2, 4, 6, 8, . . . and I counted . . . and I got to about 64! And then I stopped myself and I thought, 'I can't believe I'm doing this – I know this isn't going to help – or make him stop.'

So I stopped. I'll never forget that experience because that it totally brought me to a place where I realised that this sort of threat just doesn't work. I think I was just hooked into a desperate need to stop him. I felt huge pressure – and I guess I was exhausted. But then I realised that he was winning and I was losing. Maybe like him I had become hooked into winning and not losing. There was something about the unbearableness of losing, and of him having all the power over me. Of course I realise now that I was hooked into his transference.

He couldn't bear to lose or be bossed about (by me or anyone).

But the reality was I had all the power, because I wasn't going to let him out of the room. I guess there was something about him needing to resist being controlled by me. I think I felt helpless too, because I had been stuck in that tiny horrible room for four hours and nothing was working. It was definitely getting to me.

When I realised what was happening I just stopped. I just stopped counting. I waited and then I said – which I normally always say – 'When you're ready to leave the room we'll leave the room.' It took some time, which I knew it would. He tried to kick me a few more times and he punched me a few more times but after a few minutes he stopped – and we left the room. I guess I changed from being hooked into his pattern, to not engaging with it, stepping away as it were and waiting for him to calm down – which they always do eventually. That was such a learning curve for me. Normally whatever is happening, I can keep a little distance and I can stop and think. But this was such a powerful transference – it certainly made me sense the utter helplessness and pressure of being controlled by someone! I guess that was his experience at home!

It can be very difficult sometimes for educated teachers and TAs – who want to be successful capable professionals, to acknowledge that they are having problems with a child. In Case Study 13 an inclusion manager describes how even experienced teachers can need sensitive support and opportunities and encouragement to open up to talking things through, and how very helpful that can be.

Case Study 13 Supporting a young teacher with thoughtfulness, empathy and mentoring

We had a new member of staff in September called Miss D. She came from her previous school with a reputation for being much loved and respected by the parents. But in our school we have a different sort of parent. They often need a scapegoat to ease their own insecurities. If they see a weakness they will exploit it. As time went on there were many (about seven) complaints about this teacher from parents, so Miss D and I obviously needed to talk about this together, which was difficult for her. I tried to do it in a very sensitive way, just to find out what had happened and how we could understand and think about this together. Our parents can certainly be very 'mouthy'. For example, 'You? You're about 19 and you're crap. How can you teach my child?' Not a nice thing for a young teacher to put up with. There were two particular parents who complained about her, and I used to see them every day so I knew them well. At my first meeting with Miss D, I sensed how difficult it was for her to acknowledge that she was finding some of the parents quite difficult, even though she was clearly feeling 'put down' and undermined by their behaviour, and we talked about that. I think that was really important. It was important for her to know that I understood. We always emphasise in our school that we see it as a strength when staff come to talk things through. So we agreed that I would come into her classroom and observe, including the before- and after-school times. We also saw many parents together, and she saw how I talked with parents – with lots of thoughtfulness and empathy for their situation. It was also important for the parents to see us working together, so they could see her being strong and respected. This thoughtful reflective support between the teacher and I made a huge difference both to the parents and to the teacher. She even sent me a card in the holiday thanking me saying, 'I wouldn't be the teacher I am now without you. Thank you so much.'

In fact a nurturing school encourages all of its staff to be open to acknowledging difficulties and stresses, and to think together particularly about the challenging children and dynamics in the classroom (see Chapter 16 about a nurturing school).

The good news is that if we understand what is going on, and spend a little time thinking and talking with colleagues who also understand these processes, transference can be a very significant tool in *helping us to understand children's inner worlds*, in helping us to *make hypotheses about what might be affectively happening for the child* and thus to respond more thoughtfully to the child, as the TA at the pupil referral unit belatedly and painfully discovered in Case Study 12 above.

Acknowledging that we are struggling with a child and feeling free to talk that through with colleagues and in supervision groups can be invaluable, enabling us to respond differently and more thoughtfully. For children, these experiences of significant adults responding in thoughtful, understanding ways without diluting necessary boundaries, will slowly ease their expectations, change their relationship patterns and increase their learning resilience. Thus teaching and working with challenging children begins to bear fruit. Stress and challenge will still be around, but together it can be seen as an interesting problem and an opportunity, and with patient responsiveness, it will lead to growth. It can also be inspiring and energising for staff!

Conversely without the encouragement and opportunity to talk thinks through together, without a school atmosphere and leadership that encourages this and sees the reflecting process as valuable and leading to insight, thoughtfulness and emotional growth in children, challenging children in school can sap the energy, confidence and hopefulness of teachers and schools. Such transference can lead to a culture of giving up, grumbling, scapegoating certain children and families, stress, high staff turnover and absence. The school well-being manager in Case Study 14 later in the chapter illustrates the benefits of talking things through together (work discussion) and of having clinical supervision[5] in her school.

In the nurture base where I worked, staff had a five-minute debrief session at the end of each day to share thoughts on any experiences of projection and transference. This made a huge difference to their teaching and caring capacities with the very challenging children in the class.

Countertransference

It is not only children who have 'internal working models' (see p. 4). We all have a range of expectations, assumptions and vulnerabilities derived from our past experiences.

We might have been overcontrolled as children – causing us to find very rebellious or controlling children particularly difficult, or to tend to become a bit overcontrolling ourselves. We might have had parents with very high expectations of us, causing us to need to be 'perfect' and find acknowledging and talking through difficulties quite uncomfortable. This could inhibit the all-important 'working together' and supporting each other, which is so beneficial in this work.

We might have been overcriticised, causing us to be particularly sensitive to criticism or to become overcritical of children who can't seem to manage, or who get in a muddle.

We might have been overhelped, or overprotected perhaps from struggle and pain – causing us to find it very difficult to wait while children struggle with frustrations or make mistakes (enabling them to learn from their own experience). This can be particularly difficult for TAs, who work closely with slow or anxious learners.

In our case, such tendencies will probably be mild, many of them will be positive and hopefully we will be aware of our vulnerabilities – which is helpful because we can compensate for them.

It is certainly helpful though to bear them in mind, because they will probably have an impact on our teaching, and even become somewhat transferred on to the children (and staff too) in times of stress.

In the nurture base mentioned above the staff were very open with each other about such things and they would tell each other when for some reason they were feeling pushed towards the edge or particularly vulnerable and they needed to swap roles or take a short break.

Sometimes our own vulnerabilities can inadvertently leak out and trigger unhelpful behaviours in children. This is *countertransference* and it can be communicated through body language too. Disturbed children have often needed to become very tuned into 'vibes' and non-verbal clues and can pick up the slightest indication that we are a bit 'down', worried, tired or sick. Our 'edginess' can unconsciously remind them of troubled relationships at home, and provoke insecurity and acting-out behaviours.

Countertransference also occurs when kids (or other staff!) 'push our buttons', evoking a 'knee-jerk' or a stronger reaction to them. Unconsciously we may become identified in some way with their behaviour or their helplessness and our own vulnerabilities and reactions could become triggered by their resonating behaviour, causing us to overreact.

Unhelpful ways we might be pushed to react because of
countertransference – unconscious interference from
our own vulnerabilities

- Getting stuck in what to do.
- Easing our helplessness and pain by judging or evaluating, or making splits between good and bad.

- Avoiding the pain of staying with a child's anxious communication – by going into rational problem-solving, fixing or rescuing mode too soon.
- Becoming *overwhelmed* by the intensity of feelings, and feeling the need to switch off, react, blame, seek yet more help or get more people involved or give up.
- Overidentifying with the child/parent/adult, because of resonances with our own history.
- Psychologically merging with the child or adult – and therefore becoming overinvolved.
  I knew a TA who lost her job because she became overinvolved with a child she worked with. He came from a very dysfunctional family and also lived near her, and as she got closer to him he evoked huge empathy in her and she would invite him into her house.

- Needing or getting caught up in the vicarious satisfaction of experiencing our own unresolved issues through the child/adult.
- Blaming or putting down the child or adult because we cannot bear to stay with their pain, their vulnerability, or their acting-out communications.
- Needing to avoid conflict, leading to difficulty setting appropriate boundaries.

The secret is to notice these and have the confidence to talk them through with trusted colleagues. Relating to experiences of children 'pushing our buttons', it can be helpful to use Exercise 2.

Exercise 2   The links between our own emotional growth and the emotional growth of children we work with[6]

Reflect on these questions:

1. What did you think of yourself in your early life? What were your 'bruises'? How did you learn to live with them? How have the bruises enriched your emotional life?
2. How have your hurts and healings increased your sensitivity to others, improved your caring skills, enlarged your capacity for holding pain?
3. Are you familiar with your vulnerabilities relating to these bruises?
4. Are there 'buttons' relating to these vulnerabilities that children sometimes press?
5. What helps you to manage thoughtfully when your 'buttons' are pressed?
6. How can you use your experience and learning to enhance the emotional growth of children?
7. What have you subsequently discovered of the wellsprings of your own creativity, motivation and emotional growth?

The value of mindfulness in such situations[7]

Even with awareness the transference can be so strong sometimes that it can be difficult to 'step back' for a moment before responding. It can be difficult to 'collect' ourselves and shift out of the reactive state and move towards responding thoughtfully rather than reacting. This is where regular mindfulness practice can be so helpful, giving us a tool like a brief mindful pause (see p. 276) to aid our shifting and 'stepping back' and facilitate thoughtful responding – or not responding! A 'mindful pause' is a short quiet moment of conscious breathing or tuning into our inner body or our breath, which can shift us into a calmer or more thoughtful state. It can be especially useful in tense situations.

Professionalism

It is possible then to make an effort *not* to fit into children's unhelpful expectations and patterns, and provide them with a different experience of relationships and expectations. When in the face of strong pressure to continually fit into their pattern, we repeatedly respond with more humane understanding, with a more tolerant or a more firm or a more patient response, we give children a chance to adjust their picture of the world and grow on the basis of this new experience.

This is the professional response, and the great opportunity for teachers and school staff.

Therapists do this in a concentrated way for very disturbed children, but teachers see children day in and day out and will inevitably develop important relationships with them, particularly those who are younger and more needy.

It is a challenge, but also an opportunity, when we have particularly difficult children in our classes, to think that we *don't have to collude* with their deep-seated feelings by responding in the way they push us to. Understanding and reflecting *together* can be so helpful with this, as Case Study 14 illustrates.

Case Study 14 An assistant head talks about the benefits of clinical supervision and work discussion

At school we foster wondering and thinking together all the time – both encouraging teachers to verbalise their wonderings in front of the children and to wonder later with each other what might have been going on for a particular child. When we first started the process of being more nurturing and more reflective as a whole staff, we met in groups and individually. We had both staff and individual supervision. Lots of times at the end of the day a teacher or a TA would come to me or the head or the deputy (we have a large staff) and say, 'I'm really struggling with this child. We had a really difficult time today and we're wondering – is there a different way for us to manage this?' 'We don't understand what is going on' – and we would talk about it. After a lot of this kind of support staff are now often able to support each other. Some of them like V and C are really good at wondering what can we do differently to make it easier for particular children.

I think having that thoughtfulness and the opportunity to say 'I'm not coping' is so important. We always emphasise that as a strength. It's also having a knock-on effect on children's behaviour generally. What I see in our school behaviour log is that the number of logged behaviour incidents has fallen dramatically from when I first started, when there were hundreds of them. This last half term there were 10 incidents in the nursery (of 80 children) for the last half term. In reception we had 56 incidents for 150 children for the whole term.

If a child can experience within a trusted developing relationship that his behaviours are (on the way to being) understood, that is the first step to shifting the need for such behaviour.

As our relationships become more secure and trusting we will be able to find *opportunities to talk through* difficulties and tendencies with them. Problems, including transference, will become potential opportunities to talk things through with each other and find ways perhaps to talk with the child; and help them experience that things that *can* be talked about will *not* need to be acted out – well not so much anyway. Even if acting out happens, it will likely be less intense, and it can be talked and thought about again and again as opportunities allow. Little and often is best. All this is helpful for growth, and observing children grow is very rewarding.

Notes

1 Philip Maggs, 'Working with Behaviour Problems: Growth Through Work' (1987), unpublished paper presented at a London conference for staff at residential schools, cited in Paul Greenhalgh, *Emotional Growth and Learning* (London: Routledge, 1994), 49.
2 D. W. Winnicott, 'Ego Distortion in Terms of True and False Self', in *The Maturational Process and the Facilitating Environment* (New York: International University Press, 1965), 140–152.
3 Bessel van der Kolk, *The Body Keeps the Score* (New York: Viking, 2014), 108.
4 John Bowlby, 'On Knowing What You Are Not Supposed to Know and Feeling What You Are Not Supposed to Feel', *Canadian Journal of Psychiatry* 24, no. 5 (1979), 403–408.
5 A confidential time when staff can talk through puzzling and hurtful experiences with someone with counselling skills and psychodynamic knowledge and understanding.
6 Taken from a similar questionnaire in Greenhalgh, *Emotional Growth and Learning*, 91.
7 Chapter 14 has a fuller description of mindfulness.

Emotional containment

5

Figure 13

Emotional containment is the experience of being and feeling held and understood, or thoughtfully 'wondered about' in someone's (initially the mother's) mind.

One could say that a baby's unprocessed emotional state needs to be safely contained and modulated by his mother. Through smiles, cries, reaching out and similar behaviours, a baby is programmed to communicate with his mother or primary caregiver; who thinks about him, understands what he seems to be communicating and responds helpfully with nurturing or engaging actions, or with soothing sounds, touch and words. This leads to an experience of containment for the baby, who then returns to a calm state. Wilfred Bion called the mother's internal processing of the child's communication 'reverie', and the whole interactive process between mother and baby, (emotional) 'containment'.[1] In the words of Heather Geddes:

> He [Bion] describes the process whereby the infant, who has no experience of . . . the outside world, experiences his needs as overwhelming; and how the 'sensitive enough mother' understands her child's desperation, and can herself bear the anxious quality of it; she responds in a way which communicates this understanding. The infant is reassured by the mother's understanding response, and his or her anxiety is diminished by the experience of being understood.[2]

This interactive process is both experiential, fostering emotional capacity and security; and neurological, fostering connections and hormonal flows in the brain relating to their experiences.

In this process the parents' own capacities are crucial. This includes the capacity to bear the child's pain or anxiety. As Geddes continues,

> The capacity and sensitivity of the mother, and her ability to bear and understand the anxiety triggered by the child's fear and uncertainty, is a significant aspect of early attachment experience which Bion (1967) has linked to (the capacity for) learning and thinking.[3]

With repeated experience of their mother's reverie and emotional containment, children come to know that pain is bearable, understandable and that it can be eased. Slowly they internalise this capacity for taking in, wondering and thinking for themselves. They learn through experience that their anxieties will be bearable, because help is always there before too long when they need it. They develop their own capacity to contain experience, and to think and talk about it.

This same nurturing process occurs also in the positive interactions of joy and delight between mother and baby, enhancing their sociability and the enjoyment of connectedness and fun.

Thus their capacities for engagement and curiosity develop, and 'learning from experience' happens, which is more like realising and very different from rote learning and doing what you're told.

Through sensitively and increasingly being given space to struggle on their own without pressure, children learn not just about the 'world', but also about the bearableness of frustrations, about the rewards of struggling and about experiences of fun, interest and love.

As time goes on, for secure children an authentic inner self begins to grow within them, they become secure with their developing interests and in the knowledge that their needs and hurts will be understood and put into words they can relate to.

Emotional containment is particularly important when big hurts and losses arise. The quality of emotional support, hurting or anxious babies and children receive from their primary caregivers during and following difficult and painful experiences makes all the difference.

Children with a good secure beginning have the best possibility of coming through trauma. They can even grow through the experience, both in their inner worlds and in what they have to give.

Emotional containment in school

As they move through infant and junior school, most children manage the normal challenges of learning and socialising by drawing on their developing inner resources, and by seeking appropriate help when they need it with no problem. They can use reassurance and encouragement, and wait if necessary, knowing that help will come soon if they need it.

Changes and transitions can sometimes be painful for everyone, but in fact they are essential for growth and development. When a transition anxiety arises and a significant adult is not there, a secure child will search for a secure place inside his mind, maybe remembering his mother, or how he was understood or helped by a trusted adult in school, to help him manage and stay OK, or he will seek help from someone he trusts and find it.

Sensitive attuned adults will naturally respond to children's needs, 'read' their subtle behaviours or their play communications and slowly help them put words to their feelings. Such helpful conversations will both ease children's anxieties, help them develop their own ability to talk things through and aid their understanding of life.

For vulnerable children, however, life is different. They don't expect or even know empathy because they haven't experienced it. They haven't developed resilience, or their own containing capacities. All changes and transitions, all humiliations and hurts will threaten their secure base and get acted out in some way.

When a vulnerable child is triggered into fear or panic and there is *not an adequate 'containing person' available*, the intense feelings will burst out on to the nearest or 'safest' scapegoat – often leading to further hurt and even punishment. If such unavailability has happened repeatedly to a child, they can become programmed to project out even little hurts, because they have no idea that support *could* be available and that little hurts could be made bearable. For some children little hurts can also trigger panic linked to past trauma – leading to disproportionate reactions. All these can be difficult for school staff to bear and manage, especially if they don't understand that in the heat of the moment – the child can't help it – they need help. They need emotional containment.

The good news is that *in the school setting significant adults are around all the time*. They have many opportunities to respond to children's behavioural communications in a containing way. This involves receiving the intense feelings the child (or person) *evokes* (transference experiences – see Chapter 4), wondering and reflecting on the experience or feeling and holding it in mind until some understanding of it becomes clear – much like the mother's 'reverie' – then reflecting on whether, how and when to communicate this back to the child in a way they will be able to use. This can sometimes involve bearing and holding uncomfortable, hurtful or worrying feelings (and urges) inside ourselves for some time – even several days, before taking a suitable opportunity to respond.

I am of course aware that, while it can make a huge difference to vulnerable and damaged children when they receive emotionally containing responses from the adults they are close to in school (such repeated experiences can even shift their inner worlds and expectations), it is not always easy – especially when we are stressed ourselves. This can at times be very difficult, especially when the projections from the child are very negative and intense.

Also, when our own vulnerabilities are triggered (see p. 53) we can become stuck or reactive. We may quickly slip into rational problem-solving, fixing or rescuing mode in preference to staying with the child's pain a little longer and wondering before responding. We may become overwhelmed by the intensity of feelings and feel the need to switch off, react, blame, get more people involved or give up. Staying with a child's anxious communication is not easy when it threatens to overwhelm. Our own anxieties can also make setting appropriate boundaries difficult. We may need to bear 'hatred' and remain thoughtful, firm and empathic at the same time.

This is when emotional containment is needed for staff. 'Digesting' a child's (and our own) powerful feelings is often best done by talking things through with thoughtful colleagues. Just knowing we have trusted, caring, non-judgemental colleagues eases anxieties. Sometimes understanding and helpful insights may come up on their own as time passes. Such 'digestion' involves unconscious processes within ourselves. Staff who work most or all of the time with very vulnerable and damaged children benefit hugely from clinical supervision, when they can talk about puzzling children, painful feelings and experiences that 'get' to them, in a confidential setting. I have myself supervised such staff in a pupil referral unit and with inclusion staff in mainstream settings, as well as benefitting from clinical supervision myself.

Case discussions and debriefing sessions, involving staff supporting each other using the sort of thinking and understanding described in this book can also be very containing and facilitating.

If together we can make the link between the anxieties triggered in *us*, and the *child's* anxieties, we can come to understand the child from the inside, and our future responses will communicate that and ease rather than exacerbate the situation.

The reflection exercises on pp. 160 and 167 can be both helpful and containing for us and useful for case discussions, as well as facilitating our containing capacities and helpful responses towards the child.

A containing school encourages staff to seek help, and sees this as a sign of strength! Supporting each other is crucial (Chapter 16 about a nurturing school talks a lot about this). The capacity to offer emotional containment depends both on *our own* inborn sensitivity, and on our history of empathic experience and reflective support, both currently and during difficult times in the past.

Sensitive people need to keep their 'thinking caps' on in these difficult moments, however, and not become overinvolved, and set appropriate boundaries. Regarding sensitivity, some people feel more deeply and take things to heart more than others and this is both a strength and a difficulty, as they can be more easily hurt and affected by children's challenging or puzzling behaviours. If, however, they can manage to 'stay with' the child in their difficult moments, the child can sense that the adult *really feels for them* and is 'with them' in a deep way, which will be helpful. This is empathy – felt not spoken, but the child knows it.

We can make a real difference to the children we work with, both in the short term and in the long term – as a nurture base teacher shared with me recently:

> *The other day a child came up to me when I visited his school for a meeting and said, 'You're the only teacher I ever had who actually cared.' This is a child who left the nurture base nearly three years ago!*

That relationship and memory was obviously right inside him. Who knows where it will take him in the future.

We can all grow and develop of course, and come to terms with difficulties through first-hand experiences of caring, thoughtful, resilient friendships and relationships – just like the children!

Judging ourselves is definitely not helpful. Regarding the influence of our personal histories it is not so much what has happened to us, as the support we have received around our experiences, and whether we have been able to integrate them well enough and acknowledge and talk about our tendencies and vulnerabilities, which makes the difference. Just like for the children, a difficulty is also an amazing opportunity – to talk something through that needs to come out into the open perhaps. It's how we learn. A good place to start might be to reflect on our own emotional holding (or containing) capacities (see the questionnaire in Appendix 2, adapted from *Emotional Growth and Learning* by Paul Greenhalgh[4]) and then think about what skills we might like to develop further. We may also like to reflect on our early and formative experiences and see how we have grown through our struggles, or how our 'bruises' might still inhibit us (see Exercise 2, p. 54). All these personal explorations are life enhancing – for us and for the children. You could say in a deep way we teach what we are!

Practical containment

The containing process is 'right brain to right brain'. It involves intuition, sensitivity and thoughtfulness. In my experience it arises naturally as we come to know and understand the child both through experience, and through knowledge perhaps of what they have been through.

Sometimes there will be no verbal response at all. It may be just quietly doing or offering something, which subtly eases the child's bubbling anxiety or meets a sensed need. It may involve deciding not to say anything, as we may feel they are not in a place (yet) to receive our understanding. It may temporarily involve shifting their bubbling emotional state through suggesting something completely different – a walk around the school, a surprising question, a cup of tea. It may involve safe-holding them or guiding them calmly to a safe place for a while until they calm down, as we see in Figure 13 at the beginning of this chapter. It may be *not* responding to provocation or getting 'hooked in' to unhelpful patterns – like S' key worker in Case Study 15.

Case Study 15 The importance of calm and understanding support

S had always found separation from mum and getting into school very difficult. Every morning he would scream and cry as he entered the school, which was hard for both him and his mum – and for staff too! It was decided that his empathic attuned teacher and his one-to-one worker would use lots of 'holding-in-mind' comments and gestures, and put lots of effort into their relationships and boundary setting with him. Also, after his regular separation tantrum his key worker would calmly and quietly escort him into school through the vale of tears and screams. The school found his tantrums would ease after about 5–15 minutes and he would regularly work and play happily in the playground till the end of the day. Coupled with occasional learning mentor support for his mum, he began to settle and learn in class and his separation tantrums eased. He had clearly found secure relationships with his key worker and teacher, and a secure setting in his class and in the school, which could enable his learning, even though at home things were still ambivalent.

Box 1 presents some *non-verbal* ways to offer emotional containment – by the quality of your presence and just quietly being there.

Containment can also be facilitated *symbolically* and some examples of symbolic containers are given in Box 2.

Box 1   Containing ways of being with children

- Presence.

- Silent attention.

- Waiting patiently, not intruding.

- Not helping until asked – tuning in and bearing frustrations with the child.

- Quietly attuning to the child and their non-verbal, behavioural and metaphorical communications.

- Not commenting but attending thoughtfully.

- Empathising with, or silently bearing hurts, rather than reassuring or advising.

- Thinking about possible helpful concrete responses – *doing* something helpful.

- Surviving difficult times/breaks.

- Tuning in to transferred feelings from the child.

- Tuning into our own (countertransference) triggered vulnerabilities.

- Keeping containing consistent boundaries.

Box 2   Symbolic containers

- Box to keep special things in.

- Shared stories – written and read, played and acted together, remembered and recalled appropriately and kept safely for next time – in a book or folder.

- Small and large boxes – safe containing spaces and containers to get or hide inside.

- Clay containers and models.

- Sand box – sand worlds, sand play.

- Tray as a frame for play – with figures, Lego, etc.

- Models made and kept or photographed.

- Stories typed or 'published' with pictures or drawings and stuck in a book.

- Thoughtful games that enable contained symbolic 'acting out'.

- Use of frames or worksheets to contain and structure work.

- Use of 'frames' for writing or drawing.

Figure 14 was done by a child with a very violent history. It is interesting to see that what appears to be a very traumatised child in the painting is surrounded by a 'containing' frame – giving a sense that the horror is safely contained and in the past, or can be expressed in the safety of the containing relationship with the supportive adult perhaps.

Doing something thoughtful can be containing too, as shown in Box 3.

Figure 14

Box 3   Containing actions and ways of managing

- Same room, same layout, same time.

- Arranging thoughtful session times for particular children.

- Taking turns to write a line of a story or 'conversation'.

- Passing something – when it feels helpful to the relationship and the child.

- Tidying up together.

- Switching to a safe but similar activity when the child is becoming overwhelmed, e.g. soft-ball throw and catch.

- Arranging calm down time for particular children – calm-box activities (see Box 7, p. 95).

- Alerting school staff/parents to the likelihood of regression or acting out around breaks/endings.

- Calendar stretching from before the holiday to after next holiday with times and holidays marked – to take home and keep a copy in school too. Children can also mark on birthdays and special days (see p. 237).

- Asking a child whether it might be helpful to share a particular vulnerability with their parent or teacher.

- Reading a specially chosen story to a child (or the child's class) – see example on p. 136.

Concrete and symbolic containment is particularly important for children who can't bear too much thinking and empathy, although thoughtful empathic comments can be containing too.

Containing words

Emotional containment as described above, involves *bearing* a child's (projected?) pain because he can't bear it himself, reflecting on it and responding with thoughtfulness and practical support. Often a thoughtful sentence can ease anxieties or enable them to feel contained inside your mind, Box 4 gives some examples of emotionally containing statements.

Box 4 Examples of emotionally containing statements

- *It looks like you are really 'into' that.*

- *It can be so hard when we want something and we can't have it.*

- *When someone hurts us it can make us feel like hurting them back. It's hard.*

- *It can be hard to settle when we have lots on our minds.*

- *Perhaps we can think about that together.*

- *Sometimes it can feel a bit scary to ask for help. We might worry that people will think we should manage on our own.*

- *The group seems a bit unsettled/very concentrated today. What do you think Mrs . . . ?*

- *It can be hard to wait when we want something now!*

- *Maybe you worry that I have forgotten you when I am busy with W. . . ?*

- *I'm sensing some feelings are beginning to 'bubble'. Would it help to . . . ?*

- *That looks quite frustrating.*

- *Leaving a place where we have got to know everyone and maybe even felt at home, can make us feel quite wobbly.*

It is important to note the difference between emotional containment and ego support. *Ego support* is the encouraging and sometimes challenging way most adults work with and relate to children. Reassurance, encouragement, appropriate challenge and praise are used regularly, successfully and helpfully with many children. It is what most teachers and parents automatically do and believe in. Reassurance can make *us* feel better as well as the child. Rewards can be enticing and work quickly with most children. Even challenge can spur secure-enough children on to try harder. I call these strategies 'ego support' as they support the child's resilient ego and lift their self-esteem . . . leading them to feel justifiably proud – *'Yes! I can do it!!'*

Box 5 gives some examples of how ego support enhances and uses a child's developing ego as a way to support and motivate them, through praise, reassurance, rewards, threats and even challenge.

Box 5   Examples of ego-supportive statements

- *Wow. You've done all of them. Well done.* (praise)

- *You're managing that really well.* (praise)

- *Come on you can do it. I know you can.* (reassurance)

- *If you finish those five questions you can go on the computer.* (rewards)

- *If you don't finish by breaktime, I need to remind you that you will have to stay in and finish it before you go out to play.* (threat)

- *I went to the dentist last week for a filling. You'll be fine.* (reassurance)

- *Come and sit next to me. I'll help you.* (encouragement)

- *Never mind. I'm sure you will be all right.* (reassurance)

- *It's OK. You don't need to worry about it.* (reassurance)

- *Just have a go. It doesn't matter if you can't . . .* (encouragement)

- *You're trying really hard today. Well done.* (praise)

- *I think you deserve a sticker for that.* (praise)

- *That's great. Well done.* (praise)

- *Well done. Now try it without . . .* (challenge)

- *I'm sure you can manage it. We did that yesterday remember?* (encouragement)

Teachers and advisors have also devised many supportive 'reward' strategies (e.g. stickers, house points, monitoring targets, charts, etc.) to which most children respond well and lift their effort in response.

Most children benefit from both types of response – enabling them to feel heard and cared for, and encouraging them to learn and progress. *The problem, however, is that some children don't respond to ego support.* Their vulnerable, damaged or negative egos are threatened by praise, encouragement and challenge, because they can't *trust* reassurance, they can't *believe* praise, and challenge can trigger negativity.

Praise is actually a judgement (a positive judgement), and because of their very negative self-image, it can inadvertently trigger the *reverse* in their minds (*'It's not good – it's rubbish', 'I can't do it. I'm stupid'*) causing them to react angrily to such triggered shameful and unbearable thoughts. This means avoiding praise, and finding alternative ways to connect with them – until they grow stronger (see Box 6).

**Box 6 Some indicators a child may need emotional containment –
rather than ego support**

- A child who can't take praise, or who reacts negatively to praise.

- A child who can't manage 'big feelings'.

- A child who can be triggered into out-of-control outbursts.

- A child who has a pattern of little incidents turning into big problems.

- A child who tends to project out intense feelings or hurt on to others – particularly those closest to him.

- A child who tends to push us into particular ways of (wanting to) react.

- A child who tends to panic and disrupt others.

So when such a youngster is working well, instead of praise you can:

- take an interest in details;

- smile;

- appreciate silently;

- pass them something they seem to need;

- give them space;

- look after what they have done;

- use concrete or symbolic containment.

If their achievement is new – later you may acknowledge (for example) how previously they struggled with . . . whereas look now . . . adding, '*I think you may be growing stronger. What do you think?*'

For example:

> *Yes of course I'll help you . . . I was just thinking that last week you found it really hard to ask me for help when you got stuck. It's good to ask for help when we need it. I think you're really growing stronger. What do you think?*

(For more examples of such sentence stems see Box 18, p. 215 and also Case Study 23, p. 142).

As they grow stronger, you will observe vulnerable children begin to respond to and enjoy praise. This is a sign that their self-esteem is rising. However, when they struggle or begin to 'lose it' (and any time it flows naturally) they will benefit from emotional containment.

To reiterate – ego-supportive statements are useful with normal resilient children, and teachers use them helpfully all the time. The skill is to know when a child can't use such responses, and to understand and adjust. A child's capacity may also vary with the day and the context and any current stress factors.

I am, however, aware that probably because emotional containment is a new concept for many people, it can sometimes be difficult for staff to really understand the difference between emotional containment and ego support. I have found Exercise 3 – where the two types of comments are mixed up – helpful in this regard.

Exercise 3   Emotionally containing or ego-supportive statements?

Discuss which is which (some of them may evoke debate):

- *That looks quite frustrating.*

- *I think you are enjoying that.*

- *That's great. Well done.*

- *I think you deserve a sticker for that.*

- *It can be so hard when we want something and we can't have it.*

- *You're trying really hard today. Good job!*

- *Leaving a school where we have got to know everyone and where we have even felt 'at home' can make us feel quite wobbly.*

- *When someone hurts us it can make us feel like hurting them back. It's so hard to manage our 'big feelings' sometimes.*

- *Just have a go. If you get stuck I'll help you.*

- *It can be hard to settle when we have lots on our minds.*

- *You seem in a dream today. Are you OK?*

- *Oh dear! Never mind, I've done that too.*

- *Never mind. I'm sure you will be all right.*

- *Come and sit next to me. I'll help you.*

- *Sometimes it can feel a bit scary to ask for help. We might worry that people think we should manage on our own.*

- *If you do those three questions you can finish your model.*

- *You need to finish that before you go. If you don't you will . . .*

- *It can be hard to wait when we want something now can't it!*

- *Maybe you worry that I have forgotten you when I am helping M with her reading?*

Chapter 11 discusses the thoughtful, containing and nurturing use of language, including empathy and curiosity, both of which communicate that you are thinking about the children, for example: *'It was hard for you to try again wasn't it, but you managed it'* or *'I'm just guessing, but I was wondering whether . . .'* (Box 12, p. 163 gives many examples of empathic comments and responses).

Likewise the 'holding-in-mind' suggestions, such as: *'I just need to pop to the office. I'll be back to see how you're getting on when I get back'* or *'I remember we talked about that yesterday'*, are very containing (see Box 8, p. 102 for more examples).

It can be particularly hard to contain and not deny children's sad, hurtful and challenging comments, such as, *'No one likes me'.* Such feelings and words can be so hard to bear and go along with, that we just want to make them feel better. *'I like you. S likes you', 'I saw you playing with her yesterday'*, etc. But containing means *bearing* whatever the child communicates and not denying it, and it is not always pleasant. Of course we want them to feel better, but they need to know that we have *really heard* just how awful it is for them at the moment – with comments like, *'Is that how you really feel sometimes?' before* they can move on – and open up to other possibilities perhaps. (This is discussed further in Chapter 11 and Box 15, p. 198 gives a list of possible ways of responding in such situations.)

Boundaries

Setting firm boundaries with empathy is very containing. It enables children to know where they stand and to begin to internalise their own boundaries. The problem is that some children have had variable or very loose boundaries at home because of their parents' preoccupations, stresses, their need to please their child too much or for fear of repercussions when the child (aggressively?) resists. The more a parent gets into such patterns the less secure a child is about what is expected, and the more the child is tempted to manipulate – to get more! – and the more resistant they become to the parents' efforts to stay in the adult role and be containing. They (and the parents) will certainly need help with this. Secure boundaries in school will be important both for the children, and will help to reinforce the parents' struggling efforts.

These patterns are usually set very young, and early years parenting classes should reinforce and practically support parents who struggle with boundaries. These patterns will of course be brought into school, but with most children the teacher's calm empathic firm and consistent expectations will easily override their tendency to manipulate. With very needy and disturbed children, however, the transference will make this difficult. Supporting each other is crucial. It is also true that some teachers will have their own vulnerabilities in respect of boundaries, and the whole class can become less secure as a result. We have probably all seen classes like this. It requires some emotional strength to set firm boundaries with empathy for resistant children. Some teachers (and parents) need sensitive non-judgemental support, and may benefit from counselling support around boundaries.

Setting firm boundaries should be done calmly and firmly, and with empathy for their wishes (*'I know you want your lunch now, but we both know you have to wait till lunchtime. Perhaps you could have your crisps at break time to tide you over. Did you not have breakfast this morning?'*).

When setting boundaries, or communicating expectations – it can be helpful to use 'ACO':

A = Acknowledge the feeling

C = Communicate the limit or expectation

O = Offer help or offer alternatives

For example:

- *'Not now S. You really want it now I know. It's so hard to have to wait when you want something, but you will have to wait till . . . I will keep it for you till . . . '*
- *'You need to go to the back B. You really wanted to be first, didn't you, but . . . got there first. How about you come at the end with me and we can drop the register off in the office on the way past.'*
- *'It's time to stop now. I know you want more time, but we do have to . . .*
- *We can continue with this tomorrow. I will look after it for you.'*

But underneath all these suggestions, emotional containment is the natural outcome of understanding that in the situation the child just couldn't help it and needs help. When we understand this we can more easily *bear* what the child is communicating in a calm way (see Box 4, p. 67).

To summarise, emotional containment involves:

- a capacity to be able to hold the person and their intense and painful projections in our minds without becoming overwhelmed, and to be able to think about them;
- being able to bear quite intense pain;
- accepting that in their present state the child couldn't help projecting out their unbearable pain;
- being able to stop and think and become aware that the uncomfortable and perhaps painful feelings we are experiencing are not our own, but projected on to us from the child;
- stopping and thinking before reacting;
- finding a way to resist reacting, when we have a powerful urge to do so;
- holding the powerful feelings in our minds for some time, and seeking help with this.

Thus through our own inner growth, our developing self-awareness and self-acceptance and supported by an atmosphere of respect and non-judgemental understanding, we can grow into more thoughtful and sensitive 'containers' for our most troubled children.

It takes time of course, but through repeated experiences of emotional containment with a significant adult in school, vulnerable children gradually develop trust, resilience and a dependent usable relationship.

This is like giving them a second-chance attachment relationship (see pp. 138–143), which is secure and facilitating, enabling them to become open to teaching and learning and to listening, to asking for and making use of help and to taking the risk of having a go, knowing they will not be criticised if they make a mistake or need help.

Over time, and as vulnerable children have enough good experience of containment, slowly they begin to develop their own capacity for emotional containment. They develop resilience, although with vulnerable children transitions and stresses will always tend to exacerbate their capacities. They just need a little more containment at those times.

Thus repeated experience of emotional containment facilitates emotional growth, resilience and capacities for empathy, thoughtfulness and trust, leading to openness to learning from experience.

More concentrated emotional containment

For most children, the emotional containment provided by their significant attachment figures and by their secure predictable setting in school, together with the creative opportunities to begin to process their hurts and worries, is enough to make a difference and help them into virtuous cycles and openness to learning. But for the more damaged and resistant children the more concentrated and highly contained setting of regular therapy or counselling may be needed to open them up to the opportunities and healing relationships school can provide.

A few notes for schools on counselling, play therapy and psychotherapy for children and young people in school

(I also include some tips on working in the metaphor for child counsellors and therapists in Chapter 13, pp. 256–261.)

As a psychotherapist myself I am obviously a great believer in the value of both the thoughtful, emotionally containing therapeutic relationship, and the opportunity to slowly talk, or (especially for younger children) to play, or use art and stories in the safer once-removed setting of therapy, to begin to process their dysfunctional blockages and hurts.

In school or out of school

Many schools have an in-school counsellor or therapist. This can be extremely valuable for children whose parents would find it difficult to take them to an outside therapist on a regular basis, or for children more difficult to engage. It also saves on travel time out of lessons. Although it is essential that the personal boundaries and confidentiality of the therapy are tightly maintained, a therapist on-site can often also use their skills and psychodynamic understanding helpfully with staff who have puzzling children in their classes. They could offer after-school work-discussion groups, individual and team supervision (see Chapter 16 for many examples of how these can be very emotionally containing and illuminating for staff) and INSET for staff on attachment patterns, ways of relating and emotional containment in school, for example. This is precisely what I was able to offer at the pupil referral unit when I worked there.

It is important for schools to understand that counselling and psychotherapy are not the same as crisis support. Of course it is important to have crisis support in school for those children who need it. In my experience this is often supplied by learning mentors, pastoral support staff and heads of year in secondary schools.

Counselling and psychotherapy is not about managing behaviour better, although that may and usually will happen naturally as the child becomes more integrated. It is about offering a regular safe confidential time and space in the same place each week, for them to begin to process their hurts and difficulties in a way they can manage and engage with. Thus in the presence of a benign, empathic and containing adult they slowly open to trust and to opportunities to play, talk and explore their anxieties, hurts and fears safely through the use of metaphor. More directed group and individual approaches like anger management and all sorts of personal and social education are of course helpful and useful, but they are not therapy. Therapy may well open children who need such support to being able to engage with such groups, but it is important to keep them separate from therapy.

In my training we were encouraged as part of our educational psychotherapy intervention to have occasional reviews with teachers about how the child was doing in class. This was not to talk about anything that had come up in the therapy. Rather it was to use our developing understanding of the child and our theoretical knowledge to help school staff better understand the child's puzzling behaviours and learning difficulties in the classroom, and the powerful transference they could sometimes put into the adults around them. Thinking together of helpful ways of understanding and responding can be very helpful for the teacher and the child. We were also encouraged to have similar reviews with parents. However, the particular child and their age, and the nature of the parental relationship will all be factors here. With secondary school children, where they are beginning to develop a separate identity, it is often best or necessary to the work that there is no talking to anyone at all outside the therapy or counselling. With older students, parent meetings may be counterproductive to the confidentiality of the counselling. It is always best to sense what feels right or what might be unhelpful in each case.

It is also not helpful to have purely negative sessions with parents, although to hear and consider *their* difficulties and worries may be an important springboard, and even lead them to accessing their own counselling.

Confidentiality and trust are essential in enabling the child and young person to open up and really *use* the therapy and the relationship. For some children this may be better achieved with an outside therapist who is known not to be part of the school and who only comes in, for example, one day a week for the therapy sessions. Others may benefit from a completely separate service and place, unconnected to the school, or a multidisciplinary setting perhaps, where family work and parent counselling is also available.

(Parallel?) counselling for parents

As described in Chapter 3, in the introduction to the section on domestic violence, my therapy sessions for children who had been affected by domestic violence were only available when their parents were also engaged in their own counselling. I am a great believer in the value of counselling for parents (see pp. 105). I also know of a number of schools who have their own parent counsellor. There are so many people training as counsellors these days that it is often possible to get voluntary or trainee counsellors to offer sessions in school. This can be a great resource, but it is important to screen and select trainee counsellors carefully for emotionally containing capacity, resilience and maturity, etc. as some parents may be very difficult to engage. (Appendix 2 and also Exercise 2, p. 54 may be helpful in this screening process). Chapters 16 and 17 talk a lot about the subtle task of engaging and sensitively persisting with resistant parents. An experienced parent worker in a school can often gently open parents up to trusting and accessing counselling for themselves, and into seeing it as a privilege we could probably all benefit from. It is certainly not about failure or shame in any way (although these may be live issues for some parents) – I have certainly had years!

When to refer

A school play therapist, educational psychotherapist or counsellor will often talk with the school about the process, about when children might benefit from therapy and when to wait and use different avenues of support. It is not helpful, for example, to offer therapy to children who are currently in abusive relationships or in domestic abuse settings. Addressing safety and safeguarding issues first is crucial. Social care may be the first port of call. In Women's Aid we only ever saw children for therapy when they were safely away from the abusive setting. And from experience I know that some children are just too damaged to be ready for weekly therapy. They first need to access what Barbara Dockar-Drysdale calls 'primary experience'[5] – regular early baby- and toddler-type nurturing through a very secure, resilient and understanding (second-chance) attachment relationship (see Case Study 39 pp. 289–292). My experience at the pupil referral unit certainly confirmed this.

In a similar way to bereavement counselling typically being offered to children several months after the bereavement when the intense reactions have calmed a little, therapy for traumatised children is often better when the trauma is sufficiently in the past to be worked on safely. This does not mean that they will not need lots of support during the crisis time. But that is crisis (pastoral?) support and not therapy and should be offered by a different person.

Long-term therapy can often be very helpful for ongoing dysfunctional patterns and inhibitions.

Short-term counselling and therapeutic consultations can be helpful for milder problems, and new difficulties with an apparent cause (see my experience with C in Case Study 27, p. 176).

'Side effects' of having a child in therapy in your class

Most therapy with young children uses metaphor as a safe way to allow difficulties or buried trauma to come to the surface and be expressed – in the context of the characters or story situations. Sometimes the child will want to engage in thinking about the characters, etc., and sometimes they may just prefer to play, draw or write. Whatever happens the regular concentrated experience is likely to bring buried experiences nearer to the surface, to be slowly 'processed' within the attentive thoughtful setting of the therapeutic relationship. In my experience this developing capacity to trust and to experience that things can be thought and understood will be transferred on to caring parents and significant adults in school. I have sometimes found that the child would engage with me as a therapist through the metaphor, expressing and thinking about the dilemmas and feelings of their characters, for example; and then in school or at home they would begin to talk more openly about their worries and concerns. This is all helpful, especially if the listener can be accepting, attentive and empathic, and use the opportunity in a child-centred and thoughtful way.

Sometimes, however, therapy may facilitate children disclosing worrying or scary happenings, which need to be taken seriously and if necessary discussed with the school safeguarding coordinator. This is not the place to go into the detail of safeguarding procedure, but two things are important. First, as soon as you sense a disclosure is 'coming', gently stop the child and tell them that you may need to talk to someone about what they tell you if you feel they are not safe – in order to keep *them* safe – before letting them continue their story. This is so that the child does not feel betrayed when at the end of their disclosure, you, their trusted adult, 'suddenly' tell them that you will need to tell someone else in order to keep them safe. It is true that sometimes it all spills out so quickly there is no chance to warn them of this important safeguarding necessity, but a gentle honest warning is usually preferable to feeling let down.

It is also important to remember when a child discloses something to you not to ask them questions about it. This could be construed as 'leading them on' in some way, and get in the way of official child protection procedures. Writing down what they told you as soon, and in as much detail, as possible and then sharing it with the safeguarding coordinator is best. Schools will have their own safeguarding policies and training of course. If in doubt ask the coordinator – not your 'friend'!

As time goes on a therapy relationship will become very significant and therapists of course bear this in mind with their clients. They know, for example, that breaks in the therapy will be difficult, much as separation and loss is difficult for babies and toddlers. They will therefore address and think about any changes, breaks and endings well in advance with their clients. But teachers may also notice more regression than usual around endings and breaks with children in therapy. This will be both in relation to the (temporary?) loss of their therapist, and also relate to the loss of their significant relationships in school. This is because they are likely to transfer their increased capacity to trust on to significant adults in school – who will therefore be missed more. These anticipated losses may precipitate some behavioural regressions (see Box 20, p. 229), which need to be understood as relating to the upcoming ending or break. If, however, teachers can respond thoughtfully to these little regressions and indicators (see Box 21, p. 236) they are in fact invaluable opportunities to empathise with and contain their feelings, and support them in managing and containing the loss more effectively, for example:

> *I noticed that you put some Lego in your pocket. I'm sure you know that you can't take it home, although I do understand that it must be hard for you to feel that you won't be able to play with it for much longer, as we only have one week left in Year 3.*

Such (preferably repeated) empathic responsiveness at the same time as keeping necessary boundaries, can actually lead to emotional growth for a child as they feel contained and understood.

It is always important to have endings in mind well before a break, as sometimes a child can start to feel anxious and act this out a surprisingly long time before an upcoming loss, transition or break. To aid this process I always made an A4 term calendar for each child I saw in therapy with the dates of holidays and any breaks clearly marked on it. A copy was taken home and one was given to the teacher (see Figure 31, p. 237) Teachers, nurture group staff and TAs could do the same for their most vulnerable children (see Chapter 12 on endings and transitions).

Behaviour difficulties and exclusions

Of course children referred for therapy have a range of problems, from bereavement, anxiety and self-harm to children with entrenched behaviour problems. While the therapy offers a space for the child to *express and communicate* and therefore *ease* the underlying issues that cause the acting out, the school will have a behaviour policy that supports the *management* of such children and keeps everyone safe. Because of this, children in therapy who act out can sometimes get excluded, especially in the early stages and around breaks, and this can affect the therapy, both in their minds and in reality. They may think the therapist will similarly want to exclude or judge them. This can interfere with their capacity to trust – or to come to the session – and inhibit their expression of the very negative feelings they need to work on, even in the safer metaphorical setting. Discovering their therapist is open to them next week and things can be talked through anyway may be just what they need.

Sometimes a child may become ambivalent about coming, and even refuse to go or be late because the therapeutic relationship is becoming important, triggering them into (their default) ambivalent attachment anxieties.

These are all 'live' issues to work on in the therapy of course, but teachers may be confused as to how to manage a child who is reluctant to go. It can be important for teachers to encourage but never force, and likewise never disallow a child from going to their session. If a child refuses, uninvolved acceptance with no discussion is best.

It is best for teachers to maintain a matter-of-fact and encouraging but not particularly interested approach to the therapy, never to ask how a session went and discourage engagement with the child about the session – in a nice way. Of course a teacher may be interested, but part of the 'success' of the process depends on the very tight (and 'safe') emotional containment of the sessions – of which confidentiality and regularity are important components.

Sometimes children can effectively become excluded from their sessions because they are not allowed to be in school. As a psychotherapist this is often the very time I would wish to see the child, because the difficult issues are 'hot'. For this reason it is important to try to make an arrangement with the school – that if the child is excluded they could nevertheless be brought to their session by their parent and taken home afterwards – or you might try to encourage internal exclusions, from which coming to their sessions could be managed.

Another problem can be teachers' misunderstandings of what therapy is about. I have known teachers threaten that a child won't be able to come to their session if they *'continue behaving like this'*. Therapy is not a reward. Maybe in the early stages a child may want to 'show up well' in front of a new therapist, or when they are feeling vulnerable, but a skilled therapist will find timely ways of not colluding with this, and of accessing the more painful and shameful issues through safe and engaging metaphorical activities for example, and the sessions are certainly not a 'nice time'. A teacher's understanding of this may be especially important if the child comes back and needs to wash his painty hands, for example. It doesn't mean that they have just had some fun with their therapist (when they *'clearly don't deserve it'*). It is best for staff not to ask questions and just let them go and wash. Similarly it is best to be sceptical about what they tell you about their sessions. They may even (unconsciously) want to make you feel bad by telling you what a nice person the therapist is, or what a fun time they have just had – or that it was boring and they did nothing!

Emotional growth and change

Typically children don't make even progress while in therapy. They may actually regress a bit at first as opening up to a new and hopefully trusting relationship, and to 'things' coming up to be played through or written about in stories, or talked about little by little, can leave a child feeling quite vulnerable. They can feel pulled in two directions as they somehow know that what they are doing is helpful and they need it, but they are also scared that it might become embarrassing or unreliable, or that their 'bad' aspects might leak out and make the therapist want to reject or abandon them.

So trusting can go in fits and starts. They will also continue to be affected by happenings at home and may become more sensitive to humiliation or hurts for a while. But what also frequently happens, as discussed above, is that as they become more open in the therapy sessions, they become more open to talking things through with significant adults in school and at home – whom they can now trust more, as the positive transference (see Chapter 4, p. 80) from the therapist transfers on to trusted parents and school staff. This means that school staff and parents can be an important and significant part of the healing process (parent counselling and parent/school meetings all feed into this). Hence the thinking and interventions in this book can become particularly useful when a child in therapy becomes able to open up to thinking and talking – maybe in ways they couldn't cope with before when they needed (for good reason) to be defended and reactive.

The strengths and difficulties questionnaire (available on line at sdqinfo.com) is an easy and quick way to assess a child's strengths and difficulties, which therapists may ask teachers to fill in before and after a therapy intervention. There is also a strengths and difficulties questionnaire for parents contributing to the assessment. The Boxall Profile is a much more detailed assessment used by nurture staff to assess their children and is described in more detail in Chapter 7. Parents and class teachers also fill in Boxall Profile questionnaires, contributing to the assessment. Certainly my experience was that children always (except in two complex cases) made significant improvements. Although we didn't do long-term follow-up of clients, I have always found when I have by chance met parents and sometimes the client themselves years after the intervention, that they have changed quite significantly and settled into normal life transitions much more appropriately. (I met a parent only yesterday in a shop and she was delighted to tell me that her son is on course for becoming a prop maker!)

Notes

1   W. R. Bion, *Learning from Experience* (London: Heinemann, 1962).
2   Heather Geddes, *Attachment in the Classroom* (London: Worth, 2006), 39.
3   Ibid.
4   Paul Greenhalgh, *Emotional Growth and Learning* (London: Routledge, 1994), 186.
5   Barbara Dockar-Drysdale, *Consultation in Child Care* (London: Free Association Books, 1993), ch. 9.

Part II

Part II addresses the more practical measures of putting relationship-based ways of working into the school setting, the school day and into relationships, while drawing on the theory and thinking already described. This more thoughtful way of working benefits everyone, but in the more extreme cases as mentioned already, children really need a second-chance experience of consistent, attuned attachment relationships,[1] to enable them to internalise different expectations of trusted adults and of relationships, and become open to thoughtfulness, help and learning. Part II also uses the 'six principles of nurture' as a framework for several of the chapters in this section and addresses practical responses to each principle.

A brief introduction to nurture

The 'six principles of nurture' (also called the 'nurture principles') were developed by the Nurture Group Network[2] when they started encouraging schools to set up small nurture groups for children with social emotional and behavioural difficulties in mainstream schools in the 1970s.

The nurture principles[3]

1. Children's learning is understood developmentally.
2. The classroom offers a safe base.
3. The importance of nurture for the development of well-being (attuned significant relationships facilitate nurture).
4. Language is a vital means of communication.
5. All behaviour is communication.
6. The importance of transition in children's lives.

Nurture groups

> Nurture groups were the brainchild of educational psychologist Marjorie Boxall in 1969. Large numbers of young children were entering primary school in inner-city London with severe emotional, behavioural and social difficulties, which led to unmanageable rates of referral for placement in special schools or for child guidance clinics. Boxall understood that the difficulties presented by most of these children were a result of impoverished early nurturing, which meant they were not able to make trusting relationships with adults or to respond appropriately to other children. They were not ready to meet the social and intellectual demands of school life, which further damaged their already fragile self-confidence and self-esteem.
>
> Her remedy was to place them in 'nurture groups', classes of 6 to 12 children with a teacher and an assistant, whose brief was to engage with the children at the developmental stage they had reached and to support them in meeting learning goals step by step. As the children felt accepted and valued, their confidence grew and they began to learn, with 80 per cent returning to their base class full-time.
>
> Children in nurture groups were not stigmatised and were kept part of their base class by registering there in the morning and returning for the last part of the afternoon. The whole school was trained to give support, so that base-class teachers sent the child off with the group teacher or assistant to have a good day and greeted them with interest on their return. The reputation of the groups was so high that other children wanted to join and most schools devised ways for allowing this, such as invitations to tea, or sharing story time.[4]

The nurture principles of course can apply to the whole school community as well as to nurture groups, i.e. to nurturing relationships, nurturing ways of working with children and also to nurturing staff relationships and health. Our local Nurture Group Network is open to anyone working in a nurturing way or a nurture setting in school. Chapter 16 discusses what a nurturing school looks like, taking the example of a very large infants school with a substantial number of vulnerable children in a relatively deprived urban area. The school has recently been awarded the 'Nurturing School Award' from nurtureuk. Chapter 16 also vividly illustrates the value of nurture bases (the school has two of its own), both for the school and for the children, and also for the parents. It shows how nurture-base staff trained and supervised in this relationship-based way of thinking and working together, can make a real difference to children and to parents and families too.

The careful selection, quality, training, supervision and internalised understanding of nurture-base staff is essential. I have myself seen nurture bases fail because of lack of empathic thoughtfulness and poor selection of staff. It feels important to include a familiarity with attachment categories and with unconscious processes in the training of nurture staff and to select them carefully. In my experience that is not always there, even in people who have done the Nurture Group Network training. Perhaps it will be in the future.

Part II begins by differentiating the three insecure attachment categories, including understanding how they might come about, moving on to ways of responding to children in each category. The chapters consider this relationship-based approach that includes thinking, talking and working together both with the children, within the class team, within the staffroom, within management and within staff and parent relationships as well as in policy developments and the whole school.

Part II also looks at developing inner resources both of children and of staff and finishes with a case study showing how it can all work in practice.

Notes

1 See Louise Michelle Bombèr, *Inside I'm Hurting* (London: Worth, 2007), 57–112; and Muriel Barrett and Jane Trevitt, *Attachment Behaviour and the Schoolchild* (London: Routledge, 1991).
2 Now called nurtureuk, www.nurtureuk.org. See also S. Lucas, K. Insley and G. Buckland, *Nurture Group Principles and Curriculum Guidelines Helping Children to Achieve* (London: Nurture Group Network, 2006).
3 www.nurtureuk.org.
4 Ibid.

Insecure attachment categories[1]

6

Understanding and responding helpfully

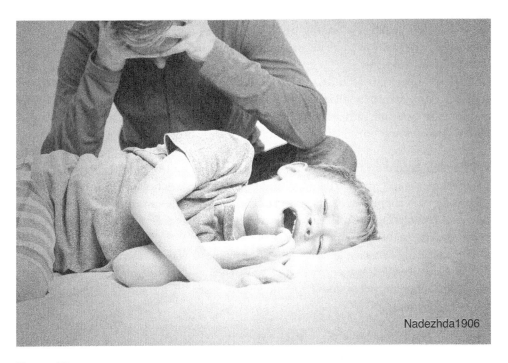

Nadezhda1906

Figure 15

Although it is rare to find a child who fits precisely into a particular category, it is helpful to differentiate and understand the different categories, as many attachment-disturbed children do fit predominantly into one category, and responding with that in mind makes all the difference. For those more chaotic children, it is still helpful to know how to best respond when they are in (for example) avoidant or resistant/ambivalent mode.

The other thing to remember is that there is a continuum from mild to severe in each case, and as we respond with understanding and skill, and with the relationship-based approach described, children will change, which is wonderful to see. But they may also regress at stressful times or around transitions of course, which we need to respond thoughtfully to.

The avoidant child

The *avoidant child* tends to avoid feelings and closeness. They can be difficult to relate to because their hurts have not been responded to with thoughtfulness and empathy or have even been ignored, ridiculed or rejected. Their mothers may themselves have had a similar experience, inhibiting their capacity to risk closeness and to empathise. Maybe they 'don't do' feelings – leading to an avoidance of feelings, which are buried and 'managed'. They may even be uncomfortable with physical contact, or prefer to engage with practical concerns.

The 'stiff-upper-lip' attitude, where positivity and toughness and 'pulling yourself together' reigns, may be a milder example of this pattern; leading to premature self-reliance and compliance within rather distant relationships. Older children and adults may develop psychosomatic symptoms relating to their insufficiently processed feelings.

At the other extreme the parents may be neglectful or even emotionally abusive, leading to their child becoming anxious around need and contact for fear of further hurt. The child may become conflicted when they are hurting or needy inside, because their hurting 'baby' part really *needs* support and closeness, but they also *fear* the (unsupported) need, and so they avoid contact and are uncomfortable with it. They may then act this out in destructive behaviours when their anxiety is aroused.

Thus avoiding closeness and relationships becomes a way of managing this inner conflict, and after a while it becomes a normal way of being – discouraging both closeness with significant adults and peers, and if not remediated, repeating the pattern in their adult and parenting relationships.

Inner and outer tendencies of avoidant children (observable to varying degrees in school)

1. Avoidant children may become very anxious when people get too close – physically and emotionally. They may therefore avoid proximity, making it hard for anyone to get close to them.
2. In school isolation and loneliness may become complications.
3. In extreme cases their behaviours and attitudes may be confused with autism.

4. They may be anxious and even angry around those they begin to love or need, because they want and need closeness, but they are terrified of rejection or of being ignored. They may act this out *not by attacking people whom they need to avoid*, but by destroying (or 'blaming') significant *objects*. This may include spoiling their own work or the teacher's things (see Case Study 17).
5. Others may run away or hide when anxious (see Case Study 16).

Case Study 16   Running away and hiding to avoid closeness

Ten-year-old P was very anxious around people especially adults. In the early days when I went into his class to talk to his teacher he would instantly run away and hide in a low cupboard specially kept empty as his 'safe place' when he needed it.

Many months later I saw him regularly for therapy and we found a manageable way to be together and to think about quite significant things through games – notably backgammon – where, for example, we could think about how being on your own on a square with no support felt so vulnerable and how we feared being 'kicked out' of the game on to the 'blot' (as happens in the game).

It wasn't easy for him to come and he would sometimes run up the stairs when it was his therapy time; but with patient support of his TA he managed several months, and even though things were very unstable at home he came regularly until he moved on to secondary school.

6. They are very uncomfortable with feelings, and therefore have poor emotional literacy.
7. They may have poor self-esteem and harbour hurts but feel unable to share these, or even to face them within themselves – making reflection difficult. When stressed they may therefore act this out neurotically or bodily, but without awareness.
8. They may have tantrums but be hard to comfort.
9. Their creativity and imagination and use of language may be underdeveloped because they have not been engaged with imaginatively. This may affect and inhibit their creative expression and writing. These inhibitions may be unconsciously associated with (not) being 'heard' or empathised with, therefore their ideas and feelings have not been validated.
10. They will find asking for and receiving help very difficult and therefore passively not engage with 'difficult' tasks, or carry on struggling without asking.
11. They may show apparently little fear in new situations; and express little enthusiasm too.
12. They may be much more comfortable with objects. They may enjoy or even become 'addicted to' computer activities or games.
13. Manageable mechanical tasks and hobbies may be the most engaging and manageable for them.

Suggestions for teachers of avoidant children

Case Study 17 illustrates an extreme version of avoidance, but also shows that understanding, and a thoughtful and practical response, can slowly ease even that level of difficulty.

Case study 17   Slowly weaning an avoidant child towards relating

Twelve-year-old P was probably the most avoidant child I have ever come across. She had a history of being passed from mother to father and going in and out of care whenever either parent had 'had enough' of her. She wouldn't look at you. She wouldn't engage. She could disrupt and destroy and make generalised abusive comments whenever she felt threatened. She was frequently absent. It was very difficult to have a conversation with her. If she felt someone was trying to get too close by asking her a question, for example, she would start destroying the nearest object to hand until the person withdrew the conversation, which made staff extremely anxious! It was difficult to know how to help and work with her.

In the school there was a nurture unit for younger children, run by a very experienced and thoughtful nurture teacher. It was decided to try placing her in the infant nurture unit as a 'helper'. She certainly seemed to feel less threatened away from her peers. The nurture unit staff agreed to give her practical jobs to do without much conversation or instruction and no emotional content, and at the same time slowly begin to make little overtures to her in the form of looking and looking away, winks, and brief thumbs up signs, etc. It was felt that just allowing her to observe their friendly, thoughtful ways of relating with the younger and very vulnerable children in the unit, and allowing her to be appreciated and useful in a warm atmosphere where she didn't have to engage might free her to relax a little. Slowly, little filling-in-the-gaps-type learning tasks were placed near her, and she started to build up a folder of work. Her relationship with the nurture teacher began to become important to her and they became able to have conversations – depending on her mood.

Relating and proximity: avoidant children's most pressing difficulty (often a shortcut to identifying their pattern)

1. With avoidant children the first thing is to recognise and respect their need for *personal defences*. This includes understanding their resistance to eye contact and conversations for example, which may heighten their anxieties, and not forcing this.
2. Understanding, thoughtful, preventative and concrete (without words) responses to their anxieties about closeness can ease the difficulty. Having the things they will need ready and to hand, for example, and understanding their preference for objects (over people) can enable the avoidant child to slowly discover that they are thought about, they are not intruded upon too much and their teacher is interested and knows what they need, or like to do.
3. So *sensitive proximity management* is very important for these children, but this does not mean permanently keeping your distance.
4. It is important for significant adults to find practical ways to move in the direction of relating even when this is difficult. Brief looking and looking away, winking and brief smiles and putting things they need nearby without saying anything, can become a bridge to increased tolerance and gradual trust, slowly weaning them into bearing the odd comment (see Case Study 17).
5. Being very attuned to them and sensing what they can take *today* is crucial, along with not taking their rejecting, negative or destructive responses too personally.

In the classroom and learning

1. Offering and *receiving help* maybe too personal and difficult, so subtly ensuring things are within reach, putting things nearby with no words, etc. maybe helpful. Patience with rejection of help is important. Persistence in trying to help may further trigger avoidance.
2. In the classroom *focusing on tasks*, rather on than conversations, helps moderate anxieties about relationships and also enables them to learn – but these need to be tasks that they can manage independently without needing to ask for help.
3. Well-delivered lessons, with plans made clear at the beginning and clear structured tasks with all materials to hand, can reduce any anxieties relating to not knowing and needing to ask.
4. The presence of another child may help moderate the difficulty of the teacher's proximity. Likewise peer learning, peer mentors or 'friends' may be easier to receive help from.
5. Living with not knowing and openness to imagination may just feel too risky for the avoidant child. So free, imaginative writing may be especially difficult. *Structured writing*, like filling in the gaps or completing sentences, may be easier.
6. A manageable structured task, with little imaginative content will feel safer, reducing anxieties between the child and the teacher. Likewise games, such as board games with clear rules – so eye contact and chatting is not necessary – may be a manageable way to relate and to learn.
7. A 'calm box' of building and fixing activities and puzzles can be manageable for *unaroused* avoidant children when they are easy and require no adult help.
8. Allowing them to hang around the edges and learn by observation of group activities may work. Nurture teachers have told me of 'new' children 'hanging around the edges of the room' until they can trust enough to join the group. Listening from the back of the class may be more manageable.
9. Written instructions and worksheets may be easier for them to access than spoken support.
10. Thoughtful differentiation and opportunity for some choice, and bearing their interests in mind, communicates that they are being thought of.
11. Practical activities with written instructions or without instructions like Lego building and computer activities will be very manageable.

Transference

1. Sometimes avoidant children can put their (unconscious) 'ignoring' feelings right into us. They can make us feel like ignoring them. We can find ourselves forgetting about them or not holding them in mind. One teacher I know found she kept forgetting an avoidant child's name! We may need to put conscious effort into the relationship.
2. Understanding that their rejection or their ignoring may be the rejection or disinterest *they* felt in their earliest relationship, transferred on to us as new significant adults, can be very helpful and enable us to distance ourselves a little from their 'ignoring' hurt.

3. Extreme avoidant behaviour can be very difficult to work with. It can leave you feeling very helpless, or make you feel like giving up or even disliking them. The problem is the child both fears but also really *needs* caring relationships. It will be important to 'hold on to the child in your mind', and not to avoid, reject or give up on them. Continuing to 'be there' but unobtrusively, and gradually making a real relationship in the ways described above, is key.

Outbursts

If they become aroused or dysregulated (indicating their 'right brain' is flooding) – it can be helpful to step back a little.

A 'calm box of 'left-brain' concrete tasks, as mentioned above, can help ease the 'flooding', either before it gets out of control or when they are beginning to calm down (see Box 7).

Box 7   Calm box

'Left-brain' activities and puzzles can shift an aroused child's attention out of their 'flooded' 'right brain' into non-emotive problem-solving/matching/sorting mode. For example:

- jigsaw puzzles;

- matching games and activities;

- dot-to-dot pictures;

- fill in the gaps;

- colouring pictures;

- pattern-making on squared paper;

- simple Lego;

- multilink – putting into tens or 'steps';

- sewing cards;

- activity books and 'sheets';

- sorting shapes, buttons, etc.;

- counting activities;

- fill in the blank – words, number patterns, 'tray';

- simple constructional activities;

- clock patience;

- solitaire;

- simple 3D puzzles;

- simple mental maths.

It may be a good idea to use a timer to limit a calm-box activity, or it could become an 'easy option'.

Safety planning

For some children joint safety planning may be needed. Good planning, reliability and empathic managing with little talking and eye contact will make a difference.

Transitions

Endings and breaks (e.g. the end of lessons/days/sessions/weeks/terms/years, etc.) may apparently present no problem and evoke little emotional response, but should be acknowledged and thoughtfully addressed as the student is open to it (see Chapter 12 for detailed discussion on transitions).

As children begin to improve

1. As children begin to open up to relationships and feelings, *transitions and endings may become more significant and difficult for them*, which, paradoxically, is good news as it means the relationship is becoming more real and important to them. Notice (to yourself) when endings become more significant for them and address this gently and more directly if they can take it. Talking about ending anxieties and related behavioural indicators with the class or group in front of them (including eye contact with all of them) may be manageable and helpful.
2. Too much praise may be difficult and threaten their old difficulties. It may be best not to say anything, but just notice and respond to their emerging openness. The odd brief comment like, *'It's a good game, draughts'*, may be sufficiently neutral to be manageable.
3. When they are open to it, working with and through the metaphor can be a good way in, and a powerful tool to explore emotions more safely, such as activities involving boxes, bridges, castles, houses and linking things together.
4. Whole-class stories with emotional content they can identify with like *A Nifflenoo Called Nevermind*, *How Hatty Hated Kindness* and *Ruby and the Rubbish Bin* by Margot Sunderland,[2] which address hurts and resistances that can't be talked about, may be helpful with younger children.
5. As trust becomes more established you can begin to use more empathy and put feelings tentatively into words. Reach slowly towards more closeness, but respect avoidant anxieties when they arise at stressful and vulnerable times.
6. Making *generalised* comments about hurts, worries about closeness and thoughts about fun and enjoyment may be easier for avoidant children to bear (see Box 9, p. 113) than anything personal. Listening to *others* share feelings and fears in 'circle time' can be a helpful way for them to pick up more sensitive and open ways of being – 'by osmosis'.
7. Attachment-based play (see Chapter 13, p. 249) including hiding and finding games, brief safe touch or tickles with little children, eye-contact games, etc. may become manageable and fun and very healing.
8. As they begin to become open to imagination, then loss, endings, feelings and friendship can be addressed metaphorically through stories, drama and film, etc. As trust develops you may see them opening up to expressing their more vulnerable side. Like S who liked the 'safety' of numbers, but through a squiggle picture (Figure 16) and within our long-term trusted relationship he managed to acknowledge the desperate 'hurt' of number 8.

The number 8 is
really 24. He is singing
but really he is crying
CRYING

Figure 16

Developmentally

The first stage is for the avoidant child to (be able to) develop a *dependent relationship*. This is progress, and enables them to access help, and express thoughts and feelings more honestly, knowing they will be listened to and understood. It also enables them to have reciprocal conversations. It can be tempting to push them too quickly towards independence, but this could actually be colluding with their avoidant preference. Slowly they will develop a more age-appropriate and secure coming and going of relating, working and learning.

Parents

If at the same time as significant adults in school are finding ways to *enable the child to trust* and develop more secure ways of relating, someone is able to work sensitively with the parents, maybe the whole relationship pattern will be able to shift (see Chapters 15 and 16). Sadly this is not always possible. What often happens is that in the school setting a child can develop an alternative and more secure attachment pattern and use this for relating and learning in school. Then as time goes on this increased security can become transferred on to new trusted relationships both inside and outside school. It may also help ease relationships at home.

The resistant/ambivalent child

The *resistant/ambivalent child* is often recognisable because they both 'cling and resist'. They consciously or unconsciously *fear separation*, because their attachment experience has been unreliable. Their mother may have been variably available, or variably attuned to them, and so these children have needed to find ways to 'ensure' she will listen and *stay thinking* about them. Maybe there have been domestic difficulties or threats of violence, which preoccupy her at times. Maybe she has/had variable mental health difficulties or (post-natal) depression, or alcohol or drugs may sometimes inhibit her attentiveness. Maybe both parents are preoccupied with their 'important' jobs or stress at work. In more extreme cases mothers may have their own unmet needs leading to their needing their child to respond to *them* rather than the other way round. This may lead to difficulties setting boundaries and allowing the child to manipulate them – for fear of losing their 'love'. They may need the child for comfort, or because they fear isolation. They may enjoy hugs when *they* need them, but not be able to tune into the needs of their child either verbally or intuitively.

Inner and outer tendencies of resistant/ambivalent children

Feeling held in mind is their most important need and difficulty

1. A very important understanding is to realise that resistant/ambivalent children can be anxious a lot of the time when their attachment needs are activated. This is because especially in *more extreme cases* they can have a structural difficulty in their inner worlds – which means that they can't feel 'held in mind' *unless* the adult is concretely in front of them looking at and listening to them *now*. They have no experience or concept of two separate people who care about each other concentrating on something else, and not forgetting about each other. They cannot imagine a relationship persisting when they are not physically connected. They only know a sort of 'merged' (joined-together) connection or no connection at all. This is what they need help with to shift.
2. So when their attachment needs are triggered, resistant/ambivalent children often 'cling' either physically, or as they get older they use words to ensure that mum (or the teacher or significant adult) doesn't stop thinking of them. This can be very irritating and difficult to manage. They can even get angry when they fear or sense that their 'special' adult isn't thinking about them or is about to move away from them.
3. They can feel very controlling because of their intense need to hold on to the adults' attention.
4. It can also make sharing a teacher or TA's attention very difficult (see Case Study 19 later in this chapter).

Ambivalence

1. Such children are described as *ambivalent* because they both 'love' and 'hate' their attachment figures. This is because they both need them, and expect to be forgotten or frustrated by them, leading them to act this out as described above through 'attention-seeking' (which is really attachment-seeking) behaviours. Their parent or significant adult's consequent irritation can exacerbate this. In more extreme cases, when tensions are high they may become aggressive and attack mum or a significant adult when they sense they are about to be pushed away.
2. This can be almost unbearable for (especially single) parents who understandably fear their attacks and outbursts. It can be tempting to give in to them for a quiet life. This unfortunately only reinforces their upside-down relationship and the power of their child's manipulation and attacks, making boundary setting extremely difficult. As time goes on this pattern becomes more and more difficult to shift – but it is very dysfunctional. Parents, as well as children, need (early) help with this.
3. This ambivalence can be acted out through *resistance* when they are asked to do something, because it can unconsciously remind them that adults always want to control them rather than listen to them.

Separation

1. This fear of not being held in mind can make separation very difficult for resistant/ ambivalent children, leading to school refusal, attendance difficulties, lateness, attention seeking and sometimes extreme anxieties for both the child, the parents and the school.
2. These difficulties can be further complicated by an 'inverted' mother/child attachment' described above, where the mother unconsciously *needs the child* for her own comfort or esteem. Case Study 18 illustrates these difficulties vividly.

Case Study 18   The difficulty of working with acute separation anxieties

S had always found separation from mum and getting to school very difficult. But with empathic attuned teachers and one-to-one workers using lots of 'holding-in-mind' comments and gestures, and with occasional learning mentor support for his mum, he managed to settle and learn in class. Separating from mum was still difficult, but after his regular separation tantrum when his key worker would calmly escort him into school through a vale of tears and screams, his tantrums would ease after about 5 to 15 minutes and he would regularly work, and play happily in the playground till the end of the day. He had clearly found secure relationships and a secure setting in his class and in the school, which could enable his learning, even though at home things were still ambivalent. But in his final year he had a new teacher, who herself was going through a crisis, and a less attuned TA, and things deteriorated. His attendance slipped down to about 50 per cent and both professionals and parents became very anxious. It was interesting to see how he tried many ways to manipulate the support around him both at home and at school. His mother complained he was unhappy for various reasons and the school made adjustments to his support – but nothing worked – leaving staff feeling like giving up and not bothering. More and more support (including outside support) was initiated, but people were beginning to resent the time he was taking up, starting not to care and even forgetting their responsibilities around him. It was very sad to see just how difficult it was to get people together to really understand how the despair and helpless giving in and giving up on him from home was becoming transferred into the network, and fostering a vicious cycle around and within him.

3. Their separation anxieties can sometimes affect numeracy, because subtraction – 'taking away' can cause unconscious anxieties and be feared (see Case Study 27, p. 176).

Learning difficulties and task resistance

4. Their difficulty and huge need to feel held in mind can have a significant effect on learning and teaching, because the child cannot let the teacher move her attention away from him on to organising the task or attending to other children, for fear of 'falling out of her mind'. This can lead to acting out or constant interruptions to keep hold of her attention, making teaching very difficult.
5. Similarly, looking at and attending to the task risks 'falling out' of the teacher's mind – making learning difficult. This means they can appear very resistant to tasks, because

they *have to keep engaging* the teacher with questions, comments and anecdotes, to stay in her mind, which can be very irritating.

6. Their 'clinging' with words can give the impression that their language is good, but it may in fact be more a way to 'hold on to' the adult's attention, rather than because they are interested in the subject matter.

7. So engaging with learning tasks may be difficult if not impossible, especially at the beginning of tasks, because this fear means they have to keep chatting. Looking down at the task risks the adult going away or turning to someone else and forgetting them.

8. Play, creativity and learning may all be inhibited because of this need to 'hold on to' the adult at the expense of the task.

Suggestions for teachers of resistant/ambivalent children

Remember that every difficulty is a 'hot' opportunity to talk things through.

Being thought about and sharing a significant adult's attention

1. Enabling resistant/ambivalent children to experience being *thought about* is crucial in shifting their unhelpful attachment pattern and expectations. Case Study 19 gives an example of such an anxiety being triggered and acted out – and how the TA might helpfully work with it.

Case Study 19   On the usefulness of talking things through with a resistant/ambivalent child

In a supervision session a one-to-one TA told me about an experience with a very resistant/ambivalent child whom she worked with every afternoon. On this occasion he had chosen to bring two friends to share in his reading time in the library. She said they had had a very intense time, and both she and the children were probably all affected. They were reading a story about a family and suddenly one of the friends talked about something a bit worrying at home, which of course the TA had to listen to and take seriously. Immediately her resistant/ambivalent child piped up with an even more worrying concern about his mother whom he hadn't lived with for a long time and wasn't allowed to see. Of course the TA knew she would have to follow child protection procedures, but we found ourselves also discussing how her special child might have felt when her attention had been on the other child in such an intense way. Maybe 'squeezed out' or 'abandoned' – as he had been by mum?

I also wondered how he was generally when her attention needed to move to other children for a while. 'He finds that very difficult,' she said.

It was helpful to think together about how hard it might be (especially at anxious times) for him to feel continuously held in mind by her when she was not actively listening to him. We talked also about how he did seem to be ready to 'work on' this, as he was recently choosing to have one or two friends to share his reading time even though he was still clearly ambivalent about it. We discussed how these sorts of experiences were wonderful opportunities to talk this issue through with them all. We wondered about addressing the issue openly when similar situations arose, and about asking both him and the other children – including the quiet one, how they felt when she was listening to one of the others; and about ensuring that none of them took too much time to talk (or read) as there were three of them, because 'it was important that they all felt included'. We also talked about openly acknowledging that her job was to think of them all and that even though sometimes she was listening to one, she still had the others in her mind, so she may sometimes need to stop one to give another one a turn. I explained how they will know that if she needs to stop one to include the others she would do the same for them. We talked about the importance of remaining the calm thoughtful adult, who stays in charge in the best interests of all of them and who talks things through with them as they arise.

2. 'Holding-in-mind' comments and gestures (including across the room) are one of the most crucial and helpful interventions for resistant/ambivalent children. They are a way to shift children's fears of being forgotten, because they communicate being 'held in mind' when the teacher is not physically there (see Box 8).

Box 8 Holding-in-mind comments and gestures

Remembering and recalling comments:

- *I remember we spoke about that yesterday.*
- *I remember you have a sister too.*
- *I remember you like . . .*
- *I was thinking about you yesterday when I was buying some . . . and I remembered that you told me . . .*
- *I know maths is not your favourite subject.*
- *So how was the trip to the . . . yesterday?*
- *I saw you at the . . . didn't I!*

Thoughtful comments – any of the empathy statements (see Box 14, p. 194) plus:

- *I was wondering how you would be today after . . .*
- *I think that might be a little hard. Do you want to try first or . . .*
- *I am aware that we only have one week left and I was thinking . . .*
- *I'll go with you the first time until you . . .*

Promises and fulfilment:

- *I'm going to leave you to finish that and I'll come back in five minutes.*
- *I think you need a little time to calm down. I'll come back when the sand runs out.*
- *I'm just going to . . . I'll come and see how you're getting on when I come back.*
- *I'm just going to help . . . I'll come and check on you in ten minutes.*

Holding-in-mind gestures:

- waving;
- thumbs up;
- five fingers – indicating five more minutes;
- shhh sign;
- any agreed sign that enables the child to feel thought about and held in mind.

3. Curiosity as to what their behaviours may be about communicates interest and thoughtfulness.
4. Empathic understanding comments, which try to make sense of their behaviours, can help to normalise and ease their anxieties, at the same time as enabling the child to feel held in mind. Remembering comments (see Box 8 above) are similarly helpful to use frequently.

(Chapter 11 on relationships addresses curiosity and empathy in more detail.)

Separations

1. It is important for school staff to recognise the *separation* anxieties described above so that the child's attention-seeking behaviour is understandable. Thinking and cooperating together on how to respond more thoughtfully can be very helpful.
2. In more extreme cases staff need to understand the real and entrenched separation anxieties described above, and think together about ways to support the child coming into school, and to support the family and each other too, so a clear, caring practical approach is agreed. This may include a 'meet and greet' arrangement when they arrive at the gate to help them separate from mum. Empathy may be crucial when the child is resistant to coming in, so they feel understood and cared for when boundaries are enforced (see p. 159). Arrangements may need reviewing on a planned basis, but should not be manipulated ad hoc (manipulation may be one of their defensive behaviours and it is important not to collude with that).
3. In some cases a transitional object (see pp. 125 and 249), or asking the child to look after something *for you* till you return, may ease separations. Allowing them to have something small from home may also be helpful, until they grow into feeling held in mind enough.
4. Encouraging mum to put little caring messages in their lunch box may help them to be thought about in her absence.
5. New beginnings, separations, endings and any class-teacher changes will all need to be thought about, prepared for and supported, understanding that the absence of their 'special' person may be very difficult.
6. For some children it may be important to develop procedures that respond quickly to absence and support return, before it becomes entrenched. This needs to involve parents.

Transference

(Chapter 4 addresses transference in more detail.)

1. It is helpful to be aware of the feelings and responses the child evokes in you, as this can help you understand them more clearly. Talking together with colleagues and thinking about their resistant/ambivalent pattern is crucial and includes resisting being 'pushed' into unhelpful responses.
2. Be careful not to replicate the neediness of mum, by needing the child to meet *your* needs (and thinking they are being kind and helpful when they just want to do jobs *with* you). Doing tasks for you but without you may be helpful for a while.
3. Be aware that *fear and anger* may be induced when the significant adult is not under their control. It may be important to find ways to manage this and to 'offload' it.

Sometimes as an attachment becomes more significant, it can be necessary to bear being disliked when their anger erupts and not take it personally. Understanding this as ambivalence and resistance, and continuing to keep firm boundaries and to hold them in mind anyway is important. Seeking help may be necessary and important here.

4. In more resistant cases staff can get *pulled into* a child's powerful wish to achieve a 'merged state' – by *seeming* to need lots of support. Again talking this through with each other may be helpful. It is also important not to be 'pushed' into ignoring them or showing irritation.
5. Likewise it is important that adults are not manipulated into giving them attention at inappropriate times. This will involve lots of conversations with the child about how you will be continuing to think of them even though they now need to do . . . until . . . It will involve reliability and keeping promises to return to check on the child when you say you will, or giving them regular, planned, time-limited periods to talk or do something together when it is convenient, or when you are with them (see Case Study 20).

Case Study 20 Noticing, understanding and adjusting

When I was a SENCO a pattern developed with a very resistant/ambivalent 9-year-old, whereby every breaktime and lunchtime she would come and see me with a little problem to talk through. At first I concentrated on thinking through the problems with her and making suggestions, but slowly I began to realise that this was more about her need to be in my mind than the little problems. I talked it through with the teacher, and we decided that I would give her a short regular weekly 'story-writing' slot when she could write and talk, and we would curtail the breaktime visits. If real problems came up there were other channels for her, and she could also have some (limited) chatting time in her story-writing sessions. The teacher and I would also use plenty of 'holding-in-mind' comments and gestures with her. We talked this through all together and she began to use the time well, and to manage the gaps with reminders of the 'special story time' if necessary.

6. Letting them know (with reference to the clock perhaps) how long you have got till you have to stop will be helpful. It will be *important to stick to boundaries* and set or reinforce them with empathy, and if necessary apologise when you are delayed.
7. Ambivalent parents can also 'push' for more and more time, and need similar thoughtful responsiveness and boundaries. It is important to remain the thoughtful adult who takes the child's and the family's needs seriously but is not manipulated.

Arousal

1. Noticing early signs of anxiety and hyperarousal, and responding with empathy or distraction may be helpful.
2. In extreme cases the child may need (many) experiences of 'dyadic regulation'. This involves actively helping them to calm down while not abandoning them, at the same time as not merging with them. Merging, as described above, means getting overinvolved, or finding it hard to wean them off dependence and set necessary boundaries. (Arousal is discussed in detail in the 'chaotic/disorganised' section later in the chapter.)

Teaching and learning

1. For teachers in class, task organisation needs to take into account that they can experience that you won't forget them. Differentiation of the task into smaller chunks may make it easier for them to manage alone (before you return as promised to see how they have got on).
2. Timers may help manage short separations and help moderate anxiety during short timed independent tasks.
3. Understanding their tendency towards initial resistance and giving them *time* (going away and coming back) may be helpful, while getting caught up in debating the issue is not.
4. Turn-taking activities and games can ease separation difficulties and task inhibitions, and give them a much needed experience of two separate people alongside each other rather than merging, because you are there both attending to the *task* together.
5. Likewise small-group work, including talking through that you are thinking of all of them when they are each having turns, can be very helpful (as shown in Case Study 19).
6. As they grow more open to tasks, the use of stories – e.g. about journeys away from home, being remembered and coming back again, can enable them to safely engage with their issues in an educational setting. Educational psychotherapist Gill Morton developed short-term therapeutic group work around journeys described in Chapter 13. Increasingly other educational psychotherapists include teachers in this very successful group process,[3] with a view to the teachers learning and replicating the process with others in their schools (see pp. 269–270 for a fuller description).
7. Such small-group journey stories also enable support from peers, plus encouraging children to have a mind of their own.

Other support

1. Engaging the parents' potential to change will be crucial. Parents may need support to understand the unhelpful patterns, to let go, to find ways to hold their child in mind and to talk things through with them. Communicating with parents, however, needs to be handled very sensitively and with respect for their own needs and patterns too (see Chapters 15 and 16). They too may be resistant/ambivalent!
2. Outside support may sometimes be necessary.
3. Multidisciplinary 'staged' support, and holding the child and the process in mind needs to include liaison between agencies, so that helplessness and ways of understanding can be thought about together and duplication does not occur.
4. Especially with TAs, therapeutic support for resistant/ambivalent children needs to take account of their possible wish to merge. This involves careful work on endings and setting firm boundaries (not being manipulated into giving more) with empathy.
5. Parent counselling (and/or therapeutic parenting support) may be particularly helpful if they are open to accessing it. Parental counselling may ease 'enmeshed' (can't let go) and 'inverted' (upside down – child controls parent) relationships including the parent's difficulty letting go of their child. Family work may be helpful because they can go together, so long as the family worker is familiar with the dysfunctional resistant/ambivalent pattern. Putting effort into making usable thoughtful relationships is crucial. A family support worker may be able to do useful encouraging work in this regard.

The chaotic/disorganised child

The *chaotic/disorganised* child is the most 'damaged' and worrying of pupils. They are also the most difficult to work with because they tend to 'panic and disrupt'. This pattern frequently involves abuse, trauma and neglect, and/or witnessing of domestic abuse, alcohol and drug abuse. One or both parents may have mental health problems or severe health problems. The parents own unresolved difficulties can mean they are frequently not able or available to support, comfort and protect their children, evoking in them anger, fear and a need to control to keep themselves 'safe'. Thus relationships deteriorate and sadly parents can retaliate and project their own anxieties back into the children. It is not so simple as to blame the *parents*, however. The pattern can cycle through generations and ranges from those who come from chaotic/disorganised homes where little things easily feel overwhelming and where attuned parenting and clear boundaries are rare; to one where the parents abuse the child or have been abused themselves. Both the parents and the children may have been in the care system and suffered multiple traumatic losses.

Chaotic/disorganised children often end up in the care system either as 'children in need', as child protection 'cases' or as 'looked-after children' (see Chapter 3, p. 26) when they are taken into care either temporarily or permanently.

Chaotic/disorganised families can be very difficult to work with as remembering appointments, being open to help, managing commitments and taking in suggestions can all be difficult because of shame and disorganisation. Even well-thought-out adoption can be difficult (see Case Study 21).

Case Study 21   The tragic effects of separations, multiple traumatic transitions and loss on a chaotic/disorganised child

D lived with and had been looked after by many different members of the family on an informal basis over the years because of family break-up, quarrels and illness, and sometimes he would move away for periods. Such changes frequently left him unsettled. Both D and the family had so many disparate needs including movement difficulties, speech and language difficulties, learning difficulties and child protection concerns that many services were involved with different members of the family. There would be professionals' meetings and frequently some of them would not turn up; D's social worker frequently changed and the parents too found it difficult to engage and turn up for meetings. They evoked a lot of helplessness and despair in the workers, some of whom gave up. Concerns escalated until D was taken into care. Amazingly he settled well into the excellent foster home and his school attendance, schoolwork and psychotherapy attendance improved. After a year it was agreed that he could be adopted, and although he really didn't want to leave his foster carers he was moved into what was felt to be a very caring adoptive family. But D was completely unsettled by (yet another) move and just couldn't settle. His behaviour even became dangerous at times and the relationship with his adoptive parents deteriorated so much that they decided that they couldn't keep him after all. So he was taken back into his old foster home where he had been so settled before, but this time it was not so easy. He was particularly challenging to his foster dad, with whom he had got on well before, and although his foster mum really wanted to keep him, his foster dad put his foot down, and he was moved to a children's home.

Inner and outer tendencies of chaotic/disorganised children

Panic and disrupt or dissociate

Chaotic/disorganised children often *panic and disrupt* any time they feel threatened with (imagined) danger or humiliation (a trauma trigger), which is just unbearable. The origins of their difficulties are almost always unsupported trauma (see Chapter 3 on trauma).

1. Chaotic/disorganised children are often in a continuous or easily triggered state of hypervigilance, because their main preoccupation is to *stay safe*. Early relationships may have been frightening, overwhelming and chaotic, and include multiple traumatic losses including feared losses. The problem is not just the traumatic experiences, but the lack of understanding, empathy and thoughtful support during and after the experiences, which would have enabled them to process the pain and even grow through the hurt. Without it they have not developed empathy, thoughtfulness, inner security or a space inside to think and wonder.

2. As well as and relating to their often severe and understandable emotional and behavioural difficulties, their brain connections and hormonal tendencies will be affected by their traumatic and especially early conditioning (see Chapter 2 on neuroscience).

3. They may also have underlying shame, which needs to be constantly defended against, leading to all sorts of 'behaviour problems'. They really need, but resist firm boundaries, empathy, emotional containment and help.

4. They are also likely to have unprocessed and unintegrated pain and trauma. The most disturbed of them may have PTSD, which is undiagnosed.

    The unbearable terror of this will be all too easily triggered by the slightest hints of the original trauma. This is why they have the tendency to panic and disrupt. Sometimes they can have so many complex disorders that they have a range of different treatments, appointments and medications. American psychiatrist and researcher Bessel Van der Kolk advocated for, and lost the battle to have the diagnosis of 'developmental trauma disorder' replace most childhood behavioural diagnoses – like ADHD and ODD – because he wanted medical staff to treat the causes rather than the symptoms and see these behavioural diagnoses as all arising out of unprocessed trauma.

5. Their need to vigilantly avoid any feelings or vulnerabilities that might threaten to arise can lead to hyperactivity, which can sometimes lead them to be diagnosed with ADHD. In reality they have a (reactive) attachment disorder. In the United States, chaotic/disorganised attachment is sometimes known as reactive attachment disorder.

6. They are easily triggered into fight, flight or freeze reactions, which they need help to manage. In extreme cases they can seem like just a bag of reactions, as if it is hard to know who they really are.

7. They are known as *chaotic/disorganised* because both the inner and outer aspects of their worlds are chaotic and disorganised. They have not been 'held together' enough to be organised. So looking after things, remembering and being neat, tidy and organised will be hard, leaving them with a tendency to lose, forget and not be able to hold things in mind. The chaotic very gluey and broken up collage in Figure 17 illustrates the disorganised world of such a child.

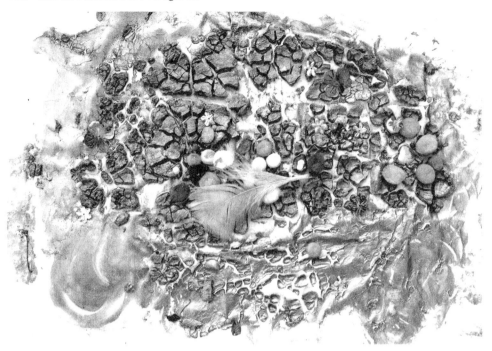

Figure 17

8. Often the whole family is disorganised, and to really make a difference work needs to be done with the whole family, or with both the child and parents in parallel. This can be difficult to start and to maintain, as the family's disorganisation and buried shame can get in the way.
9. Family relationships are very conflicted and often confound the problem as the parent(s) project into and scapegoat the children (variably – goodies and baddies). Parenting is very difficult and needs help, but this can become a shame issue and be difficult to face. Parents will almost inevitably have their own problems.
10. Both within themselves, within the family and within the school, little problems can cause a lot of anxiety and easily *escalate and get in a muddle*.

Learning

1. This *muddle* both inside and out may also *disorient* them – causing identity difficulties (who am I?), difficulties with place (where am I?), with time (when is it?) and with thinking and organising information. They may have an array of 'processing disorders' including dyslexia and dyspraxia, and speech and language difficulties as well as behaviour difficulties.
2. For chaotic/disorganised children making *connections and remembering* may be both threatening and impossible – at least for the time being. This will make learning to read, write and spell, and making links in learning very difficult.
3. Thinking, concentrating and listening will be difficult because they may need to watch out for any hints of danger, humiliation or criticism, which would be unbearable; causing

them to be easily triggered into reactivity, and to 'banter' with others, both to defend and to distract themselves. All this can get in the way of their own learning and that of others.

4. Without skilled TA support such very dysfunctional children can distract and interfere with teaching too.

Fear

1. *Humiliation* is feared above everything. Even imagined hints, or fears of humiliation can lead to avoidance of risk taking in learning, difficulty learning from mistakes and difficulty dealing with authority. They may experience teacher instructions or requests as being bossed about, which they need to resist. For many reasons they will have difficulty engaging with both the teacher and the task, as well as interfering with the teaching and learning of others.

2. They tend to be 'on the lookout' for danger, leading to excessive tale-telling, which may ease their own bad feelings, but can be very annoying.

3. Without experiences of being and feeling emotionally safe in their environment, and inside themselves, they have *not* come to expect that adults and peers will treat them (or continue to treat them) kindly. They therefore have an extreme need for both practical and emotional *safety* in the classroom, which is fundamental for their learning, relationships and emotional growth. They have learned not to trust, although they may at times need to please.

Behaviour

1. Without this safety they can be *triggered* into fight or flight, or even involuntary dissociation, which is a very primitive defence and particularly worrying in older pupils (it can be confused with petit mal). Once an outburst is triggered they can't stop until the hormones dissipate, or the 'big feelings' are contained for them, because their limbic system is flooded.

2. Their limbic system can also become 'flooded' by strong feelings of excitement – making special events like birthdays or days out quite problematic.

3. Without this auto-regulation capacity and without inner security, unsupervised settings (like the playground) and school changes can be very difficult and lead to acting out. They frequently cope with insecurity and helplessness by taking control, or they may run away or truant. Older students may 'self-medicate' by taking mind-numbing or excitingly distractive substances, which can later become addictive and lead to secondary problems.

4. They may have severe and *challenging behaviour* and need to be 'on top' for fear of being humiliated or hurt if they let down their guard (as they may have seen or heard at home).

5. Humiliation is about the fear of exposing our unprotected vulnerability, and this can be *acted out through bullying others* who express the vulnerability they can't bear to see. Sometimes there may be no apparent cause – just walking past a weak helpless child can trigger associations with vulnerability, which 'need' to be annihilated.

6. Punishments and adult reactions to their behaviour difficulties can lead them to internalise a very negative self-image, which feels more comfortable and acceptable if it is viewed as 'tough'. This again can be acted out and even delighted in – leading to perverse enjoyment and gangs. These are the most difficult patterns to change. Unremediated sadism can lead them into trouble or even prison later on.

But underneath all these observable behaviours are deprived children who have not had their feelings and wishes acknowledged and understood, and who therefore have not developed a capacity for empathy, reflection, for recognising and knowing their own feelings or for talking through difficulties. They have not grown a sense of self that is mostly OK.

Dramas

1. Dramas are easily created and can inhibit the capacities of school staff to think, reflect and act – or not act. Staff need to be mindful of not getting drawn into these. Talking together is important.
2. Both children and parents (and even groups of families) can almost become 'addicted to' dramas. Maybe the adrenalin rush provides a way for them to feel 'alive'.
3. Likewise they can be observed getting involved in other children's fights in the playground. This can also be a way of vicariously 'working on' their own issues, and sorting out injustices in a way they couldn't do for themselves when they were little.

These complex and entrenched difficulties may sound overwhelming; but school staff who see such children every day have a unique opportunity to make a difference, through the attuned consistent 'relationship-based approach' described here. Catching their difficulties young and working together with thoughtfulness and understanding will be both rewarding and effective.

Suggestions for teachers of chaotic/disorganised children

General

1. The *earlier* their problems can be identified, and multi-disciplinary interventions or EHCPs[4] can be put in place, the better. The spring 2018 issue of UKCP *New Psychotherapist* journal features articles about child mental health, including early intervention (from before birth) for the most disturbed children and families!
2. Family support and long-term (psychodynamically informed) counselling (if they are open to it) would be helpful. For real reasons often related to shame, however, this is often difficult to put in place and sustain. Gentle, sensitive persistence in building trusted relationships and practical support for parents and to help them access and remember appointments may be crucial. When I saw a child from a *very* disorganised family for psychotherapy, the only way to ensure she attended appointments was to engage the family's parent support worker to bring her and mum together. The parent worker talked to mum in another room at the same time.
3. Post-adoption or fostering support work[5] will be essential for chaotic/disorganised children in the care system – including therapeutic parenting using relationship and developmentally based approaches. All transitions and upcoming transitions will need particular care, preparation and practical help; as children who have been removed from their birth families will have traumatic memories around separations, which could be easily triggered during these times – and even lead to placement failure.
4. It is important to respect the amount of fear/discomfort chaotic/disorganised children can evoke in everyone.

5.   It is also fundamental to remember with chaotic/disorganised children that they frequently *can't help* their outbursts and reactions. They are triggered reactions in response to perceived or feared 'danger'. They may need safe holding.

6.   Many chaotic/disorganised children benefit from (or are allocated) an additional attachment person or key worker (a resilient secure adult, who is supported by the school and the network) to tune into them in a sensitive detailed way, and give them some experience of secure, resilient, consistent attachment responses and care. Their task is to tune into the child, to take the relationship seriously and implement the suggestions below as appropriate, *gradually* moving them towards secure ways of relating and expectations. Key workers need to be calm, resilient and secure. Sometimes two people might alternate to enable them to take breaks. Key workers need regular support and debriefing. The key worker role is referred to throughout this section and summarised on p. 139.

7.   Clinical supervision can be very helpful for teachers and support staff working with chaotic/disorganised children, especially attachment/key workers, to enable them to cope with the anxiety the child evokes, and to enable them to offer safety, continuity and emotional containment. Without it the child's home and school placement may fail.

8.   It will be important to watch out for child protection concerns. Trusted relationships in school are significant in lots of ways, including facilitating necessary disclosures.

Safety

1.   Chaotic/disorganised children are preoccupied with the need to be and stay safe. All changes bring some insecurity. Moving from place to place may need support. Problems frequently happen during transition times.

2.   For chaotic/disorganised children little problems at school can feel potentially terrifying. It is helpful to understand this and talk things through when they are open to it. Always ensure 'safety' and a secure base. The school staff I have worked with often say how they find it helpful to use the word 'SAFE' lots of times, e.g. *'My job is to keep everyone safe'*, *'That's not safe'* or *'We all need to stay safe here'*.

3.   Having a familiar (preferably the same) trusted person meet and greet them first thing in the morning, to settle them at the start of every new session and to meet and settle them every time they move to a new place can be very helpful.

4.   Louise Bombèr talks of the importance of a child's key adult supporting them to 'scan' the room for safety at the beginning of every session and every day to enable them to feel safe.[6] In Chapter 8 (p. 151), I describe a child initiating this for himself and how later weaning him on to do this 'internally' would be a step forward.

Ways of relating with chaotic/disorganised children

(See also Chapter 11.)

1.   The main thing is to tune into how they are now, and to put effort into the relationship, even if they are not initially responsive. Work to build a real usable relationship. Get to know and care about them.

2.   It is always important to avoid any hints of humiliation when relating to a chaotic/disorganised child, and to *pick up on and prevent any humiliation from other children (in front of them)*.

3. Positive responses and 'gifts' that surprise them can help build relationships. Sometimes giving unexpected and unconventional 'treats', e.g. for staying on a task for a specified length of time, or a cup of tea – just 'because you fancy a break' – which they didn't expect, can be more facilitating of the relationship and of inner growth than getting stuck in a reward and punishment regime – which only leads to wanting to please or rebel, and more negative self-criticism when they fail.

4. Praise can sometimes be difficult for chaotic/disorganised children to cope with – because they may become triggered into 'turning it upside down' – *'It's not good, it's rubbish'* (see pp. 71–73 for a fuller discussion of this). Taking an interest in details may be more manageable than praise. Comments or little questions about details will also help the child feel thought about. Acknowledging effort and engagement rather than their work may be more manageable.[7]

5. Tuning in to their *behavioural communications*, and acknowledging their perceived wishes, hurts, needs and inner conflicts with empathy (when they are open to it), while maintaining necessary boundaries, is helpful.

6. Just being curious about a child's behaviour can be very containing, because you are demonstrating that you are continuing to think about them.

7. Understanding their feelings and reacting thoughtfully to them, e.g. *'It can be very . . . when . . .'* plus some preventative action or boundary, can be very containing for them.

8. Use (and feel) empathy for their wishes when communicating boundaries and expectations, e.g. *'I know you want to carry on with this, but we do have to stop for lunch now. We can carry on with it tomorrow.'*

9. Having clear, *related consequences* to their behaviours, which are not just punitive, is helpful. They will still need support to manage these.

Helping them to manage feelings

(See also section on helping them with arousal states later in chapter.)

1. Chaotic/disorganised children need lots of empathy to be able to grow into feeling heard, thought about and understood. However, in the early stages of a relationship and at stressful times, empathy for their hurts and frustrations may be *unbearable* – because they do not want to bring anything painful into consciousness. As your relationship develops, offering empathy in 'small doses' can gradually ease them into appreciating and benefitting from it.

2. Putting children's hurting feelings into words helps them to recognise and know the words for feelings, and experience that they are natural and understandable and can be expressed safely.

3. A significant adult or key worker may be able to talk through their hurts when they are 'hot' but not aroused, helping them process (and therefore contain) such hurts more easily. As you get to know them and come to understand their patterns, circumstances and history, you will realise that in the heat of the moment their hormones can become triggered, and at that point they can't help it. They need help. If you can communicate something of this understanding to the child, anxieties can be eased. As they become open to empathy, regular attuned empathic responses facilitate children growing into being able to do this for themselves and for each other. Such communications also build up trust.

4. It may be easier for them to bear thinking about feelings when they are expressed in whole-class circle time, or in generalised statements, e.g. *'It can be hard to manage our feelings when someone hurts us'* (see Box 9).

Box 9 Generalised empathic sentence stems

- *It's so hard to . . .*

- *It's so hard/frustrating when . . .*

- *I guess we often . . .*

- *Sometimes it's . . .*

- *When people . . . it can make us . . .*

- *It can make us . . . when . . .*

- *It can be hard to . . .*

- *It can be fun to . . .*

5. Feeling photos on the wall with captions can help the whole class familiarise themselves with both powerful and subtle feelings, and act as a teaching aid. A poster of 'ways to deal more effectively with anger' can help anger-management strategies slowly seep into their consciousness.
6. It is important to understand that in addition to humiliation and fear triggers, *both* overexcitement, and unstructured spaces and times can be overwhelming. Making alternative secure plans and activities with a trusted adult may sometimes be needed. Making alternative arrangements for school trips that are interesting, don't feel like punishment and that are talked through sensitively with the child beforehand, may be necessary.
7. Chaotic/disorganised children are very tuned into 'vibes', so being consistent and as calm as possible yourself will help children stay calmer.
8. When a child is dissociating or disconnecting, it is important to stay connected yourself. Gentle curiosity about this communicates being thought about, even if they don't respond.

Helping them with arousal states

Chaotic/disorganised children who have only experienced reactive and punitive responses to their big feelings, may feel they are 'bad' for having such feelings. As well as experiencing anxiety and trauma, the lack of thoughtful supportive parenting may not have allowed them to internalise containing and managing feelings at all – so they can erupt out dangerously. They need help, both to manage and to slowly internalise this capacity for themselves. Key workers can support this process. Here are some suggestions:

1. All chaotic/disorganised children will have their own unique 'triggers' relating to their particular trauma history. Put effort into tuning into them and if possible preventing them occurring. Gently talking these through with them as opportunities allow, will slowly help them to acknowledge their triggers, and to accept and even ask for help.
2. Keep a record of observed triggers for a particular child, and share these with all the adults who work with them.
3. Help the child identify what he is most sensitive about, and support his efforts to protect himself.
4. Some (usually younger) children dissociate when anxious. Notice signs of this. You can help them refocus by engaging their attention, or 'surprising' them. Simple left-brain noticing activities like counting things in the environment, and heavy sensory activities like pressing their hands down hard on the table or floor can help them come back into a more grounded state. Giving them sensitive feedback when they refocus may help ease this tendency.
5. Other children become 'aroused'. Try to notice early signs of hyperarousal, such as impulsivity, dilated pupils or fidgetiness and find ways to change their state. Gently acknowledging your observation and doing something different for a while may help. A small stress ball (or similar) may be useful here. 'Time out' for older pupils may help, but it may not. It may evoke earlier experiences of abandonment or rejection. 'Time in' near the teacher or TA, or in a 'calm-down place', may be more helpful than 'time out' for some children, when they start to dysregulate.
6. Emphasise safety. Use the word 'safe' frequently around disorganised children – because underneath they are frequently anxious about staying safe.

7. A staff system of agreed procedures and responses at times of dysregulation will be necessary for some pupils. A strategy for emergencies includes emphasising safety.
8. Having a 'calm box' (see Box 7, p. 95) containing concrete, mechanical rhythmic left-brain function tasks may help them calm down both before and after (but not during) escalation. The calm-box activities may also be helpful on very stressful days.
9. To help children get out of 'aroused', 'out of control' or withdrawn, dreamy states, making rather unexpected 'ordinary' comments or questions like, *'Where did you put your lunch box?'* or *'Did you see that programme about . . . ?'* can sometimes 'hook' them into unaroused left-brain thinking states, after which they can be given 'boring repetitive tasks' until they have calmed down.

Things for the key worker to consider when the children 'erupt'

1. Explain how they are all going to stay safe, and calmly put the emergency strategy into practice.
2. Be wary of approaching a child who is in a panic state too vigorously. Approaching dysregulated children who have been traumatised too vigorously or suddenly may retraumatise them. Some children may need you to visibly step back and just give them time.
3. Other children may need to be safely and calmly held to keep themselves and everyone safe (training is available for this). Tell them calmly what you are going to do. Then allow them to calm down *without comment*. Do not engage with their arguments at this time.
4. Use the word 'safe' frequently, e.g. *'I just need to keep everyone safe'* or *'My job is to keep you all safe'*.
5. When they have calmed down sufficiently physical movement can help dissipate adrenalin.
6. Contingent and preventative consequences will need to be talked through too.

(For more detailed discussion on managing outbursts see Chapter 11, p. 205–211.)

Repairing relationships after outbursts

After a child has calmed down they will inevitably worry that their significant adult will judge them or want to reject them. This will be hard to talk about because they will tend towards shame (which can't be talked about) rather than guilt, but it may be acted out later on, or the next day perhaps in subtle ways.

1. It is important that the *adult* takes the responsibility for reparation, and that it happens when the *child* is ready. They may show you something. They may let you go first through a doorway, or they may visibly be a bit anxious around you. This is your opportunity to gently talk through how they might be feeling after 'yesterday'. It is not about going through the rights and wrongs of the incident again. It is about healing the break in the relationship, and demonstrating that we can understand and talk about feelings, and think together about difficulties and ways forward. It is also an opportunity to let them know that in a certain sense they couldn't help what happened, because you know that once their big feelings became triggered they couldn't stop them till they calmed down and that you will try to help them with that in future.

You might say:

> 'Thank you for that Sam. I'm just thinking. We had a bad day yesterday didn't we?'

> 'I think you may be wanting to know that we are still friends.'

> 'I think we both know that when you started to "go" you just couldn't stop. You needed a lot of time to calm down.'

> 'Is there some way I could help you perhaps if it happens again? Or to help you perhaps when you start to feel agitated or angry?'

If your relationship is developing towards more openness and trust, you might also say:

> 'It's so difficult when something suddenly makes us react like that I know. Afterwards we may really wish it hadn't happened, but we just couldn't help it.'

> 'I wonder what it is that makes you agitated?'

> 'Can you sense when you are getting a bit agitated I wonder?'

Changes and transitions

(See also Chapter 12 for more detailed coverage of transitions.)

1. Reliable and predictable routines help regulate brain pathways. Be very clear about the sequence of events and the structure of the day, so the child can predict what is going to happen. Help them to be clear about the timetable and the next half-hour. Visual timetables and calendars marking holidays and staff absences and any unusual events will be helpful (see Figure 31, p. 237).
2. Any change or uncertainty will be difficult. Take special care with transitions. Giving ten-minute then five-minute warnings may be helpful. Their key worker needs to support transitions practically. Preventative action may be necessary.
3. Big transitions (end of term, end of year, teachers leaving, etc.) will be especially difficult. It is important to be open to the possibility of deteriorating behaviour as big transitions approach, and put your tentative understandings into words, to ease the guilt that can arise when they can't hold their anxieties at bay. They will need more personal support at these times, e.g. 'It's hard to stay focused today I think. I'm aware that we only have two more weeks till the end of term and Mrs Brown's last day and I'm wondering if that's on your mind?'
4. Chaotic/disorganised children in the care system will need lots of support when they move to a new home and around *anniversaries* (keep a diary of these). Uncertainty and anxiety about anticipated changes should be acknowledged and empathised with *even if they are not yet finalised*. The worst thing is not to know and to fear.
5. All chaotic/disorganised children will find significant staff absences difficult, and need extra support and care when their 'trusted' person is away. Understand and plan for this, if possible prepare them beforehand. The use of transitional objects and cards to and from the absent person can be helpful. Some chaotic/disorganised children will not manage such absences at all. When I worked at the pupil referral unit we decided that even very good (but unfamiliar) supply teachers destabilised the children, and it was better for the children and the staff to have a policy of not using supply teachers at all and to find other ways of managing when staff were away.

Fostering coordination and body awareness

Often the disorganisation gets right into the chaotic/disorganised child's body and coordination. Physical therapeutic movement has been found to be helpful, for example:

1. Creating opportunities for movement, such as taking messages or offering exercise breaks.
2. Body awareness exercises, brain gym or 'activate' to music. 'Wobble board' exercises may help.
3. Sensory motor exercises like:

    (a) Whole-body actions like pushing, pulling, lifting, playing and moving.
    (b) Oral actions such as chewing, sucking and blowing.
    (c) Use of hands for squeezing or pinching with resistive materials, or 'fidget toys'.
    (d) Deep-pressure touch, e.g. weighted items or heavy blankets[8] can assist with emotional regulation. They may be worth investigating in relation to easily aroused chaotic/disorganised children. They derive from occupational therapy and different children will benefit from different exercises. Some schools have found *The Scared Gang* books for young children helpful, which illustrate 'how [children] can self-regulate through the use of food and sensory-based activities'.[9]

4. Similarly dance, drumming, rap and rhythmic activities help coordination and brain function.[10]
5. Multi-sensory approaches to learning.

Learning and work tasks

Patient and understanding support with learning and work tasks from their key worker will be essential. Engaging with both the teacher and the task will be difficult for chaotic/disorganised children, when their priority is to be alert to any hints of humiliation, or when their brain feels 'scrambled', or when not knowing, reflection and concentration feels impossible or threatening.

1. Being aware of their state of mind, and helping them scan and settle any potential disturbances will make a difference.
2. Regular routines and times and places and people are easiest to manage.
3. Especially in whole-class times, some children may 'need to be' cued into non-verbal signals (e.g. the 'holding-in-mind gestures' across the room on p. 102) to continue to stay safe enough to listen, sit still and concentrate.
4. Chaotic/disorganised children may not be able to listen and take in instructions. Asking them calmly to repeat back instructions or important information can be a way of engaging their minds. Even when something has been explained to the class, explanations and instructions can easily just slip out of their disorganised minds. It may be necessary for them to go over it again and again! Patience, simple written instructions, and putting information and task instruction into small 'chunks' may be very helpful.
5. Checking with them that they know what to do, and for how long they can work before you come back to see them may be helpful. As with resistant children, a timer might be useful.
6. Remembering and sorting things out (practically, in their minds, and on the page) are difficult for disorganised children, because both their inner and outer worlds are

in a muddle. They may need a trusted person to help them with – sorting out their papers and materials and their box or school bag, managing the layout of their work on the page and sorting out logical links in their minds. They may also need understanding (non-humiliating) support when they fail (again) to remember something, or get in a muddle.

7. They may need help with remembering previous experiences and knowledge and relating current information to things already known. Patience and understanding are crucial with all this support.

8. Visual and practical aids and exercises may be very helpful, to aid understanding and remembering.

9. Visual calendars and timetables will be helpful to prepare them for what is coming next.

10. It is important to be aware of tasks in the curriculum that may evoke anxiety or threaten to bring up painful memories, like family trees or aspects of history.

11. Mistakes are of course vital learning opportunities. Take opportunities to help them appreciate this, as they are open to it. *Apologising when we make a mistake* or when we are a bit late is helpful too.

12. Creating ten minutes of reflection time at the end of the day for the class to connect with both each other and the teacher can be both bonding and aid reflective capacity. It's also good 'modelling' for chaotic/disorganised children. For example, *'One thing I have learnt today'*, *'What has been easy?'* and *'What has been difficult?'*

Story and metaphor work

Story and metaphor can be opportunities to work *safely* on issues and concerns – as they become open to imaginative and creative work (see also Chapter 13). For example:

1. Metaphors of symbolic containment may be helpful and usable – like buildings, houses, and boats.

2. Play is wonderfully healing. Children learn through play in self-directed ways.
    Play is a natural way to 'work through' anxieties, but for chaotic/disorganised children the (feared) unpredictability of play may be unbearable. *They may need help to be able to play* (see Chapter 13).
    They may also be 'freaked' by too much 'mess', although messy but well-contained play and art could be cathartic when they can cope with it.

3. For younger children a physical container – a special (small?) containing place to feel safe in may be helpful – like a big box, a cupboard or a tent (see Case Study 16, p. 91).

Transference

Transference (see Chapter 4) can be extremely strong, variable and anxiety-making when working with chaotic/disorganised children.

Transference (the feelings and urges the child evokes in you) and *countertransference* (your own triggered vulnerabilities) can be difficult to notice and step back from, but they are also *vital opportunities to understand* the chaotic/disorganised child's inner world, and resist exacerbating their problems.

1. It is helpful to be aware of the feelings the child evokes in you, and resist being 'pushed into' unhelpful responses. Watch out for this and think before you react. Talking transference feelings through with colleagues is very helpful for all of you and the child (see Exercise 6, p. 159).
2. It is important to be aware of our own vulnerabilities and feel OK about talking them through with trusted colleagues so you can support each other and give each other a break. Such awareness and support can help prevent us unwittingly being hooked into unhelpful reactions. We need to support each other and plan for that.

As the relationship starts to bear fruit and they can cope enough with sharing the adults, nurture groups can be a wonderful healing opportunity for 'blossoming' chaotic/disorganised children (see Chapter 7, p. 123).

Finally

Finally, one of the characteristics of chaotic/disorganised children is that, unlike avoidant children who always tend to avoid closeness, and resistant/ambivalent children who always tend to be resistant to tasks and cling, chaotic/disorganised children have *not* developed a reliable way of avoiding anxiety. So they can often show (at different times) characteristics of either resistant/ambivalent or avoidant children, as well as their own panic and disrupt[11] reactions. When you notice this the suggestions for children in the relevant category noted in this chapter may be helpful.

It is also important to add that all these 'categories' are in fact continuums from mild to more extreme, so only some of the above suggestions and descriptions will be relevant to children with milder difficulties.

As already mentioned, the task is always to move the child gradually in the direction of more secure attachments, thus easing anxiety and freeing them to learn and relate more appropriately.

A secure base and a caring attuned significant relationship will make all the difference (see Chapter 8). As children develop more secure attachment patterns in school through the above experiences, they will be able to learn and settle, and hopefully transfer these capacities into new secure settings and relationships. Often the growth comes and goes a bit as transitions and stresses from home affect them. But of course difficulties are also opportunities. It can be heartening to see them slowly change and develop resilience, and to experience the relationship bearing fruit. That is the time to start and to continue weaning their support, and to facilitate some independence, while being open to increasing the support for periods when (understandable) vulnerabilities occur.

However, until things change at home, and until they have had enough experiences of love, reliability and thoughtfulness, their old dysfunctional reaction patterns are likely to become triggered in insecure settings and relationships. They may 'overlay' their dysfunctional pattern with a more secure pattern developed in school, enabling them to function and learn well most of the time. The hope is that with more secure relationships and experience they may be able to transfer this pattern into new trusted relationships and settings later on, and continue to learn and grow.

Notes

1 I am very grateful for the thinking of Heather Geddes in *Attachment in the Classroom* (London: Worth, 2006) for this chapter.

2 Margot Sunderland, *A Nifflenoo Called Nevermind* (London: Speechmark, 2003); Margot Sunderland, *How Hatty Hated Kindness* (London: Speechmark, 2003); Margot Sunderland, *Ruby and the Rubbish Bin* (London: Speechmark, 2003).

3 G. Morton, 'Therapeutic Story Groups: Educational Psychotherapy in a School Setting', in *Why Can't I Help This Child to Learn?* ed. H. High (London: Karnac, 2012), 105. The Caspari foundation staff also take this process into London schools. For details see caspari.org.uk.

4 Education health care plans (legal assessments that set out the child or young person's needs and come with binding commitments for particular support).

5 See D. Hughes, *Building the Bonds of Attachment: Awakening Love in Deeply Troubled Children* (Northvale, NJ: Jason Aronson, 1998); and Caroline Archer and Alan Burnell, eds, *Trauma, Attachment and Family Permanence* (London: Jessica Kingsley, 2003).

6 Louise Michelle Bombèr, *What About Me?* (London: Worth, 2007), 35–36.

7 C. Dweck and C. Mueller, 'Praise for Intelligence Can Undermine Children's Motivation and Performance', *Journal of Personality and Social Psychology* 75, no. 1, 33–52, emphasises the value of praising effort (rather than intelligence). See also about praise and growth mindset in Carol Dweck, 'The Perils and Promises of Praise', *Best of Educational Leadership 2007–2008* 65, 34–39.

8 See Jennifer Gray, 'Trauma and Sensory Interventions: A View From the Occupational Therapist's Mat', www.professionals.childhood.org.au, Occupational Therapist and Therapeutic Specialist Therapeutic Care Programme at the Australian Childhood Foundation.

9 Éadaoin Bhreathnach, *The Scared Gang Series* [Box Set of nine books] (Belfast: Alder Tree Press, 2011). Éadaoin Bhreathnach's website gives details of the approach and of her four-day training courses that include *The Just Right State Programme* and *The Scared Gang* books for young children, see sensoryattachmentintervention.com.

10 Bessel Van der Kolk, *The Body Keeps the Score* (New York: Viking, 2014), 242–243.

11 Barbara Dockar-Drysdale, *Consultation in Child Care* (London: Free Association Books, 1993), 34, 54.

Children stuck in early developmental stages

7

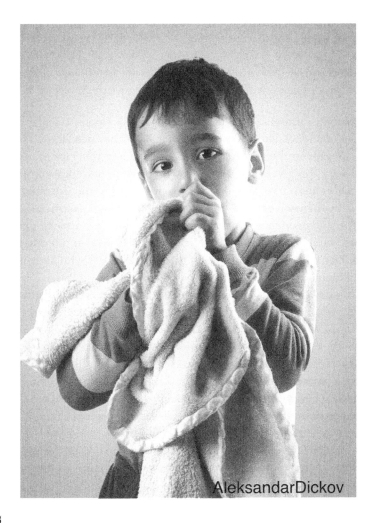

Figure 18

'Children's learning is understood developmentally' (nurture principle 1)

This chapter looks at understanding developmental stages, using nurtureuk's model of 'baby', 'toddler' and 'latency' stages, and acknowledging that vulnerable children's emotional and social development can sometimes become blocked and inhibited. As well as the likelihood of emotional damage and disturbance, there may be important gaps in children's early experience. They may need to rework the foundational bonding and nurturing experiences of baby- and toddlerhood, as well as needing 'healing' opportunities to process their hurts and anxieties. They may need to regress to earlier stages of development and nurture for a while to free them to relate and grow more age appropriately.

The chapter considers how we can notice and fill in these gaps, concentrating particularly on *early* developmental needs and gaps in the baby and the toddler stages, and moving up into the latency stage (primary age and early secondary). Understanding children's[1] difficulties in this light fits in with the aim and practice of 'nurture groups' and also legitimises teachers sometimes tactfully allowing developmentally delayed and 'blocked' children to regress in a safe and limited way. For example, a drink and a biscuit every day at the same time and place while you read them and Teddy a short story – until they grow out of needing it.

> *I remember in my early years as a SENCO giving a needy, regressed and emotionally damaged 8-year-old an afternoon a week 'helping' in the nursery, which she revelled in.*

Limited regression is also encouraged in fostering and adoption training and parenting practice for looked-after children, when children indicate they need it.

Filling in the gaps in their early experience, including the gaps of fun and delight with their primary caregivers and sensitive attuned responsiveness to their needs and hurts, will enable children to develop the capacity to enjoy and use nurturing dependent relationships themselves. The capacity for dependence is crucial and a healthy foundation for independence. Significant adults, and key/attachment workers in school who see the children every day, can play a vital role in offering such security and life-enhancing experiences to those in their care or class who have missed out on this nurturing foundation.

With severely developmentally delayed and 'disturbed' children it is particularly important for the key worker to become *involved* with the child and really hold them in mind, because they need what Barbara Dockar-Drysdale calls 'the provision of *primary* experience'.[2] This is the sort of early nurturing and bonding experience with attuned, resilient attachment figures, with frequent experiences of fun and thoughtful responsiveness, which we all need as a secure foundation for life and learning. It is important, however, that such attachment or key workers remain professional and don't get sucked into the child's manipulations and dysfunctional patterns. This needs to include the capacity to stay separate, to say no, to talk things through when the child is open to it, to take responsibility to repair the relationship (as the child offers opportunities) after 'breaks' (see pp. 129–130), and to bear the child's anger. Managing outbursts and relationship-based discipline with very vulnerable children are covered in Chapter 11.

Nurture groups

Nurture groups in mainstream schools are specifically designed to nurture and fill in the gaps for small groups of very vulnerable children, offering a high adult–child ratio and time for talking, playing and fun together, as well as learning in manageable doses. They happen in a secure, enclosed family-type space, where the day proceeds slowly with lots of talking through and short activities, a clear time structure, regular routines, preparations and reminders, including visual timetables. Opportunities for play, cooking, circle-time sharing and games, and social breakfasts as well as short curriculum tasks facilitate growth and learning.

Everything in the nurture base is child centred and attachment based. As time goes on staff in the nurture base will naturally want to think and talk together about the children, enabling them to *realise* something of what is going on *within* the child and within the relationships.

More withdrawn and delayed children particularly benefit from such small-group provision, and some who act out can benefit from the closer attention and the use of food in conjunction with nurture. It is crucial in such settings to have a safe enclosed space where children can be taken for quiet support to calm down or to have a break when things get fraught, both to ease their bubbling hormones and to ease potential disturbance on the others. Children who act out dangerously, however, may need highly attuned one-to-one support at first before they can share an adult in a nurture group setting.

For all their neediness, such children are unlikely to be able to access weekly therapy because the seven-day gap between sessions may be unbearable, the home setting is unlikely to be able to support the child through the therapy, and the challenge of opening to creativity and hurts even in the metaphor may be too much. Slowly, however, as they gain security from their daily nurturing and second-chance attachment experience, they may start to open up a little and manage to 'straddle the gaps', as I discovered at the pupil referral unit. Regarding the home setting, valuable parent (and parenting) support can be helpfully and subtly integrated into and around the nurture-base setting, as the parents are invited in to help in different and limited ways (Case Study 39, p. 289 and Case Study 4, p. 28 are examples of this).

Baby stage: bonding, trust and dependency

As described in Chapter 1, the baby stage is the time when a dependent attachment is necessary because the baby is helpless alone. Having his needs and hurts noticed and responded to, and enjoying fun and nurture together, builds trust and security within the attachment relationship. Food, fun and nurture are intertwined and enjoyed together. The natural delight and joy a baby evokes in the parent and the times of fun and laughter together facilitate a strong secure relationship and healthy brain development. These high intensity moments of fun, laughter and play together also have other benefits. They give wonderful opportunities for the parent to coregulate their joint 'big feelings', aroused during happy times together. They also prime the baby to be open to and enjoy close relationships, and prime their neuronal connections to be open to 'happy hormones' – fostering a tendency towards positive moods. Babies haven't got the capacity to manage and regulate their feelings, so babyhood is the time of coregulation of both positive and negative states, which usually happens naturally in an attuned and responsive way, even if a few tantrums and hurts have to be endured. The baby gets used to the mother's touch, tone of voice, facial expressions and cuddles, all of which nurture and build security. They also get used to receiving empathic and sensitive help to calm down, even if it is a little difficult at times. As they become secure within the trusted dependent parental relationship they begin to be curious and open to exploration in small doses. They gradually become aware that their mother is a separate person who has them in mind, and they start to take little initiatives into the environment, knowing their mother is always there when needed.

So for a child with gaps in the baby stage an attachment or key worker in school or in the nurture base can offer this 'primary experience' through the following:

1. *Close safe physical contact* (as they can manage) including rocking ('Row the Boat'), sensory exploration, touch, music, songs and rhythm.
2. *Attachment-based play* (mother-and-baby-type play like peek-a-boo or hiding and finding games) including lots of positive acknowledgement of the child, and frequently addressing them by name (Theraplay™ training teaches adults to offer attachment-based play and responsiveness to older needy children (see pp. 248–249).[3]

3. *The use of soft toys for comfort.* Very large soft toys to cuddle can be helpful. The teddy bear drawing and dictated 'story' in Figure 19 shows a very regressed primary child's ambivalence about his obvious baby needs.

4. Role playing care and affection and interacting with the soft toy can demonstrate and model a significant caring relationship.

5. For some younger, more regressed or withdrawn children, eye contact, exaggerated facial expressions and sympathetic tones of voice reflecting joy in the child may be needed. They will need both their positive and negative feelings to be recognised and acknowledged (in small doses), even if they don't respond.

6. Some children may need to regress safely and experience early relationship-building experiences with their key

I like going to the park. He is watching Angela. He is being naughty really naughty to Angela. He is making a face. He says I like watching tele. I like rolling over. I like playing and jumping up and down on my head and feet and arms. I like sucking my thumb. I am not a baby he shouted

Figure 19

worker. These will need to be well contained and in response to indications from the child that they can use a particular experience. An example might be a drink (from their school water bottle), a biscuit and a little individual story at the same time and in the same safe situation every day without fail. Barbara Dockar-Drysdale calls this 'localised provision'[4] and it lasts as long as the child needs it.

7. The availability of very large boxes, blankets and cloths for safe spaces or 'dens' may be helpful for more avoidant children.

8. Transitional objects (see p. 249) will be very helpful at this stage. It may be important to respect and value a child's chosen transitional object. This may be something from home, something in the classroom or something belonging to the teacher. Think carefully and stick to how you will manage this in the class and school setting, until it is no longer needed.

9. For children easily triggered into panic states it will be important to avoid all unnecessary changes, or make special provision, for example when their teacher or LSA is away.

10. It will also be important to avoid too much excitement. School trips, Christmas celebrations, parties and any special events will easily trigger unmanageable big feelings in some children. Prevention with compassion and empathic explanation (emphasising that we 'both' know you are 'not yet ready' for too much excitement) will be important here – so they feel thought about rather than punished. (This is also recommended for looked-after children when they are first adopted.) Special time with their key worker, e.g. cooking or doing something low-key but enjoyable, will ease many anxieties and feelings of being excluded.

11. They may find choices difficult or overwhelming and need guidance and limited choices.

12. Key workers need to be able to bear the child's antisocial behaviour and even their hateful comments, by taking them seriously but *not engaging with them* (see Case Study 12, p. 50 and Box 16 , pp. 201–202) and offering dyadic regulation with empathy and alternatives (as described on pp. 14 and 104). They may well need help with this if the child becomes out of control.

13. Sometimes thinking about a problem in terms of transference and projection might in fact be more important and emotionally freeing for everyone than *just* offering 'nurture' (see Chapter 4).

14. It is very important that key workers are comfortable asking for help and that class teams support each other.

15. Sometimes the child may indicate and/or the adult may decide that a child needs a calm-down break. 'Count downs' and incentives may not be helpful at this very early stage as the child may not be able to bear the 'pressure'.

16. Thoughtful, calm management decisions taken earlier rather than when things have escalated are best.

17. Repetition of simple routines and activities is calming and builds security.

18. The first *symbolic play* takes place 'in the space between' mother and baby.[5] Children who have not had the availability of an attuned responsive mother may be unable to

Figure 20

play, and an important role of key workers is to facilitate simple play in the space between themselves and the regressed child – maybe through 'talking to' the transitional object or a big soft toy or a painting character.

Play will develop and continue during the 'toddler and latency stages' and it is a crucial healing and integrative opportunity for all children (see Chapter 13). Play therapy is particularly helpful for such children when they are strong and secure enough. The therapeutic use of art may also be helpful.

19. nurtureuk[6] recommends and teaches a particular form of assessment (the Boxall Profile[7]) for children who might benefit from being in a nurture group, or indeed *need* some nurturing for a while, to assess their levels before they start and their 'progress' while they are in a nurture group. The Boxall Profile is a questionnaire filled in by staff who know the child well. It includes both a 'developmental strands' questionnaire, which assesses any early gaps in a child's experience and gives precise suggestions to address them; and a 'diagnostic profile', which looks at any blocks or early damage that might be affecting learning and behaviour and need addressing, again with suggestions for ways forward. I agree that both are important and need addressing, which is what I am doing here, but unlike nurtureuk who recommend working on all the developmental strands with low scores in each stage *before* moving on to the diagnostic profile concerns, I feel they should be thought about and addressed as appropriate at the same time, because they each affect the other.

20. Thinking together (work discussion) as staff teams or individually with an enlightened professional is *always* helpful to ease anxieties, as Case Study 22 illustrates.

Sometimes trauma in infancy or even before birth can lead to a particular form of 'stuckness' or acting out.

Case Study 22   Understanding very early and particular stuckness

Miss T, a nurture-group teacher, shared her concerns about the huge frustration, anxiety and helplessness that C, one of their 6-year-old children, was currently evoking because of his very 'stuck' behaviours. As well as being late almost every morning, when he came into the room first thing he always just stood there, still and apparently frozen up, unable to take any initiatives into the room or towards the few interesting options laid out for the children to have a go at. It would take staff 10 or 15 minutes every day to help him towards an activity – which he then happily engaged with. C had particular skills with maths and memory. For example, he knew all the stations to London from his home town, and he liked to recite them! He easily managed number bonds to ten, but when it came to other simple tasks, which we knew he could do easily, his initial response was to say, 'I can't do it'. He would always need lots of help and encouragement to get started.

We found ourselves wondering about resistant/ambivalent attachment patterns and even autistic tendencies, but the teacher described how he could relate well, he enjoyed relationships with other children and he evoked a lot of care and concern in staff. Miss T seemed to have a good working relationship with his very anxious mother, who tried hard to bring him in on time each day, and we wondered about the effects of her anxiety on him, and about the issue of separation, which was clearly a problem for them both when he arrived in the mornings. Being the youngest by far in the family could perhaps lead to separation and growing-up difficulties for mum and for C too, but we still both felt left with puzzling anxiety and helplessness.

Then Miss T remembered that in the course of conversation the class teacher had mentioned to her that he had had a very difficult birth and in fact he had nearly died. We acknowledged the huge anxiety that must have caused in the family at the time, particularly his mother. Then suddenly it dawned. Miss T became visibly animated. Maybe his huge anxious stuckness at the beginning of any new day, any change of room, any task or play opportunity was like a re-enactment of his very difficult, anxiety-making and traumatic birth – when he nearly didn't make it. Maybe any new experience unconsciously triggered him back into huge but unthinkable anxiety and fear that he might not manage it. Maybe this almost unbearable anxiety became reactivated in both him and his mother, and (in the transference) in school staff too, any time something new or a change of activity or place loomed up. Suddenly we could think together about ways to work with this, including empathic conversations with his mum, perhaps counselling for her (we regretted the loss of the school's play therapist for C); and while he might still need the extra support with beginnings, understanding such a good reason for his stuckness put a very different light on offering that support. Our anxieties began to ease as Miss T and I wondered about a conversation with him and his mum together about his difficult birth, and how that might make all new beginnings difficult for them both, but also how very loved and special he is to them all because of that. We thought about how 'bodily' memories of that time might still be inside them all in some deep place, and how all new beginnings might somehow 'push' those feelings up to the surface. It would be important to emphasise that it was no one's fault of course, and that understanding this could give everyone confidence that he will come through – he is well now, and his difficulties will ease, just as they did for baby C.

A few weeks later: some thoughts from Miss T

Following on from our discussion, further meetings were held with the parents to try to help them feel more secure and less anxious. I explained tentatively to them that there was probably a large amount of transference of C's beginning difficulties into school beginnings, due to his traumatic birth. This was sensitively discussed and reflected upon with the parents. I would wonder out loud with them about this, providing them with opportunities to reflect on his very difficult birth and how it could be impacting on C, and on themselves too, both in the past and in the present. This was especially powerful. They could also identify some key issues that I was able to support them with using my knowledge of attachment and nurturing expertise. We also had a meeting with C and his parents together to talk about his difficult birth and how this might be making all new beginnings difficult for him. I explained to him that I would find some special ways to help him with beginnings.

I reflected on this with my TA and came up with some practical ways to help and support him to feel more relaxed and comfortable at school, which I shared with the parents.

I suggested using the child's knowledge of train stations to 'map out' our day, with each station being a different part of the day. We talked with C about how it can be so hard to start a new journey, especially if we don't know what might happen and if previous journeys have been difficult, but that there were lots of people in school to help, just like the conductors and staff on a train platform. The use of a visual timetable helped too. We set this up at the end of each day ready for the next day, to relive anxiety about what might happen tomorrow. We ensured everything was as predictable as possible.

I wondered about a transitional object. Babies and young children typically use special toys to support them through difficult times. C's favourite teddy was brought into school and became his transitional object. Teddy became part of the class, with its own identity and special plate for toast time! The rationale behind this was to demonstrate a caring, relaxed and supportive atmosphere that valued everyone (including Teddy), while Teddy was also a 'security blanket' for C. Additionally, this 'relaxed' start to our day continues to enable all children to come into a calm, familiar environment that they have some ownership of.

Then at home time we would discuss which activities would be out the following morning when they arrived and children were allowed to choose what they wanted for the beginning session. There was always a range of activities provided, covering many areas of the curriculum. C was especially comfortable with maths, so I always ensured there was a manageable number activity for him to start the day with, if he wanted to engage with it.

To help with separation anxiety, we played simple games – such as hide and seek with Teddy (at first it was placed in very obvious places in clear sight, slowly becoming more hidden). I also shared times when I had taken my teddy to school with me when I was little! Other therapeutic games included the children sitting in a circle and then covering one child with a blanket, asking the rest to guess which child was hidden. Sometimes class items were placed outside a window – so that we could see them, even though they weren't directly with us. Additionally, a lot of holding-in-mind comments were shared and I staged a number of times when I had to leave the classroom temporarily, for short periods of time, while the children stayed with my TA. When I came back the TA and myself had lots of conversations about how I had missed the children and that I was still thinking about them, even though I wasn't in the room. I would also make personal and specific comments to C and all the children wondering about what he had been doing and how I had been thinking about them.

Months later I asked the nurture teacher if C had become more settled as a result of her conversations and practical responses. She replied:

> It took a while, but yes he did settle and manage new beginnings much more happily. He successfully transitioned back into class in Year 1, which was probably 8–12 months after the conversation we had. Whenever I saw him last year, when he was in Year 2, he seemed happy and confident.

Toddler stage: involvement with exploration

The 'toddler stage' can be thought of as the stage of 'letting go and bringing back'.[8] It is the time when a secure child starts to want to explore and investigate the world both of his mother, his family and the world around him. This exploration process, which needs a secure base and attachment experience to facilitate, is crucial for both learning and development. As described on p. 4:

> We can observe a secure baby (or toddler) with mother nearby begin to look around, or crawl or toddle about and start to explore with all their senses. Then after a while, or when something unexpected momentarily rocks their secure base, they look or

go back to mum for reassurance before beginning to explore again, and of course continuing to learn from experience that mum will be there when needed and that exploration is fun and interesting.

The confidence to explore arises out of a toddler's knowledge that his parents are nearby and available if he needs them. It can also open him to a sense of self and other, whereby he begins to experience that he is separate from his parents, but also connected and 'in their minds'.

It is also important for setting boundaries and expectations. One's physical presence nearby is important for the child, as child psychologist and attachment author Dan Hughes says:

> Maintaining physical presence is the primary way that parents discipline toddlers. Parents are aware of their toddler. They 'keep an eye on her' and 'an ear on him' constantly throughout the day. They are near their child, so that the child takes their presence for granted and gradually comes to rely on their knowledge about what to do. Their child also constantly engages in 'social referencing', whereby (s)he watches her/his parents' non-verbal reactions to know whether or not someone or something is a danger or is safe. They develop their primary knowledge of self, other and the world through relying on their parents' minds and hearts. The parents' presence gives the child the sense of safety necessary to be able to explore and learn about her/his world.[9]

In this section we are thinking about children stuck in varying ways and to varying degrees at the toddler stage of development. Each child's needs and inhibitions will be individual and particular, so the suggestions and descriptions will be useful in varying ways for children too.

For children stuck in the toddler stage

1. Following on from Dan Hughes' comment above, ensuring that significant adults are close by watching over toddler-stage children, particularly at insecure or transition times, will facilitate growth and security. So the main remediating practice is to attune to and take seriously your relationship with each child. Significant adults need to be available as promised and sometimes as necessary, to enable them to experience feeling held in mind.
2. It will be important to acknowledge their need for you if you are busy with another child, and tell them you will come soon, or when you will be back. This is very important, but it does not mean being *perfectly* reliable. Graham Music (child and adult psychotherapist at the Tavistock Clinic) argues that mistakes and imperfections are *important and even necessary*, because they provide opportunities for the crucial experience of *repair* of close significant relationships, when for some reason there is a 'break'. At a recent Caspari Lecture he explained: 'Attuning to children is best on the third time (!) – because repairing "broken" relationships and broken connections is what gives rise to resilience – perfect attunement does not *require* perfection!'[10] (See point 4 below on repair.)

In line with this, Rachel Barbanel-Fried contends that, 'Recent infant–parent studies have found that in the BEST CASE SCENARIO mothers were able to understand their infants needs only 30% of the time on the first go'.

This is good enough because, as Barbanel-Fried continues, 'the bond is created in the space between the mistake and the repair'.[11]

3. The 'conversation' around the break and the repair both facilitates the all-important parent–infant bond, and the experience of emotional containment for the baby or child.

4. This understanding of the importance of managing the mistake *and the repair*, indeed of seeing the *mistake as an opportunity to repair* the relationship with the child is actually crucial for school staff. It is linked in to our own attitudes to mistakes, so that rather than putting ourselves down when we are late or wrong in some way, we can apologise and recover. Our own mistakes and recovery can help us understand *from inside* the importance of taking such opportunities to repair and cement relationships.

5. A teacher or key worker can use this understanding to take opportunities to repair little breaks and unintended hurts by apologising thoughtfully and honestly to the child, knowing that such mistakes (like all mistakes!) are wonderful opportunities to learn something valuable – which would not have been possible without the mistake or 'break'.

> *I am sorry Sam. I know I said I would come back and look at your work in five minutes, but I got caught up with photocopying something for Mrs S. I hope you didn't think I had forgotten you. I have been thinking about your picture. How's it going?*

6. Graham Music's teaching illustrates the importance of taking opportunities to talk little hurts through as they happen, before, during and/or after an experience, particularly when it feels significant, or when you *sense* something might be affecting the child.

7. Holding-in-mind gestures and comments also help children feel thought about and remembered (see Box 8, p. 102).

8. Using the child's name frequently also helps them feel connected and held in mind too.

9. Their security is still vulnerable at this stage and they may need accompanying when they go somewhere, and help with tidying up and practical tasks. The goal is to wean them and let them manage alone in small doses as and when (but not before) they are ready.

10. They very much need a secure base from which to feel safe enough to explore and to learn. When they are feeling safe and secure in their relationships, with the available physical presence of a significant adult(s) around them and in their familiar 'homely' environment and predictable routines, their natural curiosity and openness to learning kicks in.

11. Attachment-based play continues to be important, facilitating playfulness and the nurturing relationship too (see Chapter 13, pp. 248–249).

12. Valuing their special soft toys and transitional objects also facilitates relationships, as well as helping with little absences.

13. Play is especially important. It is the young child's natural way to 'work' through all experiences and anxieties including hurtful and worrying things – and new things too. They will still often need support with play and with small learning tasks.

14. Having 'conversations' with their special toys and creations can be the beginning of pretend play with little ones who can't play. For older children I have found leaving a few 'bits' around (Blu Tack, paper clips, a lolly stick, etc.) for them to fiddle with helpful.

15. It is important to respect children's play space. Give plenty of opportunities for play, as and when they are open to it.
16. Pretend-play materials like dolls, soft toys, baby cots, shawls, drinking bottles, Play-Doh and tea sets are good to have around. Messy and sand play enables them to play through muddles and mess and things getting stuck. Big boxes and cloths can be good for making 'dens' and bridges, etc. Large amounts of early constructional toys like Duplo or megablocks model both making and breaking and then fixing again and give opportunities to help each other and cooperate.
17. Drawing and art are beginning to become possible at the toddler stage and can offer ways of thinking about sensitive things in the metaphor, things that may be difficult to talk about, or that may be outside conscious awareness. In Figure 19 we see developmentally delayed H's teddy looking rather tentative in his drawing, while his ambivalence and anxieties about 'growing up' are very evident in his dictated story. Teddy's difficulties and worries can then be safely thought about and empathised with, and returned to in the future perhaps when the picture is revisited.
18. Toddlers are very much at the egocentric stage (preoccupied with themselves) when sharing is difficult, so limit their need to share equipment at first and only gradually expect them to share and take turns. Similarly they will need *lots* of help with tidying up (for more on the value of play and use of metaphor see Chapter 13).
19. The use of rhythm, singing, music and movement activities, and of course stories together on a daily basis, all continue to be nurturing and regulating (for their brains too – see section on fostering coordination and body awareness, p. 117). The activities in Box 17, p. 207 are also about practising self-regulation and body control.
20. Continuing to structure the day with routines remains important.
21. Creating a secure base with lots of talking through and practical preparations for any unexpected and also all expected changes will be a foundation for learning and calmness.
22. Structure builds security. This includes limited choice selection, short learning activities, lots of play opportunities and limits on anything that is likely to overexcite them.
23. For children still in the 'toddler stage' it is helpful if key adults can watch out for 'triggers' and prevent them if possible, or support the child as soon as they notice a problem. Distraction is helpful in the early stages.
24. Key adults need to take responsibility to help them calm down, and prevent escalation if possible. Such children need adults who can contain their *own* frustrations and impatience, adults who never use shame, threats or bribery to control them. The problem is that in the short term, 'bribery' (rewards) and threats do work because shame and threats are unbearable and 'bribes' are enticing. When we feel exhausted and helpless with a vulnerable resistant child such approaches are very tempting. In the long term, however, they do nothing to enhance the child's emotional growth and authenticity. When setting boundaries it is much better to use ACO:

    A = Acknowledge the child's feeling or wish.

    C = Communicate the expectation or limit.

    O = Offer help or offer alternatives (rather than giving them an ultimatum).

    You really wish you could be first I know, but Simon got there first today. How about you walk with me at the end of the line?

25. Toddler-stage children are just moving in the direction of thinking for themselves. The adult decides whether they can make their own decision for calm-down time or not.

26. They need things putting into words a lot. It is not only restorative, but it also enables the child to feel they are somehow inside your mind, and begin to grow the capacity to hold you (and other significant peers and people) inside *their* minds and wonder about them. This is the beginning of empathy. As you engage in regular attuned interactions and feel more connected with them in a conscious way, you may begin to notice signs of *their* developing capacity to think of others. They may even comment on what another child might be feeling. Many teachers and school staff I have worked with report such experiences. Box 10 shows some ways of putting young children's feelings into simple words.

Box 10   Nurturing 'you' statements

- *You're trying to tell me something aren't you?*

- *You look like you're enjoying that!*

- *Are you wanting me to pass . . . to you?*

- *Yes. You've got very sticky hands haven't you!*

- *That hurt you a little didn't it?*

- *You're fitting them all together! . . . You like that!*

- *I think you're pleased with that!*

- *That looks frustrating. Would you like me to help you?*

- *You just want to know I'm still here don't you. I'm watching you.*

- *That was funny wasn't it?*

- *You had another go – and you made it . . . WOW!*

- *That looks heavy/hard/bumpy, etc.*

- *I think you need a bit of help with that!*

- *Sharing can be hard. We can worry there won't be enough for us.*

- *You're really trying so hard to . . .*

- *I'm just wondering what you're trying to tell me.*

- *WOW! You're really angry about that!*

- *I think you're a bit cross with me for not letting you . . . but it's not safe.*

- *You wish you had got it, but . . . got it first. Maybe . . .*

- *You really want another one don't you. But there's no more left.*

- *It can be hard to wait can't it?*

- *You want to say something to me don't you? I'll be with you in a minute.*

- *You're feeling a bit bad about that aren't you? Maybe you could . . .*

- *Sometimes we wish we hadn't done something – but it's too late.*

- *I wonder how we could make it better.*

27. Asking them what *they* think about things gets them used to having thoughts, even if they can't answer.

28. As with all vulnerable children, changes and transitions are particularly difficult, because the secure base we mentioned earlier is threatened or lost for a while. Transitional objects and cards from an absent teacher may help a child feel held in mind and ease the loss or separation, but at this early stage separation is still very difficult. Toddler-stage children often still need their secure adult to be nearby to feel secure. Again, handled well these are all opportunities, and can be talked through appropriately and thoughtfully, e.g.

    'Would it help if you took your teddy with you when you go?'

    'Teddy doesn't want to be forgotten/left behind today I think.'

    'Don't worry Teddy. We haven't forgotten you.'

29. There may, however, be some changes that are better avoided until the child's capacity for security and feeling held in mind is better developed. In the pupil referral unit where I worked we decided that some children were just too damaged to cope with even very attuned (but unknown) teachers and so we had a policy of not using any supply teachers. I even did an INSET on coping with absence as we were so concerned about the children's obvious regression, and the outbursts we had to cope with and endure at such times (see Chapter 8, pp. 244–245 for more details).

Finally

Dan Hughes coined the acronym PACE[12] as a helpful way of bringing to mind attuned ways of relating to little children. PACE stands for the importance of playfulness, attunement, curiosity and empathy in our ways of relating, and in our interactions with children (see p. 186 for fuller description).

Baby- and toddler-stage children benefit particularly from nurture-group provision – like C in Case Study 22 above. In fact, many of the suggestions are similar to nurture-base practice. Chapter 15 gives a detailed example of a child (and mother too) benefitting from nurture provision.

The latency stage (5–12 years)

Friendship, exploration and school learning: imagination and make-believe

For the secure child, the primary years are a time of developing friendships, knowledge and skills, a time of mutual enjoyment, fun and learning. There is a feeling of growing up and becoming your own person, developing interests and passions, while still being part of a supportive family on which you depend. Opening up to the outside world can be exciting, stimulating and challenging, but worrying too. These worries are usually under the surface. They may inhibit exploration at times and cause a little shyness, and the slightly 'obsessive' repetition of monotonous activities, which can be commonplace and calming at this age. In moderate form this diligent practice of course develops skills and confidence.

Latency is also the time when imagination and play blossoms. Younger latency-stage children especially love make-believe and pretend play. They naturally 'process' their unspoken terrors through play and stories and even quite violent games. Engaging with zombies, aliens and scary creatures (whatever heroes, monsters and horrors are in vogue at the time) through the 'safety' of stories, 'figures', TV, films and books is their natural way to play through normal childhood fears – of bigness, noisiness, strangeness, weirdness and suddenness, etc. Humour plays a large part in this process too! Fairy tales (both traditional and modern – including *Harry Potter*!) are a timeless way of engaging with fear and terror and scary impossible challenges, knowing that help will be at hand and there will be a happy ending at the end.

Latency is a time of gaining confidence and enjoyment through learning and practising both knowledge and skills. The familiar classroom and the teachers and TAs become an extension of the secure base of home.

A secure latency child is developing all sorts of skills and competencies, such as thinking for themselves, sharing and taking turns, not needing to be in control, feeling OK about not knowing and being comfortable with the adult knowing more than they do. Through experience they are learning to struggle alone for a while, and to ask for help if necessary. They trust that their needs and hurts will be understood and met well enough. They are in touch with own basic feelings, and at ease with talking about their feelings with adults. They can regulate their big feelings, with help perhaps if they are tired or pushed to their limit.

They have a strong sense of fairness and justice and like to 'sort things out', with help if necessary. They have a great capacity for creativity, and imaginative and pretend play. They enjoy creating stories and can (unconsciously) use symbolic play and stories to rehearse and process their hurts and worries. They learn through play and experience. They are enthusiastic to learn new things. Increasingly they can make links and see similarities and differences. They are learning to think for themselves and have their own particular interests. They are beginning to move from dependence to independent initiatives and skills.

These then are the 'tasks' of latency, tasks that an insecure or vulnerable child will struggle with – even to the extent of having outbursts, inhibitions and conflicts. This can be complicated by their increasing awareness that others are managing things so much better than they can, thus sapping their self-esteem in the process.

For children struggling at the latency stage

1. All latency children need emotional containment at times (see Chapter 5). The more vulnerable children will need attuned, sensitive help from trusted school staff and caregivers with the capacities mentioned earlier: to bear children's pain and be empathic; to stay with their struggles without intervening unless asked; to set firm secure boundaries using ACO (see p. 131); and to take appropriate opportunities to repair 'breaks' in the relationship after an outburst (these capacities are helpfully listed in questionnaire form in Appendix 2).

2. They may need patient help with managing their big feelings (see above).
3. This requires significant adults with an underlying capacity to contain their own pain, or feel OK about seeking help and talking things through with colleagues, especially when the child 'pushes their buttons'.
4. At the latency stage vulnerable and insecure children will need child-centred thoughtfulness and time together with significant adults, including experiences of fun and laughter, conversation and discussion and safe risk-taking activities.
5. They will need adults who take opportunities to talk both happy and difficult things through with them in a manageable way, adults who give them time without becoming enmeshed or colluding with their patterns.
6. The more insecure children will still need reliable consistent routines and timely support and talking through of transitions and separations (see Chapter 12).
7. Holding-in-mind words and gestures will continue to be important (see Box 8, p. 102). For example, talking through with them that you continue to think about them and wonder how they are getting on, even when you need to be busy with other things, will enable them to separate and still feel connected with you in their minds.
8. Becoming a separate person with interests and competencies will be important but may require a lot of talking through – as they start to compare themselves with others. Taking an interest in their developing interests and skills, and acknowledging and valuing sameness and differences in all sorts of ways will be important here, as they are beginning to discover others have skills and competencies they don't have.
9. Sharing and turn taking can be practised in all sorts of ways with and without adult help. It may be important to sense whether they need support or not with this, i.e. when they are on the way to working things out for themselves and learning from experience, or when intervention is needed to prevent hurt or escalation. Both board games and sport are great opportunities for this.
10. Play and creativity will be engaging and therapeutic. Opportunities for creative writing and art, and for imaginative, pretend and creative play will be valuable especially for the younger ones. This may need to be arranged specially, as the curriculum is unlikely to include play opportunities at this age and children may need help to access these (see Chapter 13, pp. 247–261 on play).
11. The encouragement and use of story writing is especially helpful for latency children, as they will often unconsciously create characters and situations that relate to their own issues.[13] Including regular free story writing and artwork in the curriculum and reading stories to them is particularly helpful. Chapter 13 (pp. 261–270) is all about the therapeutic value and practicalities of stories and story writing.
12. Reading stories to and with children can also be both relationship building and therapeutic. Michael Green writes passionately about the value of fairy tales for latency children in helping them to safely open up and come to terms with their 'shadow' aspects and struggles, saying that '[t]o be truly ourselves, truly whole, we need to reclaim this part of ourselves . . . this wild, dark, shadow side of us'. He refers to reading such tales to children as 'priming the pump' as it allows their imagination to kick in and open up to fears and possibilities in the safe setting of a story (and of a trusted relationship too).[14] For example he talks of how the book *Where the Wild Things Are*[15] might open a child up to his own struggles with his 'wild part'. Through the safety of his own room in the story Max 'can visit the wild part of himself and come back safely', having 'undergone a kind of initiation'.[16] Writing their own fairy tales leads naturally on from such stories, as Green's case studies vividly describe.

Relating to this I had a play-writing experience with a child after we read *The Hare and the Tortoise* together, in which he was able to express a poignant feeling of sadness and a sense of a heavy burden through the story. He was 'Tortoise' and he asked me to be 'Fox':

Fox: *Who's that over there?*

Tortoise: *It's me. Your best friend Tortoise.*

Fox: *My best friend! Come and see me Tortoise.*

Tortoise: *OK I'll be over in ten minutes. OK Fox?*

Fox: *Why don't you come now Tortoise?*

Tortoise: *If I could be a little bit faster I would get to you a bit faster Fox.*

Fox: *Perhaps you would like to be a little bit faster Tortoise.*

Tortoise: *Yes, I would love to be a bit faster Fox.*

Fox: *It sounds like you have a problem Tortoise.*

Tortoise: *Yes, I have a very big problem Fox.*

Fox: *Perhaps you would like to tell me a little bit about your problem Tortoise.*

Tortoise: *It is because I can't walk any faster.*

Fox: *You have a very heavy weight to carry round with you all the time don't you Tortoise?*

Tortoise: *Yes. I have got a lot of weight to carry all the time Fox.*

Fox: *I wonder what it feels like to carry that heavy weight around all the time Tortoise?*

Tortoise: *It makes me feel horrible all the time Fox.*

Fox: *Horrible . . . Mmmm.*

Tortoise: *It will be a lot quicker if you come over to me Fox.*

Fox: *That's an idea.*

Tortoise: *Yes. You should come over to me Fox.*

Fox: *Right. Here I am Tortoise.*

Tortoise: *Oh It's nice to see you again Fox.*

Fox: *So how have you been since we last met Tortoise?*

Tortoise: *Very very upset my dear friend Fox.*

Fox: *Very very upset . . . Oh Tortoise!*

Tortoise: *It is because I can only walk slowly.*

Fox: *It is hard to know what to say Tortoise.*

13. The most 'damaged children' will benefit from play, art and educational psychother-
    apy if and when they are open to it – particularly when the situation at home is secure
    enough to support them in coming to sessions, etc. (see section on counselling and
    therapy in school, pp. 77–83). It is often best to offer this alongside their parents access-
    ing their own counselling.
14. Most of all children will need thoughtful attuned ways of relating (see Chapter 11)
    from significant adults who tune into and stretch their interests, help them with shar-
    ing and taking turns, with sorting things out and tidying up and with learning new
    tasks – step by step.

A second-chance attachment experience will naturally grow out of all these approaches,
and facilitate a secure base from which developmentally 'stuck' children can grow,
develop and learn.

   With the most disturbed and regressed children there is often a significant adult
or 'key worker' for the child, who develops a close, dependent relationship and then
gradually weans them on to less dependence as they become more secure and confident. For trainers, the following summary and notes on the key worker's role may
be helpful.

Summary of a second-chance attachment experience with a secure, resilient, committed adult, offering a relationship that survives and nurtures

The needs of a child may include the following:

1. Attuned adaptions to their stage, which may include enabling them to reach regression and work through early unexperienced stages, using play perhaps to begin to
   process hurts.
2. Attuned responsiveness and frequent experiences of feeling held in mind.
3. Dyadic regulation with a trusted, calm, thoughtful and unobtrusive other. The adult
   takes responsibility to help them calm down – until they can manage it a little. Safe
   holding may be necessary.
4. Boundaries set with empathy as well as firmness.
5. Their behavioural communications understood, and responded to thoughtfully rather
   than just conditioned and punished away.
6. To move from shame to guilt, through very gentle and timely talking through.
7. Through containment to reach some security and personal guilt – feeling sorrow or
   regret.
8. To realise through experience that pain can be borne, talked about and survived –
   leading to a capacity to begin to learn from experience and the beginnings of integration
   (when painful and guilt-ridden or embarrassing experiences can nevertheless be thought
   and talked about).
9. Separation as a person.
10. Their projections to be 'contained' – including their hatred and antisocial behaviour.
    Their unbearable states and conflicts to be survived through emotional containment
    by the trusted significant adult or key worker. As well as necessary boundaries, this will
    require understanding support from and for their key worker.

Key worker role: to offer attuned presence, responsiveness and support

1. Develop an attuned and resilient relationship – supported by other adults. The availability and regular use of supervision is very helpful and may be crucial.
2. Offer non-collusive involvement with understanding (this means the key worker needs to have the capacity to think about and sometimes realise what is going on within the child and the relationship. This needs to include the capacity to stay separate, be able to say no, bear the child's anger and take the responsibility to repair the relationship (as the child offers opportunities) after 'breaks'.
3. Understand and reflect on each behaviour as an unconscious communication.
4. Talking things through with other staff members is crucial.
5. Offer emotional containment rather than ego support when needed (see Chapter 5, pp. 67–77).
6. Offer lots of 'holding-in-mind' comments and gestures (see Box 8, p. 102).
7. Put the child's feelings into words in small doses. Lots of talking through in small doses.
8. Develop and offer a very strong, predictable structure including visual timetables.
9. Develop a consciously nurturing relationship, and secure settings and experiences.
10. Offering food experiences can be nurturing – nurture groups include breakfast together.
11. See all life situations and problems as opportunities for attuned caregiving and nurture.
12. Make careful preparation for new beginnings, endings and transitions.
13. Offer empathy and maintain firm boundaries.
14. Some children may need dyadic regulation – staff may need extra support with this.
15. Prevent overstimulation.
16. Understand the child's chaotic/disorganised, enmeshed and frozen behaviour patterns.
17. Watch out for triggered states and if possible prevent them or talk through later.
18. Some children may need 'localised provision' (see p. 125) and fostering of dependence when necessary.
19. Use touch, tone of voice, music, rhythm, nurturing holding as they are open to it.
20. Use attachment-based play (see p. 248) when appropriate – offering fun, laughter, hiding and finding and high-intensity relational moments (see p. 14 and note 10).
21. Use transitional objects, both their own and the key worker's or teacher's, to ease little separations.
22. When necessary offer safe an emotionally contained space to express and find physical containment, e.g. cupboard, tent, etc.
23. Take and make opportunities to facilitate 'play in the space between' (see p. 126 and note 5).
24. Undirected play, art and story experiences with a key adult can be therapeutic, especially if they are timetabled, have boundaries and the contents are remembered and looked after carefully in a box or book.
25. Wean the child towards separation only as they are ready.
26. In extreme cases a child may need to be separated from other children, whom they disrupt and threaten.

As significant adults will discover, working in this thoughtful, attuned way with respect for the child's current developmental stage and difficulties will facilitate emotional growth and progress. These may be small steps, but with such regressed and insecure children we are starting from a very (and understandably) delayed base. It is encouraging for both adults and children to notice all improvements and signs of growth. Watch out for and acknowledge (even very small) signs of progress (see Box 11).

Box 11 Examples of signs of 'progress' (in approximate developmental order)

- Managing eye contact.

- Bearing and appreciating safe touch and holding.

- Enjoyment and engagement in attachment-based play.

- Being able to use a regular 'limited regression' opportunity.

- A feeling in the attachment worker that a relationship is becoming important.

- A feeling of connection.

- A move from repeated blaming and acting out to becoming upset or crying.

- Being able to manage little supported separations. Use of a transitional object.

- Increased capacity to wait, while being held in mind.

- A move from taking unbearable anxieties out on people (aggression) to taking them out on objects.

- A developing ability to allow attachment figures to put words to feelings.

- The ability to accept a boundary delivered with empathy.

- (Non-verbally) indicating a wish for 'repair' after a 'break'.

- Allowing a significant adult to initiate repair at an appropriate time.

- The capacity to acknowledge a feeling openly.

- Sharing real feelings for the first time (see Case Study 24, p. 149).

- A developing capacity to appreciate and believe praise.

- Any signs of bearing or expressing vulnerability (with empathic support).

- A developing capacity to ask for or accept help.

- Play in the attuned, attentive presence of the attachment worker.

- The ability to use play to express and work through issues symbolically.

- Being able to use an attuned response to a possible underlying meaning of their behaviour.

- Sharing a personal experience.

- Managing to engage with attachment figure in talking something through.

- Managing to stall their own escalating behaviour.

- Showing awareness of, or ability to discuss a 'trigger'.

- Managing to use suggested anger-management practices.

- The ability to manage a prepared separation.

- Calming down after an outburst more quickly.

- Enjoying cooperative play for a short period.

- The ability to share an object.

- The ability to take turns in a game.

- The ability to bear little frustrations, make mistakes and try again and manage little challenges.

- The ability to feel appropriate authentic pride.

- Signs of group togetherness, friendship.

- Less resistance to beginning tasks.

- The ability to use help with beginnings and endings.

- The ability to remember something you told them and to take in information.

- Expression of curiosity.

- The ability or wish to sort something out.

- The ability to tidy up without asking.

- The ability to concentrate on a task in a secure setting.

- An increased capacity to take risks in learning.

Noticing such signs of progress out loud to the child can be very affirming both for the child and for staff, and enhance their self-esteem, e.g.

> *'Thank you for that Sam. I really appreciated you putting all the pens away. I remember last week you went all quiet and turned away when I asked you to help clear away. Thank you'*

> *'Wow Ben! You've tidied up that game without me even asking. I think that's the first time you've done that. I think you're growing stronger. What do you think?'*

> *'You had a go at the second set with no problems. I don't think you would have managed that last week. What do you think?'*

Case Study 23 describes how an attuned thoughtful relationship enabled a child to grow stronger

Case Study 23   Growing stronger: some thoughts from an inclusion manager

I worked with F a lot. In class he could be quite frustrating and disruptive. It was fairly low-level disruption, but I think because of his family reputation he seemed to get right into the heads of staff and he would be sent out of class regularly. For example, at carpet time he wouldn't listen, he would be poking the child next to him, or pushing the child in front with his book. Then the children in front of him would shout out 'F's picking on me. F's poking me', etc.

One of his patterns was that minor things would become big issues for him. For example, if he didn't have his swimming kit. If his mum forgot to put it in, which was a problem with her large family, then that would be a big emotional outburst for him. He would stomp around and throw some pencils on the floor, and it wasn't immediately evident to the teacher what this was about and he would often end up being sent out. Later she learnt to spend time with him to see what might be on his mind, and through this sort of talking together, and though my conversations with him, we came to realise that underneath he was always feeling forgotten and let down in his big family.

When he was with me we did a lot of talking. I would put words to his feelings. We thought about a lot of different feelings, because when they are little children only really know 'happy' or 'angry'. We would look at the feeling poster on the wall and think which feeling it was that he was feeling now, or when … happened. I wanted him to be able to think in more detail about his feelings, including his swimming kit anxieties.

Then, after lots of times of talking his outbursts and upsets through, we got to a point one day (which was so exciting for me!) when he came to me in the morning and said, 'Haaaa (big sigh) I haven't got my swimming kit!' and I said, 'OK. What do we need to do?' He replied, 'Go and speak to H (lady in the office) and we can borrow a kit!' I said, 'Yes we can!' and then, 'Do you know what? I remember lots of times before when you forgot your kit you wouldn't have been able to do this. You would have been running around, stomping, and throwing pencils. You have got really really much stronger. What do you think?' 'Haaaa!' He exclaimed, 'I have!'

The next week he remembered his kit! That felt so good; like the pinnacle of my first year really. I saw that all the work we had put in had really worked. It was him who came to my office in the morning to tell me that he had forgotten his kit. I think he had had enough experience of working with me to know I wasn't going to react. Learning from experience!

He is Year 6 now. I saw him on the playground not so long ago and he just looked like another child. I think the whole experience gave me confidence as well as him – and his teacher.

It is the *first-hand experience* of relationships with empathic resilient thoughtful people that gives a vulnerable child an opportunity to grow into knowing a secure relationship for themselves, at least in the caring predictable setting of the classroom. In their secure classroom and school and with their familiar trusted adults, they can become able to relate, learn and think for themselves, and begin to regulate their own behaviour. Their old anxious, reactive patterns become overlaid with a functional secure pattern, which they will increasingly be able to transfer to new trusted adults. Sadly though the old dysfunctional attachment patterns can sometimes be triggered, for example by changes and transitions. This is not easy for the child or the school. But we can be ready for that.

Notes

1 'Children' is typically used as the content is primarily aimed at those working with younger children in preschool and primary settings, but readers may relate the content to older students too.
2 Barbara Dockar-Drysdale, *Therapy and Consultation in Child Care* (London: Free Association Books, 1993), 97 (the book arose out of her experience as a consultant at the Mulberry Bush therapeutic residential school in the 1960s).
3 See theraplay.org. I did my introductory-level training with the Theraplay Institute in London in 2011, and used it with parents and young children in a therapeutic setting, and with small groups and staff in school on several occasions.
4 Dockar-Drysdale, *Therapy and Consultation in Child Care*, 27.
5 Winnicott calls this the 'potential space'. D. W. Winnicott, *Playing and Reality* (Abingdon, UK: Routledge, 1971), 103.
6 See www.nurtureuk.org.
7 See https://boxallprofile.org.
8 Marjorie Boxall and Sylvia Lucas *Nurture Groups in School: Principles and Practice* (London: Sage, 2010), 7.
9 Taken from Dan Hughes' paper on 'physical presence' from my training at Family Futures 2010, see www.danielhughes.org/home.html.
10 Caspari Foundation lecture, London 4 March 2017, www.caspari.org.uk.
11 Rachel Barbanel-Fried, 'The Good Enough Parent' (2016), www.mindselfbody.com.
12 Dan Hughes talks about PACE in all his books and workshops, including Dan Hughes and Kim Golding, *Creating Loving Attachments: Parenting with PACE to Nurture Confidence and Security in the Troubled Child* (London: Jessica Kingsley, 2012).
13 See Angela Greenwood, 'Stories and Writing', in *Taking Children Seriously*, eds Steve Decker, Sandy Kirby, Angela Greenwood and Dudley Moore (London: Cassell, 1999), 64–86.
14 Michael Green, '*Where the Wild Things Are*: Using Fairy Tales with Children', *Educational Therapy and Therapeutic Teaching* (April 1996), 21.
15 M. Sendak, *Where The Wild Things Are* (London: Bodley Head, 1963).
16 Green, '*Where the Wild Things Are*', 21.

The importance of a secure base[1]

8

Figure 21

'The classroom offers a safe base' (nurture principle 2)

John Bowlby maintained that 'all of us, from the cradle to the grave are happiest when life is organised as a series of excursions, long or short, from the secure base provided by our attachment figures'.[2]

The first secure base is an attuned, connected 'right brain to right brain' attachment relationship with the mother. Later, as discussed in previous chapters, firm boundaries set with empathy, fun and laughter together, emotional holding, consistency and reliability form the foundation for a secure base from which children begin to explore the world. As the baby becomes mobile, the experience of a secure base with a mother nearby gives him the confidence to explore, knowing intuitively that any discomforts will be eased, and freeing him to become interested and curious about the familiar world around him. From this experience knowledge and confidence in the outside world grows. This process, however, as we have seen, very much depends on the capacity of the mother.

The problem of insecurity

Children who have not had attuned available attachment figures, will not be able to develop the sort of inner security that enables them to feel safe enough in unfamiliar but not threatening situations.

Similarly, in school, when the person they have come to trust to keep them safe is not there, and the familiar setting and routines are not as predictable as usual, anxieties will be aroused in insecure children. Without the familiar secure base that they have come to trust to keep them comfortable and calm, children's past anxieties and patterns can rise up and may become overwhelming.

The example of a young child crying outside the toilet for their stressed-out mum who is inside, who just can't settle till mum is back with them, vividly illustrates this. The problem is that vicious cycles can easily arise in such insecure relationships. The child can become difficult to settle, the mum can become irritated, helpless and need a break. But a break is the last thing the child can tolerate – leading to less reliability, more insecurity, more crying and screaming and more need for mum's 'break'. One could certainly imagine a vicious cycle developing from such a relationship pattern – leading to a child only feeling safe when they are actively engaging the trusted person *now*. No wonder they need to cling. It is *only* the presence of the trusted adult that enables them to feel safe.

We can see how such anxieties can become transferred into staff, who can then *feel* pushed into reactivity (just like mum!). Overwhelming feelings can make thinking impossible for staff as well as students. In addition, insecure children have often learnt to be hypersensitive. They can quickly pick up on any insecure vibes in their teachers, and a negative feedback loop can increase anxieties and exacerbate acting out. Maintaining calmness and a capacity to think when a child is triggered will make all the difference. We may have to think on our feet, as well as cope with children's acted-out insecurities.

One could of course argue that school staff are not social workers and their primary role is to teach and facilitate learning, but significant relationships will happen anyway in school when children project their hopes, fears and expectations on to staff. How significant adults are with the children will make a difference for good or ill – especially with the needy and vulnerable ones, who have become highly and ambivalently attuned to their attachment figures, affecting both their learning and behaviour as we have seen.

Developing some understanding of these dynamics, and having some knowledge of ways we might alleviate them, can help us maintain our capacity to think and respond helpfully, and maintain our own secure base when absences and insecurities occur.

We have thought a lot in previous chapters about how these 'disturbances' arise and manifest both within and between children and why a secure base is co crucial. In this chapter we will be focusing on the more practical aspects of providing that crucial secure base for insecure children.

The crucial importance of a secure base in school for insecure children

A secure base is essential before any child can begin to become curious to explore and to learn. We can even know this from our own experience.

> I vividly recall sailing with B, a young, very competent friend, on a rather windy day, and feeling acutely wobbly (and insecure!) when the boat tipped steeply in the wind. Several times I asked B which way to steer to make the boat lean less and he told me patiently each time, but I just couldn't take in what he said – I was too anxious!

Exercise 4 can help us to understand the importance of a secure base for learning and openness 'from the inside'.[3]

Exercise 4   The link between feeling 'safe' and being able to reflect

Think of a time when you felt unsafe or unsettled. How did this impede your capacity for reflection and learning?

Think of a time when you worked particularly reflectively and attentively. In what ways did you feel safe and settled at the time?

Facilitating a secure base for insecure children

A nurture base is specifically aimed at being secure, predictable and nurturing, but there are many ways this can be transferred into a mainstream class, especially in an infant school.

Employing or allocating the right staff

Insecure children need securely attached teachers and TAs, so head teachers and senior management need to think carefully about the staff they place very vulnerable children with, and/or those they employ to work with them. One inner-city school gets round this by only offering temporary contracts to new staff – to see how they like it, but also for the school to see how they cope with the more vulnerable children, and to observe their resilience and openness to learning, before regularising their contracts. Thoughtful knowledgeable managers can make a real difference. They need to employ:

1. Staff who are open to learning.
2. Staff with a capacity for:

  (a) attunement;
  (b) empathy;
  (c) resilience – and the ability to bear being disliked/hated;
  (d) setting clear boundaries with empathy – this is very important both for present-moment security and to enable the child to begin to internalise the capacity to set their own boundaries (see p. 195 for a fuller discussion);
  (e) managing and talking about endings;
  (f) staying with the child's current pain and not needing to prematurely reassure or make it better;
  (g) being non-judgemental;
  (h) cooperation without power implications.

3. Staff who have no problem acknowledging difficulties and asking for help.
4. Staff who are reliable and available.
5. Staff who don't collude with children's manipulations.
6. Staff (particularly senior staff) who can put effort into praising and appreciating each other.

(The questionnaire in Appendix 2 that lists emotionally containing capacities may be helpful here.)

Personally

The security and resilience of 'second-chance attachment relationships' in school will be the greatest facilitator of a secure base for learning (see pp. 138–143 for a detailed description of this).

A second-chance attachment relationship is a significant relationship with an attuned reliable thoughtful nurturing adult. Many readers will have experience of offering this to a child either in a one-to-one relationship or with a child in class they (knew they needed to) develop a particular bond with. Exercise 5 may bring this vividly to mind.

Exercise 5 Attunement experience

Reflect on a time recently when you felt particularly attuned to a child.

- What was the quality of the attunement? How was it helpful to the child?
- Was there a way in which it might it have felt risky?
- How do you think the child felt?
- What did the experience facilitate?

Attuned trusted relationships

As the insecure child comes to feel known, cared for and thought about, and begins to trust significant adults, a secure base begins to form in their mind. Relationship-building processes might include:

1. A key worker (or individual attachment worker for very insecure children) whose job is to develop a caring, attuned but non-collusive (initially dependent) relationship with the child.
2. Being aware of the child's need to make contact with their 'secure-base' (person) when (even slight) anxieties arise, and at the beginning of sessions and days.
3. Through observation trying to discern any situations, words, gestures, facial expressions, peer or adult behaviours, which might trigger their (hormonal) fear reactions. As your relationship becomes more secure, take opportunities to talk these through with them so they can get to know their own triggers. This relieves shame.
4. Sharing your knowledge of triggers with other involved staff.
5. If you become aware (even slightly) that *you* may have triggered an anxious reaction, apologise immediately, clarify your intentions and encourage the child to respond, e.g.

   > *You looked a bit upset just now. I'm wondering if it affected you when I needed to quickly go and sort out Sam's problem? I guess it would have been helpful if I had told you why I quickly needed to rush away. I'm sorry. Are you OK now?*

6. Taking all opportunities to tentatively reflect children's apparent feelings (they may only be able to cope with this in small doses, and when they are calm).
7. Being aware of their particular attachment patterns and responding accordingly.
8. Being particularly aware of their need for, or difficulty with proximity.
9. Use of active listening and responding.
10. Discipline through relationships. The use of 'moral talks' (e.g. *'How do you think you made Sam feel?'* or *'How would you feel if . . .?'*) doesn't work for very insecure children – they appear to listen but internally switch off to avoid uncomfortable shame, which may later become acted out.
11. Use of your own calm, thoughtful presence during outbursts. Seek help if necessary.
12. Developing awareness of what the child evokes in you, and discuss it with supportive colleagues.
13. Addressing and thinking *out loud* about the needs of the whole group or class facilitates a secure group. It can be especially helpful for children to experience the staff in the room cooperating together thoughtfully – like a good cooperating couple (which they may not be used to). This even includes talking thoughtfully and wondering about behaviours, feelings, moods, etc. in a benign and caring way *in front of* the children. These 'wondering' communications both model adults thinking and getting on thoughtfully together, and enable children to feel thought about, e.g.

    > *'I'm just wondering Mrs Smith, if the weather is affecting the group/class today, or maybe it's because it's Friday, but they seem a bit more unsettled today.'*

    > *'I think B needs a break for a few minutes. How about you both go and get us all a drink?'*

14. The importance of 'holding-in-mind' comments, signals and gestures can enable insecure children to bear to wait a moment, and to feel thought about at a distance (see Box 8, p. 102).

It's all about tuning into the child, thinking and not being manipulated, and also weaning them as and when they can cope. This may also involve increasing the availability of support at anxious times and transitions. This may be prearranged or they may in fact 'choose' who they want to 'use' and trust.

It's also crucial that significant adults ensure that their *own* unconscious needs don't prevent them from responding in the way the *child* needs (see countertransference, p. 53). Beware of needing to be a rescuer! Being open to your own shadow side and vulnerabilities can be very helpful. The nurture-group staff (mentioned on p. 53) who would 'swap roles' to give a staff member a short 'break' from a child who for some reason was pushing their buttons, is a very good example of this.

In special schools and units, staff teams spending time debriefing together, daily if possible, is very helpful. Acknowledging and supporting each other around transference experiences and projections from the children, can facilitate understanding and aid bonding for the team.

Case Study 24 illustrates the value of sharing and thinking together, and the rewarding fruits of a developing relationship (in a mainstream school).

Case Study 24   Sharing real feelings for the first time: an inclusion manager talks about their support for E

'When Mrs S was allocated to be the morning TA for E, a very dysfunctional and defended child with a particularly enmeshed and resistant mother, I was a little concerned, as she was not the most empathic person, she could be a bit abrupt and was used to working in a rather behaviourist way (using rewards and 'consequences' to manage behaviour), which E typically resisted. Mrs S was clearly frustrated by this, although she did really care about him. E's afternoon worker, Mrs B, was quite the opposite and was keen to support both Mrs S and E, so the three of us decided to have half-termly conversations together to think through his behaviour and resistant communications, and to try to understand his needs and his fears. This was very helpful as we were able to think fruitfully together about the very understandable reasons for E's difficulties, leading to the value of empathy when setting boundaries, and the importance of putting his possible feelings tentatively into words, for example.

E continued to be quite defensive and resistant, particularly to writing tasks, and in our conversations we were able to think about helpful and patient ways of managing those, including lots of 'holding-in-mind' comments and gestures (see Box 8, p. 102). Slowly Mrs S shared little observations, which indicated their relationship was becoming more attuned. Although she could still be quite defensive herself in response to her handling of his difficulties, things did seem to be gradually changing between them. It was particularly hard when any little stresses, like bad times at home, absences, lateness and approaching SATs destabilised him. Suddenly one day Mrs S came into the sharing meeting with shining eyes and eagerly told us that for the very first time E had shared his real and vulnerable feelings with her, when she took him to a quiet room away from the rest of the class to do his SATs test on Wednesday. As they walked along the corridor he suddenly said that he was scared. 'What are you scared of?' asked Mrs S. 'The SATs tests,' he replied. 'Of course. I understand,' Mrs S responded, 'probably everyone is a bit scared of SATs tests.' And before he did the test they were able to have a real and supportive conversation about his worries and fears, which she felt was the first time he had been able to be honest with her, enabling her to be empathic and thoughtful.

The thing that remains with me, however, is Mrs S's delight and realisation that their relationship was bearing fruit, and that she herself was really making a difference to E. A real 'learning from experience'!

Environmentally

The familiarity, consistency and nurturing quality of the physical environment can make a place feel more secure. These might include:

1. Nurturing environment:

    (a) soft home area;
    (b) 'thinking chair';
    (c) time out/quiet room availability;
    (d) comfortable place where children can sit close to you for group/class times.

2. Nurturing activities:

    (a) use of food and drink;
    (b) storytelling and reading;
    (c) rhythm and music and song;
    (d) 'Activate'[4] (exercise programme to music)/brain gym/cooperative games (e.g. parachute play)'.

3. Calming activities:

    (a) 'calm box' of easy 'left-brain' activities and worksheets (see Box 7, p. 95);
    (b) 'private' journals to write or draw in;
    (c) physically calming/adrenalin-releasing activities (outside or inside), e.g. trampoline or other PE equipment;
    (d) 'personalised' transitional objects;
    (e) listening to calming music (perhaps with earphones), short, supported experiences of silence (see Chapter 14 on enhancing children's personal capacities);
    (f) activities to *practice* self-lowering arousal levels, e.g. percussion play with lifting and then lowering of sound levels to silence, similarly with parachute play and coordinated lifting and lowering of the parachute down to the ground.

4. Thoughtful management of break and moving around times:

    (a) may involve special provision, like supported indoor options;
    (b) safe, containing outdoor spaces.

Structurally

The familiarity and supportiveness of structures, especially when inevitable changes occur, will enable an insecure student to manage better. For insecure, damaged and needy children, who can so easily be triggered into anxiety, reactivity or even into fight or flight, all changes are difficult, but the start of the school day, or of a lesson or a break time in a *different* place, can be a particularly vulnerable time. Many schools are aware of the benefit of, and the need to settle anxious and insecure children into the day or the lesson before they start their 'work'. Some people talk about 'dumping the day' or in this case 'dumping the morning miseries'. Children from dysfunctional families can sometimes come into school with painful 'unfinished business' from home that can so easily interfere with settling into school routines and learning. Attuned adults who greet them can often sense if they need a bit of time to talk things through and relieve their morning anxieties a little before the day begins. Talking while walking or drinking some juice, followed by introducing some thoughts about the coming day might help them to shift into a calmer state ready for the day. A similar process might sometimes be needed after a fraught lunchtime or break time.

> *I remember in the pupil referral unit staff would always come and greet the pupils and have a welcoming chat and listening time with them as they entered the building each day. Sometimes pupils could come into school full of pent-up rage, hurt or disappointment. A familiar empathic adult open to listening would often diffuse such anxieties.*

We have heard how some children are conditioned to be on 'high alert' for anything (or anyone) that might hurt them. They can be driven to check for safety in all new situations, or when anything different or any sudden noises occur.

In her book *What About Me?* Louise Bombèr[5] talks about the importance of allowing and helping the more insecure children to 'scan' the room before they settle down to work, to check for anything unfamiliar that might make them feel unsafe. This might include talking them through the process of looking around, noticing familiar things, particularly unfamiliar things and people, and why they might be there – to reassure them of the safe base around them.

> *I remember a teacher friend telling me of a 5-year-old who would habitually go to all four corners of the room when he came into class, before settling to any activity or responding to the teacher in any way.*

Maybe he was scanning! As Bombèr describes, talking about the importance of safety with him, helping him to scan verbally and internally from a good viewing position and gradually to need it less and less would be progress.

Other structural supports might include:

- predictable structures and setting – things in the same place, any changes pointed out;
- consistent staff and classroom;
- visual labelling;
- same way to start the day, e.g. 'left-brain' early morning or familiar 'activate' activity;
- activities done in the same place each time;
- small, cosy hidey-hole space for anxious/avoidant children;
- system of agreed procedures that respond quickly to outbursts;
- lunch and break time 'contained and emotionally safe' small group or playroom option;
- regular routines visually and verbally explained and reminded.

Thoughtfulness around changes and transitions

(See Chapter 12 on transitions.)

1. Display and frequently refer to visual calendars. A daily timetable and a termly or a weekly calendar showing activities and holidays, weekdays and weekend (home) days, on the wall, can be regularly referred to and talked through with the children.
2. 'Practice walks', photos and talking through of new routines, people or changes can fix a new routine inside a child's mind.
3. Think about endings *well in advance*, and take regular opportunities to bring them up with understanding. This includes transition support between lessons, and from class to playtime. It includes both practical and personal support, and talking through both what is going to happen next and how this will be managed, as well as talking through any possible anxieties around the change. It is especially important to talk with children about endings around which decisions are being delayed. To have an approaching ending and *not to know* what will happen next, like which secondary school you are going to, can double the anxiety. Looked-after children, for example, are often the last to hear about any upcoming changes (see Case Study 25).

Case Study 25 The importance of talking about unknown endings

A teacher I knew went to a case conference about a looked-after child and could not believe that the social workers hadn't talked to the child about the move out of her current foster home in two weeks, just because they hadn't finalised her new placement. At school her behaviour had deteriorated hugely since her placement had broken down, and no one outside school was opening to her fear, her anxiety and the horror of not knowing who she would be with in two weeks. The social worker said, 'But we can't talk about it because we still don't know ourselves where she is going.' Talk about being left without a secure base! Had they not thought of talking about how difficult it is when you don't know something that you really need to know?

4. Linking 'bad' behaviour around approaching endings to the forthcoming ending with empathy (while asserting the expectation if appropriate) can be very helpful, e.g.

    'I can sense some quite cross feelings bubbling around today. It's hard to manage when we haven't got much longer I know, but we do need to settle down now.'

    'You and Sam seem to be having some problems today. I was just thinking, it may be hard to feel that Sam will still be here after you finish next term.'

    Such thoughtful linking comments need of course to be 'from the heart' so the child can *sense* that you feel for them (which may be difficult for them to believe). Such comments may need to happen *many times* to enable anxious children to feel that their unspoken but feared anxieties around approaching transitions are understandable and can be talked about. The secret is finding (and taking) the right opportunities.
5. Transitions to new schools or places need to be managed thoughtfully and gradually with the support of an attachment worker. Photos of new people and places aid familiarity. Photos to take away of current people and places aid remembering and being

remembered. Pupil referral units sometimes have a memory board with photos and captions of significant events with past students. If leavers are remembered by photos of them remaining on the wall after they have gone, then children can vicariously experience that they will be remembered too when they leave.

6. Letters and cards to old or absent students communicate being held in mind, even after we leave. This should only be occasional! – Maybe a Christmas card on the first Christmas?

7. 'Exciting' happenings can also evoke insecurity and trigger adrenalin. Staff may need to consider the current capacity of individual children when planning school visits, having visitors and celebrations.

8. Thoughtful and preparative procedures for staff absence should be put in place.

Thoughtful ways of preparing for and coping with staff absences

1. Thoughtful and preventative procedures for staff absence may relate to all classes, or be specific to a particular class or a particular student – with no implied criticism if special arrangements are needed.

2. Prevention is better than crisis. Some particularly vulnerable pupils may be better off being placed with a previous trusted teacher during a difficult absence.

3. If possible think about any absences well in advance, and take regular opportunities to bring them up with the child(ren).

    (a) Linking 'bad' behaviour around approaching absences to the forthcoming change or absence with empathy, while asserting the expectation, is helpful (see ACO, p. 195). This may need to happen many times. It is also an opportunity to talk through this anxiety-provoking change and help them feel their difficulties are heard and understood, even while you may need to contain it. You could argue that their escalating behaviour at this vulnerable time is an unconscious sign of hope – that someone will notice that they are anxious and hear their 'cry'.

    (b) Note times and days of staff absences on the visual calendar, and frequently refer to it.

    (c) If they know beforehand, teachers can talk about their hopes and expectations during their absence with the class, before they are absent.

4. Teacher absences will be especially difficult during unstructured times and spaces (which frequently evoke insecurity and trigger adrenalin anyway) and staff may need to consider the current capacity of individual children during these times and make appropriate arrangements.

5. Be aware of the child's need to make contact with their 'secure base' when (even slight) anxieties arise.

6. With insecure children it is helpful for trusted senior teachers (in the presence of replacement teachers) to take opportunities to talk a little about a sick teacher's absence with the class/child and the alternative arrangements being made (children may have all sorts of fantasies about why the teacher is away – this doesn't mean they need to know all the facts).

7. Letters and cards (and even phone calls) communicate being held in mind.

8. Remember the calming usefulness of simple mechanical and repetitive activities at (potentially) anxious times.

9. Take curriculum opportunities to work/play through longer absences using metaphor, e.g. stories of journeys away from home, bridges, etc. (see Chapter 13).

'Therapeutic teaching' and the curriculum

Thoughtful planning and use of curriculum topics and opportunities can enhance a child's capacity to learn, and even provide opportunities for emotional processing through the metaphor. These may include the following:

1. Taking advantage of the child's interests.
2. Differentiating the work – break down tasks into bite-sized chunks with a timer to aid attention and knowledge that the key worker will return soon.
3. Being an active presence for the child – helping, patiently waiting, being there but non-intrusively, as appropriate for the particular child. This also includes weaning and stretching their capacities to manage little challenges, and be able to work alone, as the child can manage.
4. Emphasising PSHE (personal, health and social education), both formally and taking opportunities as it arises in 'small doses'.
5. Being aware of possible 'triggers' in curriculum topics and tasks.
6. Being patient with resistance. This can be a problem for resistant/ambivalent attached children (discussed on p. 161 and in Chapter 6, p. 105). Acknowledging their difficulty, stating the (small) expectation, then moving away, with the promise to return in a few minutes can be helpful. A timer can communicate feeling held in mind and enable them to more easily manage the 'attention gap'.
7. Being aware of the particular tasks or curriculum subjects that evoke anxiety, e.g. subtraction can be affected by loss or bereavement. The case of C's sudden difficulties with subtraction in Case Study 27 (p. 176) is an illustration of this. Acknowledging the possible link and separating the task from the anxiety can be helpful, e.g.

   > *Taking away can be difficult for you I know. It's only taking away numbers. But sometimes taking away can make us worry about other sorts of taking aways I know. Shall I help you with . . . Shall I get you some cubes?*

8. Taking curriculum opportunities to work and play through the metaphor (see Chapter 13).
9. Some children may need help to learn to play imaginatively – the first stage is 'play in the presence of' or 'in the space between'[6] the child and the mother or a trusted, attentive but non-intrusive adult (see Chapter 13).
10. Frequent use of telling and reading and writing stories with characters in situations children can identify with.

Thoughtful use of language (including non-verbal, heartfelt, communications)

1. Setting clear boundaries with empathy.
2. Empathic responses to children's behaviours (see Box 14, p. 194).
3. Careful use of non-humiliating language.
4. Awareness of children's non-verbal communication and language triggers.

(Chapter 11 focuses on language and communication with insecure children).

Professionally

Staff working with the most vulnerable children and in special schools and units need training and thoughtful support, including:

1. Encouragement for staff to support each other, both in a planned and a spontaneous way. Remember that acknowledging difficulties and asking for help is a sign of maturity. In Case Study 14 (p. 55) we see an excellent example of how encouraging staff to think together about children who are difficult to manage and understand can benefit both children and staff, lead to emotional growth and learning for staff and facilitate a more mature healthy atmosphere in the school as a whole (Chapter 16 gives many examples of this). With very challenging children and groups, end-of-day debrief sessions can be very supportive.
2. Clinical supervision (group or individual) for staff working with very vulnerable children can help develop understanding and ways of responding to behaviours and patterns.
3. Staff (particularly senior staff) putting effort into praising and appreciating each other. Regular appreciative 'thank yous' go a long way to alleviating stress. Apologies can be helpful too!
4. Expressions of thanks from senior management for the extra work and pressure of staff absences and 'special days', can make all the difference.
5. Training in understanding insecure attachment patterns, and ways of responding to children in the different categories (see Chapter 6).
6. Knowledge and understanding of unconscious processes (see Chapter 4). This will be very helpful and even crucial for those working with insecure children. Projections and transference dynamics can get to everyone. If they are not appreciated and understood, they can be reacted to unhelpfully and cause complications, relationship difficulties and further behaviour difficulties, hindering both teaching and learning. If, on the other hand, they are understood, distanced a little, and used as a helpful way to understand and empathise with a child's predicament and state of mind, they can be responded to more thoughtfully. They may even open up helpful conversations with the child.

Notes

1 Although much of this has been touched on in previous chapters, trainers and schools may appreciate the secure-base thinking being gathered together and organised into related sections.
2 John Bowlby, *A Secure Base* (New York: Basic Books, 1988), 62.
3 Taken from a similar questionnaire in Paul Greenhalgh, *Emotional Growth and Learning* (London: Routledge, 1994), 30.
4 'Activate in the Classroom', see info@valsabinpublications.com for details.
5 Louise Bombèr, *What About Me?* (London: Worth, 2011), 35–36.
6 D. W. Winnicott, *Playing and Reality* (Abingdon, UK: Routledge, 1971), 103 (Winnicott also uses the term 'potential space').

Behaviour as unconscious communication

9

Figure 22

'All behaviour is communication' (nurture principle 5)

When a 'hurtful' experience or memory arises for a vulnerable child – a child who is not yet able to contain and process disturbing feelings for himself – he will need either to project the unbearable pain or anxiety out on to others so he *doesn't have to feel* it; or he may develop bodily symptoms or *symptomatic behaviours*.

He will need to 'act it out' – precisely because he can't bear to feel it and think about it inside himself. As already noted, 'What can't be talked about gets acted out'. The boy in Figure 22, for example, may be unconsciously making us feel excluded, and troubled by his 'hoodiness' – so *he* doesn't have to feel like the baddie.

Understanding behaviour as communication

Understanding (especially repeated) behaviours as unconscious communications, or as 'acting out' of something children can't get anywhere near thinking and talking about, *does not mean allowing antisocial behaviour*. It is about giving the child an experience of being thought about and understood, at the same time as setting the necessary firm boundaries. D. W. Winnicott actually saw antisocial behaviours as 'signs of hope',[1] as Tamara Bibby describes: 'Familiar and recognisable difficulties for education are the forms of non-compliance that Winnicott identified as "antisocial tendencies", particularly nuisance and defiance. Despite education's current vilification of "non-compliant" behaviours these two forms of difficulty were for Winnicott, signs of hope.'[2] She goes on to ask, 'whether these emotions (anger, hate and aggression) should be . . . given more careful thought' and considers 'the challenges of working through some of these difficulties',[3] which is precisely what the reflective, relationship-based emphasis of this book seeks to address.

Significant adults in school (along with the child's family members and peers) are likely to be the ones 'projected into' when overwhelming feelings threaten. If at the same time as managing the situation, these adults can become *reflective and curious* in a non-intrusive way about the behaviour, it can be very containing, because they are demonstrating that they are continuing to think about the child and hold them in mind. Even if the child doesn't respond to their 'wonderings' a dialogue in the child's head has opened up, and the possibility of thinking about and *understanding* their difficulties has been broached.

Significant adults in school can play an important role in children's lives by bearing and thinking about the hurtful or worrying feelings within *themselves*, and then responding empathically and thoughtfully (and if necessary firmly) to the child, thus enabling them to feel 'contained'. Repeated experiences of such 'emotional containment' can slowly enable 'disturbed' and vulnerable children to become free to learn and relate appropriately (see Chapter 5).

Tuning in to children's *behavioural communications*, and responding to their perceived wishes, hurts, needs, inner conflicts, etc. with empathy, while maintaining necessary boundaries is like an attuned mother responding to her infant/child's communications, i.e. taking in the child's cry/communication, reflecting on it (digesting it) and putting it into words or responding concretely in a way that eases the need or (emotional?) pain.

It is helpful to *wonder* about the meanings – particularly of repeated behaviours – not only because tentatively putting our 'wonderings' into words may relieve a child and enable them to feel thought about and understood rather than bad (even if we are 'wrong'). It also enables *us* more easily to bear the helplessness they put into us and it can help us come up with more helpful ways of responding to them. Of course there may also be consequences – like clearing up the mess together. If you can communicate to a child *your (tentative) understanding* of the underlying anxiety, the child can be freed from the anxiety.

To reiterate, in advocating more thoughtful responses to children's 'problem' behaviours, I am not in any way suggesting we do not maintain firm consistent boundaries with children and young people. Appropriate and consistent boundaries are also very containing, and essential for the safety and security of everyone and for personal growth. It will make a HUGE DIFFERENCE if children sense that we can *bear* their 'big feelings', and we can talk benignly with them about them.

Of course it is true that a child's behaviour may be understood on many levels, so one understanding may not be the *only* way to think about it, but just to react to a negative behaviour by trying to stop it *does not*:

- enable them to feel thought about;
- enable them to feel taken seriously;
- enable them to feel and name their own feelings;
- enable them to begin to understand themselves;
- enable them to begin to forgive and be gentler with themselves;
- build a thoughtful trusting relationship;
- enable them to internalise that we can think about difficulties rather than just react.

With regard to specific repeated behaviours, Appendix 3 gives suggestions as to what a child or young person *might* be communicating through their behaviour:

We can never be sure of course, what a child's behaviour might be communicating. For example:

- *Stealing* may be communicating a need for love or a need to take what you want because no one will give it to you.
- *Hiding* may communicate shame or a need to be found and wanted.
- *Running away* may be a way of escaping unbearable situations or anxiety or of avoiding uncomfortable closeness.

Sometimes children's communications can be subtle and puzzling. For example:

- *The child who had a passion for stealing Blu Tack.* Did he want to make to make sure he stayed stuck in the teacher's mind and not 'fall out of her mind' when she went home? Or did he need it to hold things together at home?
- *The young child who couldn't sleep and was persistently wide awake and engaging his parents actively during the night.* Was he making sure he stayed awake – as he needed so desperately to do when he was precariously holding on to life in his first few days and weeks – or was night-time the only time his parents were available?

- *The toddler who had a tantrum every time he needed to go through a door if he couldn't open it himself.* On investigation we discovered he had been snatched from the car through the open door by his scary dad leaving his mum screaming – still in the car!

Although we have to ensure boundaries and safety, the most important thing to bear in mind is that often (in their current state) the child *could not help their reaction.* They need help to grow out of these default positions and reactions and to be able to bear and process both current (and eventually long-term) pain, so it doesn't interfere with their capacity to think, learn and respond healthily.

As mentioned in previous chapters, debrief sessions at the end of the day, clinical supervision, talking with more experienced colleagues can be helpful – especially for those at the 'coal face'. Sometimes the meanings can be painful. Sometimes we may be wrong. We will need to be sensitive and tentative in our reflections. It is perhaps more important, however, to express your wonderings tentatively and empathically, than it is to be right, because everyone likes to be thought about in a benign and caring way. You can say, for example, *'I was just wondering. Do you have any thoughts about it?'*

Being thought about and held in mind are the ways we (and children) develop our *own* capacity to think about and reflect on things, develop our own capacity for empathy, and our own internal space for wondering and holding things in mind – so crucial for education and emotional growth. The process is: (a) to notice the behaviour; (b) to reflect on possible links / meanings; (c) to verbalise the link in a caring, accepting and bearable way – normalising it if you like – as if anyone in that situation and with those anxieties might do the same; and then (d) possibly to offer some help. For example:

> *I can see you becoming a little bit fidgety Tom. We are going to finish this soon aren't we, and then we will move on to . . . Changes can always be a bit worrying, especially when we are not sure about the next thing. We will be moving on to . . . next, remember. How about I go with you to . . .*

Be aware that your words, facial expressions, tone of voice or gestures could be triggers. If necessary check out any startle reactions by asking them (e.g. *'I noticed you seemed startled or a bit affected when I said that. I'm just wondering if I upset you a little. Are you OK?').*

Talking together with colleagues, and reflecting on what he might be transferring into you as well as on possible meanings can be very fruitful and foster learning and caring relationships (see Exercise 6).

Exercise 6   Reflection on a particular incident

Think of an incident with a child/young person.

- What feelings did he seem to be communicating?
- Why he might have had those feelings at that particular time?

(continued)

(continued)

- What feelings did he evoke in you . . . or 'put into' you?
- How did you feel pushed to respond?
- How did you respond?
- Did the experience 'press your buttons'?
- How did you manage your own feelings?
- Does reflecting on these feelings give you any new insights into the child or into yourself?
- What opportunities could you take to talk things through in a situation like this?
- What have you learnt from this reflection?
- If something similar happened again how might you respond?

Some practical responses to behavioural communications: a relationship-based approach

(These are also fully described in Chapters 5, 6 and 11, but I include summaries of them here as trainers may find them useful in context.)

Understanding repeated behaviours in relation to a child's predominant attachment pattern

It is helpful to think about behaviours in relation to the child's predominant *attachment pattern*(s), as a way to think about how best to relate to him and help him to learn (see Chapter 6) For example:

(a) *Anxious/avoidant children* will tend to have difficulties with proximity. When they become dysregulated, avoidant children may not be able to bear people getting close (either physically or emotionally) to them, for fear of being hurt (again). They may trash work rather than have to ask for help. Clear non-challenging work is more manageable for them.

(b) *Anxious resistant/ambivalent* children may find it extremely hard to feel held in mind and need to cling or continually push for concrete attention. They may resist tasks for fear of losing your attention. Remembering little details of what they have said or done and lots of 'holding-in-mind' comments and gestures are particularly useful.

(c) *Chaotic/disorganised children* may be permanently anxious about safety and not be able to manage either relationships or tasks. Frequent use of the word 'safe' may be helpful for such children. They may also need help to take in information, organise their thinking, their possessions and their work and recall information in their minds.

(d) *Chaotic/disorganised children* may need help with remembering, making links and sorting things out and may panic and disrupt without obvious triggers. They will each have their own unique 'triggers' relating to their particular trauma history. Put effort into tuning into any triggers, and if possible preventing them. As they come to trust you they may be open to acknowledging their triggers, and to help.

A particularly difficult behaviour to manage is *resistance*. It can leave us feeling helpless, frustrated and deskilled, and easily push us into becoming controlling and threatening. Bribery can often work of course, but it doesn't alter the repeated pattern of resistance, which the child needs help to shift. Resistance could come from anxiety about the task, about being 'frozen up' for fear of failure, or about difficulty with all beginnings or beginning 'difficult' pieces of work (see Case Study 22, p. 126). But repeated resistance to tasks is probably most frequently associated with a child's resistant/ambivalent attachment pattern (Chapter 6, pp. 100–105 has lots of suggestions for how to work with such children). It often is best to start by accepting the resistance and wondering about it, and after clear instructions and *short-term* expectations, moving away for a while, giving the child a bit of space to come through his resistant state before returning to see how he is getting on or gesturing from a distance.

As you will remember, resistance occurs for the very good reason that such children can't rely on feeling held in mind by their variably available parents – who are often preoccupied by their own needs, worries, health problems or fears. This means the child has to 'cling on', either physically, or with words or with behaviour that can't be ignored, to make sure they don't slip out of their parents' (and other significant adults') minds. This can be very irritating and exacerbate relationships both at home and in school. Then their behaviour or their clinging chatter, *overrides* the possibility of them getting on with the task. Until they can begin to feel more secure and held in mind, this pattern will continue, especially at stressful times.

It makes a difference therefore to put effort into such relationships in the ways recommended in Chapter 6. Holding-in-mind comments and gestures (see Box 8, p. 102) are probably the most effective way of doing this. These will include remembering comments, such as when things they have said, things you have done together, interests they have shared with you can be recalled when they come up in conversation in the present moment, or in relation to tasks, lessons or happenings in school. Eye contact and little gestures like thumbs up, little waves or hand gestures from across the room will also help them continue to feel held in mind. All thoughtful comments including expressions of curiosity will give them an experience of feeling inside your mind. Slowly, through enough experiences such as these ambivalent children will become able to internalise the experience of being inside the minds of significant adults, and grow a secure base from which to explore, try things out and learn and they will have less and less need to cling and resist.

Offering emotional containment

It is important that we are able to bear and contain the anxiety their behaviour puts into us (using the support of colleagues if necessary) and to *think* before responding. This is called *emotional containment* (for detailed thinking about emotional containment see Chapter 5) and is crucial for more disturbed and unintegrated children. Case Study 12 (p. 50), however, illustrates how difficult this can be, and the helpfulness of talking things through sensitively and of enlightened mentoring, either at the time or in a team meeting later.

Vulnerable children need to know that whatever happens we can cope. Managing our reactions thoughtfully and staying calm and thoughtful communicates that we can contain whatever happens, but this can be difficult if their projections are powerful.

Talking things through with a trusted colleague may help us to see their behaviour as defensive – putting the unbearable feeling into others perhaps so they don't have to feel it. Seeing adults supporting each other and wondering benignly together is very containing for children. Seeking help is containing for you and them too.

The more we can contain them, attune to their anxieties and respond thoughtfully, and the more they are able to talk things through with us, the less they will need to act out. In the Preface to the book I talked about my experience at the pupil referral unit, which bore this out:

> In the whole unit we observed first hand how this attuned predictable relationship-based approach eased their anxieties and reduced their outbursts and enabled them to relax enough to begin to learn. The frequency that children needed 'holding', for example, and also exclusions from school, reduced considerably.

Emotional containment can be communicated through:

Silent thoughtful presence:

- stopping and reflecting before reacting;
- not reacting at all – silence (while still holding the child in mind).

Thoughtful words:

- understanding/empathic comments;
- benign curiosity and 'wonderings';
- putting your tentative understandings into words with empathy.

Concrete practical responses:

- relating to their patterns, needs, difficulties and interests, e.g. giving them something they need;
- moving back a step;
- having a special containing place in which they can feel safe, etc.

Responding to children's puzzling behaviours with both empathy and curiosity

Empathy

Giving empathic attuned thoughtful attention to children's puzzling behaviours, *tentatively* perhaps making links and suggestions to them (often in 'small doses' as and when they are able to cope) can lead to important and helpful insights and enhance relationships, as well as opening the way for the child to think for himself. Feeling with or alongside them will communicate anyway, but words can help too (see Box 12).

Box 12   Examples of empathic responses to children's behaviours

After you have stopped the antisocial behaviour (if that is necessary) you might say:

- *You really wanted to be first, didn't you, but . . . got there first.*

- *I think you're a bit cross with me for not letting you . . . but I need to . . .*

- *It's hard to manage when we're so full of big feelings. How about we . . .*

- *That's making you very cross isn't it. It's so hard to manage our feelings when we're cross, and not let them burst out and hurt someone. Maybe you could . . .*

- *Maybe your big feelings just became too big to manage when . . . and . . .*

- *It's time to stop now Sam, but I can see you want more time. We have to . . . maybe . . .*

- *That hurt you didn't it. Do you want to tell me about it?*

- *Sometimes we wish we hadn't done something, but it's too late.*

- *I wonder how we could make it better.*

- *It's so hard to try again when something goes wrong isn't it. It's just so frustrating!*

- *Sharing can be so hard. We can worry there won't be enough for us.*

- *Taking turns can be hard, because sometimes we feel we just need more, but . . .*

- *We don't need to talk about it if you don't want to. Maybe later we can . . .*

(See more suggestions in Box 14, p. 194.)

Curiosity

Just being curious about a child or a child's behaviour demonstrates interest and thoughtfulness and can give them an experience of being taken seriously and thought about. Being curious doesn't mean getting it right, it's just wondering with curiosity.

It can of course, be hard to maintain an attitude of curiosity when we are caught up with getting the child to behave (or not behave) in a certain way. Of course safety is important, but for lasting change and growth, tuning into the (unconscious) communication with acceptance, curiosity and empathy (ace), and helping the child slowly work through his difficulty and feel understood will be the most effective.

An expression of curiosity about a child's (hurtful?) behaviour or statement, (rather than a 'knee-jerk' reaction, or a 'mini lecture') helps us to maintain and communicate an attitude of acceptance, even when we feel somewhat hurt and puzzled ourselves. This does not preclude of course setting any necessary boundary with empathy.

Curiosity involves being in (and being comfortable with remaining in) a state of not knowing regarding a child's behaviour or expression, while at the same time knowing that there are (probably unconscious) reasons for it. It is the opposite of needing to fix it and find a solution. It is about staying with the uncertainty, anxiety or pain, and bearing it alongside the child while we wonder about it – encouraging the child to wonder about it as well. It gives the child an experience of being heard and taken seriously.

Of course, coming up with your own responses to your felt experience of what the child might be communicating at any point in time is best, but a few examples may be helpful (see Box 13).

Box 13 Examples of ways you might express curiosity about a child's puzzling behaviour

- *I'm struggling to understand what that might be about.*

- *I was thinking, is this related to your mum not turning up yesterday . . . ?*

- *I was just wondering if there was something I said, or maybe something in my expression that affected you just then?*

- *I'm just wondering what that was about. Is it hard perhaps to feel that I still think about you when I'm somewhere else?*

- *Oh! What's that about I wonder?*

- *Maybe that was the only way you could think of to stay feeling safe? Sometimes it can be hard to feel safe when we don't know what is going to happen next.*

- *I was just thinking that maybe . . .*

- *I wonder what made you . . .*

- *I'm just guessing, but I was wondering . . .*

- *Wait a second . . . I wonder . . .*

'*I wonder*' and '*I'm wondering*' can be really helpful sentence beginnings, because they open up to reflection and thoughtfulness, and they don't *need* an answer. The child can answer if they wish to, but also feel just as comfortable if they choose not to reply.

It is important though to adjust your responses to suit each individual child. Some of these may be too long for them. Just be genuine and attuned. Frequent small doses are often best.

Try to take these 'hot' opportunities to talk difficult things through with them (after they have sufficiently calmed down of course), even if it is tempting to avoid them! If they start to get resistant or aroused again you can always just stop.

We can also develop an open and understanding approach to both subtle and non-verbal behaviours by seeing them as (unconscious) communications – and using the type of responses suggested above – behaviours like:

turning away	looking down	not answering
crying	shouting	swearing
scratching	stuttering	pushing
banging	making noises	fidgeting

And as we have seen, however, the same behaviour can have various meanings, for example crying can be an expression of sadness or of hurt, or it could be manipulative (usually with parents!) We can also think and wonder about puzzling repeated 'behaviours' (see Exercise 7).

Exercise 7   Reflection on repeated patterns of behaviour or repeated reactions from a child/young person

Repeated behaviours are often difficult to fathom and may have deep and long-term roots. Schools and staff have found the following questions helpful in this regard:

- Describe a repeated behaviour or repeated response in the student.

- In what situations do they arise? What seems to evoke them?

- Reflect on what they might be communicating through the behaviour.

- How do they push you to respond?

- Do they evoke particular responses and feelings in you, e.g. irritation, frustration, anger, hurt, helplessness, anxiety, etc.?

- How might this relate to their feelings, or the feelings they are not expressing?

- Do they press your 'buttons' in any way?

- Has this understanding make you think of other ways you might helpfully respond?

- Does reflecting on these feelings give you any new insights into them – or into yourself?

- What have you learnt from this reflection?

Responding to and talking through hurtful behaviours

Alleviating, easing and managing outbursts are addressed in Chapter 11 (pp. 205–211). Managing and responding to children's worrying and hurtful comments like '*I hate you*', '*You don't care*', are discussed in Box 16 on p. 202.

Managing repeated swearing and abusive language

Explain to the child what you are going to do to help them with their problem of swearing. For example, when you sense they are getting frustrated and about to swear, you are going to catch them before they do and suggest they take it out on (for example) a piece of Blu Tack by squeezing it instead of using words. When they are calm you can teach them alternative ways to express anger.

When they start swearing explain that you can see they are angry, but you never respond to swearing. Then just wait for them to calm down. Don't give them a moral lecture afterwards! Do not engage with a swearing or attacking child. Keep yourself, any others, and the child safe, put their (apparent) feelings into words *once* (if you sense they can bear it) and tell them you are not going to respond until they have calmed down.

> I can see you are very angry. But I am not going to respond when you talk like that. We can talk when you have calmed down. I will just stay . . . to keep you safe.

Silently and safely stay nearby (it may take a while till they are ready to talk).

Later they need to hear that:

- (Although you had to stop it to keep everyone safe), you know that once it had started they couldn't stop it, but you needed to keep everyone safe, so . . .
- Sometimes big feelings can be just too big to manage and they can 'burst out' uncontrollably – and you know they need help to manage.
- They probably wish it hadn't happened.
- You know they need help with managing their big feelings when they threaten to overwhelm.
- You will always be there to help them and keep them safe if they need it.
- As they grow stronger they will be able to tell you when they are feeling hurt or upset.
- You will always listen to them, but you won't always be able to give them what they want. You know that will be disappointing.
- As they can talk about difficult things more their feelings will become more manageable.
- You will work with them and teach them ways to manage their big feelings.

These antisocial behaviours can of course get to us. They may trigger our own vulnerabilities, or their overwhelming feelings may get right inside of us, making it very difficult to think and maintain curiosity. Understanding that process is helpful, and may be crucial in enabling us to bear their projections. Thoughtful understanding support (or supervision) at the time or shortly after, can make all the difference to our capacity to respond helpfully to children, and slowly move them forward. But sometimes things can get fraught and lead to conflict and outbursts.

Acted-out behaviours can cause 'ruptures' in attuned relationships – either in the child's mind or in our mind. This can happen when:

- The child does or says something they later regret.
- The adult is busy or distracted and the child *feels* forgotten or squeezed out.
- The adult or the child is overwhelmed with strong feelings that leak or explode out.
- The child experiences something as humiliating.
- The child needs connections to others and they are not there.
- The adult needs to say 'no' or discipline the child.

Repairing breaks in your relationship with a child when your conversation has evoked shame

What matters is that the ruptures are acknowledged and 'repaired'. This matters more than making the mistake in the first place because the mistake is a learning opportunity and repairing builds trust and connection (see thoughts on the opportunities of mistakes and repair on pp. 142 and 211.

'Small ruptures' can be repaired immediately, e.g.:

> *'I am sorry I kept you waiting Sam. I hope you didn't think I had forgotten you?'*

'Big repairs' need to happen when the child is ready. They may indicate this by a placatory gesture (perhaps giving you something the next day?), e.g.:

> *'Thank you for that Sam. I'm just thinking. We had a bad day yesterday didn't we?'*

> *'I think you may be wanting to know that we are still friends.'*

> *'I think we both know that when you started to "go" you just couldn't stop. You needed a lot of time to calm down.'*

> *'Is there some way I could help you perhaps if it happens again?'*

Summary

- All behaviour is an unconscious communication, which can helpfully be thought about.
- Setting safe limits and boundaries and stopping hurtful behaviour may need to happen first.
- It is not always easy to understand particular behaviours.
- Talking puzzling behaviours through with someone who may understand more than we do can be very helpful.
- How, when and whether to respond will depend on what the child is able to cope with *now*.

- All responses should be tentative.
- Moral lectures are never helpful, e.g. 'Don't you realise that when . . .' will just cause the child to close down defensively or start an argument, which will interfere with your facilitating relationship.
- The active use of empathy is essential when talking difficult things through with children, so they feel heard.
- Remember, what can't be talked (or thought) about will get acted out.
- Once elements of a painful memory are (re)triggered the child *cannot stop* their acting out. They need help to stay safe and help to 'come down'.
- Becoming aware of our own vulnerabilities is the first step to alleviating this problem. The next step is to support each other.
- The projections of disturbed children can be very powerful (and hurt a lot). They are also adept at finding our weak spots! They may have had to learn to stay on top or in control for fear of being the vulnerable helpless one who gets hurt.

Clinical supervision (see pp. 289 and 311 and Case Study 22, p. 126) can be very helpful here in:

- facilitating a thinking space around puzzling, repeated and hurtful behaviours;
- helping us to understand each behaviour and reflect on helpful ways of responding;
- helping us become aware and think around our own vulnerabilities that are becoming triggered, and how to minimise this;
- helping us to think how we can support each other.

Because:

- Talking things through in a bearable way with an empathic understanding person is how we process difficult and traumatic experiences and emotions – and 'detoxify' them – so they don't *need* to be triggered and turn into antisocial behaviour.
- A child's 'acting out can really hurt us. We can easily get caught up in it. Understanding our hurt as their projected pain can be helpful, as we can then not take the hurt quite so seriously and bear to think about it ourselves.
- All behaviours and incidents can be complicated by the possibility that our own 'buttons' may be pressed – unconsciously triggering our own vulnerabilities, which we are then driven to defend against.
- When this happens we are in danger of (unthinkingly) 'knee-jerking' (acting out) back, for example responding in a hostile way, or giving in. If, however, we do find ourselves 'knee-jerking' we need to be gentle on ourselves and learn from it. It can happen to anyone. Talking it through with a trusted colleague can help.

In her book, *What Can I Do with the Kid Who . . . ?* Marie Delaney[4] developed the 'rethink model', a reflection tool for reviewing and thinking about pupils' troubling behaviour in order to respond more helpfully to it. The use of 're-' can be a helpful way to bring to mind the process of reflecting and revising our understanding before responding either in a quiet moment alone or in a case discussion with colleagues. I would add a few more stages, as shown in Exercise 8.

Exercise 8   Realise, resist, reflect, remember, rethink, revise, respond, rework

- *Realise*: We realise a dysfunctional behaviour or pattern is being repeated too often, or getting to staff in an unhelpful way, pushing us to react unhelpfully. Realising a potential problem is important because we may catch the problem early, before it escalates too much.
- *Resist*: We can then resist reacting – stop for a moment and consciously resist reacting unhelpfully.
- *Reflect*: We can then reflect on the child's apparent feelings and emotional state and on how we feel pushed to react. We can reflect on the dynamic between us – why it might be getting to us (transference and countertransference – see above). We can wonder with colleagues what the child might unconsciously be communicating through the behaviour.
- *Remember*: Remembering conversations with staff or with the child's parents about circumstances at home or in the child's history may aid us towards understanding. Reflecting on possible links to approaching transitions or changes may also give us a clue.
- *Rethink and revise*: We may then revise our understanding of the child and their behaviour in the light of these insights.
- *Respond*: These reflections can enable us to respond more thoughtfully with words, actions and ways of managing and teaching the child.
- *Rework*: Consciously putting effort into reworking our attachment with the child may be crucial in this process.

Think of a child who gets to you – or is just beginning to get to you – and try *rethinking*. See what comes.

Notes

1 D. W. Winnicott, 'The Antisocial Tendency', in *Through Paediatrics to Psychoanalysis* (New York: Karnac, 1975), 309.
2 Tamara Bibby, *The Creative Self* (London: Routledge, 2017), 16.
3 Ibid.
4 Marie Delaney, *What Can I Do with the Kid Who . . . ?* (London: Worth, 2009).

Learning inhibitions as possible unconscious communications

10

Figure 23

Possible (unconscious) meanings of children's learning behaviours

Although many learning difficulties are related to children's limited educational capacities, genetic factors, memory and language limitations, dyslexic and dyspraxic factors and to children's slow processing, it is surprising just how many learning difficulties are emotionally based or emotionally exacerbated. We can sense this from Figure 23 above, where the boy appears to be so preoccupied, or even traumatised by something he has witnessed perhaps, that he can't possibly concentrate on schoolwork. Emotional factors can also be secondary problems, arising when children realise that others can do things much more easily than they can, and the thought of being 'slow', 'special needs' or 'useless' enters their self-image. Or they may be related to an overdose of criticism or humiliation, causing them to fear failure or getting stuck and criticised yet again.

They could also be more primary inhibitions – relating to thinking, memory, making links, etc. (see Chapter 3 on trauma) – arising out of the effects of trauma on the brain or triggered and unconscious anxieties that what might come up will be unbearable and therefore have to be avoided at all costs.

It was this realisation that prompted Tavistock-based educational psychologist Irene Caspari to develop educational therapy (now called educational psychotherapy). The Caspari Foundation[1] is named after her. Educational therapy was specifically designed to address and work psychotherapeutically with children whose learning difficulties are emotionally based. I had this same realisation myself when I was a young special needs teacher in an inner-city primary school in the 1980s. I was giving regular special needs support to a number of children who, despite being bright and articulate, were just unable to remember or string things together and often also unwilling to work, like W in Case Study 26.

Case Study 26   The need for educational psychotherapy

One day when W's dad came in, in a drunken state, to complain and shout at a teacher and had to be escorted off the premises, I found myself imagining what it must be like at home for W with such an aggressive father. W was a child whom I had felt both puzzled and challenged by, as he just wasn't able to learn or concentrate despite seeming articulate and 'canny'. I suddenly understood how learning and having a go at things might be the last thing on his mind.

I remember also the frequent shouting of another parent when her bright articulate son ran off down the corridor every day at home time. Then of course Mum would shout even louder – in what seemed like a vicious repeated pattern. I wondered if there might be a connection between this obviously dysfunctional parental relationship and his extreme behaviour difficulties and learning blocks. He used to throw chairs!

I remember thinking that what such children needed was more counselling than learning support. With this in mind I requested a meeting with the head teacher and the special needs coordinator for the county to discuss this, and while they agreed in principle, they advised against trying to make a career out of such an approach, as there was no funding for it. Child counselling had not yet been developed and they knew of no relevant training. A few weeks later I went on a course about learning and emotional difficulties, run by Steve Decker, a local educational psychologist, and he mentioned a new discipline called educational therapy, although he didn't know any details about it. I investigated, and within a few years I was doing the training, which has offered me a profound and increasing understanding of such children and a sound psychodynamic theoretical base, as well as enabling me to offer individual (and group) educational psychotherapy to children with both learning and behaviour difficulties that are emotionally based.

I later began to support teachers in this understanding too – hence this book!

Chapter 6 considered (particular) behaviour difficulties as unconscious communications arising out of anxieties and inhibitions, and this chapter will look at learning difficulties in a similar light. This does not mean of course that all or even most learning difficulties are emotionally based, but that just to be aware of the possibility might be useful in some cases. From a teacher's, SENCO's or educational psychologist's point of view the thinking process starts with the background knowledge that learning difficulties *could* be linked to unconscious factors.

A puzzling or a suddenly developing difficulty or a very resistant one might make staff wonder if there might not be other complicating causes or emotional factors. Appendix 4 shows possible ways of understanding particular learning difficulties. You may find it useful to refer to it and see if anything 'rings a bell'. An intuition or some relevant knowledge might prompt a clue. As you will see from Appendix 4 most of the links and causes are either symbolic (difficulty beginning tasks or beginning the school day might evoke unbearable anxieties relating to separation when Mum was rushed into hospital while M was in the nursery), or the link is fairly easy to spot (chaotic world – chaotic writing!).

We might want to have a meeting with other staff to talk through our hunches, and perhaps a meeting with the parents to see if there might be some home situation that could be causing or exacerbating a difficulty (especially in the case of a suddenly developing difficulty as the case studies in this chapter illustrate). Possible understandings may lead to ways forward, usually involving talking things through with the child and family, and special needs support that includes unlinking the task or difficulty from the anxiety and perhaps some therapeutic work.

Attachment factors

Chapter 6 describes the three insecure attachment categories, including sections on typical learning difficulties and inhibitions for children in each category. For avoidant children see pp. 90–91 for difficulties and pp. 91–97 for suggestions. For resistant/ambivalent children see pp. 98–100 for difficulties and pp. 100–105 for suggestions. For chaotic/disorganised children see pp. 107–110 for difficulties and pp. 110–119 for suggestions.

To summarise, in avoidant children asking for help is inhibited because of fear of closeness, affecting all challenging tasks. They need subtle ongoing help with this. Meanwhile simple manageable tasks, with all they will need near at hand will facilitate good work. For older children, written instructions and computer work will be very accessible. Resistant/ambivalent children are resistant to settling down to work for fear of 'falling out of the 'minds' of significant adults. They need help to feel secure enough in the minds of their teacher or key worker to get started and to persist with tasks.

Chaotic/disorganised children are among those whose learning, concentration and schoolwork are the most profoundly affected. The disorganisation can get into their fingers, bodies and minds, causing dyspraxic and dyslexic difficulties and muddled and messy work. The 'three-headed dog who was protecting the fossil of the stone' in Figure 24 illustrates this vividly, as well as suggesting feelings of trauma and panic.

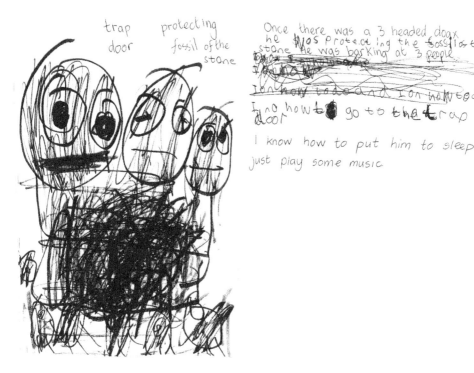

Figure 24

The disorganisation can also cause these children to frequently forget and lose things, not be able to concentrate, sit still, listen or take things in. Necessary preoccupations with safety or with proximity issues may get in the way of attending to learning tasks. Some children may need to be 'cued in' with non-verbal signals to stay 'safe'. They may need support to be able to listen and take in instructions. Asking them calmly to repeat back instructions or important information can be a way of engaging their minds.

Fear

Learning inhibitions can relate to (or be complicated by) fear of failure and/or criticism – from which the '*inner* critic' is of course also internalised – or from a huge lack of confidence arising perhaps from a very anxious or marginalised family, which M's sad writing hints at in Figure 25.

This creature is Wondring what to think.
Maybe he would go and Play With his firends.
Yes he Will go and Play WIth his firends
he Will go down the Park and Play but !

then Want Will he do I Kown he Will go
to the Siwnming Pool but he Woulldn·be a
lauid in oh Well. The END

Figure 25

*Symbolic equation: a fact gets into and inhibits symbolic
work – like maths and writing tasks[2]*

Sometimes children's learning can be inhibited in a very particular and profound way, when
for some reason symbols become concretely equated with painful reality. In this way maths
processes, for example, can sometimes be affected by family changes. In Case Study 27
I describe how as a newly qualified educational therapist and a special needs coordinator
in a primary school, I experienced taking away sums becoming impossible for a Year 5 girl
traumatised by the sudden and devastating accidental death of the girl next door.

Case Study 27   Losses and numbers: understanding the roots of C's maths difficulties[3]

Within the space of a week, three different people had come to me with concerns about C's
acute maths difficulties.

Both her class teacher and her maths set teacher were beginning to wonder whether they
had been negligent in not drawing her to my attention sooner. As the special needs coordinator in the school I was also feeling that my channels of communication and monitoring of

children's difficulties were sadly lacking. What had gone wrong? When I looked at her maths I couldn't believe that we had missed such acute difficulties. Although she could manage the process of one-to-one correspondence, and she understood how to bring numbers together to add them up, she couldn't count objects to ten, she didn't know at least four of the number values and she got in a big muddle. On the surface she seemed calm and surprisingly unworried by these acute difficulties. We tried some reading – no problem – she certainly didn't come over as a typical slow learner.

'I'm puzzled,' I said. 'Have you always found maths difficult, or do you think these difficulties have come up quite recently for you?' She couldn't really answer. 'I'm worried that we might have missed noticing them, and that you might have been struggling for a long time, getting help perhaps from your friends, but knowing underneath that you didn't really understand what was going on. Perhaps you just didn't want to think about it too much?'

'Umm maybe, I don't know,' she replied.

'Do you feel that you need help with your Maths now?' I asked.

'Yes, I do.'

'The other thought that has been on my mind is that in the staffroom the other day when we were trying to think around your difficulties, Mrs B mentioned that you used to live next door to A, the girl whose sister was tragically killed in the accident last term, and that you used to be very close to her and to the family generally. Perhaps the trauma of losing a neighbour and a friend in such awful circumstances has caused your mind to put up a block against thinking about numbers for a while.'

'Maybe,' she said, and her eyes started to tear up a little. We agreed to talk things through with her mother after school.

When I thought about her difficulties in more precise detail later I realised that it was neighbouring numbers she was muddling, or that were not in their right places. There had definitely seemed some resistance to accepting that the numbers were not as she wanted them to be. She reversed 3 with 4, and 6 with 7, 13 with 14 and 16 with 17, etc., in addition to being very hesitant generally when she was asked to count. We met all together after school and her mother was initially stunned and incredulous when she saw her daughter's difficulties. She knew C's older sister had been helping her with her maths homework, but she had never dreamed her daughter had such basic difficulties. 'Why haven't the school picked this up before?' was her immediate response, which I sympathised with. I showed her the visual aids and practice games I had devised to help C learn her numbers. Then I also shared with her our thoughts that the recent trauma of losing a close neighbour and friend could have caused C to block off her memory of the numbers, and her maths difficulty could actually be quite recent. 'They do say that it can take six months for any difficulties with the grieving process to become manifest, so this could be about the right time scale.' I said.

C's mum was immediately both concerned and fascinated, and she started to share details of a number of other recent family traumas, which she felt could also be related to her daughter's difficulties.

They had all been, and still remained, very close to P's family, although they had now moved away. They had all gone to the funeral, but unlike her siblings, C had not wanted to talk about P since the accident. C's nan had also died recently after a long illness – culminating in her forgetting C's name. This had been particularly hard for C, as she had been very close to her nan. After these two deaths, and the death of an uncle from cancer, plus the loss of her father who had recently left the family home, C had actually stopped talking altogether for a while. Mum said the only thing that seemed to get C through this difficult time was her cat. She used to talk to her cat, and gradually over the weeks she became able to talk to the family again. But that was all several months ago and Mum had thought she was over the trauma, 'as much as you could be', although a couple of weeks ago of course the cat had been run over in the road outside their house! There certainly were a lot of reasons why C might want things (and particularly numbers) to be ordered differently in her life, and why she might not want to accept things as they were. When I saw her the next day we talked about her particular difficulty with neighbouring numbers, gently making the link with the terrible and tragic loss of their friend and neighbour, P. We acknowledged how, although they continued to see A and her family regularly they were not living in their old house and indeed there were not the same number of them as there used to be.

C also joined in a little with our conversation. She seemed if anything to be relieved that we could talk together about the things that had been so hard for her to think about. We agreed that Mum would take opportunities to talk with her at home about their recent sad and difficult experiences and the people they had loved and lost. They also took copies of the number practice games and a 100 square to do 'paired counting', with no pressure to get it right until she was ready. I also offered to have a few individual sessions with her when we would both practice her number skills, and think as she was ready, about her loved ones who had died.

The next day the TA in the maths set said that when they were practising counting and naming numbers together she noticed that C seemed really resistant to acknowledging the correct names and values for some of the numbers, rather than just appearing to make slips and get in a muddle as she had previously felt. This seemed to both confirm that there was a psychological component to her difficulty, and to make us wonder whether bringing it up to the surface had been helpful.

My first individual session with C seemed to go well. When we tried counting and practising the numbers it became evident that she was having particular difficulty with 6, 16 and numbers ending in 6. I wondered whether there might be some significance in the number 6. As we began to remember and draw some things about P it came up that P had been 16 when she died. I gently made the link with her difficulty.

C also told me how P's family were keeping her room, including her clothes and her make-up, exactly as she used to keep them, indicating that C (understandably perhaps) was not the only person who was finding it hard to accept that there were no longer four people in the family (wanting perhaps, their three to be four). We remembered how the numbers 3 and 4 had often been reversed too, in our assessment session in the previous week.

Later, from the friendly looks she gave me when I saw her around the school, and from her general demeanour, I could tell that she had found the session helpful, but I was surprised when the breakthrough came so soon.

The day after her first individual session her teacher and TA came up excitedly to tell me that C had had a 'breakthrough'. Her teacher had asked the class who could recite the 2 times table. C suddenly said to her TA, 'I know that,' and started to say it. Her TA encouraged her to put her hand up and she recited it correctly to the whole class. Her TA gently pointed out that she had said the numbers in the right order, and with the correct values.

'Yes,' she said, 'My brain's become unblocked!'

The two times table, which she had known last year, before all the troubles, was obviously free to come through at last. Everyone was delighted at her success and she was rewarded with a gold star! I saw her in the corridor later and she told me the good news.

Her mother had arranged to come in after school for a review and was delighted at the news. She said they had done a lot of talking at home, and they had a new cat!

Maybe there will be regressions and ups and downs. Most of us can't imagine what it must be like to have to cope with so much loss and trauma, and so young. But C now knows she is understood, and we are there to listen and talk to her if she needs it . . . and now the numbers are free to be themselves and to stay in their proper order, as the difficult things can begin to be faced.

In this example then somehow the taking away of numbers had became equated with the taking away of her friend. Taking away numbers just 'needed to be' muddled and not achieved, as the unbearable loss of her friend and neighbour couldn't be thought about and made real. This is sometimes called 'symbolic equation'.

In a similar symbolic-equation-type difficulty, 9-year-old H developed difficulties with addition, as shown in Case Study 28.

Case Study 28   Difficulties with addition

H, a very nervy 8-year-old, had been pressured by his anxiously involved grandparents into frozen failure – to the extent that in his previous school it was felt that he needed to go to an MLD (moderate learning difficulties) school.

Now he had moved away from his grandparents, and quite recently his mum had moved in with a new partner, he seemed more settled, but he was still struggling with maths. Although he had always had special needs maths support, recently there seemed to have developed a lot of anxiety about his maths difficulties. I hadn't remembered him having such acute difficulties when he first came and I wondered whether we might have overlooked something.

I watched him try some simple addition with cubes. I could not believe the problems he was having bringing the numbers 6 and 4 together to add them up. He had been doing simple tens and units regularly at the end of the previous term, but here he was counting and checking, rechecking and counting the numbers again and again, but just not managing to bring them together. The same happened with other numbers. I tried subtraction – no problem! This seemed strange. And then I realised that for H the experience of being taken away from the unbearable pressures of his grandparents and the failure situation of his previous school had been a good and a helpful experience. In many ways he had been doing better. His writing and confidence had improved enormously. But his recent experiences of difficulty and change were in the area of adding on. His mother had recently had a difficult pregnancy and given birth to twins, so he had a new dad, and new doted-on baby siblings, both of which would probably need some adjusting to.

'I'm just wondering,' I said, 'Do you think there could be a link between these new additions in your family and your present difficulty with adding up?'

'Mmm, Yes, maybe,' he said. I was aware, of course, that he could have just been saying what he thought I wanted to hear, but I assured him that such difficulties and links could be quite understandable, particularly for a sensitive person. We remembered how he had suffered a lot in the past from learning anxieties in different ways. After our conversation I showed him how to do the adding up sums and he could do them easily! He said he would like to have a family meeting to talk things through – which we duly arranged. His class teacher commented a few weeks later that he seemed to be managing much better, better in fact than some of the other children with special needs in the class, although he still needed maths support.

These examples also illustrate how one might address such understandings by talking through the possible connections with sensitivity. First by gently acknowledging the links between the painful experiences that had been understandably interfering with the child's learning and the learning difficulties that were somewhat similar. Then separating out the problematic links from the practical learning tasks, followed by simple practical help.

Educational psychotherapy particularly offers an attitude of thoughtfulness that is open to what children might be communicating metaphorically through their learning difficulties, as well as a way of working on these safely in a once-removed setting, through specially designed learning tasks that metaphorically 'mend the difficulties' in a practical way. For example, a child from a painfully broken family who tends to trash things (as a way of controlling the 'breaking' himself perhaps) might be asked to make a jigsaw puzzle by drawing a picture of a person or even himself, cut it into six pieces, then mix them up and finally see if he can put them together again by gluing them on to a blank paper correctly. Or a similar exercise could be done with separated single sounds from a word of his choice, or from broken-up sentences. Such a child may be acting out his anxiety about things breaking apart (like his family?) by not being able to put *words or sounds* together to make sense. I remember doing a similar activity with a girl from such a family who was very stuck with making sense of reading. Instead of gluing the words into meaningful sentences, which she resisted, we attached them with paper clips on to a string – so they could come together and be separated again – unconsciously easing her anxiety about 'things' finding it hard to stay together.

Educational psychotherapy also and particularly uses stories both to read with children, and to write, play and even dramatise, sometimes jointly within the containing relationship, as a safe and engaging way to work through fears, dysfunctional patterns and trauma. This works on both the *process* of writing – motivating children to engage with the difficult writing task because their story is important and shared with the adult – and on the *content* and meaning of the writing in a supported and once-removed setting from their unthinkable difficulty. The example on p. 247 of the sexually abused boy who would only (and very primitively) read and write monster stories, which I well understood to be symbolic and therefore allowed, was a good example of the helpfulness of this understanding. This very regressed, chaotic and semi-coherent boy learnt to read and write through reading monster books!

I have found writing stories together to be a very good way to allow things to come up in just the way they need to, including perhaps violence and horrific hurts. Often initially such stories are unresolved or on repeated themes. Maybe they need to be worked through again and again until they are ready to move on to something else, or they become open to accessing some help.

Writing frames can be helpful with children who tend to become overwhelmed – to make the writing task smaller and boundaried and therefore manageable.

I have typed out my (muddled and unreadable!) 'paper conversation' with 'Roger' (not the child's real name) below, which we wrote after drawing characters together, as it illustrates both how hard learning can be for a very dyslexic boy, and how writing a story together can enable some openness, acceptance and practice.[4]

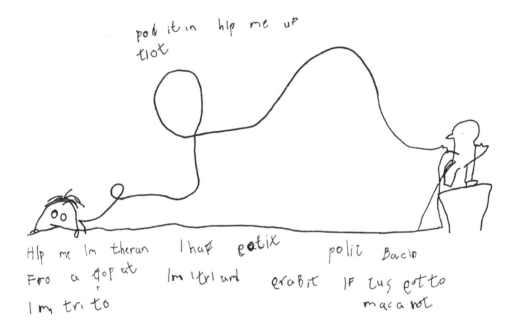

Figure 26

Roger: *Hlp me Im theran (drowning).*	Me: *How shall I help you?*
Roger: *Fro a rop at.*	Me: *Catch the rope. Here it comes.*
Roger: *Im tri to.*	Me: *It is behind you.*
Roger: *I haf got . . .*	Me: *It sounds hard to grab it.*
Roger: *If jus got to mac a not.*	Me: *OK.*
Roger: *Pol it bac in.*	Me: *OK.*
Roger: *Hlp me up.*	Me: *OK. Here you are. How are you feeling?*
Roger: *Tiot.*	Me: *Then lie down and have a sleep.*

Such creative and metaphorical activities will be addressed in more detail in Chapter 13.

Notes

1 See www.caspari.org.uk.

2 The concept of symbolic equation first appeared in Hannah Segal, 'Some Aspects of the Analysis of a Schizophrenic', *International Journal of Psychoanalysis* 31 (1950), 261–278.

3 A longer version of this case study was originally published in *Special Magazine*, the magazine of NASEN (National Association of Special Educational Needs) in June 2001, see www.nasen.org.uk.

4 This conversation, along with Roger's drawing (Figure 26), was published in Angela Greenwood, 'Stories and Writing', in *Taking Children Seriously*, eds Steve Decker, Sandy Kirby, Angela Greenwood and Dudley Moore (London: Cassell, 1999), 64–86.

Relating and relationships **11**

Using relationships as a healing vehicle

Figure 27

Ways of relating and talking with vulnerable and challenging children: 'language is a vital means of communication' (nurture principle 4)

This book is mainly about the relationships that adults have with children – both the relationships that traumatise, and the relationships that facilitate and heal. This chapter concentrates on helpful ways that significant adults can think about, relate to and talk with challenging children, including using good listening skills. Good listening skills are important for everyone of course. Indeed the subtitle of this book, *Why Can't You Hear Me?* evokes the painful experience of *not* feeling heard.

For most secure children listening skills are imbibed automatically from long-term experiences of being listened to and 'taken seriously' throughout childhood, but there are many ways teachers can encourage thoughtful, attentive listening and empathy in the children themselves, including circle-time activities (sharing done in a circle with a group or class), which make for rounded and confident individuals. The chapter begins with some of these.

Circle time: fostering children's sharing, relating and emotional literacy skills

Circle time often uses 'rounds' where children take turns to talk briefly about a topic, ranging from something neutral like 'something I like to do', to something a little more revealing like 'my favourite thing to do alone'. As trust develops they may be invited to talk about more challenging things like 'what I do when I feel sad' or 'something I feel bad about'. As well as developing confidence, such sharing can aid self-awareness, emotional literacy, mastery and social communication. Sharing topics can also be based around a theme or an emotion. They can be particularly helpful at difficult or transition times. Mrs A, a teacher I know well, used a range of sentence stems around sadness with her early years children including 'what I do when I am sad', when she had a very ill child in her class, who tragically died after a few months. She writes about it vividly and movingly in chapter 11 of *Taking Children Seriously*.[1]

Such sentence stems can also be used with pairs of children to encourage listening as well as speaking.

Creative listening and the value of silence with children

The children are given a topic or a sentence stem with the instruction that one child talks about the topic for a few minutes while the others listen without commenting, advising or saying anything at all, except concentrating with full attention. Then there is a short *silence* for a few moments before they change roles and another child speaks. A teacher friend tried this with vulnerable adolescents – using a singing bowl to mark the times. She then repeated the exercise with a related topic encouraging the listener to imagine the speaker as someone they care about immensely. She also tried it with them reading self-chosen poems out loud in a group setting – followed by a short silence before the next person's contribution.

The young people were later asked to reflect on what it felt like to be listened to so purely. They talked of how good it was to feel really listened to and not interrupted; and how having silent listeners made them feel more confident too. They also said how difficult it was to just listen quietly to others when they thought of things to say!

This is a practice that benefits everyone, although more insecure children will need introducing to it in small doses. Of course trust takes time to develop, but it is really worth investing in. It benefits from regular practice.

Fostering empathy with children

As you will have noticed both the felt sense of empathy and its expression in words is encouraged and thought about a lot in the book, and especially as we go through this chapter. So a few words about fostering empathy in children are called for here. Of course we really learn empathy through feeling it when it is evoked in us, or genuinely expressed to us by others. So taking opportunities is key. The tragic and painful experience of Mrs A's class mentioned briefly above, evoked in all the children huge amounts of both pain, compassion and empathy as they were so wonderfully supported through little D's illness and death. Both parents and teachers would come up to her quite amazed at the children's maturity, thoughtfulness and care.

> I remember one parent who was doing her ironing and her son came to tell her something that had happened in school that day, and suddenly he broke off and said, 'Mum, you're not using your looking skills and your listening skills when I'm talking to you.'

It seemed as if through their painful but real experience of so much sadness and love and sharing together, and through learning to use their listening, looking, concentrating and thinking skills, which Mrs A had taught them, they had become a real 'thinking' and caring class, looking out for each other – sometimes in ways quite beyond their years. Their subsequent teacher described them as a 'very special class'.

Another more deliberate way of engaging children in a first-hand and very natural experience of empathy is through bringing a mother and baby into a class on a regular basis for observation and reflection sessions. The children really get to know and care about the baby and to feel deeply for her when she is distressed, as mother and baby come into class and engage together in the presence of the children. *Roots of Empathy*[2] is a very successful Canadian programme doing just this on a fortnightly basis. There is even a preschool version, as well as primary and adolescent versions with more attachment, child development and curriculum connections. In the UK there are similar initiatives including *Baby Watching*[3] – an attachment-based programme where a mother and baby visit a class or nurture group weekly for 20–30 minutes, for two to three terms. Both these programmes are backed up by research. For example, in 2012, researchers at McGill University in Montreal studied the effectiveness of the *Roots of Empathy* programme in fostering the social-emotional development in primary-grade children.[4] They found a direct connection between empathy and learning capacity. Such programmes have been shown to facilitate empathy and emotional growth, even in vulnerable children. Kimberly Schonert-Reichl, a psychology professor at the University of British Columbia who has studied *Roots of Empathy* since 2000, argues that it is particularly important to teach social-emotional skills with at-risk young people: 'The evidence is so clear that when you do it [*Roots of Empathy*] . . . it actually helps them do better in school . . . It builds resilience.'[5]

Attuned, empathic and reflective ways of relating are helpful for everyone, but for very vulnerable and emotionally damaged children, working through the relationship is the only way to bring about a long-term difference and free children to concentrate and learn. In this chapter we will be thinking about thoughtful, empathic ways of relating, including practical examples, and the implications, benefits and difficulties of attuned relationships.

PACE[6]

A good summary of the sort of qualities that lead to secure attachment and emotional growth in children is given by Dan Hughes in 'PACE' – indicating attitudes of playfulness, acceptance, curiosity and empathy. In his books Hughes talks about PACE in the content of parenting adopted and foster children. Here we highlight the same qualities in nurturing vulnerable children in school. It is very applicable to key workers.

PACE attitudes and ways of engaging with children actively convey to them that all memories, feeling states and events can be accepted, understood and integrated into the relationship. Breaks are easily repaired and the flow (which includes both non-verbal and verbal aspects, and both feelings and reflection) proceeds within a sense of safety and openness to the discovery of new aspects of themselves and the relationship.

> *Playfulness* is light, relaxed, exaggerated ('*Wow!!*'), smiley and may include unexpected positive words and surprises, like '*Boo!!!*' or '*What's this?*'
>
> *Acceptance* is of whatever they express – thoughts, feelings, wishes, memories and perceptions. In relation to behaviours, acceptance is non-judgmental and unconditional, although boundaries may be needed.
>
> *Curiosity* is interested. It is open to not knowing and wondering, it includes acts of discovery, surprises and 'aha' moments together.
>
> *Empathy* is about feeling felt, feeling connected, feeling into the world of the other. It may be expressed as empathic words and/or just quietly 'being' alongside a person, as we can sense from Figure 27 at the beginning of this chapter. It is a quality of 'feeling with' or opening your heart to another person. Enough empathy eventually makes it possible for the child to acknowledge deeper underlying feelings of fear, sadness, loss and loneliness, which might lie below anger. Empathy can also enable the child to relax, trust and share hidden thoughts, feelings and memories.

As discussed throughout the book, all these PACE attitudes are important and even essential with attachment-disturbed children, facilitating enjoyable, helpful, usable and significant relationships (perhaps quite unlike what they have been used to), and opening them up to trust and readiness for learning. Within these relationships they can feel safe, and they can engage and ask questions without fear of ridicule. They can begin to bear to 'have a go', to feel felt and to feel. They can become open to listening and risk making mistakes. They can begin the journey of emotional growth and learning.[7]

Communication is not just about the language *we* use. It is about *dialogue*. Dan Hughes calls it 'affective / reflective dialogue' because it involves 'affect (feeling experiences) tuning in, and reflection, and it is a dialogue'.[8] It is definitely not a moral talk or injunction. It usually contains a blend of thoughts, reflections and feelings, enabling the adult and child to think and adjust together.

Even if the child does not engage verbally, or even if the whole interaction is non-verbal, it is a two way process of connecting with each other, and when there is a break in the connection, of repairing the break and reconnecting: connect–break–repair.

It is probably true for all of us that *non-verbal communication* is the *primary* way we express our own inner lives and sense the inner lives of others. Such conversations don't need to take much time. Vulnerable children are often particularly sensitive to non-verbal communications. They may have *had* to become sensitive to vibes – like any hints of fear, anxiety or hostility in our voice or body language – to stay safe, as we discussed in Chapter 3 on trauma, so our own calm containing presence will make all the difference.

For toddlers, non-verbal communication is naturally combined with verbal communication, and the way we relate to them includes lots of touch, facial expression and engaging in variable tones of voice. They will respond to gestures, which are animated, expansive and dramatic. Getting down to their level may be important. Vulnerable children in school need these animated qualities too, and attuned significant adults will naturally tune into children's non-verbal communications and respond or put them into words. When damaged and vulnerable children have long-term committed significant relationships with attuned significant adults who respond in these ways, they will slowly change. I regularly work with adults who tell me stories of children beginning to change as their significant relationships with them develop, even though it may take time (see Case Study 24, p.149)!

The adult's *verbal* and *non-verbal* expressions and communications need to be warm, open, interested, thoughtful and responsive. Eye contact and the frequent use of the *child's name* enhances relationships too – if the child can bear it. Even though some children take time and much emotional containment to become open to it, the use of *empathy* and *thoughtfulness* is crucial. It enables children to feel heard and therefore cared about. It enables them to reflect on how others see them and feel with them, leading to an inner sense of self.

Empathic comments will probably be quite brief, as children can't usually take too much intensity, although occasionally our thoughtful comments might precipitate a longer meaningful conversation. Whereas secure children can use and learn from comments like, *'Do you realise that when you . . . children will not want to play with you?'* disturbed and vulnerable children will feel humiliated by such conversations and quickly switch off or become defensive. Empathy is probably helpful for all of us.

The task of the significant adult in school is to be attuned to the child at the same time as teaching or helping them with their work. In school it often falls to the TA to play this role as they have more time, but teachers play an important role for their more vulnerable children too, precisely because they are the authority figure and looked up to, or feared, as the child is programmed to expect in authority figures. Taking the relationship-based approach does not need to take lots of time. Little and often, and lots of non-verbals, is probably best, as insecure children are (unconsciously) crying out for connection and compassion – even though they might resist it for fear of being let down. It is a commitment though. It can be painful to care, and children's projections can become stronger as relationships become closer – because they may fear (their usual experience of) rejection from those they are becoming attached to. So any losses, absences and endings are likely to be more difficult as through these committed relationships they can let down their defences a little, opening them to feel and take more personally such losses. In the long term however such relationships will make a real difference, as well as being priceless opportunities for growth. And such a path is rewarding, as Case Study 24 (p. 149) illustrates, and growth enhancing for both the child and for us. Sometimes we hear heartening news of a child we worked with, as a teacher friend describes in Case Study 29.

Case Study 29   Being remembered and making a difference long term with a child

I have a social worker friend who said the other day that she is currently working with a boy I know. She described him a bit and then I realised it was a boy I had worked with for many years when I was at the pupil referral unit. When he realised she knew me he said to her that he wouldn't be who he is now if it wasn't for me. He also said that loads of things had changed in his life, but I had been there for him for a long time.

One caveat though – it is crucial to manage our own boundaries and not get overinvolved. We need to look after ourselves too. Thinking what is appropriate *now* is important. We need to be very clear both to ourselves and to the child that we are just their 'special person' in school. Sometimes that includes bearing the pain of knowing about the chaotic and neglectful home they are going back to, which may understandably tug at our heartstrings. But it is imperative never to step over the boundary between home and school. Conversations with colleagues or clinical supervision may be needed and helpful when their hurts and needs and wants get to us. I knew of a TA losing her job when she invited a child into her home.

Basic listening skills

When vulnerable children share something of their experiences, thoughts and feelings with us, responding with basic listening skills can be very facilitating:

- *Tuning in* with unconditional *acceptance* (of the person – but not necessarily the behaviour), *genuineness*, and attuned thoughtful *attention*, *empathy* and *curiosity* will all enhance a child's confidence to talk and use the relationship for nurture and support.
- *Silent attention* (with awareness of our *non-verbal* communication) is also very valuable and facilitating.

- Remember that your tone of voice, speed of talking, facial expression and body language (*non-verbals*) are part of any communication, and contribute hugely to a child experiencing your attentive responsiveness.
- *Reflecting back* significant points of what they have been saying, and/or reflecting back feelings can often encourage a child to elaborate or feel confident to say more, for example:

  > *You're worried that the same thing might happen today.*

  > *Yes . . . and . . .*

  > *So you heard a shout, and you got scared and then you dropped your book in a puddle.*

  > *Yes, it was . . .*

- Acknowledging their wishes in fantasy especially if they can't be realised, for example:
  > '*You really wanted to be first today but B got there first*' enables them to feel heard and thought about.
  > '*It's so frustrating isn't it when we've tried so hard and then we make a little mistake.*'
- *Acknowledging feelings* and states of mind by wondering out loud can relieve anxieties and enable them to continue anyway, help them to know what they are feeling and enable them to feel accepted anyway, for example:
  > '*I'm wondering if you're feeling tired after our long visit yesterday?*'
- *Summarising* can enable them to feel heard and understood, for example:
  > '*So many things have been happening it feels hard to think and remember things today.*'

The helpfulness of putting things into words

Putting things into words is not only restorative, but it enables the child to feel they are inside our mind. Such conversations are 'right brain' to 'right brain' and they can facilitate the child having and becoming aware of thoughts *inside their head* too – leading to the beginnings of an inner world – like with M in Case Study 30 (described by his learning mentor).

Case Study 30   The value of talking things through

Some thoughts from a learning mentor:

Six-year-old M could be quite challenging. He came from a big family of seven needy boys. Sometimes he would stomp around and throw things on the floor, and it wasn't immediately evident what might be on his mind. Through talking together, and though conversations with him, we came to realise that underneath he was always feeling let down and forgotten in his big family. We started to use gestures and comments to enable him to feel thought about even though we might be busy with someone or something else; and we talked with him about this, so he would know that when we gave him the 'thumbs up' sign for example we were thinking of him.

When he was with me we did a lot of talking. I would put words to his feelings. We thought about a lot of different feelings, because when they are little children only really have 'happy' or 'angry'. We would look at the feeling pictures on the wall and think which feeling it was that he was feeling now, or what he felt when . . . . . . happened. I wanted him to be able to think in more detail about his feelings. Then we did a lot of:

'How can we manage . . . when we are feeling this way?'

'I was wondering, when we start to feel like we are being ignored and no one is noticing us, what can we do?'

'Is it a good idea when we feel like this to be kicking the child in front of us? Is that the best way to get attention?'

We would then practice more helpful behaviours. Then one day he came to me a bit agitated and he said, 'I'm worried.'

'What are you worried about?' I asked.

'It's my birthday tomorrow,' he said and his eyes started to tear up.

'Are you worried about your birthday?' I asked.

'My mum's always busy with J. He's sick. I want a birthday cake,' he said.

'How about we have a chat with your mum to talk about this?' I replied.

'Yes please.' He said quietly.

This was the first time he had shared a real worry with me. I was very touched. We had a little 'meeting' after school and he got his cake.

Thinking and wondering about feelings together, and experiencing others thinking about us, both models and leads to the development of empathy. Just being curious about a child, or a child's behaviour, demonstrates interest and thoughtfulness and can give a child an experience of being 'inside our minds' and thought about.

Sometimes, however, a child may suddenly 'switch off', causing what feels like a 'break' in the dialogue. It can be helpful then to wonder if something happened or came into their mind to upset them, or if perhaps you inadvertently said or indicated something that affected or upset them.

Although is is important never to press a child if they don't want to say more, acknowledging and healing little breaks in the dialogue or relationship can be crucial – at the right time. We thought earlier (in Chapter 7, pp. 129 and 130 – points 2 and 4) about the importance of talking through and healing little breaks in the relationship, like when you are prevented from keeping a promise to a child, or when they have 'lost it' and have needed to be stopped, reprimanded or even held. I gave the example of child psychotherapist Graham Music's suggestion that, paradoxically, *such breaks or misattunements are actually valuable* because they give an excellent and real opportunity for talking through such difficulties with honesty, regret and compassion – leading to 'repair' and even strengthening of relationships, which would not have occurred otherwise. Such 'break–repair–reconnect' experiences build resilience as well as making the current relationships more secure.

This importance of repair and talking 'mistakes' through honestly links in to Winnicott's 'good-enough mother' – who only needs to be perfectly attuned *some* of the time.[9] Just as the mother's near perfect attunement to her newborn needs to ease into some little supported frustrations to enable children to bear to wait and to trust in the face of some difficulty, so the newly fostered or adopted child's need for close dependent availability (or the very vulnerable child's need for a closely attentive new key worker) needs to slowly shift into the reality of little frustrations and disappointments that can be talked through and survived. This whole process, which is carried out as the child is open to it, can make us both feel better. It both builds secure relationships and enables the child to grow more secure within themselves (see also Winnicott's understanding of acted-out behaviours as 'signs of hope' on p. 157).

In the context of supervision discussions with school staff I have often found myself saying that it can be better to make a mistake and talk it through with a child than not make the mistake at all – because you have a 'hot' opportunity you wouldn't otherwise have had. It is not always easy though.

The disruptive boy (in Case Study 23 on p. 142) who could not contain his 'big feelings', including his swimming kit anxieties, and who would frequently precipitate 'breaks' between himself and school staff, is an example of this. We read how the school well-being manager described him benefitting from lots of talking through of his anxieties and hurts and his feared relationship breaks – leading to a real and stronger relationship and an observable growth in his resilience. This example illustrates how talking things through can make a difference for *both* teacher and child. Exercise 9 encourages us to recall our *own* experiences of the helpfulness of repairing a 'broken' relationship.

Exercise 9   Reparation exercise[10]

Consider an occasion when you have been able to make a reparative gesture with someone you had 'hurt'.

- Reflect on the emotions that you had to face up to in order to make the gesture.
- What facilitated this?
- What impact did your reparative gesture have on your subsequent relationship?

I remember a visiting psychologist telling us in a lecture how a child she was working with suddenly turned away and became very resistant, and she said (something like):

> *Something's happened hasn't it? I'm just wondering what made you suddenly turn away. Is it something in my face I wonder? Sometimes when I listen to people I screw up my eyes a little as I wonder about what they are doing or saying, and sometimes people can think my screwed-up eyes mean I'm frowning at them.*

He turned round.

I'm just wondering if there was something I did that upset you?

He visibly relaxed and carried on with his painting.

It's hard to know what people are thinking and feeling sometimes. We can worry and feel hurt and scared – until we realise it's OK.

Empathy

Scattered throughout the book, and in this chapter in particular, are a lot of suggestions and sentence stems relating to empathy. It is important to emphasise, however, that empathy is not just words. Words are an important tool, but being really tuned in to the child will make all the difference. Of course we will often use words to express empathy, but empathy is a feeling, a felt sense of being with someone. Really *feeling* alongside them because we know them well enough to care and *want* to put our understanding into words, will communicate to them. We can also know this from our own experience (see Exercises 10 and 11).

Exercise 10 Experiences of empathy

Think of a time when someone was particularly empathic towards you.

How did it ease your hurt or pain?

How did it affect your relationship with the person concerned?

Exercise 11 The benefits of empathy

Think of a time when you were able to empathise with a child's wishes, even though you couldn't go along with them.

How did your empathic response ease the child's frustration or hurt?

My experience as a psychotherapist was that as I got to know a child, even those difficult to like or be with, I found I would always come to care about them and *feel* their stuckness or their closed-upness or moodiness or whatever they communicated, alongside them. Of course our own openness and resilience makes a difference to our capacities for feeling and thinking clearly, and our capacity for aliveness too. This work is a rewarding adventure all round – as well as a challenge!

Some thoughtful ways of responding

The best way to do this is to develop *your own thoughtful responses* 'in the moment' – to use your intuition!

In my long experience, however, schools have found the empathy sentences in Box 14 particularly useful and practical. In some infant classes and nurture groups staff have blown them up and stuck them on the wall as an aide-memoire to glance at when they are faced with an anxious or a difficult acting-out child. Sometimes in the heat of the moment we can go blank and a prompt can be very useful!

Box 14 Ways of responding empathically to children's (difficult) behaviours

- *You really want another one don't you, but . . .*

- *You really want it now. It's so hard to have to wait when you want something, but you will have to wait till . . .*

- *When he said that I think it hurt you a bit didn't it?*

- *You're feeling a bit bad about that aren't you? Maybe you could . . .*

- *People can really hurt you when they say things like that.*

- *It can be so hard to try again when something goes wrong.*

- *It was hard for you to try again wasn't it, but you managed it.*

- *You want to say something I know, but I'm just listening to . . .*

- *I think you need help with that.*

- *You look like you're enjoying that.*

- *It's hard when you both want to talk to me at the same time isn't it.*

- *I think that hurt you.*

- *It must be so hard to manage . . .*

- *It can be SO frustrating when . . .*

'*I wonder*' and '*I'm wondering*' can be helpful sentence beginnings, because they open up to reflection and thoughtfulness, and they don't *need* an answer. The child can answer if they wish to, but also feel just as comfortable if they choose not to reply:

> '*I'm just wondering why you reacted like that*'
>
> '*I'm wondering. Is it . . . ?*'
>
> '*I wonder what made you . . .*'

An expression of *curiosity* about a child's behaviour enables them to feel thought about:

> '*I wonder what made you say that?*'
>
> '*Mmm, I'm puzzled. There are some things that are just hard to understand.*'
>
> '*I'm just guessing, but I was wondering . . .*'
>
> '*What do you think?*'
>
> '*Do you often feel . . . when . . . ?*'
>
> '*Do you usually find . . . ?*'

Whereas a 'knee-jerk' reaction or a 'mini lecture' may make them do, or not do, what you want them to, but it will evoke defensiveness and resistance to the relationship too.

Curiosity also helps to maintain and communicate an attitude of acceptance, even when we feel somewhat hurt and puzzled by their behaviour. This does not preclude of course setting necessary boundaries with empathy.

When setting boundaries or communicating expectations the use of 'ACO' can enable children to feel thought about at the same time as not getting that they want:

> A = Acknowledge the feeling
>
> C = Communicate the limit or expectation
>
> O = Offer help or offer alternatives

For example: '*I know you want to talk to me, but you will have to wait until after lunch now. I will be in the classroom this afternoon.*'

Then even if we have to discipline a child they will sense at some level that we care, and our (sometimes tentative) words or body language will communicate that. We can communicate understanding and acknowledgement of a child's feelings even if we can't go along with their wishes, e.g. '*It's frustrating when we have to wait isn't it. It can even make us quite cross*' or '*I know you want it but you need to let Sam finish with it first.*'

Empathic responses are not always easy though. Children's feelings can get right inside us, which is not always positive. In other words, they can evoke anger, helplessness and irritation too. We may even decide to communicate that to them – in a clear calm way – without 'dumping' our resentments on to them, e.g. *'You're making me very cross. Just stop – now. We all need a few moments of quiet to think.'*

For the most damaged children, however, empathy may evoke reactivity. Any talk of feelings may trigger the negative feelings like fear, shame and hurt, buried just under the surface. They *still need* empathy and attunement of course, but it may take time to develop enough trust and security in the school or class setting, and in their relationship with their 'special person', for them to be able to bear it 'safely'. For these children thoughtful *practical* responses may be more manageable. Silent thoughtful attention may be best for the time being; a gesture perhaps, or giving them something they seem to need.

Generalised empathy sentences (not directed at the child) may be easier for them, as they refer to everyone. For example:

> *It's so hard to . . .*
>
> *It's so hard/frustrating when . . .*
>
> *I guess we often . . .*
>
> *Sometimes it's . . .*
>
> *When people . . . it can make us . . .*
>
> *It can be hard to . . .*
>
> *It can make us . . . when . . .*
>
> *It can be fun to . . .*

Similarly empathic responses to *other* children, or in class or group circle times, or even to big 'wounded' soft toys, can model the use and helpfulness of empathy for such children to see, without their feeling personally affected, e.g. *'Oh Teddy. We haven't forgotten you.'*

Empathy for little hurts is easier too. I remember a girl at the pupil referral unit who was forever wanting sympathy for her tiny marks and scratches, while we all knew there were much more worrying things she couldn't get near to thinking about. We wondered about a vague but understanding response, e.g. *'So many hurts. That feels so difficult for you.'*

Preschool children and toddlers can benefit from empathy too. Box 10 on p. 133 gives examples of the sort of attuned nurturing comments most parents might naturally make to their children. Young children who sadly haven't had such a good beginning, particularly those who have been abused or neglected at a very young age, will really benefit from these nurturing conversations with their preschool 'aunties', their adoptive or foster parents and their early years staff, to give them a different and a nurturing relationship they can build on and use. The earlier damaged children can start to *rework* their attachment patterns and expectations the easier it is, especially if the parents are open to help too. Feeling thought about and understood may enable them to become empathic to others too. That's real progress!

Secure, reliable, usable relationships

As these ways of understanding, reflecting and relating begin to bear fruit, children can become more securely attached to their key workers, and this increased security can facilitate both learning and calmer behaviour. As these trusted relationships develop we can gently encourage them to take small steps towards independence.

Moving them gently on

When children are resistant, anxious or needy it can be difficult for them to shift out of their default patterns and responses. Sometimes a little shift is all they can manage. But that is fine. It is a step in the direction of health and confidence and can be encouraged and acknowledged. Within their trusted relationships with vulnerable children, key workers and significant adults can encourage 'small steps' in the direction of health. Small challenges and little forays out of their comfort zone may be possible – using a timer perhaps, or with *their* adult nearby but not with them. Teachers are good at encouraging and supporting children to 'have a go'. The sentence stems in Box 15 give a flavour of the sort of encouraging and supportive words that might enable children to take little 'risks'.

Box 15   Gentle curiosity-based questions to encourage 'small steps forward'

What would it feel like if you . . . ?

What would it feel like I wonder if I . . . ?

Perhaps you could try just . . . ?

How about you just . . . ?

How about we think together about . . . ?

How about we just . . . ?

I wonder if you could . . . while I . . . ?

How could I help you with . . . I wonder?

These could be combined with empathy and acknowledgement of their difficulties:

I know getting started with something is difficult for you. How about if . . . ?

It's always hard when we have to stop before we've finished I know. How about I . . . ?

I know you can do it, but I also know you are anxious about having a go. What would it feel like I wonder if . . . ?

It is the *first-hand experience* of relationships with empathic resilient thoughtful people that gives vulnerable children the opportunity to grow into knowing a secure relationship for themselves, at least in the caring, predictable setting of the classroom. In their secure classroom and school and with their familiar trusted adults, they can become able to relate, learn and think for themselves, and begin to regulate their own behaviour. Their old anxious, reactive patterns can become overlaid with a functional secure attachment pattern, which they will increasingly be able to transfer to new trusted adults and use as a secure base.

Sadly though the old dysfunctional pattern can sometimes be triggered, for example by unexpected changes and big transitions. This is not easy for the child or the school (see Chapter 12 for more about change).

When trusted relationships become wobbly

Some children (as described in previous chapters) have only ever known close relationships that are conflicted, judgemental or even hurtful. We are all programmed to need attention and connection, and such children will feel that too, but for them closeness *includes* conflict.

Fear of closeness

For such children, therefore close dependent relationships may be both necessary *and scary*. They may expect close relationships to be conflict ridden (as they are at home). As significant relationships become closer, attachment-disturbed, ambivalent and chaotic/ disorganised children can become reactive, hurtful and resentful towards those they are beginning to value. For all that they need to be loved, they can become (unconsciously) terrified of closeness, for fear that the person they are coming to value will reject or abandon them (as those closest to them have always done). They can become driven to reject or attack first. When these anxious attachment anxieties are around, they may be triggered into rejecting us, for example:

> *Look what you made me do!*
>
> *Go away. I hate you*
>
> *Shut up. Don't talk.*

They may even attack us if they feel threatened, overwhelmed or unbearably uncomfortable. This is *transference* (see Chapter 4 for a fuller discussion).

These behaviours and vibes can get right inside us. Even if they don't act them out we will feel their feelings in the transference, which are not always positive. We may even become *pushed to wanting to reject them* by saying and doing hurtful things. In other words we may feel anger, helplessness, pain and irritation too.

It is helpful to remember though that this sort of regression happens precisely because the relationship is becoming significant to the child, and if we can (be supported to) stay with them, while setting the necessary boundaries (and having the breaks we need), then we can help them into calmer waters and into using secure relationships for help and support most of the time. We can help them grow stronger! (Case Study 23 on p. 142 is an example of this.)

Supporting each other is essential. Talking things through later with trusted colleagues and supportive managers may be helpful and necessary. If through training, supervision and supportive conversations we have some understanding of these dynamics then we can be ready for them, and stop for a moment before responding! Knowing that it is projection makes it easier to manage. We can also feel OK about needing to take a short break.

When children 'get' to us we need to be aware of own countertransference tendencies too. That is, to be aware that a child's behaviour or manner may sometimes strike an uncomfortable chord in us, pushing us to react more strongly than is really warranted. Awareness will make all the difference. If we are aware that a button has been pressed, we can stop for a moment and find ways to resist the urge to retaliate. We can take a minute to manage our heightened emotions, exposing our own hurts and fears. A deep breath may be helpful – to enable us to *maintain our capacity to think* before responding. Neuroscience teaches us that slow out breaths activate our parasympathetic (rest and digest) nervous system – easing tensions naturally.

Children who hurt need to experience over and over again that we can bear their hurts, *even if we have to stop them hurting others*. As my supervisor used to say, 'They need to know that whatever happens we can cope'. Our calm but firm boundaries in the face of their powerful projections demonstrate that we are not fazed by their destructive feelings. We can contain for both of us. We can stay calm.

Silently staying calm and attentive is very containing. We may also communicate clearly that we have 'heard' their pain and we empathise with the *level* of feeling that prompted their strong reaction *even though we had to stop them* and that we can talk about it later – as and when they are open to such conversations.

Reflecting and responding to children's sad, worrying and challenging comments

Other children's hurting words may express more depressed feelings like low self-esteem, feelings of uselessness, self-loathing or self-pity. Sometimes they need us to bear and contain these too.

When children say sad or depressing things that are hard to hear, and that we really don't want them to say or feel, like 'You don't care. Nobody cares', it can be very hard to know how to respond. Our instant reaction is to want to placate them, to make them feel better, to tell them that *we* don't feel like that, e.g. 'No it's not like that' or 'Of course I care about you'. This is probably because to really take in how they are feeling now is too difficult to bear. But is that *really hearing* what they are saying? What they really need is to feel heard and taken seriously.

Each child and each time is different of course. Only the receptive listener knows in the moment what a particular child might be open to. Sometimes silence and full empathic attention is best for now.

Probably to stop and reflect for a moment, to wonder internally (or even out loud) what might have made them feel or say that *at this point in time*, is the first thing. As with their projected hurtful comments it is important to communicate that we have *heard* what they have said, and that we can think about it with them if they want that. It may be that they have never felt taken seriously, never felt really heard. They need us to accept that this is how they feel right now – and it is horrible!

This way of responding is accepting, both of the content and of the feelings they are expressing. If they engage with our 'tuned-in' response, we may have an opportunity to talk some more about it with them, not so much to make them change their minds before they are ready or because *we* want them to feel better, but because empathic and thought-ful responses to our hurting feelings enable us to process things into becoming less hurtful and more integrated.

Box 16 offers some suggestions for the sort of accepting attuned comments we might make to such sad or challenging words – not as any sort of correct response, but to give a flavour of the sort of responses that might enable them to feel heard, responses that include empathy and openness to a child's current pain and that may paradoxically open up their hearts to processing and healing their hurts.

Box 16 Some ways to respond to children's hurtful and sad comments

(Make one comment then wait and see is usually best – it's all about tuning into their communication in the moment.)

I hate you.	*I can see you are very angry with me. It's hard when we can't do/have . . .*
	Maybe it's hard for you when I have to get cross with you and stop you . . .
	It doesn't mean I hate you because I can't allow . . . but I do sometimes need to say STOP quite loudly to stop . . . getting hurt.
	You are not happy about . . . are you.
You hate me.	*It's hard when I need to say 'no' or 'stop'. I know it is . . . but I can't let you . . . because . . .*
	Does it make you feel I hate you because I sometimes need to say no to you?
	That must be very hard for you if you feel that.
	I don't hate you. I just need to keep us all safe.
No one likes me.	*Is that how you feel sometimes? That sounds so sad.*
	Oh, Sam. That sounds so sad. Is that how you really feel?
No one ever cares about me.	*Does it really feel like no one cares for you? I/we care about you, but perhaps that's hard to believe.*
It would be better if I were dead.	*Oh Sam. Is that how you really feel? That sounds so sad.*
I'm just stupid/rubbish.	*I wonder what makes you say that Sam? It makes me feel very sad to think that you feel like that.*
I'm useless. I'll never . . .	*It's really hard to keep going with difficult things I know.*
	It can make us feel so useless sometimes. Is there any way I can help you?

I wish I was still with my mum.	*I'm sure you think about your mum a lot, and you wish you could still be there with her It's so sad that she can't look after you.*
I hate my dad.	*You hate your dad. That sounds a very hurting feeling.* *I think you might be very cross with your dad, (only say things that won't trigger further pain or humiliation)*
Why does everyone pick on me?	*Does it really feel like everyone picks on you Sam?* *What makes you think that I wonder?*
Yes! You pick on me all the time.	*Does it feel like that Sam?* *I have had to stop you doing . . . haven't I.* *But we both know it's not safe. And it's my job to keep everyone safe.*
It's not fair. You never let me . . .	*I'm so sorry if it feels unfair.* *But I think we both know that if . . . you will (both) get too excited, and then you will do something you will later wish you hadn't.*
I'm/she's never going to get better.	*Do you worry about that Sam. (SILENCE) That sounds a very difficult worry. Is there anything I can do to help you? Does it help to talk about it?*

The other thing to say is that conflicted children are always ambivalent. What they say at any one point in time may not be the whole truth. It is helpful to bear that in mind. We may even find them *changing or modulating* what they say as they feel heard, and as they experience their hurts and fury being accepted and wondered about. For example: '*Well you listen to me, but . . . .*' or '*Well, my sister was kind to me yesterday*'.

Repeated swearing and abusive language (discussed in more detail in Chapter 9, p. 168) can be particularly hard to respond to in a helpful way. It is important not to come over as rejecting or judgemental of the child, but also not to let them take advantage and treat you and others disrespectfully.

Sometimes abusive language floods out – like an adrenalin fuelled verbal outburst. When they start swearing explain that you can see they are angry, but you never respond to swearing. Then just wait for them to calm down. Later on you will want to have a conversation with them of course, and there may well be school rules and school consequences, but 'moral talks' can just make vulnerable children feel judged and become defensive – either in their minds or outwardly.

Explain to the child what you are going to do to help them with their problem of swearing. For example, when you sense they are getting frustrated and about to swear, you are going to try to catch them before they do and suggest they take it out on (for example) a piece of Blu Tack by squeezing it instead of using words. When they are calm teach them alternative words ('*Oh sausage!*') or alternative ways to express anger. There are many examples of anger-management techniques on the market (see also Box 7, p. 95).

Containing secure boundaries

Angry disruptive children need firm secure boundaries. They need to feel that whatever happens we (or the school) will contain and control their outbursts in a way they cannot (yet) do for themselves, even if we need to get help.

If they are allowed to 'get away' with antisocial behaviour because of weak or ineffective boundaries they will not only learn that they can manipulate us, they may also (unconsciously) feel that their anger is uncontrollable and even frightening. (There is a wonderful story about this called *Angry Arthur*,[11] the story of a little boy whose anger was so bad that he destroyed the whole world and disappeared into space on a piece of rock – because *nobody* could contain it.) Children will in fact, need to act out *more*, not less if they are not contained, because they will unconsciously need to struggle again and again to try to find someone who *can* hold it – and them, safely in check – someone who can slowly *work and talk* things through with them – as they are open to such conversations (Winnicott talks of the extreme case of such children ending up with the containment of a 'prison cell'[12]).

Children need to experience over and over again that, although we understand that in the heat of the moment they are 'triggered' and often they can't help it, we will always stop any antisocial behaviour. Whatever happens we will cope *and we will still care about them and be there for them*. These difficulties, however, are also an invaluable opportunity, when they have calmed down, to talk things through and help them process their relationship anxieties. Even if you don't get it quite right, *taking opportunities to talk things through will* make all the difference to their feeling heard and understood. Asking them what *they* think can be helpful too, for example:

> *'It can be hard for you I think when teachers ask you to do something – to do some work maybe. Does it feel perhaps that they or we are wanting to boss you, or make you do things out of meanness?'*

> *'I guess it takes time to trust that teachers just want to help you to learn. What do you think?'*

Responding thoughtfully to behaviour difficulties

Understanding particular behaviours as unconscious communications was discussed in Chapter 9, but in addition to wondering what they might be communicating and setting any necessary boundaries, the *way* we respond – thoughtfully, calmly and firmly, acknowledging the child's feelings perhaps, but not getting caught up in ongoing debate, makes all the difference. Behaviour difficulties are often because a child has *had* to become defensive for fear of being hurt or humiliated.

Although it is possible to manage such difficulties with strong enough rewards or punishments or threats, you will not alter their underlying dysfunctional expectations, and their ongoing need for defensive resistance or retaliation (when they get the chance) through behaviourist approaches. They need consistent, trusted, emotionally containing relationships and secure boundaries to shift their dysfunctional patterns and enable them to begin to learn and relate.

Some thoughts about regulating and preventing arousal with disturbed children

Because outbursts evoke understandable anxiety and even anger in staff, and because managing them through relationships is rather different from what we might be used to, I have organised the following suggestions into groups and kept this section in note form. I hope this is helpful.

General and preventative strategies

1. Have clear rules, routines and expectations, but rules that *you may choose* for good reasons to adjust with particular children at particular times.
2. Always be firm, quietly assertive, clear and thoughtful.
3. For very chaotic/disorganised children it may be better to make choices for them and structure their activities.
4. In the case of traumatised, chaotic/disorganised children who have been programmed to be on the look out for danger and humiliation, frequent use of the word SAFE can be helpful, e.g. in nurture bases or behaviour units: *'I need to make sure everyone is safe'* or *'My job is to make sure we are all safe'*.

   If they know and are frequently reminded that their teacher or TA is keeping them and everyone safe it will relieve them a little of this anxiety, leaving them freer to engage in learning tasks, etc.

5. Always and visibly support each other. It is crucial for disturbed children to experience cooperating adults. This may be new to them!

6. Recognise *your* responsibility to help vulnerable children with their overwhelming feelings, and to help them lower their arousal levels. Through your attuned attention (even at a distance) you will often know the signs of their escalation and may be able to diffuse or distract them before they escalate.

7. Agree a *strategy for emergencies* for children who have regular problems with outbursts.

8. Clinical supervision will make a huge difference for those working with disturbed children.

9. It is helpful to understand (particularly repeated) behaviours as unconscious communications (see Chapter 9). Reflect with each other on what their behaviour might be communicating, and on responses that might meet the child's needs more appropriately. Put your tentative understandings into words in small doses, as they are open to it.

10. Provide natural and *logical consequences* (rather than punishments) for antisocial behaviors. For example, you may decide that a child who is going through a difficult patch and is clearly not managing his big feelings at the moment, should not go out to play this week, or go on a particular visit, etc. as you both know he is likely to be easily triggered into doing something he will later regret, get himself into trouble and that he or others may get hurt.

11. Offer empathy for children's wishes and hurts when setting boundaries, and secure but non-punitive alternatives. You may use choices with children who can manage them.

12. Offer emotional containment (see Chapter 5) through understanding and empathic comments, benign curiosity, 'wonderings' and concrete responses based on understanding their patterns, needs, difficulties and interests.

13. Remember that change, endings, transitions and *excitement* all arouse anxiety in insecure children (see Chapter 11). This is neurological as well as emotional – because their stress and arousal hormones become more easily triggered at such times. Help with beginnings, endings and transitions involves thinking, planning and preparing the child beforehand. It also includes empathising with their behavioural communications around endings and transitions (see Box 21, p. 236).

14. Individual repetitive or simple 'left-brain' activities ease anxiety and foster security. Gather together a 'calm box' of mechanical 'left-brain' activities (see Box 7, p. 95).

15. Provide a quiet comfortable calming-down/thinking area that can be used preventatively to give children a break. It can include a calm box, as well as blankets, cushions and soft toys. It is important to differentiate this preventative calming-down place and its use, from somewhere you take an out-of-control child, or what you will do when you need to remove a resistant child from the class for safety reasons, otherwise the calming-down place will lose its calming potential and become resisted itself!

16. Teach children ways to 'self-regulate' and relax (see Box 17).

Box 17　Helping children to relax and self-regulate

Ways to help children relax

- One minute's quiet before lessons, at the beginning of each day and afternoon.

- Everyone put their head on the table and relax your body. Quietly count your breaths.

- Quiet humming.

- Meditation music.

- Benign guided visualisations with quiet background music (I recommend Relax Kids CDs, see p. 275).

- Mindfulness activities (see pp. 284–285).

- Peer massage, e.g. gentle stroking or patting like gentle rain.

- Gentle attachment-based play (see p. 96) activities with a special adult.

- Sleeping lions.

- Cuddle teddy and close your eyes.

- Roll in a blanket.

- Have a slow drink of water.

Ways to help children self-regulate

Practising managing the rise and fall of emotional states (adrenaline) enhances self-regulation capacities:

- Parachute play, carefully held and manage, e.g. 'lift *up* . . . bring *down* to the ground'.

- Musical instruments. 'Conduct' their playing of the ups and downs of sound level and rhythm.

- Run and stop games.

- Dance and melt.

- Dramatic ups and downs in movement.

- Rainstorm – acting out the coming and going away together.

- Going-round-the-circle games like Zoom and slow down.

17. A significant adult sitting calmly and attentively near a child enables security.
18. Prevent exposure to situations that are very likely to cause a particular child too much anxiety (see point 10 above). In this vein it is interesting to note that adopting parents are recommended to keep their newly adopted children nearby with them at home and to just do quiet activities together for the first few weeks, avoiding exposure to other people (even other relatives!) and unfamiliar situations that could easily trigger insecurities and acting-out behaviours. This is because it is understood that bonding with and creating a secure enough base for very insecure children and helping them to manage their vulnerable inner worlds is *so* important. This doesn't mean having a boring time. With a consistent attentive secure base and relationship they will grow stronger. Cooking, gentle stories and art can be nurturing.
19. Use understanding and supportive language when communicating such decisions, e.g.

    I think we both know you are not strong enough yet to manage the fairground visit. I will help you practice the skills you need, and then maybe you will be ready to have a go next time. Meanwhile we will have a nice, quiet time doing cooking together.

20. Be aware of the child's attitude towards proximity. As discussed in Chapter 6, some (resistant/ambivalent) children find it very hard if a significant adult is not think-ing about/attending to them *all the time*, while others (avoidant children) can't bear anyone to get too close. Respect these patterns as a necessary defence *particularly at stressful times*, and engage with them appropriately to ease them (see Chapter 6).

    Respond to their needs at the same time as weaning them into more security:

    - For *resistant/ambivalent* children and young people) show them they are being 'held in mind' in lots of ways, e.g. remembering little details of what they have said or done. As they grow more secure slowly stretch their capacities from close and frequent relating to less attention, less frequency and using hand signals.
    - For *avoidant* children take lots of little opportunities to connect briefly with them and then look away. Provide them with what they need without engaging with them. As they grow more secure slowly stretch their capacities from keeping a safe distance to more engaged relating.

    In both cases discuss these subtle shifts and their growing strengths with them.
21. Provide a reflective time to think about particular children causing concern with other staff involved with vulnerable children.

When they are open to it . . .

1. Acknowledge states, feelings and behaviours for them by wondering aloud.
2. Help them talk experiences and feelings through as they indicate they can manage.
3. Accept and tentatively verbalise their possible feelings, wishes, intentions and percep-tions, but *do not dilute necessary boundaries*.
4. Acknowledge evidence of little signs of emotional growth in a child. e.g.

    'I was just thinking – a little while ago you would have rushed out when that happened.'

    'I think you're growing stronger.'

    (For more suggestions see Box 18, p. 215.)
5. Help them practice ways of being that are helpful and new to them, e.g. relaxing, calm-ing down techniques, asking for help, resolving conflict, having fun, showing affection.

For particular children

1. Identify any specific triggers and share them with other members of staff.
2. Help the child become aware of specific trigger situations and body indicators when they are open to it.
3. Notice how the child/young person communicates anxiety, and talk about it with them.
4. A coloured card, non-verbal communication system or non-verbal hand signals and gestures may be helpful for particular children.

When anxieties begin to arise

1. Notice early hints that they are becoming anxious and offer preventative empathic comments and actions.
2. At times of crisis it is important to hold on to your own thinking capacity.
3. Be wary of reacting to the child's projections. It can be helpful, however, to acknowledge projections and other defensive acting-out behaviours to yourself and with colleagues to enable you to keep a little distance and continue to think and not get unhelpfully 'caught up' in children's 'dramas'.
4. Be firm and set boundaries in a neutral voice.
5. Decide for the child (initially) when they need to 'take a break'.
6. Decide if any preventative action is required, e.g. movement, distraction, a walk, a cup of tea, a job to do, can all help shift an anxiety state. Perhaps discuss this with a colleague.
7. Use your own calm presence to help reduce anxiety.
8. 'Big feelings', 'wobbly feelings', 'bubbling up', 'fizzing around' may be helpful words.
9. If they are known to have a problem with escalating out-of-control emotions and behaviours, recognise *your* responsibility to help them with their overwhelming (big) feelings when they become aroused and to help them lower their arousal levels. Remember dyadic (you and them together) regulation (see pp. 14 and 104) precedes self-regulation.
10. In the early stages of escalation try distracting them with a surprising comment or question, e.g.

    'I don't know about you but I could really do with a glass of water.'

    'Where did I put my pen? Can you see it?'

If an outburst arises

They need to experience empathy *and* firm boundaries – and a benign, calm, confident adult who stays in charge. These suggestions may help:

1. Concentrate on remaining calm yourself. Know that it will peter out eventually.
2. Set and maintain *your* favoured emotional tone, not the child's.
3. Convey with calmness and empathy that you are not overwhelmed by the child's problem.
4. Put in place your agreed strategy for emergencies.
5. Tune into your 'gut' feeling as to the best way to be with them during the outburst. Silence and keeping your distance may be the most appropriate and helpful for now.

6. They, or the others, may need to be removed temporarily for safety.
7. Be wary of approaching a dysregulated (or an abused) child too quickly.
8. For some children it may be helpful to *take a step back* and avoid eye contact. But stay nearby. Say as little as possible.
9. Other children may need safe holding ('team teach holding'): www.teamteach.co.uk.
10. If you need to keep some physical distance, do not ignore the child – ignore the behaviour.
11. If the outburst continues, be firm and set the boundary in a neutral voice.
12. Greatly limit the child's ability to hurt you, either physically or emotionally. *Seek help if necessary.* It is crucial for an escalating child to know and feel you can contain them, even if it takes two of you.
13. Enable the child to feel your continued connection by reassuring comments, and perhaps a reassuring pat on the shoulder as they recover – maybe using the word SAFE even if they don't seem in a state to hear. This does not mean condoning the behaviour or engaging in a debate.

When the outburst is over

1. As the outburst eases offering a repetitive mechanical activity like sorting or counting can help them calm down.
2. They may need a drink or a cup of tea!
3. Let them know that you understand that once the rage had erupted they couldn't just stop it. They needed help to come down. Let them know that you will be helping them with their overwhelming (big) feelings in all sorts of ways.
4. Acknowledging that they really wish it hadn't happened will be helpful (if it is true) when the child is open to it.
5. Later (maybe much later) they may benefit from a chance to talk things through in a safe place. They will need to experience being heard, but this does not mean colluding with their bad behaviour or going along with untruths. They may also feel a bit bad about what happened and *want* to connect with you again. But try to resist making the conversation into a moral talk or giving lots of advice. Asking them what *they* think or how they feel now may be helpful.
6. Supporting them with a reparation activity (e.g. clearing up the mess, making a card for anyone who may have been hurt, etc.) will help to 'complete the rage cycle' and ease their secondary bad feelings, which otherwise could get acted out later on (see next section).
7. You may also need to support and listen to other staff affected by the outburst, and when it feels appropriate help staff understand the child's severe unmet needs and difficulties and triggers. A conversation about their possible anxiety in relation to your developing relationship (see 'fear of closeness' p. 199) may be helpful. Thinking and wondering together about the possible meaning of a child's outburst can be very helpful for everyone.
8. Consequences may need to be put in place. It is important that these are appropriate, brief and not manipulated by the child. They may be preventative limits to keep them and everyone safe in the near future or until they have grown stronger. They should be regularly reviewed in the light of what they (and you) feel they can manage 'now', and dropped when it is safe to do so.

Repairing the relationship (see also Chapters 6 and 7)

Very disturbed children and young people may find that to openly acknowledge that they have done wrong or hurt you may feel just too humiliating and arouse too much shame. Nevertheless if it was a big incident it will certainly be on their minds – possibly for days.

So be open in the following hours or days to any hints from the child that they want to repair the relationship or build a bridge. Acknowledging such initiatives with sensitivity and acceptance can be very helpful. Particularly, it can demonstrate that relationships can survive difficult times, and that you care about them anyway even though you don't approve of their behaviour. It is best to wait for *them* to give you an opportunity to 'repair' things – even if it is a very small 'gift' or opening – like opening a door for you or waiting for you. Comments like:

> *'Thank you for . . . '*
>
> *'I'm just thinking that we had a hard time the other day didn't we.'*
>
> *'I think you might be wishing that . . . hadn't happened.'*
>
> *'Perhaps you are also needing to make sure that we are still friends.'*

Afterwards

1. A big outburst is likely to leave you feeling overwhelmed and puzzled (at least!). Feel OK about finding a trusted person to talk things through with afterwards. It can be helpful to reflect on the feelings the child seemed to be expressing and what might lie underneath, the feelings the child evoked in you and in other staff and your own reactions and after-effects. Did the child press your buttons? Use supervision if you have it. Ask for it!
2. You may also need to support and listen to staff, and when it feels appropriate help staff understand the child's severe unmet needs, patterns, difficulties and triggers. Learn from the experience.
3. Identify any specific triggers and share them with other members of staff.
4. For repeated peer conflicts *mediation*, facilitated by a trusted member of staff, may be very helpful, especially if both parties want it resolved. In my experience, however, it may be too risky when there is a significant power imbalance between the two parties – like ongoing bullying. Any agreement in those circumstances will need very regular monitoring. I am very much aware that to confront someone who has hurt or humiliated you takes a lot of courage. We can so easily fear a repeat of the hurt. But mediation can sometimes be really helpful.

Brief description of mediation[13]

I think of mediation as like creating a bridge between two sides, and finding a way for each side to cross it through talking and listening in a secure setting. The aim is to find a possible way forward that everyone can agree to, and not to assign blame or rights and wrongs. The mediator keeps the 'secure base' by not allowing debates and sticking to the process.

The 'mediator' gets together with the two parties (they could be individuals or each individual plus a 'friend') who take turns to describe the problem or what happened, including how they felt about it from their own point of view – *with no interruptions.* Everyone listens.

The mediator then asks each party in turn to say how they think the *other* party is feeling – again with no interruptions. He then checks the feelings out with each party – with no discussion. He then asks them all if they can think of a way to make things better *for all of them. They make suggestions* one at a time with no interruptions. He might write the suggestions down. He checks with the other party, either each time or at the end to see if they think any of the suggestions might be helpful. This process continues until they come up with an agreed way forward, or not.

After a certain time, if there is no way forward they agree to go away and have a think and meet again at another time, which they now arrange. If they do find an agreed way forward, you may decide to finish by each person having a chance to say one positive thing (uninterrupted) to the other. They shake hands (across the bridge) and agree a date to review.

Discipline works and lasts because of trust and real relationships

Underlying these more thoughtful ways of responding to vulnerable children is the value and importance of putting effort into developing real, resilient, reliable, caring relationships. This does not mean investing a lot of time (which you may not have), but it does mean responding thoughtfully and if appropriate empathically in the moment to children as opportunities arise, and taking them seriously even when you can't go along with their wishes, and you need to set boundaries. When a vulnerable child, through first-hand experience, has learnt to trust and respect a teacher or TA, they no longer need to be so defensive – so there is less need for discipline. (This is why, after adopting this attachment, relationship-based approach at the pupil referral unit where I worked, the number of incidents went down significantly – see p. xvii.) Of course both inner- and outer-environmental factors will still trigger anxiety and negative behaviours, but their trusted adults will know that and respond clearly and thoughtfully. If a child is triggered into acting out in some way, their thoughtful resilient teachers will not 'knee-jerk' or overreact and exacerbate the situation or the escalating feelings. They may need to set boundaries, but they will do this firmly, calmly with empathy for the child's wishes, and without engaging in debate with the aroused child. This is a completely different experience from an irritated brusque reaction with threats or exclusions, which can leave the child feeling humiliated or rejected *again* and all alone with their unbearable frustration and fury.

This is not easy I know. Staff may need to bear and contain more emotional pain and anxiety when working through the relationship. If a disturbed child senses that a teacher or special TA can bear their resistances and contain their badness and hurt and stop their anti-social behaviours too, at stressful times they may unconsciously *use that person* to contain their anxieties and find release. This is actually a compliment, but it can be both difficult and *an opportunity to help them process their hurts and grow stronger,* through thoughtfully reflecting and responding to their projections.

This way of working with vulnerable children is very different from the way teachers are usually trained to work, especially when they are communicating boundaries or expectations or when they discipline children. For most children rewards and punishments or consequences work and often work quickly, because the child wants to please and doesn't want others, including teachers, to think badly of them or humiliate or punish them; but with some vulnerable children this direct 'no nonsense' approach can actually exacerbate their behaviour. It can also undermine the possibility of them developing a therapeutic relationship with significant adults, from which they can internalise their own thoughtfulness, security and resilience. In Case Study 42 (p. 213) we see a vivid example of this. In the beginning a student teacher is struggling to appreciate the value of working in a more thoughtful and less punitive way with a boy who had experienced severe domestic abuse. Then we see how the class teacher and inclusion manager were able to support her through empathy, thoughtfulness and training in the value of trying to *understand* the child, and also modelling for her more thoughtful ways of working. We see how this support and observation enabled her to be persuaded and gain the confidence to try working differently and how through her own transforming experience she found and acknowledged that it worked. She was immensely grateful. This example shows not only the effectiveness for the *child* of working through the relationship, but also the rewards that teachers and school *staff* can experience, both in their own personal growth and when they see their very vulnerable children growing stronger.

Through these trusted relationships children will come to know from first-hand experience that their caring, trusted adults will be interested in what they have done and what they achieve, and that they can return to them any time for help, conversations and little experiences of fun. They will gradually develop their own capacity for thoughtfulness and empathy and begin to appreciate praise. They will start to develop pride in their work as we all do. They will start to become 'their own person'.

Becoming our own person: the important move towards inner directedness

Moving from being '*outer controlled*' to becoming more '*inner directed*' is important for everyone.

It enables us to think for ourselves and to become our own separate person with likes, interests and capacities. It enables us to reflect on experiences, to change our minds, apologise and tolerate differences and mistakes. It enables us to grow in confidence as we experience the fruits of our thoughtfulness in reciprocal relationships, interest in learning and in our capacity to manage our own behaviour and even stress. It includes saying '*No*'! It has direct links into internal control of our behavioural urges, reactions and feelings; and our capacity for empathy for others.

This usually happens automatically as children grow older and naturally internalise thoughtfulness and appreciation from their attuned nurturing parents and teachers. The problem is that needy and damaged children, the children who act out because they 'hurt',[14] often rarely experience this sort of thoughtful responsiveness from the adults they care about and who care about them, responsiveness that would enable them to grow internally. So the very children who need the most help with this crucial capacity usually end up having an overdose of *outer control* in the form of *criticism* or even *punishment* or *consequences*. They may get praise too of course. Praise is lovely if you can take it – but it comes from 'outside' and if it is not really believed it may actually *not* enhance a vulnerable child's self-esteem. I have even known myself to think, *'Oh she's so kind to say that'*, when someone has praised me (rather than appreciating the truth inside the praise). Perhaps readers can resonate with that too! Praise and punishment can of course often 'work' in the short term for such children, but as described above it doesn't encourage their emotional growth. Offering advice, warnings and moral injunctions like, *'If you keep on behaving like that you'll never have any friends. No one likes to be shouted at. Why don't you . . . '* is tempting because it makes the *adult* feel better, but it can push children into humiliation and defensiveness.

There is another way

This involves *staying with* the possibly quite uncomfortable feelings the hurting child is expressing and evoking, which is not easy I know, but it helps the child feel *contained* (see Chapter 5).

It also includes thoughtfully noticing small signs of growth, with curiosity but without overt positive or negative judgements. This will make a lasting difference to such children, but it is not something school staff are normally trained to do. The problem is the behaviour and irritating resistances of dysfunctional children may not give us much opportunity, and may even discourage us from *wanting* to notice little positive signs of growth. But this is precisely what the child needs.

Acknowledging growth

Acknowledging observable signs of improvement as indications of 'growing stronger' really supports children's emotional growth and their improving self-image, as well as their learning. Signs of 'growing stronger' will be different for each child of course, according to their developmental stage and difficulty. Box 11 (p. 140) helpfully lists possible signs of growing stronger (progress) in developmental order.

Putting your observations of delight and appreciation into words will reinforce growth in a child.

Asking *'What do you think?'* – and engaging *them* in thinking about (and appreciating) their own growth processes – in relation to their slowly easing and understandable needs and anxieties is very helpful. It is fostering their own capacity to reflect, their self-awareness and the development of their own inner world.

It is often helpful to end conversations that indicate emotional growth with: *'I think you're growing stronger'* and/or *'What do you think?'*

Box 18 Growing stronger conversations

- *I think we both know how hard it was for you to say that. What do you think? I think you're growing stronger. What do you think?*

- *That's the first time I've heard you say you're sorry and really want to make up. I think you're growing stronger. What do you think?*

- *It took such courage I think for you to say that. How do you feel now that we have talked about it? I think you're growing stronger. What do you think?*

- *Did you notice that you played with G. . . for the whole playtime with no problems, even though you had to wait sometimes? I'm just thinking that that's the first time you have done that for so long. I think you're growing stronger. What do you think?*

- *I noticed you asked for help just now. It can be hard to ask for help when we think we should be able to manage. But it's good to be able to ask for help if we need it. How did it feel? I think you're growing stronger. What do you think?*

- *Do you know something . . . I think you're growing stronger. What do you think?*

We are not necessarily expecting an answer here. It is enough that the seed is sown. If they respond negatively just accept that for now! It's all about tuning in to a child or young person with thoughtfulness and empathy, taking them seriously, not judging and not needing a reply!

From the point of view of the growth and development of the child's inner world, taking even tiny opportunities to make positive and thoughtful comments (from the heart) is helpful. For an example of a child who was helped to 'grow stronger' and the helpful use of such comments, (see Case Study 23 on p. 142).

It's particularly helpful to notice subtle signs of growth and authenticity (see Box 19).

Box 19   Fostering inner growth and thoughtfulness in children

- *I can see you're cross about that. But somehow you managed to hold those feelings and not act them out. How did you manage I wonder?*

- *Oh dear . . . you probably wish that hadn't happened.*

- *That hurt didn't it. I'm so glad you told me. It can be so hard to manage hurting feelings. Does/would it help to talk about it?*

- *I think you're really wishing you hadn't done/said that.*

- *I think you wish you could make it better. It's so hard when we can't make something better. But we/you could talk to him about it. I wonder what you/we might say?*

- *I'm so pleased you told me that. I wonder what makes you think . . .*

- *I think you know that I know about that. And I think you don't want to talk about it. Talking things through can be very helpful. Maybe later.*

- *Sometimes we wonder what other people are thinking. Sometimes we might even ask them if it's OK with them to . . .*

- *Sometimes we think about things don't we?*

- *How do you feel now?*

- *I wonder what made you say that?*

- *Maybe you wonder what I think about that?*

- *You think . . . and A thinks . . . I guess we're all different. How does it feel to think something different from A?*

- *Yes B's upset. I wonder what upset him?*

- *You think it should be done differently don't you?*

- *Everyone seems very calm in here today. I wonder what's helping people feel calm today?*

(continued)

(continued)

- *That's very thoughtful of you. A was finding that difficult, I could see that too, and you let her take her time. She got there in the end didn't she! Was it hard not to tell her the answer?*

- *It looked as if you nearly . . . and then you stopped yourself. Is that right? It can be so hard to feel a strong urge to do something, and then realise that it wouldn't be helpful, can't it.*

- *You started to do . . . then you changed and did . . . what made you decide to change I wonder?*

- *Sometimes we find ourselves doing something without thinking, and then we realise what we've done and we feel bad. Have you ever had that?*

- *So, I'm wondering, how many times this week do you think you have stopped yourself doing something when you realised it would not be a good thing to do?*

- *What does it feel like when you don't come and check with me first, and you just do something because you know it's OK?*

- *Is it hard to trust yourself? I wonder what that means – trusting yourself?*

- *How does it feel when you don't have to check in at the beginning of the day anymore?*

- *Ah, you've changed that I see. Sometimes we do something, then we think, 'No I don't think that's quite right', don't we – and then we change it!*

- *I think you're beginning to trust yourself. What do you think?*

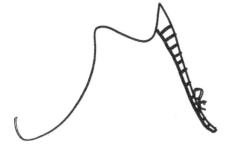

One day there was a boy who needed courage to go down the big slide

he was really scarded of slide but he want to be call. He wanted his friends to see how cool he was.

he was really really scarded but he nearly slipped down the stairs. The stairs were slippery and he was shaking.

his Friends went shout at him saying go Down the slide. He was worried that his friends might not be friends with him if he didnt do it.

So he went to go Down the slide but he was sweating. It was really scary this head was thrown back and it felt like it was going to come off.

He did'nt like what he was doing. He was Nearly at the bottom of the slide. and there was a bend upwards at the bottom which threw him up in the air. it felt like he was on a porer shoot. Then he fell into the ball pit. It felt to him like he had just dived into loads of rocks, he felt very Happy beucase his freends said he was call.

Figure 28

Usually these are evident in behaviours but P's shared writing in Figure 28 illustrates both an anxiety about being excluded, and a lot of persistence and courage – which could be acknowledged and talked about perhaps.

Responding to children's anxieties around loss, endings and transitions and new beginnings, is especially important, as anxieties arise for all of us both in anticipation, during and after such times. It is normal for new places, people and experiences to bring up some anxiety, but for most of us we know we will eventually adapt, and anyway we can always ask for help. Talking through changes with friends and family is both appropriate and normal. 'Playing through' new experiences and changes is the normal way for little children to process such experiences.

But for children who have a history of unsupported and traumatic losses, any changes, new places, new people and losses are extremely difficult. Without the history and expectation that both emotional and practical support will be available and helpful, they can be triggered into huge anxiety with no thought attached, because the last thing they want is to think about loss and change (see Case Study 27, p. 176). This is a big topic and will be covered in the next chapter.

Notes

1 Kate Ashby, 'Danielle: A Class Teacher's Account of Circle Time and Beyond', in *Taking Children Seriously*, eds Steve Decker, Sandy Kirby, Angela Greenwood and Dudley Moore (London: Cassell, 1999), 184–191.

2 *Roots of Empathy*, developed by Mary Gordon in 1966, brings a parent and baby into the classroom on a monthly basis to learn about and naturally evoke empathy with the vulnerable baby and with each other. See rootsofempathy.org for inspiring You Tube clips and details of the programme.

3 See www.base-babywatching-uk.org/what-we-do.

4 K. A. Schonert-Reichl, V. Smith, A. Zaidman-Zait and C. Hertzman, 'Promoting Children's Prosocial Behaviors in School: Impact of the *Roots of Empathy* Program on the Social and Emotional Competence of School-Aged Children', *School Mental Health* 4 (2012), 1–21.

5 Ibid.

6 Dan Hughes talks about PACE in all his books and workshops, including: D. Hughes and K. Golding, *Creating Loving Attachments* (London: Jessica Kingsley, 2012).

7 Paul Greenhalgh, *Emotional Growth and Learning* (London: Routledge, 1994).

8 Dan Hughes' books and training courses are full of examples of affective/reflective dialogue, including Dan Hughes, *Attachment Focused family Therapy* (New York: Norton, 2007), 100–102.

9 D. W. Winnicott, *Playing and Reality* (Abingdon, UK: Routledge, 1971).

10 Adapted from Greenhalgh, *Emotional Growth and Learning*, 95.

11 H. Oram and S. Kitamura, *Angry Arthur* (London: Andersen Press, 1993).

12 D. W. Winnicott, 'Aspects of Juvenile Delinquency', in *The Child, the Family and the Outside World* (London: Penguin, 1964), 231.

13 Ruth Musgrave writes about taking conflict resolution including peer mediation into schools in 'Creative Conflict Resolution: A Workshop Approach in Schools', in *Taking Children Seriously*, eds Steve Decker, Sandy Kirby, Angela Greenwood and Dudley Moore (London: Cassell, 1999), 195–207.

14 Louise Bombèr helpfully reminds us that such vulnerable, damaged and acting out children are 'hurting' inside. That's *why* they 'act out' in her book *Inside I'm Hurting* (London: Worth, 2007).

Coping with change 12

Figure 29

'The importance of transition in children's lives' (nurture principle 6)

Supporting vulnerable children through beginnings, endings and transitions

The ability to bear new beginnings, transitions, endings and losses will relate to how much support children have had with previous changes and transitions. A new beginning, for example, can only be managed successfully if the ending preceding it was acknowledged, thought about and let go of enough. For children this involves the various and complex feelings being expressed and acknowledged not only by them, but by trusted adults in their presence. A parent or trusted adult will help the child to bear and process the experience by thinking and talking about it to and with them. All separation evokes some frustration, pain and possibly anger and anxiety, as Figure 29 vividly illustrates.

Change is inevitable in life, and difficult at times for everyone – including staff (see Case Study 31).

Case Study 31   A primary head plans a meeting with staff about impending staff losses

Three teachers are leaving in the summer and it's really rocking morale. We don't lose many staff, but those leaving are all young with no families and they have had an opportunity to go and teach in Africa, and of course we have encouraged them to go, but staff are also feeling abandoned, some even said, 'They shouldn't be going, we are such a strong team.' Some of them are anxious about getting the right staff to replace them and some are understandably envious. So we are going to have a meeting. After some team building (involving chocolate!) we will have a discussion around the losses and leavings and how it's making us feel, and then we will have an opportunity to talk in small groups led by experienced teachers, and we will see if anyone needs some individual time after that. We will be thinking both about our own feelings and about how best to talk to the children about the losses, and how to recognise when a particular child has the ending on their mind and needs a bit of time and understanding. Of course we will think about the more vulnerable children especially.

And then we've got SATs coming up for Year 2 and the end of the year already being on everyone's minds. So there's lots to discuss.

For all of us birth is the first big change, including the loss of the warmth, comfort and security of the womb, and ejection into the unknown, cold boundary-less world. Secure babies cope with it by clinging on to, feeding from and indeed still feeling part of the mother, who as a good-enough parent responds with loving availability and joy. Slowly, secure babies are eased into their new environment, experiencing and opening to the world and to their relatives in small doses and finding it good. The next transition is weaning, which can evoke resistance and anger in the baby and some anxiety in the mother. The success of this transition (as with all early transitions) depends partly on the capacity of the mother to tolerate the anxieties around it, both within herself and in her baby.

Parents typically talk to each other about these early transitions, and to their own mothers too. This is normal (and often delightful) processing.

Children vary in their experience of early loss and parental modulation, and in their corresponding abilities to learn, or not to learn, from experience. Acknowledging and talking through changes is both supportive and preventative. Changes always need some processing according to their severity, but if a change is well supported it can be an excellent opportunity for growth.

Any ending evokes feelings connected with earlier endings and the threat of losses in the future. It makes a huge difference whether supportive loved ones can themselves bear separation, loss, uncertainty and change or whether they are avoided. Perhaps the adults around prefer to avoid feelings, or maybe they are too caught up in their own fears and anxieties to have room to think.

> *H, the very first child I saw for educational psychotherapy, was a child whose mother had suddenly died, and whose family were understandably visibly shaken and couldn't talk about it. H coped by collecting a pencil case full of rubbers he would 'tout' around the classroom every day instead of working, in case anyone wanted to rub out or change a word they didn't like!*

Any panic and stress of significant adults around a change or loss is communicated to the child of course, and if it can't be talked about in a child-centred way, it will exacerbate the normal fears and anxieties in the child, especially if the child senses a big change is afoot that no one is talking about. The child may overhear anxious or even angry conversations, for example, and even develop doom-laden fantasies of being left behind. Such overheard conversations and worries that can't be talked about can have a profound and even a lasting effect, as John Bowlby, the 'father of attachment theory', wrote in an article entitled, 'On Knowing What You Are Not Supposed to Know and Feeling What You Are Not Supposed to Feel' in 1979[1] – the title speaks for itself! (Case Study 25 on p. 152 illustrates this.)

Repressing traumatic losses and transition anxieties almost inevitably leads to acting out, causing problems for the child and for others. My experience with 'H' above vividly illustrates this.

Some children, however, have not just had unprocessed endings and transitions, but *traumatic* losses linked to violence, tragedy, fear, breakdown or depression. For them, approaching or even feared endings evoke acute anxieties, which cannot be processed, and need to be avoided, denied, expelled and *acted out* in some way.

Attachment aspects

(See Chapter 6 for a detailed description of attachment categories and patterns.)

In attachment terms *avoidant* children, with mothers who are less sensitive, less available or even rejecting will tend to avoid facing endings. They will tend to avoid close relationships and talking things through, fearing the painful expectation of loss and rejection again. Of course, such children will still be affected by transitions, losses and endings, but the feelings will be buried. Depending on the particular separation or transition, and the level of their avoidance, they may just 'jolly' superficially on, or *appear* unaffected. However when anxieties are too intense, experiences of change and loss are likely to trigger acting out – *particularly involving the destructiveness of objects* (see Case Study 32).

Case Study 32   An avoidant child's acting out around change and fear of closeness

Ten-year-old C had a history of going in and out of care whenever either parent had had enough of him. In school he wouldn't look at you. He wouldn't engage. He could disrupt and destroy and make generalised abusive comments whenever he felt threatened. He was frequently absent around the end and the beginning of terms. He found all sorts of transitions difficult. It was clear that his anxieties increased at these times but he couldn't talk about it. Sometimes he would provoke a conflict towards the end of the day and walk out – unconsciously avoiding the ending. If he felt someone was trying to get too close by asking him a question or making a thoughtful comment to him, for example, he would start destroying the nearest object to hand until the person withdrew the conversation. I remember once towards the end of term trying to have a conversation with him in the dinner hall, and instead of answering a very simple question, he started to rip the displays off the wall. This was not the first time he had done that. It made me feel something of his acute anxiety – they were not my displays!

Children with *resistant/ambivalent* attachments have many difficulties with separations and transitions because their mothers have been unpredictable or variously available. Fear of separation from significant attachment figures is around all the time for them and insecurity is unbearable. Separating from activities, from particular things, from familiar places and from 'special' people is likely to evoke the fear of 'falling out of their minds' or of abandonment. They will tend to *act this out and project it into significant others*, sometimes causing staff (much like mum) to get overinvolved (enmeshed) and then to want a 'break' from them, which they could then experience as abandonment. Beginning tasks may be impossible too, as discussed in Chapter 6, until they have developed a sufficiently containing relationship with a member of staff who can enable them to feel held in mind anyway.

When their attachment anxieties are triggered they may cling (with school children this 'clinging' is with words) to make sure their significant adult (or mother) stays close, otherwise their fear of her absence (again) will leave them helpless and fearful and or impulsive and tense. The ends of lessons, days, weeks and especially ends of terms will evoke big anxieties. Likewise teacher absence, new beginnings when they know no one and loss of significant adults will be especially difficult. For others, coming to school and leaving Mum may be the difficulty, and may be Mum's difficulty too (as discussed earlier, see p. 99). They may both fear these losses and changes, and their irritating acting out may push people away, thereby exacerbating their pattern.

For the more *chaotic/disorganised children* the absence or unavailability of their mother will have been commonplace. They may have a history of anxious or sudden losses and relationships at home with little security. Their experience of (especially big) changes will probably include multiple traumatic losses with no thought, support or processing available, leading to unintegrated 'bits' inside, which can all too easily become triggered by any change or loss. Little transitions like the end of a spelling test or the end of a game may sometimes also trigger reactions, with no conscious thought of the underlying anxiety.

At school as they begin to develop trusted secure relationships their anxieties will ease, but when that trusted familiar teacher or TA is absent or unavailable, and particularly when their unexpected absence is replaced with a stranger, their anxieties will return. One of the features of chaotic/disorganised children is their tendency to 'panic and disrupt'. They can react anxiously and even panic or run when just the *thought* of a transition (feeling 'dropped' or hurt) threatens to enter their minds (see changes and transitions (for chaotic/disorganised children) p. 116).

Understanding this dynamic will help us think fruitfully together about supporting such children with their insecure times and their management of transitions, insecurities and endings. For these children teachers and TAs can become educational attachment figures who will benefit from the thinking in this chapter and the many practical suggestions beginning on p. 237.

Unconscious aspects

Some of the anxieties experienced by individuals in relation to endings relate to their *imagined reasons* for these losses or endings, although for vulnerable children these may be less of a thought than a hint that quickly gets acted out. These may be of a *persecutory* nature, for example that the teacher's absence is to punish them for their bad behaviour, or that she doesn't want to teach them because she dislikes and has had enough of them. Or they may be more of a *depressive* nature, for example they may feel guilty that they have tired the teacher out or made him ill.

In addition there may be feelings of rivalry, injustice and envy relating to fantasies about the nice time the teacher is having at home or in the new place, or with other people rather than them (in relation to her holiday or her move to a new place perhaps). Relating to this, when working with vulnerable children it is never helpful to talk with them about our own personal 'stuff'. As they quite naturally become attached to us they will become very interested in our lives, so it may be tempting to use that interest to engage them (especially when they are difficult to engage), but they will also be very easily provoked into envy and this could be acted out.

I remember once, when working in a special school for children with emotional and behavioural difficulties, observing again and again teachers becoming caught up in responding to children's questions about their families. It was almost a way to get them engaged and have an easy time with them, but I worried about it as the children were also clearly envious, which would be acted out at times too. It also got in the way of attending to the curriculum, and maintaining an appropriate teacher–pupil relationship with the children.

Children who have been in situations of domestic abuse can have particular anxieties and difficulties relating to endings, as their experiences of loss are likely to have been sudden and traumatic and linked with conflict and fear or associated with danger and hurt. Often they will not have been able to talk and work through these (and perhaps previous) losses, for fear of adding to the family burden or because their mother herself was unable to bear the pain. Guilt or shame (unbearable feelings that can't be thought about) that the traumatic losses or endings were largely their fault can be a complicating factor here, particularly for the sibling who carries the 'baddie' role in the family. Such children will find it especially difficult to be open to thinking through and processing endings, fearing such conversations might expose their 'badness'.

Adopted children, or children in long-term foster care who seem to have settled in well and be functioning securely can (even after several 'good' years), can have particular and sometimes severe and unexpected difficulties with endings and transitions, which can devastate the family (see p. 295). Especially a big change can sometimes trigger a regression to an early dysfunctional (but functional at the time) reaction pattern. Understanding this and reacting thoughtfully can help everyone to 'work through' it successfully.

For all children endings mean change – the loss of something familiar – as well as anxiety or even fear relating to what may happen next. Children in violent, neglectful or abusive homes may be very anxious about the forthcoming evening, weekend, holiday or even the coming lunchtime for good reasons. They may find 'home time' acutely difficult – like the child who would frequently run away from his mother at home time, provoking her to shout down the corridor after him (see Case Study 26 p.173). For such children, as an ending *approaches* the anxieties that they try to avoid thinking about and outwardly deny become harder to hold at bay and can be more easily triggered.

When working with troubled children then, potential or actual conflicts can become *heightened* just before the ending. It is helpful to be aware of that, and to find some way to support them and prevent escalation and the necessity of discipline. For example, children may burst out of the group, as if they didn't want to go through the painful experience of ending and leaving. Or a troubled child might misbehave or leave in a manner that makes the teacher feel 'dumped on'.

A teenager's sarcastic remark at the end of the lesson may seem to destroy all the good learning in the lesson, or an insult may project the anxiety and pain of the ending into someone else, leaving *them* hurting and angry.

Conflicting emotions at separation[2]

- Fear of loss of the holding/containing presence (their trusted teacher or TA) or the secure setting.
- Fear that things might fall apart.
- Feeling of helplessness and panic (especially chaotic/disorganised children).
- Feelings of abandonment.
- An uncomfortable feeling of neediness, which may need to be denied or reversed.
- Feelings of rivalry or envy.

These fears and feelings can lead to . . .

- Anger with the person for leaving, or for abandoning them for the holidays or for putting other things before *them* (e.g. for going on a course and abandoning them to a strange supply teacher).
- Destructive feelings, which need to be projected and acted out – against people they are close to (e.g. revenge, anger, hostility, refusal or on to objects in the case of avoidant children).

- Inability to hold on to the good learning or experience and grow through it.
- Inability to acknowledge any need or accept any help – because the special person will soon be gone.
- Denigration of the old relationship and idealisation of the new one. This is a form of splitting (see Chapter 4, p. 46). Understanding this personal denigration as defensive acting out can make it easier to bear and respond to (this can happen with staff too – see Case Study 41, p. 302).
- Denial of sadness or any feelings in relation to loss. 'Good riddance' may feel more manageable.

Endings are also opportunities for growth

Endings in school offer valuable opportunities in the present moment to make a difference. They evoke many opportunities for empathy, and for 'real' and manageable conversations, which in the long run enhance growth and self-awareness. In educational settings, the endings faced by teachers and pupils are too often under-recognised. It is possible to talk about missing and thinking about each other over the holiday, for example, and to experience that we might be or have been held in mind – in a way that's not possible with traumatic losses and separations. In my experience school staff often know this, but somehow and for good reasons they are frequently reluctant to bring up forthcoming endings because they fear children's behaviour will escalate – which indeed it probably will, especially when staff are still struggling to develop their empathic relationship-based skills. I am very aware that what I am recommending is not always easy. We know at some level that they can evoke powerful and even scary and painful emotions. Loss is particularly difficult. We can worry about bringing such powerful feelings into the open, and about how we might handle that. But we can also give them first-hand knowledge of the value of talking things though and perhaps experiences and memories to treasure forever.

Stories about loss can be a great resource (see Box 22, p. 126). *Amos and Boris* by William Steig[3] is a wonderful story of friendship and loss and never forgetting each other, which I have used many times to help children with losses. It touchingly sows the seed of still feeling held in mind, and having a precious memory inside.

Supporting each other

If we can *support each other* to manage such fears, we will develop confidence. If we can take opportunities to acknowledge the understandable feelings around school losses and transitions, and make a tentative link between the inevitable acting out behaviours from the hurting child and a forthcoming change or loss (or even a death), we are giving them a valuable gift (see sentence stem suggestions in Box 21, p. 236). If we don't avoid acknowledging difficult feelings when a child indicates an ending is on their minds, we are giving them a valuable experience – like a gift, even though it may be painful for us too – as a deputy head teacher shares in Case Study 35 on p. 241.

Supporting each other, staff training and supervision are all crucial in developing these very valuable relationship-based and empathic skills. That is part of the purpose of this book!

Prevention and 'catching difficulties early' is always best of course. So every time there is even a slight indication of escalation, or that a forthcoming ending or change is on a child's mind – even months before a big change – it is important for the adults to tentatively acknowledge this, and with lots of empathy, link the difficulty with the forthcoming ending and 'normalise' it, e.g. *'You and Sam seem to be having some problems today. I was just thinking, it may be hard to feel that Sam will still be here after you finish next term.'* In other words we need to acknowledge and normalise that changes are difficult for everyone and perhaps give them a bit of extra support or nurturing. Thus they will learn to share and work through their own emotions appropriately, and have something valuable to give to others, in terms of support and understanding, and realistic hope and trust.

School staff are in a unique position to give vulnerable children a (difficult but very valuable) opportunity to experience that one *can stay with difficult feelings*, and find ways to express them and work through them. Adults who have the capacity to face and acknowledge losses, separations and endings, and stay with children with understanding, resilience, knowledge and empathy, are giving them a great gift that they may not be able to experience in any other situation.

So noticing signs that an ending is on a child's mind or being acted out is the first thing (see Box 20).

Box 20   Some possible indicators of ending/transition anxieties

1. Wanting to leave early to avoid the ending.

2. Wanting to stay on longer, have extra time or manipulate boundaries.

3. Bravado, e.g. *'I don't need this time/you any more. I'm fine. Everything is fine.'*

4. Difficulty coming to the last (few) days (not wishing to face the ending).

5. Rivalry with other children (who may continue seeing the teacher or TA after they have gone). This may only be hinted at (e.g. other children using the room or equipment, who did that? etc.) or it may be expressed in the metaphor (e.g. lots of babies or children in stories, rivalry in stories, etc.).

6. Papering over the cracks, by saying nice things.

7. Jollying along, even at the end precipitating hysterical behaviours and laughter. (I remember a whole class getting hysterical for half an hour once on the last day of term!)

8. Finding it unusually hard to ask for or accept help when they are struggling. (*'I don't need you any more!'*) Avoidant children will tend to withdraw more.

9. Implying that the room/equipment/teacher are not good enough/useless, etc. Likewise, talk of things at home, things in the new situation or with the new person being better (like the teacher in Case Study 41, p. 302).

10. Being forgotten may come up in stories and play, or through direct comments.

11. Being rejected. This can show up in either direction. They can 'push' to be rejected through their acted-out behaviour, they can themselves reject (better to reject than to bear the pain of feeling rejected) or rejection can come up in stories or play.

12. Regression. It is quite normal for children to regress at home or at school when an ending is approaching. Regression may show in needy or infantile behaviours or in ways of talking, in the class, the playground or in the finishing of small-group sessions.

13. Doubts. Regressed behaviour can evoke uncertainty on the part of the child, the teacher, the SENCO or within parents, as to whether the right decision has been made to finish a particular intervention, for example (this does not necessarily mean that a wrong decision has been made).

(continued)

(continued)

14. Acting out the experience of breaking apart or chaos either within or outside the class, e.g. rubbishing or destroying their work (or other children's or even the teacher's work).

15. Anger with the teacher or the TA. Little hints of this can be picked up and empathised with, and linked in to your not being there for them any more soon. Sometimes anger and hurt can be acted out dangerously against a significant adult who is leaving soon. This will need lots of resilience, understanding and support for the adult as well as the child. It is best *not to change the support person or class at this ending time as that will exacerbate the long-term difficulties.*

16. Expressions of sadness. For some children sadness may be easier to acknowledge. The child may wonder (privately) whether the teacher or LSA may also be sad. It may be helpful to acknowledge that possibility, if an opportunity arises. For other children sadness can be unbearable, because sad and hurting feelings in relation to previous losses and endings have not been supported and empathised with. It can even feel like a black hole. Culturally, boys can often feel encouraged to hide their sadness and vulnerability and act tough.

17. Taking things from the room or the teacher could be a way of concretely taking what they will no longer be allowed to have.

18. Wanting to take special things home, and to give and receive presents can be a form of denial of the sadness, although it could also be an appropriate response to an acknowledgement of the loss of something good and to a genuine feeling of gratitude.

19. Unacknowledged feelings that their teacher or LSA will be having a much nicer time/having much better presents than them over the holiday can lead to acted out envy or rage.

I often notice that schools and staff start working on ends of terms, leavings, ends of years and moving schools much too late. The amount of time children need to really process losses varies of course with the scale of the change, and developmentally with the age of the child. Nursery children are very much 'in the present moment' so they need less time or they may think it is happening tomorrow(!) whereas for older children, a few weeks or even months (for changing schools or finishing counselling or therapy) will be needed. An enlightened infant teacher said their Year 2 classes had started thinking about going up to the juniors already – in April!

Christmas is a particularly difficult time for vulnerable children in this regard. Christmas holidays are not just difficult because of anxieties about the upcoming ending, but they can also be times of parties and concerts, etc. with lots of changes involving unpredictable timetabling, waiting around and Christmas activities, evoking excitement but also insecurity and anxiety for vulnerable children. Underlying the 'high hopes' and excitement are big fears and resentments that *'others will have a nicer time/nicer presents than me'*. I knew of an adoptive parent who requested her child not be involved in the festivities much, and also kept him away on occasions when she knew he wouldn't cope.

Uncertainty

With the advent of academies that can make their own decisions about which children they accept, an increasing problem is that while most children know the secondary school they will move on to in plenty of time, for the most vulnerable and disturbed children the decision is too often delayed or uncertain until very near (or even after) the end of term. This has often meant that staff avoid thinking about the ending and the move to the new school with such children, because no one knows where they are moving to. I feel very strongly that although you can't talk about the next school if it is unknown, you very much can talk about the forthcoming change, about leaving the familiar secure base and the loss of trusted staff and friends; and particularly of how it is so difficult *not knowing* where you are going or what is going to happen when you leave – especially when other children do know, as the inclusion manager describes in Case Study 33.

Case Study 33   The importance of talking through 'not knowing'

We have a little girl at the moment who has just been taken into foster care, and her mum is now pregnant. The little girl has started acting out at home and a bit in school, because she wants to know what is going to happen when the new baby is born. No one can tell her because no one knows (the baby might go straight into care but they haven't decided yet). So I explained to the social worker just how hard it was for her not to know, and how it was affecting her behaviour and the social worker said, 'Well, we can't tell her anything because we don't know yet', and I explained that although we might not be able to tell her what will happen, we can acknowledge with her just how hard it is not to know and to keep wondering and thinking about it. The social worker found it very hard to see how it would help, and I tried to explain that through such conversations she would feel 'held' and supported in her anxiety. The foster carer found it very helpful and she said she would try it.

Loss of significant adults

It is important to remember that a child's relationship with a teacher or TA can be very significant, and losing it may be very painful for (and overtly denied by) the child. Acting out in all sorts of ways (including dangerous ways) can be a disturbed child's reaction to this painful loss. Staff will need lots of support in these situations, and may need some time out, but should not be removed. If such acting out is not understood in context it can sometimes tragically lead to the school suddenly transferring the child to a new support worker, just when they need the relationship to survive and help them process the ending.

A well-worked-through ending involves processing the experience of loss and mourning. Mental states associated with mourning a loss or an ending (and a death) include:

- *shock* – a state where we can't think or feel;
- *disbelief*;
- *denial*;
- *anger* for being abandoned to face dangers alone, or at teachers probably preferring to be with other 'nicer' children;
- *guilt* for what should have been done differently, for not doing enough, for wasting time or being too difficult or too exhausting – these may be unconscious of course and 'leak out' in behaviours;
- *despair* arising out of guilt, that it may now be too late to make reparation;
- *grief* at losing someone or something good, forever;
- *sadness* that something good is coming to an end;
- *yearning* for what was lost – sometimes the pain is just too much and it feels like things have fallen apart – like B's picture in Figure 30 vividly communicates.

Figure 30

Whether we can mourn current losses and endings successfully depends to a great extent on the help and support we have been given in the past to bear the painful feelings surrounding previous losses.

All children benefit from support and understanding when major changes and losses occur, but whereas secure children can use *'ego-supportive' (reassuring) responses* (see pp. 69–70). Based on talking through conscious feelings and experiences, very damaged and insecure children are often completely out of touch with and defended against their more vulnerable and subtle feelings and so talking things through precipitates avoidant or resistant reactions. Such children need *emotional containment* or *emotional holding* of their anxieties by attuned and trusted adults. This means they need to experience adults bearing their anxieties, taking them seriously and thinking about them in small doses and with empathy (see Chapter 5).

The problem is that vulnerable children may well have learned from experience that painful feelings need to be avoided or expelled. It is only through first-hand experience of a trusted adult talking and empathising with them about endings, transitions and losses that they will discover that they can be acknowledged and survived, they can be talked about and even grown through. It may take time, and many little experiences of thoughtful, timely and empathic support, but it is a lifelong gift to children to enable them to shift these past unhelpfully learned patterns.

For successful 'mourning' or processing of a loss or an ending vulnerable children need a supportive, understanding trusted adult who can:

- understand that as endings approach and are beginning to be anticipated they can evoke anxieties and the need for defensive reactions, so that the sadness and inner pain is not felt;
- understand that such anxieties are acted out, *precisely because* the endings and transitions and the underlying feelings they might evoke cannot be contemplated and talked through – the acting out will be an unconscious way of managing the unbearable anxieties evoked when losses or changes are around;
- perceive, tolerate and understand signs of ending anxieties (see Box 20), and of mourning and some children's inability to process these;
- have the capacity to stay with uncomfortable feelings and empathise, and not avoid;
- offer emotional containment and take opportunities to ease anxieties by talking things through as the child indicates they are open to it.

In this way behaviours that may be *indicators* of ending anxieties (see Box 20 above) can be 'picked up' for thinking about by significant adults, when an ending is either planned or feared.

Talking about little endings is of course much more manageable, and helpful too, e.g.:

> *I can sense some wobbly feelings bubbling around at the minute. It's hard to manage when we haven't got much longer I know, especially when we only have ten more minutes till home time, but we do have to stop in ten minutes. Shall I set the sand timer so we can see when five minutes is up?*

It is easiest when *slightly observable emotions* surface and can be briefly acknowledged because children are not too aroused and they can think and actually feel the connection. Even if the child doesn't respond much, they will experience some relief, begin to grow in their ability to process losses and learn from experience and to value and even treasure past relationships.

Emotional containment processes are helpful at times of approaching change, loss and ending

1. The process is to notice the behaviour or indicator, put it into child-friendly non-judgemental words and then make a possible link between the behaviour and the ending or transition.
2. Noticing and empathising with possible feelings *when they are first indicated* can be particularly helpful and preventative, as discussed above, as well as educational for the child, e.g.

    > *I can see you becoming a little bit fidgety. We are going to finish this soon aren't we, and then we will move on to . . . changes can often be difficult, especially when we are not sure about the next thing. I will go with you to . . .*

3. Timing is key. Tune into when the child indicates an ending is on their mind, and sense what they can take before commenting.
4. Brief comments may be all they can bear, or all they can take in at the moment. Sometimes brief, thoughtful talk *at the same time as* concrete containing action can enable thinking to be accepted 'in small doses', e.g. passing a child a calming activity or task while commenting empathically that their feelings are probably 'bubbling up' as the end of the session approaches.
5. Unintegrated children (see pp. 20 and 224) may not yet be ready for any thinking at all. Concrete containing action like giving them a visual timetable to take home, or a job to do at the end of a lesson, may be all you can offer for the moment (see Case Study 34).

Case Study 34   An example of containing action from one-to-one therapy

Frequently at stressful times with L (e.g. towards the end of term) my 'thinking' was greeted with 'you're wasting time!' On reflection I realised that L experienced me as containing only when I was able to shift the thinking into concrete responsive action.

For example, L made a prison out of a box, and when she was playing with it, it got broken. She was distraught. I empathised with its falling apart and then helped her with the rebuilding – leading to a story and a meaningful symbol, which calmed her down.

The following week she started some dangerous destructive throwing, which I shifted into a safe throwing game that I engaged with, incorporating the ball's feelings and treatment (of being dropped) in a dramatic and jokey way – leading to again relief and a calming of the destructive feelings.

6. Enabling children to experience that their hurting and angry feelings are understandable, can ease unnecessary guilt. For example, that their anger may have been partly triggered by the teacher or TA who was absent yesterday.

7. Be aware that tolerance of frustration and resilience can decline when endings are beginning to be anticipated. As mentioned above it is easier to intervene and have empathy and thinking accepted at the point of the *first hints* or indications of *frustration*, rather than wait until the angry reaction sets in.

8. Acknowledging that relationships and memories can continue to be important and to nourish after they finish, facilitates emotional growth (see Box 21).

Box 21 Some ways of responding to ending/transition anxieties

1. *I noticed that you put some Lego in your pocket. I'm sure you know that you can't take it home, although I do understand that it must be hard for you to feel that you won't be able to play with it for much longer, as we only have a week left in Year 3.*

2. *I'm just thinking. We only have . . . left. I guess that must be on your mind too?*

3. *I can see you're finding it a bit difficult . . . I was wondering . . .*

4. *It's never easy when we have to finish . . .*

5. *I can imagine it may be hard to let me help you with that, when we both know I won't be there to help you after . . .*

6. *It's so sad when we have to say goodbye. But sometimes it can be hard to feel sad.*

7. *I can sense some cross feelings bubbling around today. I can understand you may be feeling quite cross that I won't be around for you next term when you . . .*

8. *Lots of things dropping today! Maybe it feels a bit like I might be dropping you when . . .*

9. *It's so hard to think I/we won't be . . . I'll never forget you though. I will always remember . . .*

10. *Wow, thank you. I'll keep it on the wall in my office. I shall think of you every time I look at it.*

Some practical suggestions in relation to holidays, ends of terms/years and leavings

1. Make any decision relating to ending a special intervention well in advance.
2. Use a visual calendar to draw children's attention to the number of days or weeks till an ending. The calendar should be long enough to show the date of the next return after the holiday, and a few days (at least) into the coming term (e.g. from the half-term before the break to after the beginning of the next term) (see Figure 31).
3. At the same time as acknowledging the coming ending it can be helpful to remind children of when we may see them again in various situations – next term for example.
4. Discuss the ending, or the coming break with the children well in advance, when it feels right, and *revisit this discussion regularly* when opportunities arise. Acknowledge to the child that the ending might be a difficult time because it may make them feel sad, angry or anxious, or even that things aren't fair – and that's normal.

Calendar Autumn 2010

September	Mon	Tues	Wed	Thurs	Fri	Sat	Sun
	20	21	22	23	24	25	26
	27	28	29	30			

October	Mon	Tues	Wed	Thurs	Fri	Sat	Sun
					1	2	3
Birthday	4	5	6	7	8	9	10
	(11)	12	13	14	15	16	17
	18	19	20	21	22	23	24
Half term	25	26	27	28	29	30	31

November	Mon	Tues	Wed	Thurs	Fri	Sat	Sun
	1	2	3	4	5	6	7
	8	9	10	11	12	13	14
	15	16	17	18	19	20	21
	22	23	24	25	26	27	28
	29	30					

December	Mon	Tues	Wed	Thurs	Fri	Sat	Sun
			1	2	3	4	5
Party!	6	7	8	9	10	11	12
last day	13	14	15	16	17	18	19
Holiday →	20	21	22	23	24	25	26
	27	28	29	30	31		

January	Mon	Tues	Wed	Thurs	Fri	Sat	Sun
						1	2
	3	4	5	6	7	8	9

Figure 31

5. Take opportunities to remind children of the approaching ending, bearing in mind both the painful and the sad aspects, and the hope and the positive aspects of moving on at the same time. Notice also the length of the coming break on the calendar and the date of return.
6. Some particularly vulnerable children may need previously agreed arrangements (mentoring time, etc.) to support them in managing and understanding their difficult feelings around endings.
7. Do not expect children to talk through outbursts when they are emotionally 'high'.
8. Take opportunities to express your own sadness at the end of the year with a class and remind them that you will still think of them, see them around and be pleased to have visits from them, if appropriate.
9. Holidays generally can arouse conflicting feelings in vulnerable children, especially Christmas (see above).
10. Apparently secure adoptive and long-term foster families may need particular awareness and alertness to signs of regression around big transitions. Conversations with

school staff and parents around (the possibility of) unexpected triggered behaviours may be helpful and important. Encouraging them to seek support and not to take any such regressions personally may also be important for both teachers and parents.

11. Maintain firm boundaries with understanding when a child tries to manipulate, but give extra time for talking the ending anxieties through if necessary (at another time).

12. Communicate with the new teacher in front of the child(ren), letting them know you have a good relationship with her and that you will be interested to know how they are getting on next term.

13. Make a time to talk to liaison workers/heads of year/teachers/TAs/parents, etc. well before a significant ending, about children's possible acting-out behaviours. This can facilitate more understanding of such behaviours and of how ending anxieties can start surprisingly early. Such discussions can also enable new staff to better understand and manage endings in good time, including how to respond to any 'ending regressions' when they notice them. It will also support new staff in catching any escalations early.

14. When a child is leaving a class or group, it is good for them, *and for those left behind*, if the ending can be *marked* in various ways. Those left behind will experience that the same would be done for them if they were leaving.

15. Review the past year's highlights and the hopes for next year.

16. Ways of marking an ending might include: a final drawing; writing to each other, to the new school or teacher, to the friends they are leaving, etc.; writing letters or cards; making cakes or sweets; a memory/poem board or photo album – photos of those who have left in an album or on a memory board can enable those leaving to know that they will be remembered too.

17. Circle time hopes and fears around next year.

18. At the end of the year, or when special groups are ending, a circle-time sharing session on sadness, memories and loss can be very helpful, including acknowledgement of the more negative feelings that can be around.

19. Reading special books to children can be a way of acknowledging difficult feelings through the story.

20. Use of creative work to express anxieties in the metaphor, can be helpful, for example:

    - writing stories, poems and plays or making a shared book;
    - drawing and art work;
    - putting a puppet or big soft toy in the middle of the circle and letting the children speak to him (or for him) about the ending can be engaging for little ones – modelling talking about the negative feelings *yourself* to the soft toy can indicate that such feelings, including giving thanks, are OK to acknowledge;
    - paper conversations (child-centred speech-bubble conversations that a significant adult writes) with a child around loss, ending or change – this could be prompted through reading a story together, like those in Box 22.

Box 22   Some books about loss, endings and bereavement[4]

Charlotte Zolotow, *Wish You Were Here* (London: BBC Longman, 1990)

> The book includes 'Janey' and 'My Grandson Lew', two stories of love, loss and remembering.

William Steig, *Amos and Boris* (London: Picture Puffin, 1997)

> The most evocative story of loss and ending I have ever read. A whale and a mouse become close friends in difficult circumstances. The description of their sadness and loss at the inevitable parting will mirror many children's feelings at such times.

Gabrielle Vincent, *Ernest and Celestine* (London: Picture Lion, 1983)

> Celestine's beloved soft toy Gideon is lost, causing sleepless nights and grief. Her father Ernest tries to make a substitute.

Shirley Hughes, *Dogger* (London: Picture Lions, 1979)

> The story of the loss and finding of a much beloved soft toy.

Susan Varley, *Badger's Parting Gifts* (London: Anderson Press, 2013)

> Much loved friend Badger reaches the end of his life. All the animals are very sad. Remembering his special gifts to each one helps to ease the sad feelings.

Hans Wilhelm, *I'll Always Love You*   (London: Hodder, 1987)

> The story of the love of a little boy for his dog. How the sadness of the dog's growing old and death is eased by the boy remembering that he always told his dog every night, 'I'll always love you.'

Valerie Flournoy, *The Patchwork Quilt* (London: Penguin Books, 1987)

> A grandmother shares with a little girl the memories evoked by the patches on a much loved patchwork quilt.

John Burningham, *Granpa* (London: Picture Puffin, 1984)

> The sensitive story of the death of Granpa.

Bob Graham, *Pete and Roland* (London: Picture Lions, 1982)

> A story of friendship and loss.

(continued)

(continued)

L. Komaiko and L. Cornell, *Annie Banannie* (London: Harper Collins, 1988)

> A story of friendship, loss and endings.

Doris Stickney, *Waterbugs and Dragonflies* (London: Continuum, 2004)

> A delightfully simple way of thinking about death with children through the change waterbugs experience when they leave their underwater world and mysteriously become transformed into beautiful dragonflies in a whole new world of air and lightness, which the little waterbugs in their water world just can't appreciate or know about!

Margot Sunderland, *The Frog Who Longed for the Moon to Smile* (London: Speechmark, 2014)

> Frog was totally preoccupied with his yearning for the moon's smile. He was closed to everything else. Slowly his friends managed to help him face reality and open to other joys and friendship.

Margot Sunderland, *The Day the Sea Went Out and Never Came Back* (London: Speechmark, 2003)

> Eric the sand dragon is distraught when his beloved sea suddenly disappears forever. He goes 'down and down', wasting away with yearning and pain. He just can't think of anything else. A friendly, understanding dog brings him a drink, which he spills, and miraculously a flower grows. So begins the slow transformation into memory and having something precious to give.

Josephine Croser, *Letters to Leah* (Flinders Park, Australia: Era Publications, 1993)

> The story of Tessa, who struggles to adjust to the loss of her best friend through writing touching and engaging letters to her. A very sensitive book that leads gently into discovering what the letters are about.

After reading *Letters to Leah* to a class whose teacher, Mr S, had tragically died after an illness, and a spontaneous sharing time about him, I gave the children 20 minutes to respond in any way they chose to the sad news. Some of them just sat quietly, some drew or painted. Others chose to write letters to him, like S (Figure 32). G wrote a story about an elephant who had come to the end of his life (Figure 33). P asked if he could write about his grandad who had recently died (Figure 34).

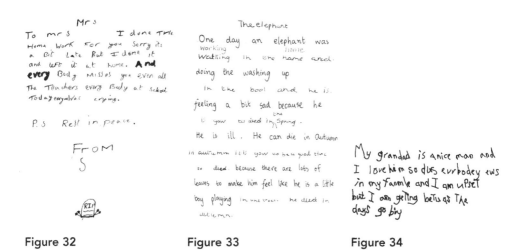

Figure 32   Figure 33   Figure 34

Coping with death and bereavement in school

Stories like those in Box 22 can be very helpful at such times, as can thoughtful circle-time sharing sessions when a death is 'around' (see p. 184). But essentially it is the 'being there beside them' that helps most, not avoiding talking things through when opportunities arise and supporting them when unbearable sadness is around. Case Study 35 illustrates how being supported to stay with the pain and hurt can make all the difference – to the school staff as well as the child.

Case Study 35   A deputy head talks sensitively with staff about a child whose mum is dying

We have a little 6-year-old girl called E in school. Her mum is dying. They have a great support network at home, which is good. They are supported by the church and the whole family talk about it. E is the second eldest and she finds it really difficult when her mum goes into hospital. They don't know if she will be coming out. They know she is dying. We have all talked about it because it's so much part of their life that when she goes into hospital she might not come out.

E has emotional outbursts. Sometimes she closes up, sometimes she will have a little explosion and sometimes she will get very angry with Mrs H, the TA in the classroom, and say that she hates her, which is of course very difficult for Mrs H. Sometimes it builds up to a point where Mrs H thinks, 'What am I doing wrong – because whatever I do is wrong.'

I spent quite a lot of time working with Mrs H (and with Mrs L, the teacher), helping her to understand that E is not angry with her. She is actually angry with her mum. She really loves her mum, and of course she doesn't want her mum to go, to die and to leave her. We think about how in fact this behaviour towards Mrs H is actually evidence that E is really close to her, because she feels safe to take it out on her. Last year, because of E's very understandable difficulty with endings, we kept Mrs H with her when she went into Year 2. That was really difficult for Mrs H and she needed a lot of support to manage, which we gave her. E wasn't difficult every day, just occasionally – around the end of term, half-term and the end of the year mainly – and when her mum was taken into hospital. So on those occasions the teacher Mrs L and Mrs H would often come over for a bit of time and support to talk things through, even though they knew why it was happening, because we needed Mrs H to be strong and Mrs L needed Mrs H to be strong too, to bear all the painful, worried and hurting feelings that E was 'putting into' her. Mrs L just needed us to say, 'Mrs H, actually you are doing a really good job.' They were both doing a really good job. We all recognised how difficult it must be for all of them, and how emotionally draining it must be, and of course these difficulties have helped us to know just how difficult and painful it is for little E, because she is letting us all know how difficult it is for her when mummy goes into hospital yet again.

We also knew that Mrs H needed to offload sometimes, so that she could go home and be with her family without carrying the pain around over the weekend.

Next year E is going up into the juniors. So she is going to lose Mrs H too at the end of the year – in six months when she goes into the juniors – so we mention that too sometimes – in an understanding way of course. Life is not easy sometimes. But E is developing hidden strengths.

Mrs L and Mrs H don't need supervisory support all the time these days. They have got to the point when they can support each other, which is good.

There are many excellent books about coping with bereavement in schools and I have decided, because of space limitations, not to include very much on this subject, although I know bereavement, especially in traumatic circumstances is the worst loss of all. It has of course been touched on in the Case Study 35 above and the story of C in Case Study 27 (p. 176), who developed puzzling maths difficulties in response to her friends sudden death, and in the very touching story of 5-year-old Danielle who developed leukaemia and tragically died while in Kate Ashby's class (see p. 185) – such a moving and inspiring story of how she, the children in class, the helpers and Danielle's mum too, coped and 'grew' through the terrible pain and loss of Danielle's decline. I really recommend her chapter in *Taking Children Seriously* to infant schools and staff coping with dying children in school.[5]

I was also involved in a rapid-response initiative in my local authority when a teenage driver accidentally swerved and drove into a crowd of adolescents on the pavement, killing one and injuring several more. The team of local counsellors, psychotherapists and psychologists was set up within hours to offer counselling and support to children, schools, staff on an as-needed and request basis, addressing both the loss and grief and the trauma. Hopefully many councils will have such strategies in place these days.

Coping with staff absences

For secure children, class teacher and TA absences do not often present a problem. They will probably miss their familiar teacher and way of doing things, but there will be no complicating factors. They will know their teacher will come back as soon as she can, that she will remember them anyway and be pleased to see them when she returns. They may even like a change.

But very vulnerable children can be profoundly affected by the absence of their teacher and their secure base. Without the familiar secure base that they have come to trust to keep them secure and calm, children's past anxieties and patterns can rise up and easily become overwhelming. Overwhelming feelings need to be got rid of, and are likely to be acted out hurtfully at the first opportunity.

Even if they feel ambivalent about their regular teacher, their behaviour when she is away will deteriorate and affect both their peers and staff, causing anxieties all round. They may act out their guilty fantasy that they upset her and have driven her away or made her ill. They may feel painfully abandoned and forgotten and act out their fury. Even an excellent supply teacher can feel like an unpredictable stranger to some children, and any trust they had with their familiar teacher will have gone and been replaced by their default fear, defensiveness and reactivity.

In school, such anxieties can also *get right into staff*, particularly if the absence is unexpected, inadequately prepared for and no one knows what was planned for the class. Staff may have to think on their feet, as well as cope with the children's acted-out insecurities. Where there are just one or two vulnerable reactive children in a class, schools and staff will probably be able to cope OK with a few adjustments, but in units and schools for the more disturbed and needy children, and in mainstream schools with a higher proportion of such children, staff absences can be quite a problem. A vicious cycle of a teacher becoming stressed and repeatedly sick puts pressure on everyone. Hypersensitive children quickly pick up on any insecure vibes, and a negative feedback loop can ensue, which can increase anxieties and exacerbate acting out. In extreme cases classes can lose their secure base. Staff left behind and a succession of supply teachers may feel helpless and overwhelmed, struggling to know what to do, even becoming 'pushed' into 'knee-jerk' reactions themselves, which they later regret (see Case Study 12, p. 50). On these occasions it is particularly important for staff to help and support each other. Such overwhelming feelings can be complicated by a mixture of resentment for the extra stress and responsibility they are having to carry, along with guilt that they shouldn't be feeling like this.

Insecurity and anxiety of course, are also very 'catching'. In extreme cases and settings a whole class can be triggered within minutes. Developing some understanding of these dynamics, and having some knowledge of ways to alleviate them, can help staff maintain the capacity to think and respond helpfully, and maintain the secure base when absences occur.

All the ways of understanding, containing and managing outlined above will be helpful, but there may be other preventative, structural and preparatory measures that can make a real difference to the more unintegrated children. Some children and some units may be better off not being exposed to strangers or even excellent supply teachers. They may be better placed with those they know, even if it is inconvenient.

When I was working at the local pupil referral unit – a small unit for the least resilient and most damaged children in the area – we had a staff training day on coping with absence, because we knew we needed to think together about managing these very precarious times. We needed to develop the skills and supportive structures necessary both to manage the children, and to develop our own skills in this area. As a result of our discussions we decided reluctantly to manage without supply teachers – because even though it was a considerable strain on staff, it avoided overwhelming anxieties and outbursts.

Below are the notes I used and that we discussed at the training session.

Ways to prepare for and cope more specifically with staff absences in a pupil referral unit

1. Make thoughtful and preparative procedures for staff absence. These may relate to all classes, or be specific to a particular class, child or staff team.
2. If possible think about any changes or absences well in advance, and talk them through thoughtfully with the children.
3. The current capacity of individual children may need to be considered, so that appropriate arrangements can be made for them during teacher absences.
4. Prevention is better than crisis. Some particularly vulnerable pupils may be better off being placed with a previous trusted teacher or TA during a difficult absence.
5. Link 'bad' behaviour around *approaching* absences to the *forthcoming* absence with empathy, while asserting the expectation. This may need to happen many times.

   > *It seems hard to concentrate today. Perhaps you're thinking that tomorrow is Mrs K's college day. I know it's always hard for everyone when she's not here. She always likes to see what we've done on Thursdays though doesn't she?*

6. Display and frequently refer to a visual calendar and timetable for the day.
7. It is helpful for teachers to talk through their expectations during their absence with the class before they go, and leave planning and materials ready if they can.
8. When their familiar teacher is away, unstructured times and spaces and unusual happenings also evoke more insecurity than usual and trigger adrenalin.
9. Be aware of the child's need to make contact with a 'secure base' when (even slight) anxieties arise. Consider what, where or who that secure base might be.
10. Letters and cards (and even phone calls) to a struggling child from a teacher who is absent or ill for longer, or vice versa, communicate being held in mind.
11. Remember the calming usefulness of simple mechanical and repetitive activities at (potentially) anxious times (see calm box – Box 7, p. 95).

Ways to support staff who are left to cope during absences

1. Staff should support each other, in either a planned or spontaneous way.
2. Encourage and normalise staff asking for help. Acknowledging difficulties and asking for help is a sign of maturity.
3. Regular appreciative 'thank yous' from senior management go a long way to alleviating stress, including appreciation for the extra work and pressure absences sometimes involve. Staff (particularly senior staff) should put effort into praising and appreciating each other.

4. Staff talking thoughtfully together in front of children communicates care, and the helpfulness of talking things through.
5. Staff who take over, or remain and cope when a colleague is absent, need to practice:

   (a) attunement;
   (b) empathy;
   (c) resilience – bear being disliked/hated;
   (d) setting clear boundaries with empathy;
   (e) managing and talking about children's feelings in relation to the absent teacher;
   (f) staying with the child's current pain and not needing to *prematurely* reassure/make it better.

6. It may be helpful to involve the whole class or group in thinking about ways of supporting each other during the absence.
7. Heads and senior management may need to think carefully about which staff they place very vulnerable children with during absences.
8. Debrief any difficult incidents and experiences together, learning from experiences.
9. In-service training, policies and staff discussion on coping with absences in the unit or school, or with particular children, will be helpful and important in such units and schools.
10. Senior management helping to support classes themselves will be much appreciated.

Notes

1 John Bowlby, 'On Knowing What You Are Not Supposed to Know and Feeling What You Are Not Supposed to Feel', *Canadian Journal of Psychiatry* 24, no. 5 (1979), 403–408.
2 I am grateful to Isca Saltzberger-Wittenberg here whose chapter on endings in *The Emotional Experience of Learning and Teaching* by Gianna Henry, Elsie Osborne and Isca Salzberger-Wittenberg (London: Karnac Books, 1983), influenced my thinking many years ago.
3 William Steig, *Amos and Boris* (London: Puffin Books, 1977).
4 Extracted from my own list of 'Books That Touch on Emotional Issues Children Might Identify With', which can be found in the eResources for the book at www.routledge.com/9780367025465.
5 Kate Ashby, 'Danielle: A Class Teacher's Account of Circle Time and Beyond', in *Taking Children Seriously*, eds Steve Decker, Sandy Kirby, Angela Greenwood and Dudley Moore (London: Cassell, 1999), 184–191.

Working through the metaphor 13

Figure 35

The therapeutic value of play, drama, creative work and stories

Artists, as well as children, allow images to come through into consciousness and 'work their magic', rendering the unthought or unthinkable thinkable, subtly shifting our perception perhaps, while both pleasing and disturbing us. Dreams and deep creative work, especially when taken seriously and engaged with, can lead to emotional growth for all of us. As Matthew Fox says:

> We need to ride our images as one would ride a giant eagle, soaring up and down wherever they may take us . . . Who knows what lies behind and beyond our images, until we trust them enough to ride them fully, even into the darkness and into the depths like a seed in the soil. Perhaps we will never know the gift that our images are until we ride them through to the other side, and only from that perspective will we see them for the first time.[1]

Through 'playing out' conflicts and wars, playing and drawing monsters, reading, writing and even 'watching' scary stories, and through all sorts of pretend play in a secure setting and relationship, children engage with difficult, new and puzzling experiences and feelings. Play activities can be symbolic too, like hiding and finding, dropping things and constructional toys and games – helping children to process anxieties and fears that they aren't even aware of.

It is natural for young children to amuse and express themselves through play, not only because they may not yet have the words to talk about and process their feelings and experiences, but because play is vivid, engaging and fun. Play doesn't require words. Sometimes even if the words are there, it may be unbearable to speak or think directly. Some experiences may have *needed to be buried* and therefore cannot be talked about, because they are not consciously known.

Play and creative expression naturally accesses this deeper level of consciousness. Children can become vividly involved in a story *as if it were real*, without linking it in any way with themselves. Play can enable children to find meaning in painful, puzzling and difficult situations, although typically they will need to play through painful and traumatic experiences over and over again to 'detoxify' them.

Through play children can express their emerging concerns to a trusted attentive adult without actually talking about them. This is the reason for play therapy, child psychotherapy, art psychotherapy and educational psychotherapy, which work through the metaphor, using play, art and stories (as well as the relationship).

As painful experiences are repeatedly played and talked through, they slowly become less toxic and no longer need to be acted (or played) out.

> *I vividly remember P, a 7-year-old slow learner I worked with who had been sexually abused and who was obsessed with monsters. Every book we read together, every picture and every 'story' he wrote with me was about dangerous hurtful monsters. Luckily I understood the symbolism and let him continue, until about nine months later he one day wrote a story about a helicopter! I was amazed!*

But creativity, art, play, drama and story-writing opportunities are available for everyone in school, and this is what the chapter will address.

Concerns

I confess that I felt very ambivalent about even writing this chapter, because although I believe fervently in the healing power of play, creativity and stories, I am sadly aware that in recent times play is being ever more squeezed out of the school curriculum. I have even heard of Year 1 classes where there are no toys, and the children are concentrating on teacher-led instruction and teaching the whole time. I am also aware that teachers' time can be increasingly taken up with preparing PowerPoint presentations, laminating learning outcomes and filling in data sheets, etc. So preparing creative resources and opening to and facilitating children's creativity could easily feel like just another burden. It can be lots of fun though – as I remember vividly from my teaching days!

Also in our more top-down, busy, competitive and digital culture, the too early conditioning of children on to electronic devices and arranged activities can also prevent them from maintaining their spontaneity, play skills and their imagination at home. Sadly, in our digital culture there is an increasing dearth of free, child-centred play opportunities for older children.

One could argue of course that play and creativity are needed more than ever today, in this time of increasing stress and disintegration in families and our increasingly technologically addicted world. Both in schools and in families our mass media culture fosters a more addictive, controlled and less imaginative way of relating to objects and to each other.

In addition, in chaotic or preoccupied families the frequent lack of a caring attentive adult can interfere with the secure base children need to *develop the capacity* to play, inhibiting their natural spontaneity, creativity and concentration, and their natural ability to play and process their experiences first hand.

But as the reader will see, I really believe in the value of play and creativity, not just because it can be therapeutic, but because it opens children up to their authenticity, their natural spontaneity and the inner life force that bears such fruit in our culture and civilisation, and that makes life worth living.

Imaginative and creative free play is a health-giving, emotional resource. It is fun too. Older children can derive the same therapeutic benefits and fun from creativity, art, drama and story writing.

Stages and types of play

Attachment-based play

The earliest play is the interrelating between mother and baby using eye contact, touch, rhythm and song, movement, rhymes and laughter – developing, for example, into peep-bo and hiding games – sometimes called *sensory and mirroring play*. A good experience of attachment-based play fosters secure attachment and bonding. It also activates the play and care circuits in the brain, releasing life-enhancing hormones like opiates and oxytocin (see Chapter 2, p. #).

Adoption agencies encourage their new adoptive parents to do this type of play with their children as it encourages and builds attachment. This is usually in the form of 'Theraplay',[2] which is attachment-based play for older children. 'Theraplay' is a delightful and fun way to build the bonds of attachment for children who haven't had this essential foundational beginning. I completed my 'Theraplay' training at PAC UK, one of our premier adoption agencies, and have used it in various settings. Adoption expert Dan Hughes also recommends it in his lectures and books, for example *Building the Bonds of Attachment*[3] (which is extremely accessible for foster and adoptive parents). I would recommend both Dan's book and the 'Theraplay' training to school staff who work closely with such parents.

Play 'in the space between'

As the baby begins to feel secure and contained within the mother's mind he will begin to explore the world around him (initially this is the mother's body), slowly coming to appreciate 'what is me and what is not me'.[4] This could be thought of as transitional play, when babies start to make use of objects to bridge the gap between themselves and their mothers. Thus they *begin* to manage separation and experience themselves as separate people. A 'transitional object' like a blanket or a teddy can be experienced sometimes as a separate, familiar and comforting object, and sometimes it is almost *as if it is* the absent mother comforting them. Later transitional objects can be very helpful to comfort and reassure an anxious child who is finding separation and absence difficult in school.

Exploratory play

Curiosity develops out of a good-enough mother–child relationship – out of an infant's or a child's experience of good-enough attunement and emotional containment (Bion – see Chapter 5). When a mother or trusted adult can provide a secure base for the child, so the child will naturally begin to explore. Every so often (or if something happens to make him a little anxious) he will need to 'touch base' to restore his security and enable him to be free to explore again. Exploring and trying things out is how we learn and discover things. Margot Sunderland describes how a child's 'seeking system' in the brain is *activated by a stimulating and enriching environment*[5] – something a good nursery teacher knows so well. This does not just mean physical toys and fascinating objects, but imaginative ideas and thoughtful and vital responses from significant adults.

Symbolic play

Tina Bruce suggests that children are born 'symbol users'.[6] By the end of the first year babies typically begin unconsciously to 'play' in symbolic (as well as sensory) ways. So, for example, putting things into holes, pulling things out, bringing things together and dropping things, can have deep symbolic significance. Later symbolic play becomes very important and together with metaphorical play and stories (often in the presence of a thoughtful, attentive and trusted adult), it forms the basis for growth, adjustment and child therapy (when needed).

Physical interactive play

Physical interactive play enhances the development of the higher rational brain, including the capacity to regulate emotions (e.g. 'Activate in the Classroom', see p. 150). Boisterous play can transport children into states of joy. The 'tickle monster' was very popular in the PRU Nurture Base! Physical challenges and practice lead to mastery and enhanced self-esteem. (Safe-enough) risk taking is important for emotional growth and confidence. One study found that children deprived of playtime at school developed ADHD symptoms![7] Box 17 on p. 207 includes self-regulation exercises.

Some useful theoretical frameworks for understanding play

Active imagination[8]

Jung placed great importance on the power of the imagination to transform and heal. He talked of the need we all have to integrate our 'shadow parts'.[9] Active purposeful creation is a means by which the conscious mind can tap into the unconscious. Through imaginative work, unconscious material is brought to the surface – giving expression to the powerful images that can come into consciousness in safe, containing situations. Opportunities to play and create metaphors in this way can open up the channels between the conscious and the unconscious, allowing creativity, play and imagination to begin to transform and heal. Through reflecting on a story we can see that there are often good reasons for aggression, hate, envy, greed and regression. Thus some of our own uncomfortable reactions can come nearer to the surface and be thought about.

Images and stories can have a life of their own, and will develop in their own way if we are careful not to interrupt the flow with premature words and questions. Drawings, painting, stories and the imaginative play engaged in by children within safe, trusting relationships can be symbolic representations of changes going on deep within the psyche.

Thus through the free play of their imaginations, children are able to work at a deep level on their unresolved conflicts. Michael Green talks of the creative arts (writing, drawing, painting, music, sculpture, drama or dance) as ways we can all use to

> free damned up forces in the psyche which hold back growth, and which in severe cases can cause mental health problems. The driven quality – the need to create, which is a feature of great artists' lives, points to the importance of such imaginative work for them.[10]

Containment/emotional holding

Unintegrated children (who have buried unintegrated traumatic experiences) are unable to make use of play, because they cannot contain experience,[11] and cannot risk unknown outcomes. They may even disrupt the play of others (destroy toys, smear paints, etc.) because they need to defend against the unbearable anxiety it evokes (for this reason they may sometimes need to be separately managed during play sessions, until they grow stronger).

I observed at the pupil referral unit how they would prefer to engage in banter or 'sparring play' that is controlling and can quickly turn to conflict they can 'win'. This can have a direct effect on their capacity to process their pain and reach their potential, to create, to learn and try new things. Unintegrated children need help to play. They need a secure attachment and a secure base.

Secure attachment and a secure base

A *secure attachment* and *secure base* form the foundation of the capacity to play. As with mothers and babies, creating a secure base is essential for play in school and playgroup. Of course a secure base includes secure attachment relationships (see Chapter 8). Underneath the security a trusted adult is able to create for the children in the moment, will be the attachment patterns they bring with them. Chapter 8 gives a detailed description of these. To summarise:

- *Insecure anxious/avoidant* children may find proximity and unpredictability difficult because of too many rejecting, neglecting or abusive experiences. Such children will find both the imaginative content as well as the attention from an adult uncomfortable. They may need to make sure to keep in control, which can make playing with others difficult. Playing alone may be easier for them. *They need slow weaning into being able to trust and use sensitive support.*
- *Insecure resistant/ambivalent* children will find letting go of actively engaging the adult's attention with 'chat' in order to attend to the play or creative task difficult, for fear of the adult losing interest in them. They may become so 'clingy' that they drive interested adults away, or they may demand so much time that staff become conflicted about working with them. *They need very firm clear boundaries and lots of 'holding in mind' on a daily basis, to develop a secure base for play.* Discussing with them how you will just watch them quietly and think about their developing play may be best for both their separation and their play, as Case Study 5 on p. 31 vividly illustrates. Try it and see.
- *Insecure chaotic/disorganised* children, described by Heather Geddes as 'the most worrying pupils', cannot play.[12] They need practical help, as well as emotional containment, to become secure enough to develop the capacity to play, although they may only be able to access and use this 'in small doses'. *A secure resilient 'educational attachment person' who is always there and puts long-term effort into attuning to them, can help to facilitate this.* I found throwing beanbags, balloons and soft toys could be a 'way in', as could engaging (their) soft toys with friendly chat and curiosity. Something to 'fiddle with' like plasticine, Blu Tack or paper clips, can also be calming and facilitating with older pupils.

Significant and repeated play experiences with a key worker will necessarily evoke a significant attachment. It is important to take this seriously and be trustworthy and reliable. A regular time, place and materials will feel containing. It is important not to be persuaded into giving more time unless there is a crisis; rather remind them when they will see you, or have a play choice time, next.

As well as a containing relationship, a reliable uncluttered environment will be facilitating. Play items for unintegrated children might include large boxes to get into and items suitable for making dens and 'nests' – like blankets, string, elastic bands, pegs, cushions, tables, water in bottles to drink and big soft toys. Glove puppets, finger paints, bubble-blowing equipment, soft balls and balloons, etc. can also be engaging. As described above, they particularly need *containing, resilient and trusted adults* to turn to when needed, or possibly one-to-one thoughtful attention, to enable them to feel safe enough to play. This is exactly what the children at the pupil referral unit nurture base were given and engaged with so enthusiastically. The move towards integration and the capacity for symbolic play for such children may take time, but it will be an *important achievement*.

Taking the relationship and the child's attachment pattern seriously also involves good preparation for endings, and acknowledgement of unexpected breaks in the sessions, because they will miss you and they may not be able to acknowledge that. They may regress.

As discussed in Chapter 12, children with unresolved and traumatic losses will have particular difficulties with all endings. The end of sessions, days, weeks, terms, etc. may show in their play, stories and images. It can be helpful to acknowledge such difficulties with them in the once-removed metaphorical situations of their stories, linking them perhaps with real and approaching endings and transitions.

> You don't want to finish it? Mmm . . . maybe just at the moment finishing is not what we want to do. Your time here will finish next week won't it. I will miss you too.

Practical transition help may be needed. Reading 'ending' stories to them around big endings can be helpful in this regard (see the list of stories about endings in Box 22, p. 239).

Transference and countertransference

Sometimes a child's play may evoke strong, poignant feelings in us. Noticing the feelings the child and their play evokes can help us resist being 'pushed into' unhelpful responses. It is also important to be aware of our own vulnerabilities and tendencies (e.g. to need to be the helper, to need problems to be sorted or to avoid certain or difficult issues) when watching a child play. If we are not so aware we can unwittingly become hooked into unhelpful, or overly helpful reactions like making or doing things for them rather than bearing their struggles – which can actually erode their developing confidence (see more on transference and countertransference in Chapter 4).

Different types of play and how they can be helpful emotionally in school, nurture bases and preschool settings

The following notes are given to enable school staff to value and respect children's chosen play, and to motivate staff to facilitate such play and creative opportunities. Although it can be helpful to bear these 'thoughts' in mind, it is never helpful for school staff to talk to children about them. Comments in the metaphor can be engaging though – when they feel right. Use your intuition.

Some thoughts about music and rhythm

- Beginning in infancy, music and rhythm are very valuable for emotional health. Tuning and joining in with a child's musical and rhythmic playing and singing is fun and it also builds the capacity of the limbic (emotional) system (this can be crucial for traumatised children, see p. 15 note 11). It fosters a concrete experience of attunement as you play and sing together.
- Nursery rhymes, action and finger-play songs and rhythmic clapping with key workers fosters bonding and secure attachment and also builds brain connections. This is attachment-based play.

Some thoughts about pretend play

- Pop-up tunnels and tents and small hidey-hole spaces, offer children a safe space. They are especially helpful for avoidant children.
- Big boxes, sheets, cushions, chairs and sofas, etc. can be used for dens, offering a 'concrete' and a symbolic experience of a secure base from which to venture in and out.
- A cooker and utensils, Play-Doh, a tea set and accessories (also real cooking, toast making and shared dining experiences) can be very valuable. Cooking and food are both nurturing and symbolic of love and nurture, and 'taking in' of good things, as well as an opportunity to play out anxieties and conflicts around food and home.
- Hospital and medical items like bandages, stethoscopes, big cushions, a sofa bed, blankets, dolls and uniform accessories offer opportunities to play through experiences of (and anxieties about) hurts (symbolically including emotional hurts), hospital visits and needing care and healing.
- A play house (including a window and a door), with accessories and dolls offers opportunities to play out domestic situations, roles and conflicts.
- School items like a white board and pens, a blackboard, an easel, small cushions, soft toys and dolls, offer opportunities to play out school roles, experiences, conflicts, rivalry, bullying, etc.
- Dressing-up clothes, hats, puppets and masks facilitate trying out different roles and dramatic story making. Engaging with the characters in role may be helpful (or not). Only join in if the child wants to engage you. Asking them, *'What do I say?'* or *'What do I do now?'* before taking any initiative helps the adult keep to the child's agenda. ('Why' questions are often not helpful as they shift the child out of imagination into rational thinking.) With older children I have at their request role-played dramatic conflicts and scenarios with them, always asking (out of role) *'What do I say?'* or *'What to I do now?'*

o   Pretend play with *miniatures* (e.g. in a sand tray) offers opportunities to play through things being buried and coming up again (repressed experiences emerging into consciousness), things being suffocated, things being attacked and hurt and explorations of death. Stories naturally arise from sand worlds, which can be understood metaphorically and engaged with *as if* they were real. Adults can offer to scribe stories and photograph sand worlds for children.

Sand world (or pretend) play miniatures useful for eliciting stories include:

- animals – wild and domestic, plus fences, gates, walls, trees, etc.;
- buildings or building components, e.g. Lego, wooden blocks;
- vehicles – including emergency vehicles and warning signs;
- people – positive and negative figures, mythical figures, family members, people in roles, e.g. nurses, policemen etc.;
- monsters;
- bridges and fences;
- 'precious' and natural items, like crystals, cones, rocks, etc.

Caring, secure, reflective adults, who take a distant interest without needing to control the play unless danger threatens, keep the play safe enough. This may include empathising with or just observing the characters' dilemmas, *but not changing the sad outcomes* if that is how the child needs it to be. Silent attention is often best.

Some children may need weaning into playing alone or with peers

Some thoughts about messy play

- All sorts of messy play (including clay, paint, finger paint and gluing) gives opportunities both to create images and to try out a different (less controlled) part of a child's personality. Mess can symbolically link with the 'mess' inside us – things getting in a mess, being in control or out of control, anxieties about being good/bad/told off and the need for emotional and physical containment. Anxious, inhibited and controlled children benefit from messy play.
- Play-Doh, soft plasticine and clay (possibly with accessories, but not 'cut-out templates') offer opportunities to create anything in three dimensions, which can be understood (but not talked about) symbolically. Engaging with created 'characters' in role in a facilitating but bland way, e.g. *'Hello snake . . . so, what's up with you today?'* may facilitate (metaphorical) stories developing – or not.
- Water or dry sand and containers (along with a funnel and Sellotape) offer opportunities to play through anxieties about containment, holding and change.

    But some very chaotic unintegrated children may become overwhelmed by too much mess or too many things and could end up trashing the toys or materials. They may in fact need a much simpler or blander experience, until they grow more contained. It is important of course to think first before offering creative or messy play opportunities to such children. If they do 'lose it', try to stay calm, and *don't offer the experience again next time*. In extreme cases you may need to remove the child from the setting for safety. When they ask about it you can have a conversation about how they need to grow a bit stronger before they can manage such exciting play. Explain how you are going to help them and suggest that, *'Maybe we can try the sand (or whatever) again when you are stronger'*. After a while (a few weeks perhaps) you may want to ask them if they are feeling strong enough to try again. I know about this from experience!

Some thoughts about games and board games

The value of playing games with children is not just the metaphorical content of the game, but the conversations and comments you can make about the feelings that come up naturally as the game progresses in its ups and downs. Children can experience safe empathy in the context of the game for themselves and for the 'characters' in the game, as well as hear your hurt and frustration expressed naturally and 'survived' when the game goes against you.

'Oh no not again!'

'I don't believe it! These snakes are all out to get me today!'

In this light:

- *Jenga* can be metaphoric and engaging, as the tower is built with some anxiety and falls with horror, devastation and lots of laughter. It can be played with individuals or small groups.
- *Frustration* or *Ludo* enables thinking about moving, loss, hurt and anticipation as the counters metaphorically 'move house' amid an opponent who is out to knock them back.
- *Snakes and Ladders* similarly evokes fear, excitement and frustration.
- *Draughts* involves both thinking and feelings as opportunities arise and our plans are thwarted.
- *Chess* is more complicated but similar in its opportunities, and introduces rules and differences.
- *Backgammon* is quite a complicated game where you travel a difficult journey in opposite directions, and when you are alone on a space you are vulnerable to being kicked off 'on to the *block*', which feels like a horrible punishment that you have to endure until you gain the wherewithal to come back into the game. I found it particularly helpful with an intelligent but very avoidant boy to be able to talk about vulnerability and hurt in the context of the game.
- *Ball games* can be helpful and relationship building too, evoking opportunities to connect, share and 'beat' each other in the safety of the game, as well as displaying admirable skill. You can even playfully go into role as the ball, especially if you are the butt of any negative comments, e.g. *'Oh no, dropped again!'*, *'Wow! You caught me! Thank you!'*

Some thoughts about constructional play

Large quantities of bricks, megablocks, sticklebricks, Duplo, Lego, etc. offer great opportunities for group and cooperative play. Symbolically they offer opportunities to work on things falling apart, building houses, bridges and vehicles, and on frustration, resilience and starting over again.

Art and painting, especially art with an element of free choice and expression work, offer wonderful opportunities for surprising, evocative and vivid expressions of 'shadow' and buried aspects that benefit from opening up to the light of day. This of course is the basis of art psychotherapy, but children have art lessons in school too, and teachers may notice when a child becomes particularly engaged in a work of art, or when they create a powerful expression of something, and treat it with respect and appreciation even if it's messy (e.g. Figure 17, p. 108) or somewhat disturbing (e.g. Figure 36). Valuing it as a 'work of art', which like all great art has 'something to say' to all of us, may even facilitate a hidden 'shift'. P's huge smile in Figure 36 seems as if it might be hiding something else doesn't it? Comments in the metaphor, like, *'Wow that's a big smile. I wonder what she's feeling inside?'* may be helpful and manageable.

Figure 36

Working individually with a child: a few tips for counsellors and play therapists

Something that troubled children really need is a way to let their anger, aggression and antisocial tendencies come safely into the room to be acknowledged and thought about.

This is what a therapeutic relationship can offer. It is particularly important therefore that counsellors and play therapists do not *need* to be liked, they don't even subtly collude with a child's need to impress them and *not show* their shameful angry parts. Metaphor is a way to allow, express and even facilitate aggression safely. For example, after reading *The Ghost Eye Tree*[13] to J (about the terror evoked when a boy's mum asked him go through the scary forest to the farm to fetch the milk), he looked back through the book and drew the image shown in Figure 37.

Figure 37

I noticed that his picture included a knife and an axe piercing into the scary tree trunk and a sinister eye looking down from the top of the tree (these were not in the story!). Also the 'boy' was trying to look away from the tree, but his eye seemed to be seeing all the horror of it. J didn't want to talk about it, but it was there on the page and we kept it safely in his box.

Joining in with their dramatic stories, dramatisations and puppet plays can be powerful and facilitating experiences as the child discovers first-hand that negative feelings can be expressed and thought about, and that their therapist can bear them. 'Paper conversations', as we saw in Figure 26 p. 181, can be engaging and metaphorical in one-to-one work. They can also be used more challengingly in child counseling and psychotherapy by, in the context of the dialogue, inserting more provocative comments into the story to encourage otherwise closed-up children to express their buried anger and discover it can be thought about.

But be careful if the child wants to engage you actively in his play, don't let his character bully yours without responding (in role) that you don't like it etc. – verbal arguments are OK to *act* out as long as you *always* follow the child's lead, e.g. *'What do I say now?'* And don't *ever* allow yourself (even in role and with a puppet) to be drawn in to fighting with him physically – although it is OK for *him* to safely act out fights with toys while you watch quietly. If a child gets actively involved in a very angry or sadistic scene, be careful how you respond. Silence may be best. Any response that is felt to be judgemental may inhibit the future use of the relationship or time.

Ways of facilitating a child's engagement, play and creativity

- Having a trusted empathetic adult beside them while they create can make a potentially significant experience into a containing one.
- Creating a model or a picture with someone beside them who *can bear the pain and stay with* them can enable more to be contained, and possibly processed a little. You may not need to talk much.
- If the story is unresolved or very painful, be aware that the child may not be ready to think about making things better just yet. It is OK to allow sad and painful endings (like in Sean the Sheep in Figure 38). It is best not to comment too much – or they may change it just to please you.

Shawn the sheep

One day there was a farm and on the farm was sheep called Shawn he was all done in the den. How he wished he wasn't all alone. He wished he could have a brother or a sister. But he didn't have a brother or a sister. That night he planned an escape, out of the horrible farm. He cried and cried 'Boo'

Figure 38

- The story characters, or aspects of a sand world or picture can relate to parts of the child's inner world or to experiences. These *do not need to be talked about* although it can help to be silently aware of links and possible meanings.
- The emotional quality of the whole play or story may also convey an important message.
- Serial 'story' making can feel more containing than 'one-offs'. A child in educational psychotherapy, for example, will often engage with a similar theme or character week after week, slowly shifting the emphasis and content.
- Themes may (need to) be repeated, because unprocessed experiences and emotions are pushing to be worked through. The child may need someone to really hear how awful it is over and over again (in the context of the story), until he can assimilate it himself. The same story theme week after week can be a rehearsal of a different way of being or responding to a problem – which can take time (see my example of P's monster stories on p. 180). This could indicate that the child is stuck and needs you to *really* understand. It may mean that the child feels that you are not really hearing or feeling what it is like. Contain any anxieties the story evokes (just 'hold' them within yourself).
- Resolutions or changes in themes may indicate that the emotional containment is working, and emotional processing is beginning or reaching bearable proportions.
- Trusted peer groups (in the presence of an adult perhaps) can sometimes contain more than individuals. My experience with therapeutic art groups for junior children was that things came up through the creative, convivial free-play opportunity more quickly than they did in individual therapy. Therapeutic groups need more containing management though, because adrenaline can be more easily triggered. (I found it helpful to have a very tight space – with no room for running around!)
- Pictures, stories or models kept safe in a special box or book can be like a container for a child, particularly if they are also *looked at and thought about* on subsequent occasions with the trusted adult.
- Having a previous story or play theme *remembered*, and making links with previous stories or pictures, can feel containing for a child.
- A containing frame can facilitate a practical experience of emotional holding, e.g. a sand tray, play mat, writing and drawing book or a storybook.
- Having the same time, the same place and the same materials each week or each time will create a safer, more boundaried space and experience.
- However, at crisis times for a child a one-off story or picture-making session can become very significant and may be more manageable and helpful than talk, for now.
- Predictable non-stretchy time boundaries are very important and containing.

Ways of listening and responding to their play and imaginative or creative work

- Take an interest in the aspects the child focuses on.
- Follow the child's lead.
- Do not give advice or help unless they ask for it.

- Resist the need to take over when things get difficult. Instead, empathise with the difficulty.
- Be patient when the child is struggling. It is OK to allow them to struggle for as long as they need to, or until they ask for help. Empathise perhaps with their struggle. Empathise if they decide to give up. Don't discuss. They may have had enough.

When a child is engaged in imaginative play

- Silent and respectful concentration is often best. Don't intrude while they are creating.
- Stay within the metaphor.
- Imagine yourself into the story/characters.
- Going into role can be helpful and fun, e.g. speaking the feelings of a character may engage them – or not. Try it and follow their lead
- They may like you to write the story to their dictation as it unfolds or at the end.

If the child is deeply engaged in creating a drawing or story

- Respect their creative process. An attuned empathic response is essential.
- Asking the odd question to clarify may be OK, but consider whether you need to ask the question at *that* time, before asking it. It may be better to ask it later.
- Notice/ask/reflect tentatively (e.g. *'I'm wondering'* or *'I'm just thinking that . . .'*).
- Bear the pain or dilemma with them without needing to resolve it.
- The 'helpful' intervention (e.g. *'I'm wondering if there is anything he can do about this'*), should be used *sparingly*. It is more important for a child to feel you can bear to stay with the situation as it is.
- If they rubbish their picture, maybe reflect back their feelings, without agreeing with them. Making generalised comments about how we can feel when things go wrong may be helpful, or just be silent. Don't judge the rubbishing. Keep the picture safely if you can.

When they finish creating

- Open questions can lead to active imagination in the here and now (e.g. *'So, tell me about your picture'* or *'So, what's happening here then?'*).
- Notice/ask/reflect tentatively (e.g. *'I'm wondering . . .'* or *'I'm just thinking that . . .'*).
- Sometimes summarising the story back to them may feel helpful.
- Frequently they may not want to talk about it, which may be understandable in the circumstances.

The most important thing is the process of actively being with the play, story or image, feeling any feelings that come up and experiencing any tragic happenings with them. This may be a bit painful for you, but it can be very supportive for the child. It is being beside them that is therapeutic. Checking out how they are at the end may be helpful. Tune in to the child. Feel the feelings alongside them. They will know when you are *with* them. You may not need to say much at all.

Story writing and stories

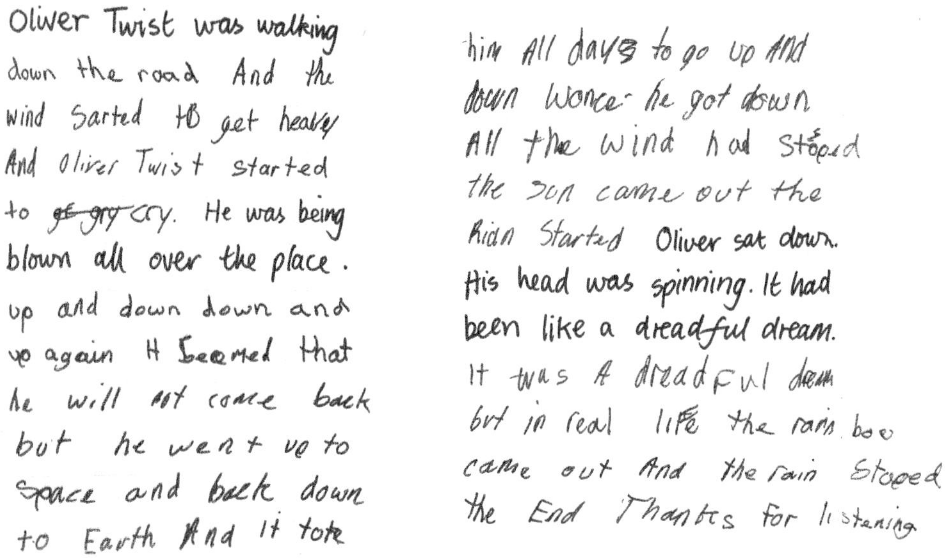

Oliver Twist was walking down the road And the wind Sarted tB get heavy And Oliver Twist started to ~~gf gry~~ cry. He was being blown all over the place. up and down down and up again H Seemed that he will not come back but he went up to space and back down to Earth And It tok

him All days to go up And down Wonce- he got down All the wind had Stopsd the Son came out the Rain Started Oliver sat down. His head was spinning. It had been like a dreadful dream. It was A dreadful dream but in real life the rain boo came out And the rain Stoped the End Thanks for listening

Figure 39

Caspari educational psychotherapists regularly use both writing and reading stories with children as a safe way to open to any buried or stuck feelings or experiences which might be getting in the way of their learning and behaviour. In a similar vein, Michael Green talks of reading evocative stories, especially fairy tales to children as 'priming the pump' (see p. 136).

Sharing stories together is fun, engaging and relaxing too. It can also be calming for the more hyperactive children to be supported into quiet listening and imaginative states, although they may need to sit very near you to stay calm. Teachers are good at putting the most needy children close to them when they read to the class.

I am aware, however, that reading to children can often become squeezed out of the busy teacher's day, but to stimulate enjoyment of stories, and especially to give poor and reluctant readers the experience of stories, story language and vividness, it is crucial to read to them as often as possible. Book-loving parents do this frequently for their children – often throughout the primary years – opening them up to imagination and familiarising them with written language by osmosis. Especially in these increasingly technological times, however, and with preoccupied, busy or depressed parents, the more vulnerable children can miss out on such imaginative and literate 'food'. This makes reading to them in school especially important. Even when children can read well themselves, there is something special and shared and relationship building about being read to. It also enables poorer readers to access age-appropriate stories and books that they are not yet up to reading and enjoying alone. Watching TV and films is just not the same!

Vulnerable children will often become quite attached to particular scary or sad stories that probably resonate with their experience in some way. Experiencing such stories within a safe setting and relationship can be very therapeutic.

The availability of story CDs also encourages enjoyment, motivation and story familiarity, but there is no substitute for reading *to* children. Choosing the 'right' book can be a gift for a child.

Many years ago I made a list of evocative story and picture books that touch on issues children might identify with, organised into themes like 'fears and overcoming fears', 'bullying and being bullied', 'being different/being yourself', 'loss, endings, bereavement, 'anger', 'feeling left out/rejected', 'being loved/needing love', etc. This list, which could always be added to, is available as an eResource at www.routledge.com/9780367025465.

The language of story and imagination is vivid, colourful and engaging. Stories and images are amazingly rich, evocatively linking past present and future. They can involve subtleties, complexities and full, rounded experiences. They can be experienced on many levels and from many points of view. They can involve unbelievable terror. They can also involve magic and helpful characters. A rich diet of stories fuels the imagination for creating our own stories.

With older children free creative writing provides a similar therapeutic opportunity

Writing stories offers a chance for children's imagination to flow and become expressed on the page and thus be shared with others, as well as developing their writing skills in a meaningful context. More inhibited and traumatised children will need practical and subtle help to let their imaginations flow and to feel confident enough to get started (see Box 23).

Box 23 Suggestions for fostering creative or free story writing in class or with small groups

- Regular and frequent writing.

- Quiet beginning for concentration.

- Element of free choice, although you may need to limit the theme, e.g. football stories.

- Stimuli available, e.g. magazine pictures, suggested story beginnings.

- Stories could relate to a particular topic of work or to a real purpose for writing.

- Clear expectation of process, e.g. what to do when one stage is finished – read it to a friend, start to edit, etc.

- Firm consistent boundaries.

- Peer support.

- Collaborative work (sometimes).

- Talking with children about their writing – focus on content first, then *later* focus on one or two technical points.

- Availability of word banks, appropriate-level dictionaries and spelling visual aids can be helpful, but they may inhibit having a go at spellings and also the 'flow' of the first draft.

- Inventive spellings in first draft are OK.

- Spelling partners are helpful for editing work later.

- Encourage having a go at difficult words.

- Teach spelling and grammar skills separately so their writing flow is not inhibited.

- Teach editing skills separately.

- At the end of the lesson, share stories with the class or group – the author of the story answers questions.

- Story of the week – display in class.

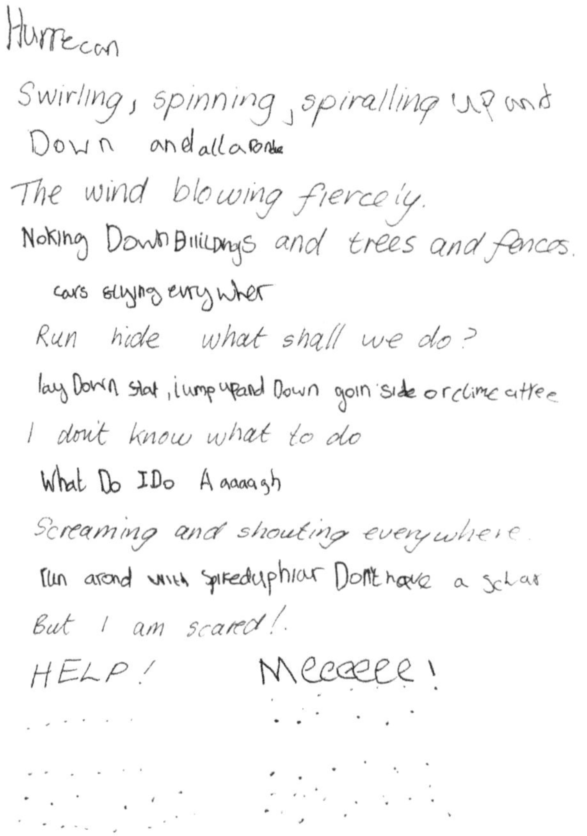

Hurrecan

Swirling, spinning, spiralling up and
Down and all around
The wind blowing fiercely.
Noking Down Biluings and trees and fences.
cars sliyng evry wher
Run hide what shall we do?
lay Down staf, iump upand Down goin side orclime a tree
I don't know what to do
What Do I Do A aaaagh
Screaming and shouting everywhere.
run arond with spiredyphiar Dont have a schae
But I am scared!.
HELP! Meeeee!

Figure 40

Poetry too can be very evocative, whether prompted by a stimulus or not. The shortness of the lines and the power of phrases that don't need to make narrative sense can free the mind to vivid expressions, especially when a class has a rich diet of poetry. J had had a hard life, which got him into many scrapes, but he could 'come alive' in his tempestuous poems, which we could all appreciate, like 'Hurrecan' in Figure 40.

Many years ago I was fortunate to work in a school where regular 'free' writing was encouraged and supported along the lines listed above. The sessions would last about half an hour and the teacher would begin writing with the children in silence for the first few minutes. As they were ready the children moved gently into sharing and editing mode with each other and with the adults in the room. At the end of the session a few children would share their writing with the class.

Making their stories into books for others to read or into class books was also very motivating.

Ways to facilitate stories with reluctant and needy children on a one-to-one basis

- *Read stories to them.*
- *Stimuli:*

  o Children's own pictures.
  o 'Sand worlds'.
  o Key words.
  o Their plasticine (or other) models.

o   'Squiggle pictures':[14] draw a simple, quick, spontaneous squiggle (a 'twirl' or a jagged shape – as it comes) for the child to turn into something. Then through conversation their picture can often lead to a story. This may be enough – or they may also do one for you. The instruction to look at the squiggle and wonder about it and turn it into something (maybe turning it upside down in the process) frees up the thinking mind, allowing spontaneous deeper images to arise and be thought about within a safe and trusted relationship. Figure 41 shows how little K turned my square shape into a room with mouse holes. Then he drew a mouse and a somewhat needy and scary story arose.

the mouse is eating the cheese all by him self so. no one else own eat the big Cheese with him along came a cat!

Figure 41

In therapy I would often begin a session with a squiggle picture and a story for this very reason. Within this setting it was often fascinating to watch the slow change from 'unresolved' stories to stories where the character in the story either sought or received help with the scary situations or dilemmas (see p. 267).

- *Drawing and writing.* As with squiggles, a child's spontaneous drawing often accesses deeper levels of the psyche, allowing the story to flow from a deeper place and go where it will.
- *Shared story writing,* e.g. writing alternate lines, keeping your part bland or reflective or engaged with what they seem to want.
- *Child dictates and adult scribes,* then adult dictates back one word at a time for the child to write. This separates thinking about the content from the writing process, enabling the child to write a more fluent story in their own handwriting.
- *Shared play writing.* This can be done with a partner or an adult (see example on p. 137)
- *Paper conversations* (e.g. see Figure 42).

    You and the child draw a little character that can talk in opposite corners of a double page spread or a large sheet of paper. Then you start a conversation by

Figure 42

writing a bland comment beside your character, which you then surround with a speech bubble (e.g. '*Hi there*') – and wait. The child will often be intrigued and respond with a reply beside their character. Show them how to put the speech bubble around each comment *after writing it*. Then let the conversation continue by joining on new comments to each character's previous comment, thus linking each character's speech bubbles into a chain of bubbles. You each take turns to write for your character, allowing the child to 'control' the content. Just respond in a bland way or 'reflect back' their character's comments or apparent feelings in what your character says. Continue until they indicate they want to stop. My 'conversation' with 'Roger' (see p. 181), a very dyslexic and struggling learner, is an example of this.[15]

As described on p. 258, a therapist can use this technique in a more challenging way to purposely provoke a closed-up child into expressing anger or resistance in the containing setting of the characters.

- Serial story writing allows characters and situations to change over time, and also enables previous happenings to be remembered and held in mind. For example, 'The Baby Bird' and 'The Spooky Moon' stories written by the same boy, show the development from an unresolved bird story to a still painful, but resolved moon story (see Figures 43 and 44).
- Respond in writing with your comments (e.g. '*I should think he needed a rest after that J!*').
- Publish/type it out for them or maybe help them with this – it shows you value them and the story.

The Baby Bird.

One day there was a bird in an A 's garden. It was hatching out of its egg. It was little. A thought it was ~~cute~~ cute. A wanted to show her mum A's mum ~~sd~~ ~~it~~ ~~was~~ cute A mum wold to cep the baby bib A mum woth the baby bib she pool the baby bib in a big cagle and the baby ~~bi~~ bird thloow a rad and rad and rad and rad and ra it lut the cage.

Figure 43

The Spooky Moon

Once there was a boy and he stayed up and played in the street until it was 8o'clock and he never knew that there was a terrifying mobn above him and when it stut 7o'clok and that was when the terfing spooky moon strst to hunt for children to eat for teatime and the boy didn't realise that the moon was coming towards him. Then the moon was an inch away from the boy. The the terrifying spooky moon strted to open it math then the boy's mum and dad sctfied out to the boy they ~~seed~~ said ~~LOOK OUT THE MOON IS GOING TO EAT YOU!~~ LOOK OUT THE MOON IS GOING TO EAT YOU! the boy was sath ~~becaues~~ because his mum and dad kill the terfing spooky moom. THE END

Thank you mum
Thank you dad.   You saved my life

Figure 44

- Make thoughtful comments about the writing (e.g. *'So how was that?'* or *'I wonder why/ how . . . ?'*) and see if they want to talk about the experience.
- Scribing enables reluctant writers (or non-writers) to produce an amazing story and get into 'flow mode', when deeper images and metaphors can more spontaneously arise.

One day it was snowing and reluctant writer W dictated the following story.

> **Winter Boy**
>
> It was winter. Winter boy liked to play in the snow and no one else used to play in the snow. No one liked him. So he built a frog out of snow to amaze them. But it didn't work and he went to school and he sat down and no one sat next to him. When the children went up into Year 2 the boy had to stay in Year 1 because no one liked him and the teacher didn't like him.
>
> Because it was winter the snow stuck up the door and the door wouldn't open. Everyone was stuck inside with no food. Winter Boy said, 'I might be able to open the door,' and the teacher said, 'I don't think you could open it but you can try.' When he opened the door everyone ran to the door and they said, 'Thank you Winter Boy!' And they all went home and told their mums all about it and Winter Boy was happy for the rest of his life.

Sharing a story with a trusted adult can give a child a new way of thinking about his troubled feelings. It can provide a character or a situation *he* can identify with and think about with support, facilitating experiences of acceptance and understanding.

Stories and play can bring a child's buried hurts and worries nearer to consciousness, and enable them to be thought about and understood in the safe context of the character. Sharing a story can give a child an experience of being profoundly understood. It can touch both of you deeply.

It is crucial for the child to feel that you can stay with the painful/scary aspects of the story without needing him to resolve or change it before he is ready. This may be the first time someone has been able to *bear* such scary things with him.

Responding to their writing through 'reflective and engaging marking'

Teachers are so busy these days that it may feel hard to put more than a tick, underline a mistake or write 'well done', etc. on children's work, but children (like all of us!) like to feel that their teacher has really read and thought about what they have written, and writing little thoughtful responsive comments or questions in their book (preferably not in a red pen!) can both foster the relationship and the learning and make them feel 'taken seriously', for example:

'Wow! That was exciting!'

'I was wondering if he was going to find it in the end.'

'Yes. I think so too.'

'This must be the longest story you have ever written! Was it fun to write?'

'This sounds very scary.'[16]

Writing groups

Small writing groups can be great for reluctant or special needs writers. The writing materials and picture stimuli are available but there is no pressure – beyond knowing that there will be a time at the end when they can each (if we wish) share their writing and respond to each other in a respectful way and that their stories and writing will be made into books for others to see and read. There are no expectations for correct spelling or grammar, although editing and help is available. It is mostly about finding their writing 'voice', and it certainly works. One child I remember won the annual school writing award for her poorly spelt but heartfelt story and got to read it out to the whole school. The books we made were regularly shared in assembly. Sometimes they would type out their stories, but often I would type them out – so the vividness could be appreciated by all and boost their confidence. Sometimes they would write stories, like:

> Once upon a time three boys were waking up creatures and they woke up a really big one. All the boys were saying help help I need help. There is a big monster down here. One of the boys got bit. The rest never. They all were crying for help. Mum help me please. And just then a cloud came and the monster turned into the biggest monster ever.

I would also write at the same time, often in response to issues that were 'around' and in an encouraging vein:

> *'Ben came today with questions about dinosaurs and Tim could tell him a lot.'*
>
> *'In the writing group we can listen to each other and help each other. It is fun writing stories in the group.'*

Caspari Foundation educational psychotherapists frequently use, teach and encourage teachers to use stories in their therapeutic work with children. One of the interventions that has really taken off in Caspari's work in schools is Gill Morton's 'Storymaking Around a Journey'.[17] Briefly, an educational psychotherapist and a teacher together facilitate a shared dictated story about a journey with a specially selected group of children. The process involves drawing as well as creating the story, which is both to keep them engaged while others have a turn to speak or tell their part of the story, but also because drawing tends to open to a deeper level of consciousness, allowing whatever is ready to be worked on to come into the picture and then perhaps become incorporated into the story.

For several weeks the group go on an imaginary (sea) journey together, involving lots of thinking and wondering around hopes and fears, and about what to do, what to take and what might happen next, etc. Every week the children talk and draw together around a theme, like 'getting started', 'taking with us or leaving behind', 'dangers ahead', 'a new place', 'a discovery', 'falling out and getting back', 'arriving and exploring', 'leaving and travelling home' and 'arriving back home'. The facilitators foster a sense of connectedness within the group. They hold the space and the group in mind. They pose questions and name difficulties rather than offering solutions, and they encourage thinking and talking things through together. Everyone's contribution is accepted (even if it conflicts with others) and written down by an adult in the child's special colour and then stuck in the group book alongside their picture for the week. At the end of the 'journey' each child is given a copy of the book to take home, and the experience is evaluated together, both with the children and later with school staff.

For those interested in the therapeutic value of story writing there are many great books available, including (Chapters 3 and 4 in) *Taking Children Seriously* and Trisha Waters' *Therapeutic Storywriting*.[18]

Notes

1 M. Fo, *Original Blessing* (Santa Fe, NM: Bear & Co, 1983), 204.
2 See www.therplay.org.
3 D. Hughes, *Building the Bonds of Attachment: Awakening Love in Deeply Troubled Children* (Lanham, MD: Jason Aronson, 2006).
4 D. W. Winnicott wrote about this in *Transitional Objects and Transitional Phenomena* (London: Tavistock, 1958), ch. 1.
5 Margot Sunderland, *What Every Parent Needs to Know* (London: Dorling Kindersley, 2006), 96.
6 Tina Bruce, *Learning Through Play* (London: Hodder & Stoughton, 2001).
7 Pellegrini (1996), quoted in Sunderland, *What Every Parent Needs to Know*, 96.
8 Michael Green, 'Active Imagination in Schools: Unlocking the Self', in *Taking Children Seriously*, eds Steve Decker, Sandy Kirby, Angela Greenwood and Dudley Moore (London: Cassell, 1999), 25–63. 'Active imagination' is a term that was coined by Jung in 1913 and written about in C. G. Jung, *Memories, Dreams, Reflections* (London: Fontana, 1961).
9 Green, 'Active Imagination in Schools', 25.
10 Ibid., 27.
11 See Barbara Dockar-Drysdale, *Consultation in Child Care* (London: Free Association Books, 1993), ch. 3.
12 Heather Geddes, *Attachment in the Classroom* (London: Worth, 2006).
13 Bill Martin Jr and John Archambault, *The Ghost Eye Tree* (New York: Square Fish, 1998).
14 The 'Squiggle' game was invented by paediatrician/child psychiatrist D. W. Winnicott, see his *Collected Papers: Volume 8* (Oxford: Oxford University Press 1953), 35.

15 The conversation was published in Angela Greenwood, 'Stories and Writing', in *Taking Children Seriously*, eds Steve Decker, Sandy Kirby, Angela Greenwood and Dudley Moore (London: Cassell, 1999), 64–86.

16 I saw on *Dragon's Den* that someone has developed a voice-sensitive computer app through which you can speak your thoughtful comments and they will be automatically typed on to students work!

17 G. Morton, 'Therapeutic Story Groups: Educational Psychotherapy in a School setting', in *Why Can't I Help This Child to Learn?* ed. H. High (London: Karnac, 2012), 105. For further details see caspari.org.uk.

18 Steve Decker, Sandy Kirby, Angela Greenwood and Dudley Moore, eds, *Taking Children Seriously* (London: Cassell, 1999); Trisha Waters, *Therapeutic Storywriting* (London: David Fulton, 2004).

Enhancing our own and children's personal capacities

14

Figure 45

This chapter considers how in many ways we teach who we are, and so putting a little effort into developing self-awareness, self-knowledge and self acceptance, and becoming aware of our own vulnerabilities can be very valuable. A self-assessment questionnaire is introduced (see Appendix 2 at the end of the book) along with a link to a drivers questionnaire as tools to better understand ourselves. The chapter discusses the value of mindfulness practices for both adults and children, as important ways of looking after ourselves and of enhancing our capacity to facilitate stopping and thinking before reacting and to 'stay in the moment'.

Looking after ourselves

I remember many years ago being impressed by Jenny Moseley,[1] including the idea of 'looking after ourselves' in one of her circle-time courses. She talked about 'nurturing our wells':

1.   Our *intellectual well*: having interests and pursuits outside school.
2.   Our *physical well*: looking after our bodies and enjoying exercise or sport.
3.   Our *social well*: having friends and social involvements outside school.
4.   Our *emotional well*: using family, friends and perhaps counsellors for support when things feel overwhelming, and enjoying fun and uplifting experiences.
5.   Our *spiritual well*: opening to experiences of depth, present-moment awareness, connectivity, awe and meaning, etc.

She emphasised how these were important both for ourselves and for the children we work with. I have always adhered to this way of thinking in my own life, but I am painfully aware that teaching can be so stressful these days that some staff may feel such an ideal is just impossible – for all the value they can see in it – both for themselves and for the children they work with. For this reason perhaps it is even more important to include a chapter on our internal worlds and capacities, as balance, lightness, resilience and depth, etc. are more important than ever in our complex and sometimes very pressured society.

Developing our internal capacities and self-awareness

The philosophy of this book is that through our consistent, resilient, attuned relationships we can make a huge difference to the emotional growth and learning of vulnerable and insecure children in school. This is like an offering of ourselves, at the same time as teaching and helping the children we work with. Relationships will happen, the children will attach to us anyway – 'for better, for worse(!)' – so it is worth putting some thought into this.

When working with disturbed and vulnerable children it is important to develop our own containing capacities, as severely deprived children need our uncomplicated availability and capacity to keep thinking under pressure. The calmer we can be in turbulent times the better it is for both for them and for us. This is not about being perfect but about putting sensible effort into becoming as secure and integrated as we can for the sake of the children (see discussion of 'good enough' on pp. 130 and 190–191).

Whether we like it or not, at stressful times disturbed and vulnerable children will push our buttons. They will often have needed to become adept at sensing vibes, vulnerabilities and anxieties in others for their own survival, and if we are feeling fragile or triggered into irritation for some reason they may unconsciously become driven to attack or challenge us. So it is in our own and the children's interests that we are as aware and accepting of ourselves as we can be. This need became clear to a number of staff at the pupil referral unit when I was there, and at one stage I think there were about six members of staff having counselling! Some of us had had years of counselling and psychotherapy to prepare us for such work. This is not a sign of weakness but of courage and maturity, and it often fits us for particular and special contributions to schools and society later on.

Of course we will all be different in our capacities, from our genetic make-up, in relation to our early experiences and in relation to the support and emotional containment we ourselves received. There is no judgement in this, and anyway we can always change and 'grow' – just by living and reflecting honestly on our experiences as they surface and resurface. And it is not so much about what *happens* to and around us, as about how we *respond* to what happens. As with the children, all experiences are opportunities, some admittedly more difficult to take and to bear than others, but always offering potential for growth, which is rewarding and life enhancing.

The questionnaire in Appendix 2 at the end of the book may be a good place to start. It is derived and expanded from a similar questionnaire in Paul Greenhalgh's book, *Emotional Growth and Learning*.[2] The questionnaire is a numbered list of skills in emotional holding, containing and strengthening, which also helpfully illustrates the precise skills that facilitate emotional containment. By reflecting *briefly* on each skill in turn as we respond, we can use the questionnaire to think about our own capacities and those we might want to work on. In this context it is important to be gentle on ourselves, and to let go of any self-judgements that might pop up. Too often in our competitive, dualistic culture we can be conditioned into judging ourselves – so just noticing this is helpful. Then we can just drop our intention to work on a skill into the depths of our mind and leave it there. It will come into our consciousness occasionally, along with opportunities to practise it!

The suggestion at the end of the questionnaire in Appendix 2 is that we choose just three particular areas to work on. Try it and see. It is probably a long-term process, but those of us drawn to work with needy and damaged children are probably also drawn to developing such qualities. For trainers using the questionnaire in training courses it is important to be aware of the risk of arousing shame through such questionnaires however. Just gently acknowledging that and watching out for those who might need support may be helpful. This is not though (in my opinion) a reason not to use them, as they can be very enlightening.

Exercise 2 on p. 54 is similar, but goes deeper, as it encourages us to reflect on our personal histories and formative experiences, as a way of developing self-awareness, self-understanding and self-compassion. It is even more important with this exercise to be aware of the risks of arousing buried hurts in using this questionnaire, because some people may understandably not wish to think about their personal histories and bruises. I did once have a problem with the questionnaire (which we talked through) in that some staff who were *required* by their school to attend the course (and were therefore much less motivated and sympathetic) found it quite uncomfortable. Luckily we decided it was best used optionally at home as a reflection tool, but trainers will make their own decisions. I have used it helpfully with school staff who came voluntarily on courses linked to the material in the book. As you will see from the questions they are very relevant to the topics covered in the rest of the book.

The drivers questionnaire[3] is another self-assessment tool that gives us an insight into our tendencies and those of others – facilitating understanding and acceptance. The drivers are: 'be strong', 'be perfect', 'hurry up', 'try hard' and 'please people'. The questionnaire also includes the 'strengths' and 'weaknesses' of each 'driver', the situations when each is helpful and not helpful, some ways to grow from each position and ways to work with such people. People are usually intrigued to try it out, and see which ones fit them more than others, usually a combination comes up.

Understanding ourselves 'from the inside' can lead to empathy for children and parents too. Indeed it is what we are hoping to move the children towards. It is of course about developing maturity and even wisdom.

Mindfulness

Mindfulness is a practice that in many studies has been shown to improve emotional and mental well-being, in that it facilitates clarity and engagement in what we are doing *now*, without worrying about or being preoccupied with the past or future. Its secular application originated in helping people to manage stress,[4] but it is now used widely by the general population (myself included) as an aid to living more healthily and happily in the moment. Child-centred versions of mindfulness and relaxation techniques are also being used more and more in schools in the Western world. So this chapter offers the reader an introduction to the practice for adults and an introduction to some versions for children, including the notes on two courses I ran, which may be helpful for trainers and school staff too. The chapter also includes some details of helpful resources and some interesting case studies from school settings.

Mindfulness is essentially present-moment awareness. It sounds simple, but it takes practice to manage it for more than a moment! Through practice though it can bring moments of peace, joy and aliveness – something we all sorely need. Walking mindfully in nature can be wonderful!

I have done the eight-week mindfulness course,[5] and participated in a monthly group thereafter for several years now. I have also done the Relax Kids[6] training along with running some Relax Kids classes in school, so I have some experience, but interested readers will find many articles, videos and details of mindfulness courses from more qualified mindfulness teachers on the Internet, and there may be qualified mindfulness teachers for adults and for children in your area, so this is just an introduction.

My original 'mindfulness' Internet search put me in touch with Susan Kaiser Greenland, an experienced practitioner from the United States, who teaches mindfulness to children there. I have found her two books, *Mindful Games* and *The Mindful Child*,[7] and YouTube videos extremely helpful and practical. In her TED talk she describes mindfulness as a 'way of looking' – *a way of looking with attention, balance and compassion*. We begin with attention.

Attention – includes focusing and noticing

Focusing is a skill we learn through practice, practising with kindness, bringing our minds back to the object of our *attention* again and again. It includes *noticing*, noticing when and where our attention has drifted, and bringing our attention back again and again, to our breathing, or sounds or a flower, etc. We are reminded that all minds wander and get caught up – that's just what minds do – so we need to be *kind and gentle* on ourselves when we discover we have lost our focus. Mindfulness gives us countless opportunities to practise being kind to ourselves (rather than critical). The more we practise this noticing and coming back into the present, the more the brain pathways in that area of the brain are strengthened.

Balance is achieved through quieting and calming

Practised regularly mindfulness can facilitate our right-brain capacities (see reference to Jill Bolte Taylor's experience on p. 11) like peaceful consciousness, calmness, unconditional love and quieting. Quieting is the capacity to quieten our busy minds and our big 'spinny' feelings like anger, disappointment or frustration. We start by noticing (seeing) with our aware thinking consciousness that these thoughts and feelings are there, and then *stopping* for a moment and consciously putting our attention on something calming like some slow out breaths. In life *stopping* is not easy. It sounds easy, but we can get so entangled and driven to get things done that even if we become aware that we could stop, we are reluctant to do so. So *practising stopping* is helpful. I remember learning the 'mindful pause' in my eight-week course, when you consciously stop for a few seconds in the middle of an activity, relax your body and take a few conscious breaths, before continuing your activity.

> *Try it now! Stop reading for a moment and take three mindful breaths. How was that? How easy was it? Did you resist it? Could you be gentle on yourself if it was difficult?*

I also find stopping and putting my attention on my 'inner body' – feeling my whole body calming – and tingling a little, helpful. But it is not easy to stop I know, which is why we need practice and exercises.

A good exercise for children to practise is dancing or shaking to music, and then when the music stops, stopping our moving bodies and standing still and balanced with our breathing in the centre of our belly – feeling our quiet, still centre for a moment, becoming aware of our tingling body – then doing it again and again. Practice builds (self-regulation) pathways. The exercises and games in Box 17, p. 207, may be helpful in this regard.

Like Jill Bolte Taylor, I also believe that both we and the world need to move towards a balance of right- and left-brain capacities for both compassionate effectiveness and peace.

Compassion – includes caring and connecting

It's about learning (through experience) that the more we understand and bring compassion, empathy and awareness towards ourselves, the more we will naturally become empathic and understanding towards others and vice versa. We will become more caring and connected to others and more connected to ourselves.

I was very heartened when I heard Susan Kaiser Greenland include compassion in her mindfulness 'Way of Looking' (TED talk on YouTube, which I highly recommend),[8] as it provides a link between the teaching of the rest of this book and the more interior work of mindfulness that I have valued and practised for some time. It reminded me of an insight I had personally some years ago – that attuned attention to children (actively noticing their subtle behaviours, apparent needs and emotional state in any given moment), which children need so much from their parents and attachment figures, is like an attachment version of mindfully attuning to our inner selves and noticing what *we* see, hear and feel in each moment within and around ourselves. Both these processes happen in the present moment. But it is not about being perfect.

At the end of her TED talk Greenland says: 'Wisdom does not come from being perfect, but from being present.' I like that! When we are in the present moment and not caught up with busyness, sometimes amazing things can happen. Inspiration can flow, from some deep place, connected to our experience. Suddenly, probably prompted by my yoga and mindfulness class today, the following 'Noticing' poem came to me – in response to the subject here in this chapter and in the class of course, but even the 'in and out' layout came – like a wave of experience or a wave of the breath perhaps:

Noticing
Noticing what is here in this moment
Just noticing   Not thinking or labelling
Just feeling the feeling – or the sensation
Hearing the sound, or noticing the thought without pursuing it
Becoming aware of all the subtleties in our experience right now
And if we stay with the noticing
What can happen – is three things
The first is it's difficult. We so easily get caught up and distracted
So we need to return to noticing – again and again – with gentleness –
and with kindness
And that is good. We become kinder to ourselves – less critical
And we realise we are just like others – struggling and judging ourselves too much
But that's OK.
We become more compassionate and gentle with ourselves – and with others
Then we come to realise the richness of the present moment
There is so much more to it than we would have thought
So many aspects to be appreciated. To link to each other.
To enjoy.
And then we discover a different way of experiencing
A different way of *being* with experience
We discover
A space around experience
An openness to experience in the present moment
Including a different way of *being* with difficulties

With pain even, or with worries
We can just notice them,
Notice where we feel them in our body.
Notice the intensity of the feeling, or the depressing thought. Just notice them.
Notice all the different senses, the feelings and thoughts attached to the pain
Just staying with the experience
But not contracting on to it
Just watching it shift and change
Just see what happens, and how it affects us.
Try it!

I include now some notes on mindfulness courses I have run, both for school staff themselves and also to introduce teachers to mindfulness and relaxation exercises with children. For those who are interested there are a lot of short mindfulness practices on YouTube and also many CDs available.

Notes for an introductory course on mindfulness for school staff

Brain connections build through repeated experiences

We can think of the analogy of walking through a grassy meadow. As we repeatedly walk the same path the grass gets trodden down and a path develops that we subsequently tend to follow. We can, however, always choose to make a new path.

Purpose and practice of mindfulness

- To bring mindful (conscious) attention to what is happening now. To accept 'what is'.
- To practise letting go of any expectations or control over what we want to happen.
- To let go of any judgements of ourselves.
- To practise *just being*.
- To accept whatever is happening and develop our capacity to stay with it for a while.
- Slowly to develop the capacity to STOP for a moment when we become aware that we need a break in life, or we are too 'caught up' in a conversation, a task or an issue.

Benefits of mindfulness

Mindfulness can help us:

- relax body and mind – I find just *noticing* relaxes muscle tension;
- calm down – calm down physical tension and calm the nervous system;
- become more non-judgemental – of ourselves and others;
- move away from our tendency to 'live in our heads', towards tuning into our bodily and heartfelt experience;

- attune to our own and to other people's states;
- have experiences of 'being in the moment';
- gain a 'space' around our movements, our thoughts and our responses;
- become aware of the observer part of ourselves;
- stay present in a difficult situation, rather than becoming resistant/resentful/reactive;
- develop our capacity to respond and speak from a place of stillness;
- facilitate the flow of creativity – in the silent spaces between thoughts creativity can flow.

Mindfulness can enhance our capacities for:

- acceptance;
- balance;
- concentration;
- action with awareness;
- being here now – without being caught up in past or future anxieties;
- compassion;
- empathy.

Some mindfulness exercises

1. *Raisin experience* – feeling, biting and eating a raisin mindfully, plus feedback.
2. *Breath-awareness introduction* – focusing on the breath is useful because:

   - It is always there.
   - You can practise returning to it again and again (with 'kindness') after drifting on to thinking about something else.
   - Sometimes 'naming' the distractions (*thinking, feeling, judging, sensing, worrying, etc.*) can aid the letting go of them and returning to the breath.
   - This returning to the breath again and again with kindness facilitates an accepting non-judgemental attitude towards ourselves.
   - The breath is both controllable and automatic. It is a borderline experience. One can 'ride the wave' of the breath as it breathes us.
   - The breath is the interface between the inner and the outer worlds. It comes from outside to inside and back to outside, etc.
   - It is both relational (we all breathe the same air), and embodied within us.
   - The 'in breath' activates the sympathetic autonomic nervous system (getting us ready to act/move).
   - The 'out breath' activates the parasympathetic autonomic nervous system (calming us down after excitement). It is said that if every human being on the planet focused on the breath for five minutes a day we would have a different planet.

3. *Breath-awareness practice* – posture/half-smile/eyes gently closed (use CD or YouTube) (five minutes).
4. *Mindfulness of breath and body* (use CD or YouTube) (5 minutes).
5. *Walking meditation* – feel your feet on the ground as you slowly lift and place each foot. This can be combined with breathing – one breath to one step, or two steps or three as you wish.

6. *Opportunities in everyday life to practise mindfulness:*

- When you wake up consciously observe three mindful breaths.
- As you rise up or move, be aware of the subtle movements in your limbs and back (try it now).
- When you are about to move, become aware of:

  (i) your intention to move;
  (ii) your decision to move;
  (iii) your bodily experience of moving (try it now).

- Climb stairs slowly paying attention to your feet and your breathing as you go up.
- Any time you think of it during the day, stop and take one or two mindful breaths and tune in to your inner body.
- When waiting in a traffic jam or a queue, use the opportunity to take mindful breaths and tune in to your inner body.
- Use the sound of the phone or doorbell ringing, of a car door shutting, a car horn or church bells as a reminder to take one or two mindful breaths.
- In difficult situations it can be helpful to stop and take a mindful breath.
- Take opportunities when walking alone to walk slowly and mindfully for a few steps.
- When something hurts you, stop and tune into your bodily experience of the pain.
- *But above all be gentle with yourself.* Remembering and taking these opportunities will develop gradually. That is fine. They are only suggestions.

7. Finally, something to take away – stones. Blind choosing of a stone, then feeling, anticipating and discovering without looking, and then opening our eyes and tuning into our feelings about our choice. Put the stone in your pocket to remember to be mindful any time you feel it or think of it!

It's a lot to take in. Yes. Some of you may feel inspired to do the eight-week course, as I was. You may also be beginning to see the value of mindfulness in our busy lives.

Another reason for introducing mindfulness practice to school staff is because it is always recommended to practise it yourself before introducing mindful games and exercises to children in school. All children will benefit from mindfulness and relaxation practices, interestingly a number of public schools were the first to take it up.

On the back cover of her book *Mindful Games*, Susan Kaiser Greenland writes: 'Mindful play is a great way for kids to develop focusing skills while learning to regulate their emotions and respond to any situation calmly, with kindness and compassion.' It is also true, however, that the more chaotic/disorganised children (who probably need it most!) will find it very hard to sit still and focus without embarrassment and will need personal support and patience. They will need a slow and thoughtful introduction with lots of support and talking through. I have even heard of a 'mindfulness with children' teacher (the '.b method') who gave up because she was repeatedly given a group of the most disturbed children in the school to work with, with no support. There are ways of managing that include a mixed group with 'good' role models (see Case Study 36).

I myself ran several Relax Kids sessions with primary classes, and I was very aware of the difficulties some children might have with the quiet and still activities, so I asked the teachers and the TAs to join in too and to consciously offer a supporting hand to the children that we knew might find it difficult (including an autistic child). I think we were all surprised by how well they managed. The staff benefitted by learning the practices too, which they then used in their own way with the class.

One experienced learning mentor and meditator I know has run a 'creative relaxation class' first thing in the morning at her school, which anyone in the school can opt into, for many years with great success (see Case Studies 36 and 37).

Case Study 36   Ms O's creative relaxation class

Ms O has been running the creative relaxation class in her primary school for six years now. Being a meditator just about all her life, she is passionate about opening children to a quiet calm place inside their minds, where they can feel safe and supported. Ms O is also a learning mentor, so many of the 'needy' children know her and are keen to come to the class.

The staff are very positive about the creative relaxation class and sometimes refer children to it (parents sometimes refer children too, for example children who find concentration or settling down difficult), but basically the group is open to any child who wishes to come, which is good because it includes many secure children who make good role models for those who are less secure. The class is held first thing every morning during assembly (about 20 minutes), which gives those children who find assembly challenging a nurturing and life-enhancing option, as well as easing the pressure on teachers and providing a calm start to the day for those who need it. The atmosphere in the whole school is quiet during that time, which prevents distractions and facilitates a good transition both from and back into class.

Ms O talks of having a continuous eye on the security of the class. The daily regularity of time and place feeds into this secure base of course. Also any changes, forthcoming breaks or new directions in the class are thought about in previous days, so children are prepared and secure in what to expect. Ms O wants these classes to be a safe and calm place for all of them, and indeed children who are sometimes notoriously difficult in class will usually settle after a few days or even minutes. If new or insecure children want to just watch from the back until they are ready to join in that is fine. They can come as often, or for as many days or weeks as they like. Mostly they stay for several weeks or months, or even till they leave the school, some come occasionally.

Understanding the importance of being heard (particularly for the more needy children) has led Ms O to begin the class with a sharing time, when children can share briefly anything from their experience that comes to mind. This used to happen in a circle, but as the class has now grown to up to 50 children they are just scattered across the dining hall each on a mat and they put their hands up if they have something to share. This also enables them to feel thought about and held in mind, as Ms O often remembers and briefly refers back to a child's previous sharing in response to their contributions. Sometimes they might share how they have been doing the latest visualisation at home, or teaching it to their siblings! The sharing lasts about five minutes. Of course there will be days when there is not enough time for all those who want to share, which is acknowledged, and they are given the option of waiting till tomorrow or going to Ms O's room at break time to tell her their news.

Then they move quietly into the relaxation or meditation (Ms O is comfortable with both descriptions). They can either lie down or sit cross-legged on their mat – whatever works best for them (about half choose to lie and half to sit). They are encouraged to close their eyes and are regularly reminded not to make eye contact, as this can get in the way of other people's concentration.

> 'If you think you may be tempted to make eye contact you can come to the front and sit or lie facing the wall to make it easier.'

Occasionally if they are all a bit fidgety (as Christmas is approaching, for example) Ms O will get them to stand and jump up and down on the spot for a few minutes to dissipate the adrenalin, and then stop and 'feel' the energy slowly fizzling out in their body, before sitting or lying down to begin the relaxation.

They are guided gently into ensuring that their back is straight, and into becoming comfortable, still and relaxed. For a few minutes they are guided through a brief body scan – from their toes to their head or vice versa, or focusing on the sensations they can feel in different parts. They then are encouraged to soften and feel warm for about five minutes.

Then they are guided through a calming visualisation, usually a scene in beautiful nature. This always includes trees, plants, scenery and water in some form, which they visualise in their own way. After a few weeks they are encouraged to visualise a safe place, again out in nature. Ms O says she has tried using the Relax Kids CDs for this, which I know to be beautifully and calmly presented, but interestingly she says the children always prefer her voice. She may take ideas from various books of meditations, or read the wonderfully evocative visualisations in the Relax Kids book, but their attachment to her is obviously a factor in their enjoyment and valuing of the class – and her calm voice and presence will be part of that.

She consciously provides unobtrusive support for children who need it – by standing near them, or with a gentle touch or a quiet whisper in their ear – but she never singles out a child in public as she says this 'goes against the grain'.

After the visualisation they have a chance to briefly share their experience (hands up if they want to share), and Ms O says she is often quite amazed by the vividness of their experiences and images.

Finally as they leave they each share 'one thing I'm thankful for' with the class. As each child is named they stand up and share, and then quietly go and stand in the line ready to go back to class (while listening to the others' thankful comments).

To support the class Ms O has a noticeboard outside her door about creative relaxation, which currently includes pictures of famous people who meditate and what they say about it.

The original process was designed to last six weeks, but in reality most children stay much longer. The more needy children come to 'need' it perhaps, and the daily regularity facilitates a secure group that children can really come to value – and that is fine. There are brief before and after feedback forms for teachers, but the real benefits are observable in the children and their enthusiasm!

Case Study 37   Some thoughts from Ms O

> One child with a diagnosis of ADHD spent the first two weeks quietly wailing and clinging to a chair in the corner at the beginning of each session and couldn't join in the sharing time. He later became one of our most regular attendees – right up until he left in Year 6!

. . .

One very ill child who used to find attendance at school very difficult, now comes to class (and school!) every day. She says this is 'her safest place in school.'

. . .

It is very rare that I have to exclude a child, as the 'rolling programme' where children can start and finish at any time means there are always many confident secure children who model appropriate and calm behaviours and attitudes for the new and insecure ones.

There was one child, however, who found sharing me with the others in the creative relaxation class just too difficult. He had a diagnosis of ODD (oppositional defiant disorder), so I also saw him individually. His teacher referred him to creative relaxation and he managed it for a while, but he couldn't settle. He would do all sorts of things to get my attention – like clinging on to my leg and running around the room. I had to have a quiet word with him and said, 'Look S, I can see this time is just too difficult for you. We can do it one-to-one, but it's not working out in the group is it. So we can't do it at present in the group.' I was aware that his relationship with me was becoming important and that we needed to work on developing a secure enough relationship – with lots of holding in mind – before he would be ready to share such a relationship with others.

. . .

Of course we do get distractions sometimes – a teacher walking through the hall for example – but I teach them that distractions are natural in life, and it is useful when something distracts us, as we can practise using our concentration skills to take no notice and just carry on. Many of them manage this perfectly – better than me!

. . .

I really like this quote: 'Most adults think it's natural to be stressed(!) – so it's really important to teach children that relaxation and choosing to practise relaxation and meditation is natural – so that as adults they can have that resource.' I put it up on our noticeboard!

. . .

Beginning the school day with creative relaxation really benefits me too. I really miss it if we can't have it for some reason.

There are many excellent training courses on using mindfulness and relaxation with children, for example, 'Paws b', '.b', and 'creative relaxation' are just a few I know about. Yoga for children also provides similar benefits. The 'Yoga Pretzel' cards and the 'Enchanted Wonders' cards are engagingly presented picture cards that introduce yoga to children in a fun way. Andy Puddicombe at headspace.com also offers free and very accessible mindfulness, yoga and meditation practices for children (and adults too) in graded and themed short programmes. As mentioned above, Susan Kaiser Greenland's two books, *Mindful Games* and *The Mindful Child*, are full of very usable ideas, in addition to very clear descriptions and arguments for the value of mindfulness for a full and healthy life, and for freeing children up to learn and reach their potential.

There are also many interesting YouTube videos about the value of mindfulness for children, for example on 'The Mindful Classroom' from Opening Minds. Trainers may find the notes on the introductory course that I ran for teachers on fostering the Inner development of children (which includes some Relax Kids[9] CD tracks) useful.

Fostering the inner development of children: a course for school staff[10]

Mindfulness is:

- present-moment awareness;
- observing/witnessing our experience as it happens;
- attunement to ourselves;
- noticing feelings or thoughts as they come and go.

Mindfulness develops our:

- capacity to attune to others:
- capacity to observe and reflect;
- capacity to choose to stop before responding;
- capacity to focus and concentrate;
- awareness of space around our words, actions, busyness;
- creativity, concentration, relaxation, calmness;
- own observer part;
- internal resources.

Some mindful practices to try with children:

We can tune into our:

- Breathing – with guidance (Relax Kids 'Anger Management' 10 – 'Becoming').
- Movement and stretching:
  - Qi gong exercises.
- Sensory awareness:
  - *hearing* – outside noises, gong, other sound triggers;
  - *sight* – look at a flower in detail, observational drawing;
  - *taste* – eating mindfully, e.g. a grape;
  - *touch* – feely bag and guess.
- Body awareness:
  - *body scan* (Relax Kids 'Relax and De-Stress' no. 3, or 4, 5, 6);
  - *movement and stillness* – energy flow;
  - *dancing and stopping* and feeling the energy drain away.

Facilitating quiet breathing with children – rock Teddy to sleep (with Teddy on your tummy as you breathe):

- with quiet mindful music;
- snow globe, singing bowl or sand timer to look at as you breathe;
- gong or special sound to listen to;
- three breaths;
- 'breathing in I know I am breathing in' ('Thich Naht Hanh') poem.

Relax Kids seven-step programme process – examples from each step:

Step 1. Self-regulation: 'go . . . stop . . . go' (tingle game).

Step 2. Body awareness: 'fizzy lemonade' (fizzy body shake and calm).

Step 3. Yoga stretches: three simple stretches ('pose of a child').

Step 4. Peer massage: guided pizza massage on a partner's back.

Step 5. Breathing exercises: icy breaths in, and AAH out through mouth.

Step 6. Self-image affirmations: *'I am calm'*, etc.

Step 7. Silence and visualisations: CDs and book of guided visualisations.

Ways to practise in schools (*Mindfulness in School* Relax Kids booklet).

Parents' meeting – ways to practise at home (Relax Kids '21-day plan' – download and print once).

Resources to buy:

- Schools have found the Relax Kids CDs and visualisation books particularly helpful.
- You can download 'Chill Skills' for free.
- Susan Kaiser Greenland's books *The Mindful Child* and *Mindful Games*.

I myself did the Relax Kids training with Marneta Viegas. The lessons include self-regulation and awareness activities, relaxing stretches, soothing peer massage, positive affirmations, mindful breathing practices and guided visualisations.

Reflecting on the value of mindfulness activities and approaches for needy and reactive children, it is clear that some of them may need a lot of support and patience to become sufficiently calm to manage to access them. Some children, for example, may be touch aversive and may need adaptions or gentle assistance to feel OK with peer massage. But I believe that such support would be invaluable, as it would both introduce them to an awareness of an inner world inside themselves and help them grow a capacity to access that. It would develop inner resources too, which they can draw on in times of stress. Indeed that is what regular mindfulness practice can do for all of us. Ms O's creative relaxation class demonstrates that it's possible!

Notes

1 Jenny Mosley has written many books and is credited with pioneering and popularising the use of circle time in schools. See, for example, Jenny Mosley, *More Quality Circle Time* (Cambridge: LDA, 1998).

2 Paul Greenhalgh, *Emotional Growth and Learning* (London: Routledge, 1994), 186.

3 See www.brefigroup.co.uk/acrobat/drivers.pdf.

4 Jon Kabat-Zinn first used mindfulness for stress reduction in 1979 in his Mindfulness-Based Stress Reduction (MBSR) programme, see Jon Kabat-Zinn, *Full Catastrophe Living* (New York: Random House, 2012).

5 The eight-week mindfulness course is offered in many locations, see https://mindfulnessworks.com/8weekmindfulnesscourse.php, to find a course near you.

6 Relax Kids offers mindfulness and relaxation classes and resources for children and was developed by Marneta Viegas. The Relax Kids seven-step process is available online, see www.relaxkids.com.

7 Susan Kaiser Greenland, *The Mindful Child* (New York: Free Press, 2010); Susan Kaiser Greenland, *Mindful Games* (Boulder, CO: Shambhala Publications, 2016).

8 See www.youtube.com/watch?v=LpMvTTIr2p4.

9 See relaxkids.com, which has many wonderful guided visualisations in CD and book form.

10 Numbers in brackets relate to Relax Kids CD tracks.

Working with vulnerable parents

Some thoughts

15

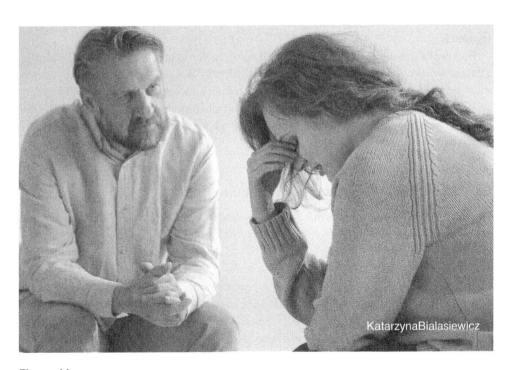
KatarzynaBialasiewicz

Figure 46

Work with vulnerable and disturbed children is so much more effective if we can engage with the parents at the same time. We all know how children's problems can be intricately interlinked with, and even caused by the unmet needs and unprocessed hurts of their parents. As described in Chapter 1 (p. 7), 'attachment patterns cycle through generations'. The task is to break that cycle. This chapter is about the importance of engaging parents and having a relationship-based approach to them much like we have with their children. It is not about parent workshops or strategies, which are well covered already in the excellent books and materials about parenting vulnerable and looked-after children, including those by Dan Hughes and Caroline Archer. There are also many agencies that work with and specialise in parent work, to which schools and social care will often refer families. The problem is that often the most vulnerable families find accessing and continuing to access such services very difficult. This could be because shame and anxieties are aroused, either inadvertently in the sessions, or because the very *thought* of (having to) go for such support brings anxiety and shame, even though it may be helpful. In addition the most chaotic and disorganised families can find remembering and getting to meetings very difficult. Coming to trust and to remember, and to *feel* remembered and respected, takes time and investment. As with vulnerable and poorly functioning children, vulnerable parents often need something a bit different – a relationship-based approach.

Because of this difficulty, when I was at the pupil referral unit we thought of employing a parent worker who would be like an available friendly face, taking time to make relationships with parents and befriend them, to listen to their concerns with empathy and interest and slowly move them towards honest sharing or outside help as the time was right. Case Study 38 includes an excerpt from a proposal I wrote at the time (sadly this was not taken forward because of lack of money).

Case Study 38 Proposal for a parent worker

The parent worker we have in mind would probably have counselling skills and maybe social work skills, but would be employed as a befriender, as someone who would visit or chat to parents regularly, take an interest in their lives and the lives of their children, as well as offering practical help when they became open to that.

The parent worker's relationship with the parents would not replace the teacher–parent relationship but enhance it. They would be a link person between the school and the home, and their main role would be to develop trusting workable relationships with parents, relationships that hold both the parent and the child in mind. If and when the parent is open to it they might facilitate parents accessing their own counselling. They would be able to signpost parents towards statutory or voluntary services. They would be available to transport parents and children to supportive and therapeutic services (chatting while driving and waiting) – certainly in the initial stages.

They would also liaise practically with involved services to ensure arrangements are secure and revised if necessary, understanding (without blame) the tendency of the family chaos and disorganisation to eat into the systems around the child, and into the arrangements to support them.

In line with the thinking in the book this would be a relationship-based approach, because the sort of parents we are thinking about first need to trust an adult enough to open up even a little. They may automatically expect other people to judge them, put them down and even abandon them when they get too close. They may well be conditioned to be hypervigilant to any hints of judgement or criticism. As with the children, the optimal attitude for the parent worker and for staff dealing with a parent is sensitivity, empathy and curiosity, with lots of thinking about whether and when to comment or make suggestions. Suggesting ways of relating and understanding may need to come slowly. I know from my own experience how vulnerable people can so easily interpret well-intentioned comments as judgements that they are not good enough. The attunement suggestions and ways of working and relating described in the book would be very helpful for parents too – in respectful adult format.

Parent workers themselves need to be highly attuned to the parent and their subtle communications, offering empathic responsiveness and thoughtful noticing, and even surviving and repairing the inadvertent 'breaks' in the relationship. Working in this way with vulnerable parents is not easy, and such staff benefit from clinical supervision, much like we have discussed for teachers 'at the coal face'. I was employed for a couple of years by a children's centre supervising their parent workers and it seemed to be appreciated (until the management structure changed), both to 'debrief' and think about their difficult to engage and disorganised parents, to enhance their knowledge of attachment and unconscious processes in the context of their difficult cases and to think about their (and the children's) behavioural communications. To illustrate this, an extended example of working in this way is given in Case Study 39, as a primary school inclusion manager talks about her experience with a very vulnerable mum.

Case Study 39   Relationship-based support for parents

Today we had a meeting about 6-year-old R, who presented when he first came to us a year ago as a bright but very inhibited, regressed and disturbed child with a speech impediment.

When he started with us we picked up quite quickly that he seemed to have quite severe emotional difficulties. He was both developmentally delayed and he acted out – mainly by throwing himself on the floor and screaming like a toddler when something didn't go his way. He couldn't bear even the slightest frustration. He wouldn't eat, and he would throw chairs. He was very controlling, and because of his 'huge' size he would really intimidate the other children.

Our initial meeting with his parents quickly indicated that he needed extra nurture – so we timetabled him into our nurture base. Because of his extreme difficulty with frustration we needed to think very carefully about the work we gave him to do. It also depended on how he was feeling at the time. We had to tune into him very closely. To start with we wouldn't give him any challenges because we quickly found he couldn't cope. We have often found playing games is a good way to get to know new children in the nurture base – but we found in his case we couldn't give him a choice of games, as any frustration in the game would 'freak' him. We also thought a lot with him about how to manage his 'big feelings'.

When I met Mum it was quite evident why. He still had a dummy and a bottle, he was still in nappies, and he was still sleeping in her bed. He would have the dummy in his mouth almost permanently and his speech was very affected by this. He was also very overweight.

Shortly after R arrived in the school I started having meetings with Mum. She would come to see me every morning and my first step was to build a strong relationship with her, at the same time as building a relationship with R in school.

In the meetings with Mum I would use lots of empathy and gentle curiosity, much like I might with a vulnerable child. But I was also aware that I needed to be careful not to give over any hints of judgement or even surprise. Soon Mum started to share how R would have huge tantrums at home, and how she found these impossible to manage and would often end up giving in to him.

I was aware that she became attached to me quite quickly. She was very needy and so I guess that facilitated the work, but of course it was also important for me to set boundaries with her and not overstep the available time, at the same time as enabling her to feel accepted, cared for and thought about.

In the meetings she also talked about her mum, who seemed to be quite involved with the family. So I suggested a meeting with Mum and Nan together. It was interesting to discover that Nan was still treating R like a toddler as well – wiping his bum – and he was sleeping in her bed too, etc. In the meetings Nan was always wanting to 'keep the peace' – saying, 'You don't want to leave him' (in school by himself if he cries), and one day Mum actually stood up to her. Maybe the fact that I was there made it safe to for her to say that.

Initially we had him in nurture (the school nurture base) full-time so we could assess his attachment pattern, skills and developmental stage. This left me the opportunity to work (for short frequent spurts) with his teacher while he was out of the room.

One day they had a circle time in nurture, and he started talking to the other children about having a 'bot-bot' (bottle); 'At night I have my bot-bot,' he said, and the other children laughed at him. One child called him a baby, and then all the children called him a baby (of course such children like to have a baddy or a baby in the group who is not them!) and staff had to intervene immediately, but it was too late. He was really upset and had a massive outburst. We understood the reason of course. He had probably never had such an 'honest' reaction before. The nurture teacher and I met with Mum after school to talk about this experience and it soon became clear that at home he was given in to all the time. There weren't any other children, and Mum wasn't 'allowed' (by Dad) to have friends home, so he was never challenged. I guess in the long run, however, this painful experience sowed a helpful seed, because this was the first time he saw that other children his age don't have bottles.

Then I started to have meetings with Mum and R together about these things. It was very helpful for him to see us talking thoughtfully together, trying to find manageable ways to work with him. After several meetings he slowly began to be open to the possibility that perhaps he didn't really have to have these things like his bottle and his dummy. But it was not easy.

Dad would come to the meetings sometimes, but that was very difficult. He was not only very critical of Mum, but he was also very rude to me when I started talking with Mum around R's baby needs and behaviours – like thinking together about how to get rid of the dummy. I think he felt threatened. I don't think he liked that Mum was listening to me at all. It was not easy. He could use quite abusive language towards me and even became threatening.

So in consultation with the head we decided we had to stop him coming to the meetings, which was difficult I know for mum. She then went through a period when she wouldn't see me, and Dad would wait outside for her when she dropped R off in the mornings. We were monitoring it carefully. After a while she popped back to say hello and we had a little chat. Things were difficult. She was obviously very needy and helpless. She was a total victim, unable to stop being controlled by both her partner and her son. She seemed very (unhelpfully) enmeshed with both of them. It felt important for a while that I saw her every day for a few minutes when she dropped R off for school. Slowly she shared how with everything she said, and everything she did with R, her partner put her down.

Getting rid of the dummies was not easy. It was complicated because he had about eight dummies! So getting rid of one was only the start. We offered to help with that. At school we made a fairy box for him, and he would bring his dummies in one at a time and put them in the fairy box, and the 'fairy then took the dummy away to give to a baby who needed a dummy'. Every time he put a dummy in the box he would say – 'Well I've still got two more at home!' and I would say, 'Well, I think the fairy wants those two as well. Because what the fairy does, is the fairy gives those dummies to little babies who haven't got dummies'. Then eventually there were none left, and we were all really really pleased, and he was pleased with himself too!

But setting boundaries like no more dummies when you have always given in for an easy life needs huge strength. Perhaps understandably Mum could get very down and preoccupied at times and become quite negative. We began to think about his resistant/ambivalent behaviours – because of Mum's unavailability and 'absence' at times – and his chaotic and controlling behaviours too, all of which were understandable in the circumstances.

We helped Mum to try out some of the nurturing songs and games from the nurture base with R, which she had seen and joined in with when she came in to 'help'. She began to see the value of the holding-in-mind gestures and rememberings, and to try them at home.[1]

Witnessing all the thoughtful and empathic conversations in the nurture base slowly enabled R to feel part of the group, and to want to be like them and want them to like him. Interestingly he now says, 'I'm a big grown up boy!' and he has started to join in a little more in the group.

In a meeting recently it was encouraging to hear his class teacher talking to staff about her experience of having a very delayed and challenging child (R) in her class who was now improving and settling, and how both she and R (and mum too) had been supported through the experience. This included his support from the nurture base, which is now (after eight months) mostly finished. Actually he has made a surprisingly quick turnaround. It has been so heartening to see him calming down, and start making academic progress. We are of course aware that the transition into Year 2 will not be easy for him, so we will keep part-time contact with the nurture base available until October – to see him over the change.

When I think how things have changed in eight months, I think what made the difference was the trusting and honest relationship we developed with mum – which included challenging her at times – as we felt she was open to it. We would say for example that 'things need to change'.

> What we're doing in school is not going to work unless you make some changes at home too. As you can see we are trying to support him to develop independence and to feel like he can be away from you, and that you will still care about him and think

about him even when he is not with you. He really needs you to let him go a little. I think it helps a lot when you tell him that you have been thinking about him when he was in school today.

Of course this took time, and mum did understand, even though he was still having massive tantrums at home. But she also knew things needed to change. It was not easy. Sometimes she would come into school and be very angry with me because I was the one who had suggested she take his dummy away. I tried to suggest that even though it was difficult it would be a positive for both of them if it could be achieved.

One of the things we had to work on with Mum was the importance of bearing hatred – because he could certainly express lots of hatred when he didn't get what he wanted. And slowly she came to understand that it wasn't personal – he was just very angry and scared of being out of control and vulnerable. And we could all understand him 'kicking off' because he was being deprived of the 'comfort' he so desperately needed. And we found we could talk about the times when she hated me too.

The nurture staff also continued to welcome her into the nurture base regularly – and of course they were modelling respectful, thoughtful and empathic ways of relating to him.

Recently Mum has made the decision that she wants to leave Dad, although managing it still feels very difficult. We probably still have a way to go.

As Case Study 39 shows, the helping relationship is supremely important. Especially with professionals, such parents can easily be triggered into experiences of shame or of not feeling good enough, and that is unbearable. If that happens they will probably not want to come back, but if enough trust has been built up – with sensitivity, thoughtfulness and time – the relationship can usually be repaired. If handled with empathy and honesty, both parties can also learn a lot from the 'repair' experience. Even the most experienced and thoughtful professional can inadvertently trigger a vulnerable parent's sensitivities. I once had a parent stop coming to a group because she felt judged. A lot of work and time was needed to heal her hurts, which were not apparent in the group at all.

It is also important to say that there are other agencies who specialise in this work, and school staff of course are not social workers, but the advantage of having someone in the school with the skills and emotional capacities to spend time listening to the parents of our most needy and dysfunctional children is that they are more available (see Case Study 40).

Case Study 40 The benefits of 'casual' supportive relationships with a social work student

When I was a SENCO in an inner-city primary school we used to have final-year social work students in the school for placement. They worked a lot with parents and one student, Mrs M, ran a lunchtime sewing group for several vulnerable girls, which they loved. Then every morning she would sit in the reception area sorting out sewing muddles. Often parents of our more dysfunctional and needy children would be there too, waiting to see the head teacher, and they would take an interest in the sewing and chat. Mrs M was very friendly, motherly and approachable and they would often strike up a relationship. Thus a natural and unthreatening channel opened up for Mrs M to visit parents and support them in their homes. She would listen to their dilemmas around home and school and point them towards the help they needed, and on a couple of occasions she saw them on a regular basis for a while (she had supervision for this role).

When children are young the school and the children's centre (including its cafe) are safe and familiar places for the parent as well as for the young child, and the parent will need to go to there frequently. It is quite normal for parents of young children to liaise with teachers and school staff in the course of delivering and collecting children – so the possibilities of developing good working relationships are often better than in a clinic that is unfamiliar and may feel daunting to attend – until a relationship is established. I also know of a primary school that has specially selected final-year student counsellors who see parents.

But some parents and families may really value having a different place to take their worries, which might feel more confidential. A regular hour in a neutral setting can be very containing if handled well. Also, staff in clinics usually have particular and specialised trainings.

Case Study 39 also illustrates the helpfulness of a nurture base in supporting vulnerable parents, both practically through friendship and as a manageable way in to helping them feel comfortable in the school. Having them in the nurture base for short periods enables them to feel that they are becoming part of the 'healing process' for the child. They can also observe how nurture staff relate to each other and share ways of thinking with each other, and how they relate thoughtfully and empathically with their child, which they may then take on board. This is so much better that just being given advice, because they can try out these new ways of relating in the 'safe setting' of the nurture base.

Setting boundaries for long-term dysfunctional children who have been used to having whatever they want is especially difficult, as we can see in Case Study 39 (also discussed on pp. 306–307). Other boundaries like bedtimes, mealtimes and saying 'no' can be similarly difficult for vulnerable parents. As the case studies in this chapter show, relationship-based ways of working with parents can help them in this slow and sometimes painful journey towards being strong and in control.

Long-term foster and adoptive parents

A group of less vulnerable or even secure parents who have *very* vulnerable children are long-term foster and adoptive parents (see also section on looked-after children on pp. 26–28). Such parents are basically confident, even if slightly anxious about their totally 'new' life. They will have been screened and trained to some extent, and the children are often relieved to be safe and warmly welcomed. The parents are encouraged to put a lot of effort into bonding with their new children including lots of availability, 'attachment-based' play, regression when needed and special one-to-one and nurturing activities like cooking together (see also section on the baby stage in Chapter 7, pp. 123–128).

The parents have often successfully brought up their own children and their new children may seem to settle in remarkably well. Slowly, in their new secure setting with their resilient caring parents, the children will come to experience that their feelings are understandable and can be contained, their worries can be talked about and hurts and guilt can be resolved. They can often develop security and strong, dependent relationships, which surprisingly at first perhaps, survive the little ups and downs. They can grow stronger. With caring, attuned and resilient foster or adoptive parents, who love them and are committed to them, and freed of the pervasive fear and anxiety, they can thrive and even eventually have a lot to give from their experience. Author Alan Burnell, who with Caroline Archer wrote one of the most helpful books for adoptive parents, was himself an adopted child.[2]

Frequently adopted children have a honeymoon period in their new family, which is evidence of the love, security and nurture they are now receiving and can even last years. But it is never easy. In some cases, as they get closer to their new parents such children can start to feel anxious. Sometimes parenting and relationships can become more difficult just as a child seems to be settling in. Anxieties relating to past family relationships can become transferred into their new 'forever' family and the ensuing closeness can arouse fear of rejection. What is also often not acknowledged enough when things are going well, is that underneath such very real and usable (second-chance) secure attachments, there can be underlying and earlier dysfunctional attachment patterns, fears and expectations, which can become triggered. This can happen particularly as puberty kicks in or around transitions. Buried and unprocessed trauma can become triggered too. Even if such parents are primed to expect this it can be devastating. Trusted, informed and sensitive LAC (see Chapter 3, p. 26) coordinators can do very useful preventative and supportive work in the form of regular 'supervisory' conversations with parents when they notice hints of things deteriorating. This may be especially valuable both well before and during big transitions, or they may encourage parents to go back to their agency for support.

Even when everything is fine it is important to be aware that the cumulative effect of past traumatic separations and losses can make all transitions difficult for looked-after children. Parents who understand something of this may be able to take emerging difficulties as opportunities to help their adopted and foster children play and talk through their buried hurts, thus integrating them little by little.

But *big* separations or losses (like moving house) can trigger unbearable anxieties and lead to acting out, evoking huge anxiety in both parents and school staff.

A child's increasingly challenging behaviour after a long calm period, can sometimes trigger parents into feeling helplessly disappointed. They may try to smooth over the cracks and carry on as best they can – not wanting to acknowledge any signs of difficulty perhaps. Asking for help can be very difficult when you have always thought of yourself as good capable parents. They can even shift into seeing their child as 'damaged goods', something they may not wish to face openly. In extreme cases things can begin to fall apart.

Adoptive and foster parents will hopefully be well chosen and have good attachment-based support and training, but even years after a child has settled into their new home I have seen adoptions break down or wobble dangerously as a previously settled child moves (for example) from their familiar, trusted junior school to a big, new, unfamiliar secondary school with unfamiliar people, which is differently organised and much less nurturing and secure.

One adopted child I knew had two good years with her adoptive family. Then shortly before she moved to secondary school she started stealing her mum's jewellery, which she vehemently and repeatedly denied. Lying and stealing were obviously communicating a need for love and understanding, but for the parents they demonstrated criminal tendencies that were unacceptable. The school persuaded them to seek help but by then it was too late. Sadly a few weeks later the adoption broke down.

Being clued up about the very real risk of triggers and escalation around big endings and transitions can help LAC coordinators become open to subtle signs that a family might need help, and handle such situations sensitively. It can take a lot of courage and humility to go back for help. Often the skill and natural confidence of adoptive parents means they do not expect to need more than a little help. So when things slip a bit they think they can handle it. They may not even realise how *just anticipating* a big upcoming transition can be an unbearable and understandable trigger for their child. When things start to deteriorate they may privately wonder if they are slipping in their parenting skills. An attuned observant LAC teacher's thoughtful enquiries and normalising of such regressions can gently open them up to the possibility of these devastating triggers and preventative support.

Agencies are usually very good at training and inducting adoptive parents before adoption and in the early days, but I think they should have a system of automatic reviews around all big transitions both substantially before and after the transition, to remind parents of the likelihood of regression and to support them. Maybe some do.

The early and extreme trauma some of these children have experienced will also need addressing. Adoption agencies vary but the value of body-based trauma work of the kind offered by Family Futures in London[3] is increasingly coming to be appreciated as part of the healing support such children may need. These sensory motor exercises (see p. 117) originate in occupational therapy (see notes 8 and 9 in Chapter 6, p. 120). They aid the processing of buried trauma and ease emotional processing and self-regulation through bypassing the thinking and feeling parts of the brain. All these interventions, however, including psychotherapy, are better being offered before things deteriorate too much, otherwise the child may think it is a punishment or because they are 'bad', which will exacerbate their difficulties.

The other big challenge for such children is the move into puberty and adolescence, which is a challenge for all young people even without the complications of multiple traumatic and early losses and family changes. This book is not the place to go into the details of the complexities of adolescence, (briefly listed in Chapter 2, pp. 16–17), except to alert coordinators to watch out for the possibility of unconscious repeated intergenerational patterns (e.g. drugs or teenage pregnancy of their birth mother of which the young person may be only dimly aware).

Investing in the relationship and supporting adoptive parents to continue to give the children *ongoing* concentrated attuned relating, including setting firm boundaries with empathy, thoughtfulness and nurture (see suggestions in Chapter 7) and especially regulating arousal and managing outbursts, will continue to be important. This is of course covered in most Part II of this book, but to enable LAC teachers and pastoral workers to have a concrete framework for their discussions with such parents I recommend both Dan Hughes' very readable *Building the Bonds of Attachment* and Caroline Archer's two parenting handbooks, *First Steps in Parenting the Child Who Hurts* and *Next Steps in Parenting the Child Who Hurts*.[4]

Another group of vulnerable parents and families who may need particular help are those recovering from domestic violence and all the painful dynamics, after-effects and inhibitions, etc. that can result. This is discussed in detail in Chapter 3 (pp. 28–41).

Notes

1 The nurturing 'you' statements (see Box 10, p. 133) are also very helpful for parents of younger children – when they are open to it.
2 Alan Burnell and Caroline Archer, *Trauma, Attachment and Family Permanence* (London: Jessica Kingsley, 2003). The notion of 'internal working models' of attachment stems from John Bowlby, *Attachment and Loss* (New York: Basic Books, 1969), 12.
3 For interested professionals, adoption workers and LAC coordinators I recommend Alan Burnell and Jay Vaughan, 'Family Futures' Neuro-Sequential Approach to the Assessment and Treatment of Traumatised Children: Neuro-Physiological Psychotherapy (NPP)', www.familyfutures.co.uk/wp-content/uploads/2015/05/family-futures-rationale.pdf. These very detailed, complex and interdisciplinary interventions including specialised occupational therapy (which some early traumatised children need) should be more well known.
4 Dan Hughes, *Building the Bonds of Attachment: Awakening Love in Deeply Troubled Children* (Lanham, MD: Jason Aronson, 1998); Caroline Archer, *First Steps in Parenting the Child Who Hurts: Tiddlers and Toddlers* (London: Jessica Kingsley, 1999); Caroline Archer, *Next Steps in Parenting the Child Who Hurts: Tiddlers and Toddlers* (London: Jessica Kingsley, 2000).

A nurturing school

16

Some thoughts from an assistant head

Figure 47

The thinking and relationship-based way of working emphasised throughout the book is not only helpful for individual children and for vulnerable parents, but for whole schools too. Especially in these stressful times when schools and teachers are minutely evaluated and appraised and curriculum and behavioural expectations can sometimes feel overwhelming, staff need to feel cared for, thought about and supported to work in the most effective way with the children who challenge them the most.

This chapter is a case example of a nurturing (infant) school that focuses particularly on supporting staff to understand and nurture the children and is taken from the words of the assistant head teacher.

Nurture

After several years of preparation we have just been awarded nurtureuk's Nurturing School Award. This means we are a school where we think together about children, try to understand their difficulties and consciously respond to them from that understanding in a thoughtful, empathic and respectful way.

It means having 'nurture' at the heart of our way of working within the whole school. This means embedding the 'nurture principles' (see p. 85) in our relationships, our policies and our ways of working and responding to children. With the more vulnerable and disturbed children – of which we have quite a lot in our school – it means consciously using significant relationships as a way to both support, care for and teach them, to enable them to experience a more secure relationship and setting within which they can grow and learn. It means having a basic understanding of attachment, attunement and attachment categories, so staff can respond to children in attuned and appropriate ways according to their patterns, needs and difficulties. It means thinking of ways to meet their unmet needs for nurture and a secure foundation. It means viewing the whole nurturing process developmentally – as a work in progress – and discovering from experience that nurture and thoughtful responsiveness make a difference to damaged and vulnerable children, and to our own teaching experience too, because we see children slowly change and grow, which is rewarding and validating.

Everything we do is based around nurture. When thinking of a nurturing school it is important first of all to make sure that all staff are aware of what it means to nurture children. It's more than being nurturing of course, it's about understanding what it means to nurture. And this understanding particularly comes from supervision, which is having a confidential space to talk through the inevitable difficulties and the often challenging and puzzling feelings such children can 'put right into us' on a regular, and an as-needed basis.

So as I say, being a nurturing school is about knowing the nurture principles and about understanding attachment and unconscious processes, but it's not just knowing what they are. It's about having a true sense of their meaning through reflecting on them, and sometimes through struggling with our own experiences with children and developing our thinking and responding skills so we grow into using them naturally with children, with the parents and with each other.

Safe base

'The classroom offers a safe base' means putting thought and effort into creating a safe base with consistent, safe and predictable structures and relationships, within which the less secure and more easily triggered children can remain calm and secure enough to function and learn. From our own experience I guess we all know the difference it can make if we feel secure (or not) in a challenging situation. In our school we have done quite a lot of work around what a safe base is. One problem was that to emphasise the importance of a secure base (particularly for insecure children) was not how they had been trained to work in schools. The emphasis these days in teaching is so much on management and targets, and how to plan and teach the curriculum, which can mean that relationships and the importance of a secure base is perhaps taken for granted.

In addition some staff find the safe base concept quite confusing because a 'safe base' gives the impression that it is a place, but it's actually more about a relationship that holds the child in mind, remembers him and thinks about him. It's true that the big playground can feel less safe and secure for a vulnerable child than the small familiar classroom, so a safe base includes the familiar place, but it's mostly the secure resilient 'holding relationship' that gives the security. It took some staff quite a time to understand that the security relies on us as attachment figures, as significant adults for the children, on us being consistent and reliable and holding them in mind whatever the circumstances. Even when we are in a different room they can come to know that we are thinking of them, and we will be interested to hear what they have to say when we see them again. We did a lot of work on attachment and loss around this and we related it to staff experiences in class with the more needy children, and particularly to their relationships with the children. They could all recall experiences when they or the teacher or the key adult was away from an insecure child and the child would act out in some way, sometimes quite disturbingly. Relating things to their own experience was always helpful.

Of course working on creating and enabling a secure base is important for parents as well as for children, especially the parents of our most needy and damaged children who are often defensive, vulnerable and needy themselves, for good reasons of course. What do they say, 'attachment cycles through generations'?[1]

Training

When I first started at the school we spent a lot of time training. Even now in our weekly staff meetings we have 'nurture' on the agenda every week. We don't talk about it every time, but it is there in black and white, and if an issue has arisen it can be mentioned and if necessary a time will be made to address it.

We began with an overview of what nurture is. We broke down each principle into small parts, and we continue to do that all the time. We had a separate training on each of the nurture principles, and on attachment and the three insecure attachment patterns. In the training we included both teaching and discussion around current case studies. We always try to integrate training with experience.

Behaviour as communication

So when we thought about the principle, 'all behaviour is communication' we asked staff to bring along puzzling behaviours and we did the 'reflection on a repeated puzzling behaviour together' exercise (see Exercise 7, p. 167).

For example, we had a child who was continually taking school things home. We tried to think about what that child might be communicating, what feelings he might be experiencing, inner conflicts or needs perhaps. We wondered if he wanted some connection with us to keep at home, whether he tended to want things as a substitute for love or whether he had learnt to grab what he wanted as the only way to get his needs met.

Puzzling and problem behaviours also come up frequently in the context of our regular (often daily) debriefs at the end of the day. We do this both individually and in class groups, and also in year groups sometimes, because we are a very big staff. We have this sort of informal supervision regularly. All these little discussions reinforce the way we think and work. In fact we have found that if staff haven't got an understanding and experience of how this way of thinking is helpful, then they just won't do it. Talking things through together is the best way to cement their understanding.

The importance of language and talking things through

The nurture principle about language emphasises talking things through, acknowledging feelings and the use of thoughtful reflection and empathy, and that's what we do. We take little opportunities to talk things through with the children as they arise (little and often is best), and we also sometimes 'wonder' with each other in a thoughtful caring way in front of them. This can be supportive for the staff of course, but it can also be important for the children to experience their special adults thinking and cooperating together in front of them in a caring, 'wondering' and supportive way. It enables them to feel thought about and cared for, and it also enables children from conflict-ridden families to have the 'amazing' experience of observing staff talking in caring ways about them and helping each other manage and support them together! They may be used to quite the opposite at home!

So taking little opportunities to talk things through is important and encouraged. But sometimes engaging our vulnerable ones with words is difficult because we have young children and a surprising number have language difficulties. So we may use signs, offer them thoughtful things or practical help instead or as well. We are aware of course that quite a lot of speech and language difficulties are emotionally based. A number of children have speech and language therapy, and that's important. Maybe one day we will be able to share this thinking with the speech therapists too.

We make a big thing in the training, and in all our interactions, of using thoughtful empathic language and of talking in a 'wondering' way, which is both curious and reflective and opens up thinking in a non-judgemental way. Wondering about something also doesn't require an answer, so it is less threatening to a child who is reluctant to engage. It just 'sows a seed'. In this context role modelling makes a huge difference. When I first worked at the school, I role modelled 'curiosity' and 'wondering' all the time, e.g.

'I wonder what that's about?'

'I wonder what's going on here?'

'I'm just thinking about that. Could it be that . . . ?'

'That's interesting. I wonder if it relates to P's early history. You know, he . . .'

We even have such sentence stems in our policies and all staff have copies to refer to, because in the heat of the moment you can get quite flawed, and it can be useful to have a crib sheet till it becomes second nature.

It's important to emphasise, however, that using such thoughtful empathic responses does not mean having 'loose boundaries', but rather having very predictable and firm boundaries and setting them in a thoughtful and empathic way, e.g. *'I know you want to carry on for longer, but we do have to stop now. I will look after it for you till tomorrow if you like.'*

Changes, transitions and endings

'Transitions are significant in the lives of children' is a very important nurture principle, and of course we have a policy around it. Because we understand how crucial it is to really work through children's ambivalences around transitions and endings, we start doing ending work quite early. We have already started our transition work (in May) with children, especially with the older ones (the nursery children still live very much in the present moment of course so it will be a bit different for them). We have a calendar on which we mark significant endings and days, and we have a countdown of weeks till the end of term for example, and we take frequent opportunities to think about how that might be making us feel, etc.

Sadly not all childcare professionals see it this way. I was at a looked-after children meeting recently and we started thinking about a child who was moving into a new school in a few weeks, and one professional said, *'Don't you think it's a bit early to think about this. You would just make him worry more about it,'* to which I replied,

> But he's already worrying about it. We can already see little indications in his behaviour that it's on his mind. What we will be doing in school is support him to have an ending with us that can be thought about and talked about, so that all his difficult and ambivalent feelings around it can be acknowledged and empathised with as we notice them coming up. I think this is such an important opportunity – to support him as well as we can through his grief and loss in a way he probably hasn't had before in all his sudden and traumatic changes.

What happens is we start to see changes in the behaviour – particularly of our most vulnerable children as an ending approaches – and that is how we know it is on their minds. So we talk with the children about how it can be quite worrying when we realise we haven't got many weeks or days left in the school or with their teacher. I have to say that when I first came to the school staff didn't really talk about endings at all until about two weeks before the summer holidays! Sometimes transitions can be quite complicated when the future is unknown.

I think it is very sad to see that this kind of psychodynamic and attachment-based thinking is so rarely there, even in social work and other children's services. Maybe it's not in their training, I imagine they know the word attachment, but in my experience they don't seem to appreciate the implications of separation and loss, even though you would think they would need such understanding all the time! Maybe they would find this book helpful! The problem is that if you don't talk about something with a child it gets repressed and then it gets acted out and then they get into trouble! Sometimes such acting-out behaviour can even lead to a child being moved into a new foster placement – and another loss! It works on all levels of course (see Case Study 41).

Case Study 41   Staff projection around loss and leaving

Loss and endings can be difficult for everyone. We currently have a member of staff who is moving to Hong Kong and I noticed recently that she has started to become quite defensive. It has felt as if she has started to distance herself from us a little bit. And she's also tried to rubbish some of the ways we work. So I have had some conversations with her about how it can be easier to go away from something that hasn't been particularly good, than to walk away grieving a loss of something that has meant a lot. Of course I do understand that she may feel the need to do that, as the loss of our close and supportive school may be very difficult for her (and for us too). But the reality is that leaving can be painful. I guess this is what grief is about. And of course the time of year (as we move into the final term) will also make it harder for her because she will be doing ending work with her class, which will be difficult, but important, for all of them.

Small changes can be difficult too. We have recently put the older children into sets for maths and English, because we needed to maximise their learning and teaching and so sets were considered necessary. We were aware, however, that the more vulnerable children would find these changes difficult, but we did what we could to make this manageable for them. We put the vulnerable children's regular one-to-one support TAs in with them too, and that was helpful.

Supporting attachment workers

In school we are aware of the difficulty some very insecure children can have with their attachment workers. Although most dysfunctional children need a 'second-chance attachment', for some of them it is not easy. Their experience of close relationships may have been conflict ridden or even rejecting – so they may get very anxious when they start to get close to a significant adult – until they can learn from experience that they will not be rejected or abandoned when they misbehave. We include such thinking in our trainings and we prepare staff before they start one-to-one support with a vulnerable child. But it can still be difficult, as Case Study 42 illustrates.

Case Study 42   Supporting and surviving rejection of M's attachment worker

Even though M's attachment worker had a lot of preparation work before she started working with him (he has developmental and language delay, quite aggressive behaviour difficulties and he has a 'statement'[2]), he soon became so difficult that the attachment worker actually said she didn't want to work with him anymore. We then supported her more intensively around understanding his behaviours and his patterns, highlighting the fact that his negative behaviour towards her was actually a sign that he was very attached to her. What he used to do was blank her (not respond when she spoke to him), while he continued to respond to other people – so it wasn't dissociation. We would talk about how this was actually an indication that he was starting to become attached to her, because being hurt and rejected by those closest to him was probably what he was used to – he was rejecting first before he got rejected. Her initial response had been to start pushing him away and ignoring him – as he was ignoring her – but as she began to understand a bit, she changed her approach. At first though she overcompensated. She even brought biscuits in one day! And then when he still wouldn't respond she would get annoyed. It took time and lots of supervision, but eventually she became able to have conversations with him, saying things like, 'It's hard when you want to work with someone and you think they're not going to like you isn't it?'

And now six months down the line things are a lot better. Interestingly his language is getting better too and he is verbalising more. He used to do quite a lot of 'Makaton' (sign language), and now he uses it less and words more.

The attachment worker even said to me the other day that she was so glad we didn't let her stop working with him!

> Because actually we now have a fantastic attachment, I can really understand him and he can let me help him now. It was so helpful when we talked about his attacking behaviour as being related to his fear of getting close to me in case I might reject him and to know that that has happened to him in the past.

The example in Case Study 42 shows how patiently working with staff around the child is an important aspect of our work, but how it can be complicated and take time to bear fruit. It also vividly shows how the child can shift and grow more open to trust and to help, and how the attachment worker can grow too!

But we are also aware that when you consciously and helpfully develop a trusting relationship with a child, both little separations and the loss of that relationship during holidays and end of terms will need more attention and thoughtful acknowledgement with the child because the breaks are more felt.

Relationship-based way of working

So our whole way of working both with the children and with the teachers – and with the parents too – is a relationship-based way of working. That's just how we work, what we have found makes a difference and of course we come to care for each other. We talk everything through without judgement. In our practice the principle of non-judgement is like a foundation. We taught it and thought about it from the beginning. It's not easy though. I might feel the need to say to staff sometimes, *'I'm just wondering if you felt a little bit criticised when I said that. Because I'm certainly not meaning to be critical, just to think about all aspects and to wonder about our relationship and about feelings too.'* Then we might have an honest and thoughtful conversation. And they know they are cared for and they can become surprisingly open.

Talking through staff difficulties

One thing we have noticed is that when we discuss a child's difficulties, we can sometimes end up talking about our own role and feelings in particular communications. Sometimes teachers might even share their observations of each other's ways of reacting to children, in front of them in a supervision group for example.

> *S, I don't know if you are aware, but I have noticed that often when you talk to P you can have quite a brusque or even a critical voice. Maybe he evokes that in you (he certainly makes me feel a bit critical at times and I have to watch myself). I wonder if that might be happening with you?*

We are even open to talking about such difficulties between staff. For example, there are two members of staff in the office, who are really not getting on at the moment. It's a little bit like a conflict of power. One has been there for ten years and the newer member has been there just two years. They are both strong characters and they both like to be right. So we have been addressing that in supervision, which includes the office manager who is a real advocate for this way of working – and that really helps. One day an office staff member brought the conflict up with all of us present. She said they are both very lovely people and actually very similar characters, but what she has noticed is that when they talk to each other they can have a bit of an attitude in their voice, which isn't there normally. They found it uncomfortable talking about this, but we always stay together and deal with such problems caringly until it is sufficiently talked through and eased. It is really important to talk enough to enable them to go home without feeling too bad. Eventually they both were able to admit that they do find the other quite difficult, which was very brave, and it has now eased. However, it does slip back at times of stress (just like with the children). Like today, for example, as the end of the financial year and the end of term approaches and as we are moving towards becoming an academy, which means a lot of extra admin work. When I went into the office they were both shouting at each other – really inappropriate of course! And I found myself saying, *'We need to stop this. I know it's stressful for everyone at the moment, but we need to just stop and talk things through.'*

A minor disagreement had escalated and of course we needed to talk about it. We have found that when emotions are heightened you often need someone else to help you calm things down. This is a bit like mediation of course. Having a neutral third party, who is not involved in the conflict, can really facilitate everyone thinking together. This sort of thinking can be quite impossible without a trusted person who is not involved or judgemental, someone who can really listen to both sides. In this case both the staff ended up having a good cry, which was good. I stayed in touch with them on and off, and put effort into checking that they were both OK during the following weeks. They are getting on much better these days.

Our journey towards becoming a nurturing school

This relationship-based, 'thinking-together' way of working is not easy. In my experience it can only work if everyone is on board, which takes time and effort but is really worth it. It's not enough just to use the recommended phrases as a token just because they are in the policy. That wouldn't work.

What we have found is that if new or reluctant staff can really *experience and see the difference it makes* when they understand a particular child, and they see staff responding differently out of that understanding, it makes all the difference. They might start to notice little positive changes in the child, the easing of anxieties for example, or the lessening of incidents. Then they begin to become convinced and have a go themselves, and that is the beginning. The student teacher in Case Study 43 is an example of this.

Case Study 43 A student teacher's growth: managing resistant/ambivalent behaviour

Learning that threats don't work

We once had a student teacher (S) placed with us. We put her with one of our very skilled and thoughtful Year 1 teachers (R). We are always mindful of which classes we put student teachers with, because we don't want a student teacher to be in a class with a child that is very needy and needs lots of extra support. S started off just doing 20 per cent of the teaching. The class were really settled.

However, just before S joined us a new child (B) joined the class, who turned out to have some problems. We weren't given any background on him, which is not helpful but not uncommon. Anyway after a while the class teacher (R) came to me to say that she thought S was being a bit too punitive with B. So we set up some training for staff around managing needy children, and around the language we use – lots of empathy and 'wondering' – and the expectations. And we explained that we did have some very needy children in the school, and so we had supervision on offer and you could always come and ask for some time to talk about a child if you felt that would be helpful. We always encourage that because we really believe in lots of talking things through. I observed in passing that S was a bit negative about that. I think she felt she was really strong in her behaviour management and she felt her way would work.

This came up again later when I had a meeting with her about her work. I said that it was really good that she felt confident about managing children.

> I expect you've noticed that we have a [certain] way of doing things, and we all work like that because it respects the children and their needs and seeks to understand their issues, but it still keeps firm boundaries. And we will support you to work in this way of working.

A couple of weeks later the teacher, R, said that the student teacher, S, was still quite punitive. I watched once when she was teaching writing. S explained what they had to do but B wasn't going to do it. He just turned away and made noises. We normally give those who need it a border to write in, when a whole page feels overwhelming. I wondered if the task was overwhelming him, or if there was something else getting in the way of his engaging.

When he didn't settle S straight away gave him a 'consequence' – 'If you don't do it you will miss your playtime' – then when he continued to resist she said he would miss playtime and lunchtime! It was all going wrong, so R, the class teacher, decided to intervene. She said to S, 'Why don't I sit with him?' S agreed and he settled and did a little work. Later that day R came to see me to talk things through. She wanted some guidance as to how she should speak to S about what had happened. She wanted to find a way to explain to S about why it doesn't work when you just give a disturbed child consequence after consequence after consequence. We both agreed that that would be a good conversation to have, and wondered how we might approach it differently and why perhaps he was pushing her to keep giving him consequence after consequence. R then spoke to S about this and asked her what she thought his behaviour was communicating.

In our supervision meeting later, S said that she could understand R's point of view but she felt that her way was quicker. She said that if you give strong enough consequences then children will see that they have no choice and so they will do the work quicker.

I guess if you bribe or force children through enough rewards and consequences it can work. It conditions them. They may do the work, but with no real internalisation of the knowledge.

What S was saying was she just wanted them to do their work quickly – then they would learn and achieve more. What she feared was that the way we were asking her to work with the boy would take forever, and still he probably wouldn't do the work, whereas with her way he would get the work done. And I could see from her perspective as a trainee teacher that she might feel she had to show results and get him to learn.

But what I was saying was that they may do the work, but probably with no real internalisation of the knowledge and love of learning, which comes through enjoyment, interest and engaging with challenges, and this is what they need to shift long-term.

This is the reason we want to *understand why* children resist or behave in negative ways. After all it is a very small proportion of children who will refuse to do their work (usually based on something in their experience or their attachment pattern). If we can understand what is prompting their resistance and have conversations with them about it, and then if we can help them feel heard, or make adjustments in how we relate to them, they can begin to grow emotionally as well as become more open to learning.

Whereas in the situation where they are pushing and pushing us to set firm boundaries, and we don't try to understand or develop a thoughtful relationship, it's a bit like putting them in a cage where they have no choice! The problem is if we don't reverse this pattern at a young age and give them an experience of understanding and thoughtful responsiveness, they will get stuck in the vicious cycle of resistance and 'forcing' and more acting out.

What they really need is both understanding and firm boundaries, and a setting within which they can manage because they feel thought about and secure, both within the teacher–pupil relationship and in the classroom. This is like building a secure base rather than just force-feeding the learner. I guess it's like building a foundation for learning. In truth I care less about the child doing the work, than about observing the child growing stronger and more secure, because this leads to them little by little having a go at things *by themselves*, and then they will be able to learn anyway. They will learn that taking little risks brings success and their confidence will rise.

Case Study 43 (continued)

So as I listened I could understand S' point of view, even though I didn't go along with it. But I also felt she needed to know that I understood why she might think that way. So I acknowledged that her approach probably would work with many children, although with the more needy and damaged children like B it was clearly not helping, and in fact it was exacerbating his relationship with her. I said something like,

> You know what, I totally get where you are coming from. As a student teacher your primary task is to teach and get the children to do the work. But as a school our primary task is different. It is emotional growth. Emotional growth and learning.

I guess emotional growth is learning. It's about learning through experience that you can get to a point with your teacher where you feel thought about and understood enough that you have a secure base and then you can feel safe to take a risk and learn. And when you get to that secure base on a regular basis, you know that you can try things and then you can feel good about that and so the vicious cycle begins to turn into a virtuous cycle.

So what happened after that was that she said she would try our approach. We gave her lots of support. We explained how it seemed that he had developed a resistant/ambivalent and very enmeshed attachment pattern with his mum (for very good reasons from both of their points of view) and I explained all about that pattern (see Chapter 6).

I said that in school we could start by giving him a special adult – his teacher, R – who would be very closely available for him when he worked (even safely and gently touching him some of the time, like a mum at home), and she would also give him lots of holding-in-mind comments and gestures so he could slowly come to experience feeling held in mind at a distance and not need to have her sitting beside him all the time. And we would see if that enabled him to become secure enough to begin to work and to learn with increasingly less attention and support. We also placed him part time in our nurture base for more concentrated nurture and holding in mind.

I gave S supervision regularly to talk through and try to understand the children's behaviour in class (especially B's behaviour) and to think how to respond to it. I also had a lot of conversations with B's mum about her very understandable relationship with him, his attachment pattern and his need for lots of holding in mind at home and at school to help him grow more secure. I also put her in touch with the local Women's Aid support services.

The class teacher, R, also modelled holding in mind excellently all of the time. What B needed was lots of holding-in-mind gestures like thumbs up, and her availability and proximity (he sat next to her when it was carpet time). Then S started doing holding in mind with him too, when she was not too busy with the class. Four or five months later when S was teaching over half of the time and we had weaned her off lots of the guidance, you could really see how it was beginning to bear fruit.

One day she was able to say to me that she could 'now see that the TS way works!' She had come to realise that 'thinking about what's happening for the child makes a difference'. She had experienced first-hand that just giving such children punishments didn't work. She could see that B was now able to take a risk. She could see that having R sitting with him had enabled him to work even when he was clearly quite anxious. Then gradually with all the holding-in-mind comments and his part-time nurture group placement, she could see that as we weaned him away from having his special adult available all the time, while continuing to give him encouraging gestures from across the room, for example, he could still take the risk and have a go at the learning tasks.

She could see that managing him in that way gave him the skills and the security to be able to learn for himself. We had given him a secure base – and that is the aim for all of our children and classes.

I have modelled this way of working, wondering and thinking from the beginning, both with children, staff and parents too, and of course I still do. It's just how I work. And gradually it has entered the whole school's way of thinking and relating, both individually and together. Increasingly I see staff using this language and way of thinking with each other, which is of course role modelling for the newer and more sceptical staff at the same time. We do have some weaker staff though for whom this reflective thoughtful approach doesn't come so naturally, and we also have some exceptionally strong staff who are naturally curious and expressive, and when this way of working becomes mainstream in the school they just fly with it!

The importance of a supportive head teacher

I was lucky. I didn't have to get my head teacher on board, because that was why she employed me. This was related to the fact that I had supported the school and the head to set up a nurture base here some two years previously. So her enthusiasm and belief was key. I think the head is the key person. In fact she supported me.

I won't pretend, however, that this journey has been an easy one. In my first term at the school I really wasn't liked very much. I have since talked about this with staff. Some staff found it very difficult to work with me because I was very honest, and I did quite openly talk about 'how that made me feel' and 'how that might have made the child feel'. I openly acknowledged that it might not be easy for them to think about personal aspects, to hear me wonder about my own feelings and their possible feelings too, and the possible effects of my moods, for example, on the children. Becoming aware of what the children 'put into' us and what we might unintentionally communicate to them was not easy, as staff might take such thinking personally and of course we talked about that too. So I understood that they could have had good reasons for becoming a bit defensive. And there have been a few adults who just couldn't cope with this way of working, and they tended not to stay. I guess it was a bit like walking a tight rope, while staying present and connected.

Working through resistance

I would say that for about the first year of working there it was quite a struggle, but as I say the head was very supportive. Sometimes staff could be quite vocal, asking, for example, if I really knew what I was doing when I encouraged them to think about their own feelings in a situation. It wasn't easy. I do understand this. Staff can easily feel that you are like an expert and such conversations might make them feel that they aren't good enough. No one likes to feel not good enough. And of course we would talk about this. We talk about everything.

Having this whole-school approach and way of talking everything through is helpful in so many ways, and over the weeks, months and years we have found staff have become much more open. They now have no apparent problem even including talking about their own issues as well, because they understand how these might impact on the children, and on their teaching and confidence at the same time. Sometimes if they have a problem outside of school they can be really open. Then I think, 'I can't believe they've told me that.' It's because in every way we really believe that the best way forward both with children and with each other and for the school as a whole, is to talk things through, even if it's a bit painful. I guess staff have discovered that we don't judge and we always try to understand and think about how we can support each other. We've built up trusting relationships, which are both valuable and precious. We treat this knowledge (and each other) with respect too. I think it is obvious to everyone now that the relationship-based way of working pays off, and is rewarding too, although that doesn't mean hurtful and worrying things don't happen. We just view them differently and have faith that we can make a difference.

So as I say the journey was not easy. At times I would find myself wondering if we were going to come through. But even in the difficult times I was modelling all of the time the empathic and 'wondering' ways of relating and reflecting, with both children and adults alike. For example, when you become a significant adult for a child, and you consciously use the relationship as a thoughtful restorative healing factor, you often have to bear to be hated. So I was experiencing and demonstrating that I could bear the painful or resistant responses from some staff and not become judgemental, but wonder how we can work through this together and support each other. It was important I think that *I really believed in the approach*. I knew from experience that it worked and made a difference for the children. I had seen it for myself at the pupil referral unit. And I was very supported from both within and from outside the school. The head as I say was fully on board, 100 per cent behind what we were doing. I guess we were both holding each other, and at different times we needed that.

The importance of selecting new staff carefully

From experience we have seen that staff can definitely grow and develop emotionally containing capacities through training and supervision, and through the struggles of experience and trying things out for themselves. But we are also very aware that some adults, and even some highly qualified teachers, just can't open to developing the capacities to work in a reflective empathic way that doesn't collude with the children's inappropriate 'needs'. Maybe their early conditioning or buried hurts just can't allow them to shift from their more rigid behaviourist ways of managing and teaching. Something gets in the way of them adopting the nurturing relationship-based approach we have in our school. So we take selection of staff, especially the selection of TAs who might work closely with the more damaged children, very seriously. Maybe like other schools though we have found that you can't always tell from an interview how a person might be under pressure, even including several visits and trial sessions. So our tendency has been, especially with people we don't know, to offer short-term contracts initially, thus preventing the need to keep staff who sadly turn out not to be suitable.

Incorporating and inducting new staff

When we have a new member of staff join an established team in a class we build up the supervision slowly. We start off with one-to-one supervision. Then, when they feel ready, and in consultation with the established staff, they join the class supervision and then later the year-group supervision too. We don't have year-group supervision very often, but it is important sometimes when children work with more than one set of adults, because we have sets for maths in Year 2, for example. In that case it can be very helpful to get all the staff who work with a particular child together to talk things through and share observations, transference, projections and attachment patterns. We also share the ways we have found helpful to relate to the child in question, or we might discuss the ways we could work with him.[3]

Emotional containment

Emotional containment is important for the children. It's important for them to know we can bear to really hear their pain, or think about the difficult or embarrassing things with them, or wait patiently while they struggle for example.

But it is also very important for staff too – in the sense of containing each other's anxieties enough in school, so that we don't 'take things home'. People vary of course. Some are naturally more sensitive than others, which means they have a lot of empathy, but they also need more containment and supportive listening because they can get hurt more easily. It may be important for leaders to be quite thick-skinned, as well as mature and resilient. One of the worst things is if managers are themselves defensive and act out their needs or blockages in some way. Of course they won't realise it, but I have certainly experienced this in the past, and it is very unhelpful for both the staff and the school.

Bearing fruit: learning from experience

It was interesting because after that first year when things were getting easier and bearing fruit, I actually had some staff come up to me and say, *'For a while I didn't like you much at all. I thought you were a bit mental! But now I realise what you are doing, and I can really see that it's working.'* Now things are a lot better. It's true that some staff still find this way of working difficult because it makes them feel vulnerable, but we just have to accept that and take opportunities to work with it when it feels possible.

Sometimes we share very deep feelings with one another because we know that our stresses can so easily affect the children and our teaching too, and if we feel supported by our colleagues it makes such a difference. It can feel risky of course to be open. It's not easy to hear staff sharing truthfully (but non judgementally) how they felt when you acted in a certain way in a certain situation.

Of course you have to pick this up and acknowledge that we can all be triggered, and as I say we are not in the business of judging, just of trying our best to work together thoughtfully, supportively and optimally for the sake of the children – who are sometimes quite damaged and so easily pick up on vibes. It's about having that non-judgemental supportive environment, where asking for help and talking things through is seen as a strength. It truly is seen as a strength and it highlights the fact that sometimes we all need support from other people.

Tuning in

I guess we have to tune in to each other (and to the parents) in the way that we might to a child, and *sense* when we can bring something up in a helpful way. And as I say some people tend to just leave, and I really understand that. Not everyone is ready or up for this challenge, even though it really works and makes a difference. I also acknowledge that perhaps not all schools can be nurturing, because it requires a certain maturity, or a willingness to open to developing that maturity, among the adults and particularly among the leadership. Maybe it requires a particularly mature, internally strong and convinced leader who can carry the staff and the school through the difficult, risky beginning time, when defences will understandably try to undermine such an innovative and nurturing, but unfamiliar and potentially challenging approach.

Supervision (a confidential space to talk things through and develop understanding) has been talked about a lot in this chapter. I don't think we would be where we are without our regular supervision sessions, because the supervision is where you help embed the staff learning and training – just like my learning came from my own supervision when I was at the pupil referral unit. That's where my learning got embedded.

We find we need to have supervision weekly. A child or a situation can get to you at any time. The thoughtful curious attitude may be there – to wonder and think and reflect with colleagues – but we can still be irritated, frustrated or feel undermined or emotionally triggered at times. We really need the space to think and bounce off each other, and we need the foundation for thinking too, which is the training. The difference, I guess, is that in our school we don't just allow for that, but we actively value and appreciate and even praise staff when they spend time thinking together, or when they ask for help. But also as we gain experience we actually need less supervision. We can talk to *each other*. We know the theory – we understand unconscious processes, for example, and the importance of thinking about the precise attachment needs and tendencies in a child, and we understand the inevitability of regressions in certain children around transitions. And so the insights flow quicker. The fear of what others might think is usually not a factor these days. Staff really value supervision. As much as they have their planning meetings, etc. to do, they will take time to do supervision. I guess they know it bears fruit, and problems naturally ease when we understand and respond thoughtfully. It makes everyone's job easier, and the children become open to learning. They see that.

The importance of a good foundation in attachment, nurture and thinking for all teachers and school staff generally

I think all teachers, including and especially teachers in training, should have an understanding of nurture and the nurture principles, of attachment and attachment categories (see Chapter 6), and of unconscious processes (see Chapter 4). These (like projection and transference, for example) happen all the time in schools whether you understand them or not. It makes such a difference if you understand them.

We have a continuous flow of teachers in training and NQTs (newly qualified teachers) in the school and what is interesting is that after a period with us all of those teachers say, *'I wish I had known this when I was training'*. I think this book will be a great resource for teachers and trainee teachers. And I think it is so helpful including the case examples too, because it makes it come alive and believable. It relates the theory to what is actually happening in schools. Then when we try it out in a supportive setting, it becomes clear how these ways of working and understanding can make a difference.

Theory might sound a bit heavy but it's important. We have five training days a year to include everything – curriculum, policies, etc. – and we try to have one half-day a year when we go through the underlying theory and thinking about nurture and attachment, etc. as a whole staff. Take defences, for example: When we have supervision and an example of defensive behaviour comes up – like projection (see Chapter 4, p. 47) – I find it's helpful to use the terminology. Not in an all-knowing way, but just as a way of communicating. Of course I explain when people don't know a word or a concept, and then later they will use that language too to explain a child's behaviour and to help understand it. Then often people will go away and read about it and they become motivated sometimes to read more. So I think this book could be really useful. I've got books at school too and staff borrow them. Sometimes they will say, 'Oh I read about that', and then they will explain a little. As educators we all want to learn as well and then with understanding and experience we grow more relaxed and confident in our thinking and our practice. We become motivated to develop the resources within ourselves to think and understand and help each other too. It can be very rewarding. What we are doing and facilitating of course is 'learning from experience' – going back to Bion – definitely. I know this from my own experience, because if I had just read a book about nurture, and never actually worked in a nurturing way and seen the difference it can make, I wouldn't be as passionate as I am about it.

Other schools

What I would recommend to any school, or any head who is thinking about creating a nurturing school, is to visit a nurturing school and see for yourself the differences in how staff talk to one another, how staff interact with the children and how they understand the children's communications.

As a school we also have the Flagship Status Inclusion Quality Mark, which talks about nurture and how nurturing we are, so we already have lots of schools visiting us from across the area. The *Centre of Excellence* report is online for everyone to see. This process includes us doing a report for the assessor. In the report we talk about our 'nurture statement', which includes all the nurture principles and how these are included in all of our policies, so interested schools can read these and know that we emphasise nurturing.

Visitors from other schools

Recently I have been showing potential new SENCOs around the school, as our SENCO has unfortunately had to move to London. Of course I am very aware that employing the right person for the job is very important. I know that the interview and the showing around process is an important opportunity for us to get a feel for a person's potential. It was interesting that a lot of the staff when introduced to a prospective SENCO told them, 'This is a fantastic place to work. We're just a big family!' And that's true.

Recently we've had the head and deputy head from a school in a neighbouring borough come to visit, and they wanted to talk about nurture and inclusion. I'm always very honest with interested schools. I explain that it's not something to be taken lightly, and just 'ticked off'. As I said in a conversation with a visiting head last week, *'If you take this on, you're probably going to get a lot of knocks.'*

The head replied, *'That's all right. I'm a head teacher. I'm used to that!'*

> *'And you as a head teacher yourself will need supervision.'*
>
> *'That's all right. We have a school counsellor.'*
>
> *'Well that may be OK. I'm sure your counsellor will be a good listener, but not all counsellors know about psychodynamic thinking. They might know something of attachment, but they might not know all the details that can be so helpful.'*

So the door is open to her and we talked about her coming again whenever she needed to, about staff visiting, observing classrooms and coming to staff meetings. We talked a lot about supervision too. She was very interested in that. What I wouldn't do is I wouldn't ever let anyone come into any of our supervision meetings as they are confidential. I don't even think I would want to *ask* staff, because people trust and share sometimes at quite a vulnerable level, so it wouldn't be fair.

I emphasised to her that it is a continual path that is ongoing. I could, or a psychotherapist could perhaps offer to model a supervision session for at her school, or a series of sessions, but that would take time and have financial implications of course.

Policies and behaviour intervention plans

In our school the last 12 pages of our behaviour policies, and our learning policies too, are appendices including: 'containing ways of relating' (see Boxes 1, 2, 3, and 4, pp. 63–68) 'nurturing "you" statements' (see Box 10, p. 133), 'holding-in-mind statements' (see Box 8, p. 102), 'indicators of ending anxieties' (see Box 20, p. 229) and ways of relating. We have all the 'wondering' and 'empathy' sentence stems in our behaviour policy too (see pp. 163–166).

Our behaviour intervention plans are based around nurturing language and reflecting together on what a child's behaviour might be communicating. The plans usually include suggested ways of relating and working with a particular child. For example with B: If we see that B is starting to get agitated, tapping his foot for example, it can be helpful to distract him. We might say, *'B there's a pencil under the table, could you get it for me please?'* Then when he's down there he may become distracted from his agitated state. Or we might say, *'B, I notice that you are tapping your foot a bit. How are you feeling?'* Then there may be an opportunity to start thinking with him about what was upsetting him. All staff who work with B will know these strategies, which can help him shift out of the moments when he could have escalated. So we use distraction, acknowledgement and then exploration – if they are open to it.

I think senior staff in other schools who want their school to become more nurturing could use the thinking in this book, and these ways of relating, etc. in their policies. Particularly Chapter 8 about a secure base is very helpful for policies. All the information about the key worker is so important and of course the details about attachment, especially the ways of responding to the different categories.

So it is about doing the training, offering supervision, modelling and talking things through without judgement, but as I say it's not just a tick-box exercise. It's about real relationships and real change, which is wonderful to be a part of. It's rewarding for us all and challenging too at times, but as readers will see, support is always available – and that's life enhancing too!

I would like to think that other schools will become nurturing schools. Maybe some are already. The new National Nurturing Schools Award, which we have recently achieved, has also opened up opportunities for more schools to visit us and for us all to learn from each other. Maybe your school would like to work towards it.

The word is out.[4]

Notes

1 K. Lee Raby, Jamie M. Lawler, Rebecca J. Shlafer, Paloma S. Hesemeyer, W. Andrew Collins and L. Alan Sroufe, 'The Interpersonal Antecedents of Supportive Parenting: A Prospective, Longitudinal Study from Infancy to Adulthood', *Developmental Psychology* 51, no. 1 (2015), 115–123.

2 'Statement' here refers to a special assessment and legally binding 'award' for a particular support package, now called an EHCP (Education Health Care Plan).

3 This is a bit like the 'context profiles' described by Barbara Dockar-Drysdale, where all the staff working with a particular child at the Mulberry Bush Residential School would write down their observations during that week and then in supervision they would share them and think together with Barbara as consultant about the child.

Barbara Dockar-Drysdale, 'Provision of Primary Experiences', in *Therapy and Consultation in Child Care* (London: Free Association Books, 1993), ch. 10.

4 In relation to this chapter and to our nurture work in the borough, educational psychologist Dr Tina Axup and I devised a nurturing school questionnaire (see Appendix 1), which we hope to trial locally. The school described in this chapter filled it in and scored very positively in all areas.

Conclusion

The example of a nurture school in the final chapter of this book speaks for itself and validates the thinking, understanding and practical relationship-based approach described in detail in the rest of the book. It works. All children will benefit from a relationship-based approach of course, but it is the more vulnerable and disturbed children who really need it. They need it not just because it works. Behaviourist approaches may work short term, but when vulnerable children find themselves failing again and again, such approaches can sap their fragile self-esteem, lead to secondary self-image problems and more defences – including addictions, antisocial behaviours, mental health complications and even vulnerability to criminal involvements.

These children need a 'second-chance' opportunity to know and benefit from secure attachments and thus to learn and function more appropriately. The most chaotic and trau-matised of them may need the newer sensory and body-based practices (see Chapter 6, notes 8, 9, 10 and Chapter 15, note 3) to enable them to self-regulate enough to be open to a second-chance attachment and relationship. Through reliable caring relationships, which survive their understandable outbursts and sense the intense anxieties under the surface, children will naturally become able to open up to their inner worlds of thoughts, feelings, preferences and interests a little. They will slowly grow into becoming more inner directed and authentic, like their secure classmates, rather than feeling driven to please or rebel. Their 'banter' will morph into conversation. They will become able to think and to learn from experience. Within the secure base of school and trusted relationships they will grow into more openness. Talking things through naturally and courageously as they arise will begin to ease their buried hurts and anxieties a little, as they experience being understood, respected and valued. Then, when they are ready and open for it they may be able to access their own counselling or therapy as it becomes available in more schools and colleges. They may one day have something to give of themselves to the world – or even to vulner-able children and families – who by then they will really empathise with, because they have learnt from experience.

I hope universities and teacher-training institutions will take seriously their responsibility to learn and train teachers and other school staff in this understanding and thoughtful relationship-based practice.

I hope the government will listen too, and cease squeezing and straightjacketing schools so that the wonderful staff who can put these approaches into practice within their normal teaching and working days can remain there and continue to improve the lives of vulnerable children.

Appendix 1

Nurturing school checklist[1]

A. Children's learning and needs are understood developmentally (rather than purely chronologically)	Yes/no

1. Children's/YPs social/emotional needs are assessed and taken into account when setting targets and planning ways of working with them, e.g. in EHCPs. ISPs, PEPs, LAC reviews, etc.[2]
2. The Boxall Profile is used for assessing, formulating interventions and monitoring children where social emotional factors in are severely affecting their access to school life.
3. Staff have training in, and are supported to address children's unmet social emotional needs, this may include the Safe to Learn course and/or similar training.
4. Transitional objects are used when necessary. This is when a child/YP has something belonging to a significant person to help them cope with being away from that person or moving between settings (e.g. home and school) (transitional objects can help the child/YP feel held in mind).
5. The response to the individual child/YP is 'as they are', underpinned by a non-judgmental and accepting attitude.
6. Children/YP who cannot yet manage unstructured spaces/times have a secure supervised option that is preventative not punitive, e.g. at lunchtimes.

B. Attachment patterns and needs are understood and taken into account by staff

1. Staff have training in identifying and understanding attachment patterns and ways of responding to each pattern.
2. Staff have training in, and awareness of, the long-term impact of attachment relationships on mental health and emotional well-being.
3. Working towards social emotional/security is taken at the child's/YP's pace (strategies such as 'holding in mind' are used and understood).

(continued)

(continued)

B. Attachment patterns and needs are understood and taken into account by staff

---

4. Staff understand that when an insecure child/YP becomes stressed or triggered there can be a neurological/sensory response and defence mechanisms are activated and Staff adjust to these appropriately (*The Scared Gang* books are useful in helping to understand these).[3]
5. Secure resilient additional attachment workers are used with very vulnerable children.[4]

C. The classroom offers a safe base

---

1. Staff are consistent and there are predictable reliable routines and organisation.
2. Disorganised children/YP are given extra help with remembering and sorting out information, work and objects.
3. There is frequent use of the word 'SAFE' in relation to supporting and calming children/YP.
4. Designated places to go to calm down/take time out are available both within classrooms and outside.
5. A 'calm box' of 'left-brain' activities (i.e. concrete, repetitive activities such as sorting, matching, jigsaws, etc.) is available in all classes and the playground.
6. Children/YP who need it are given empathic help to calm down. This may involve trained staff using positive handling as a last resort.
7. Staff set appropriate boundaries and expectations with empathy and firmness. When setting boundaries, or communicating expectations – use 'ACO'

   A = Acknowledge the feeling
   C = Communicate the limit or expectation
   O = Offer help or offer alternatives

D. Nurture is important for the development of self-esteem
(attuned significant relationships facilitate nurture)

---

1. Significant adults take seriously their relationships with disturbed children/YP. They are consistent, fulfil their promises and apologise if they get it wrong.
2. Staff have training in attunement and in ways of relating and responding.
3. Staff understand and can think together about transference (the often powerful feelings and urges children can put into significant adults). Staff can support each other in managing this and in using transference to further understand the child.
4. Experiences together are facilitated and supported as children/YP are developmentally ready. Children/YP are only challenged as much as they can bear.
5. Opportunities are given for imaginative activities during the school day and week.

E. Language is understood as a vital means of communication

---

1. Everything is talked through with empathy and thoughtfulness according to the capacity of each child/YP, and at a time and place suited to child/YP and adult.

---

2. Feelings are regularly put into words and acknowledged
3. At an appropriate level, photographic feeling cards are on display in classrooms to enhance children's capacities to talk about feelings in a natural way.
4. Reflective (wondering) conversations are encouraged at appropriate times.
5. Adults take opportunities to rebuild any possible relationship 'breaks' after necessary discipline.
6. Reflective approaches such as conflict resolution, circles of friends, talk time, playground peacemakers, worry boxes, peer mentoring and the no-blame approach to bullying are embedded in school life.
7. Adult-supported peer mentoring and buddy systems are properly set up and monitored – (mature) older children paired with (more vulnerable) younger children).
8. Age-appropriate circle time/sharing – using relevant sentence stems as thoughtful 'starters' are built into school life.
9. Naming, shaming and sarcasm are not used. Staff are conscious of the sensitivities of each pupil and adjust their approach accordingly.

F. Behaviour is understood as (unconscious) communication

1. Repeated behaviours are observed closely and thought about by adults to enable them to respond more thoughtfully. Supervision in the form of individual clinical, peer and/or work discussion groups is evident.
2. Significant adults make tentative links between a behaviour, the child's internal state and any school or transition anxieties or experiences (and home anxieties if they are openly known).
3. Staff are trained in how to understand, reflect upon and manage their own emotional processes and vulnerabilities.
4. Staff are trained in basic emotional containment. This is where they are able to remain the containing adult within the situation, rather than resorting to a reactive response. In situations where staff find this difficult, support is given to help them reflect and understand their own emotional processes.
5. Staff understand children/YP who can't (yet) use praise, encouragement, challenge and constructive criticism, and who need emotional containing practices to enable them to function well.
6. Staff understand their responsibility to help a vulnerable deregulated child calm down, this includes understanding sensory regulation. Ideas from *The Scared Gang* books (see p. 117) are useful for younger children.
7. Strategies for emergencies are agreed for particularly vulnerable and potentially disruptive children/YP.

G. Transitions are significant in the lives of children/YP

1. Staff are trained in understanding how (upcoming) transitions destabilise insecure children/YP, including observable indicators that a (little or big) transition is on a child's/YP's mind, and how to put that into words with empathy and appropriate support for the transition
2. Strategies for transitions for vulnerable children/YP are agreed between significant staff and where appropriate parents/carers.

(continued)

(continued)

G. Transitions are significant in the lives of children/YP

---

3. Changes and transitions are communicated to staff and children in plenty of time.
4. Staff who work closely with vulnerable children are respected as being best placed to know if a particular child/YP or class is able to cope with a particular new experience or change.
5. Age-appropriate calendars showing significant events and timetables are on display in classrooms.

H. Staff needs, team and whole-school communication is taken seriously

---

1. Clinical supervision is available for particular staff working with challenging children/YP.
2. There is good communication and respect for everyone within the school.
3. Significant information is shared with all who work closely with vulnerable pupils (while maintaining confidentiality), this includes regular and as necessary 'thinking time' for adults around the child
4. The well-being of staff is taken seriously – including team building and nurture for staff.
5. Significant staff (e.g. pastoral team, managers and front-line staff) working with vulnerable children complete the Safe to Learn training. The local Nurture Network Group is open to all.
6. Staff are able to recognise when children evoke powerful negative responses in the adult (intense dislike, etc.), and have the confidence to express this openly to colleagues/be secure that colleagues will not think badly of them, etc.

I. Other

---

1. A nurture ethos is evident in the school literature.
2. Nurture principles are displayed in every classroom.
3. The school is welcoming to young people, parents/carers and other visitors.
4. Every day is a fresh start.
5. Instead of excluding young people, their needs and difficulties are thought and talked about with all significant adults, in terms of how and in some cases where they can be met.

Notes

1 This questionnaire was compiled with the help of educational psychologist Dr Tina Axup in 2014.
2 YP (young person), EHCP (educational, health and care plan), ISP (individualised service plan), PEP (person education plan), LAC (looked-after child).
3 Éadaoin Bhreathnach, *The Scared Gang Series* [Box Set of nine books] (Belfast: Alder Tree Press, 2011).
4 See Louise M. Bombèr, *Inside I'm Hurting* (London: Worth, 2007); and Louise M. Bombèr and A. Daniel Hughes, *Settling Troubled Pupils to Learn: Why Relationships Matter in School* (London: Worth, 2013).

Appendix 2

Self-assessment of skills in emotional holding, containing and strengthening[1]

(Circle: H = high, M = medium, L = low)

1. To contain and know your own tendencies and vulnerabilities so they don't become acted out on the children.   H M L
2. To be aware of your *own* present-moment internal experience (what you are feeling or thinking *now*).   H M L
3. To concentrate on the present experience with the child, and suspend your own preoccupations and concerns.   H M L
4. To be able to contain and suspend any current anxiety you have and not project it out.   H M L
5. To get alongside the child non-intrusively.   H M L
6. To be able to remain silent and attentive.   H M L
7. To be able to be non-judgemental.   H M L
8. To stay with where the child's 'at', and resist the urge to encourage, or advise – to make *yourself* feel better.   H M L
9. To bear a child's pain and stuckness, and resist premature reassurance and solutions.   H M L
10. To bear to be 'hated' – and not take it personally.   H M L
11. To be patient and empathic as the child struggles, without offering help, unless requested.   H M L
12. To have a space within oneself to wonder about the child and the meaning of his behaviours.   H M L
13. To listen and reflect back on the child's feelings.   H M L
14. To be able to contain extremes of behaviour without retaliation, while setting appropriate boundaries.   H M L
15. To be able to set boundaries in a non-threatening way.   H M L
16. To be able to be non-directive as well as directive.   H M L
17. To be able to take opportunities to address difficult issues empathically.   H M L
18. To demonstrate awareness of the child's inner world.   H M L

19. To help the child make connections between experiences.   H M L
20. To frequently communicate 'rememberings' of the child's interests,
    stories and images.   H M L
21. To communicate your 'holding in mind' of the child around separations
    and transitions.   H M L
22. To facilitate the child's capacity to play.   H M L
23. To be able to respect confidentiality.   H M L
24. To know your own limitations.   H M L
25. To be able to ask for help.   H M L
26. To appreciate and respect colleagues' feelings, concerns and anxieties,
    even if they are different from yours.   H M L

Consider and prioritise those skills you would like to work on personally in order to develop your own containing capacities in order to develop your own containing capacities. You may want to tick three points above to work on.

Note

1 Based on an idea from Paul Greenhalgh, *Emotional Growth and Learning* (London: Routledge, 1994).

Appendix 3

Possible unconscious meanings and causes of common behaviours

Behaviour	Possible meaning	Possible causes
No tolerance of frustration Easily gives up	Frustration is unbearable and must therefore be eliminated	Because their parents could not bear to watch them struggle and bear frustration they solved their children's problems for them, so the children haven't learned to bear frustration This could be because the parents have not had enough experience of their needs and struggles being supported
Can't try something new Hard to have a go at difficult things	Fear of failure Fear of getting stuck Fear of neediness or vulnerability	Failure is unbearable because they have been hurt by too much criticism Neediness, struggle, failure and vulnerability have been ignored or ridiculed
Tends to avoid tasks Reluctant to engage with tasks Difficulty with attending to and getting started with all tasks	The fear of the loss of supportive, containing attention and the secure base is unbearable. This requires them to keep the significant adult constantly engaged in any way they can If they turn away from the adult to look at the task they may be forgotten	They can't risk focusing on the task because they have to (continue to) engage the significant adult *now* – otherwise they might be forgotten or 'fall out of her mind' (a feature of the resistant/ ambivalent attachment pattern)

(continued)

(continued)

Behaviour	Possible meaning	Possible causes
Always finding fault or criticising others	As a way of making *others* the ones who are wrong or bad – not them To ease their own feelings of not being good enough	Could relate to too much hurtful criticism and ridicule in the past
Difficulty separating (from mum?) and difficulty with separations generally	They have to stay engaged with mum/significant adult as this is the only way they know to make sure they are still thought about Mum needs them or seems to need them	Because their mum/parent has been variably and not reliably available (see resistant/ambivalent attachment pattern, pp. 97–105) Or because depressed/vulnerable/sick mum communicates neediness
Difficulty with all beginnings	Beginnings may evoke (unbearable) separation from mum, or other significant adult (see above) Beginnings may evoke trauma triggers	Unconsciously repeated anxiety related to difficult/traumatic beginnings, e.g. birth/early life/health difficulties and/or resistant/ambivalent attachment anxieties (see above)
Adverse reaction to particular subjects topics, words, tone of voice, facial expressions, etc.	Fear of particular (threatened) meaning Fear that they are going to be 'hurt'	Their primary need is to stay 'safe', because they have been hurt too much and too easily in the past Conditioned anxious need to not think about particular traumatic thoughts, feelings or situations – which threaten to be triggered They have not had the necessary, attuned responsiveness to be able to process their trauma – so it can be easily triggered
No capacity or inhibited capacity to think	Their chaotic inner world means all thinking is muddled – especially when they are stressed They can't think. They can only react	Too much scary chaos in both their inner and outer worlds that has to be avoided, plus not having been thought about has meant they have not developed the capacity to think themselves It is safer to keep things muddled
Acting out in various ways in response to anxiety, e.g. they have an outburst, run or turn away, curl up, switch off/dissociate or cry	Difficulty with bearing anxiety Anxiety observed in others is also unbearable	They haven't had enough emotional containment and thoughtful attuned responsiveness from their attachment figures to be able to internalise the capacity to bear, think about and process anxiety for themselves – so feelings that can't be contained and thought about just *erupt* out They have been traumatised/abused with no support

Difficulty taking food from mother or significant adult	Food has become linked with (not) having their needs met, or being 'force fed' feelings (or foods) that are unbearable – so they have developed the need to feed themselves or to resist (particular?) food(s)	No experience of attuned caregiver who will give them what they need so they have learnt to *resist food* from mum (or significant adults in transference) because mum's wants are associated with ambivalence. *Or* they have needed to rely on 'looking after themselves They can therefore only sneak or take food for themselves
Inability to take in information from significant adult Difficulty with remembering and holding in mind instructions and information	'Taking in' anything (including information and instructions) too easily evokes not having their needs met, which is unbearable Everything gets in a muddle and can't be retrieved Closed or preoccupied mind to stay safe	Because information from adults is metaphorically experienced as the nurture that they didn't get – which needs to be avoided No (or not enough) experience of being held in mind/kept safe by attachment figures
Inability to contain information and things they need to do	Limited capacity to make links with previous knowledge No clear space to keep memories/information	Because their inner world is so chaotic and disorganised Multiple trauma and losses Chaotic/disorganised attachment experiences
Constantly losing/ forgetting things	Losing and forgetting is acting out their uncontained muddled inner world	Their inner chaos leaves no space inside to put or keep anything – they haven't internalised a capacity to 'hold things in mind' themselves
Omnipotence – I can do everything	Managing everything themselves is the only way to feel OK	Not being able to manage and feeling helpless is unbearable, because helplessness has not been supported or has been ridiculed in the past
Omniscience – I know everything already	Knowing everything already is the only way to feel OK and avoid unbearable vulnerability	The experience of not knowing something and needing help is risky and unbearable – as it may be ignored, or ridiculed (again)
Switching off/ freezing/ withdrawing engagement	Unconscious fear of being overwhelmed by what might come up	Could be defensive freezing to avoid criticism Freeze is a primitive defence in young children who can't 'fight'
Dissociation – extreme form of withdrawal – 'out of reach'	Could be an automatic extreme reaction to unbearable fear (repeated dissociation in older children is pathological) Could be petit mal – may need to check with GP	Relates to extreme unprocessed (maybe ongoing) early trauma

(continued)

(continued)

Behaviour	Possible meaning	Possible causes
Difficulty with change Difficulty with new people	Change brings insecurity People have been critical/hurtful/rejecting in the past Avoidant difficulty with all people	New places or new people have been scary, unhelpful or neglectful in the past Trauma Unexpected and painful changes
Clingy behaviour Persistent attention-seeking behaviour Interruptions	Only OK with a present, personal, secure base *now* They can't feel held in mind by their trusted attachment figure when they are not here and listening to them *now*	Unreliable, anxious and ambivalent attention from parent figures
Peer conflicts	Projecting difficulties on to peers so *they* don't have to feel their own 'uselessness/badness'	May relate to sibling rivalry, jealousy Taking things out on siblings may feel safer than getting angry with parent, for example
Stealing	Taking what he needs now may be the only way a child can feel his needs will be met	Taking things may be a 'symbolic' or 'concrete' replacement for an unconscious need for love Stealing can also become addictive because of secondary gains (enjoying what you have taken, peer kudos)
Hiding (doesn't include *normal* hide and seek games, which are about attachment and fun and very age-appropriate with younger children)	Could relate to a need to be found and wanted Or to not wanting to be seen because of shame, acute shyness Or a defensive measure to avoid being rejected or hurt	Parent(s) too preoccupied to notice them Avoidant attachment pattern involves not wanting to be noticed, for fear of being noticed and rejected, and thus only being comfortable with *not* being seen
Picking on/telling tales of other children (not including the need to tell of something hurtful or bullying, which is appropriate)	Finding fault with others makes them feel better – when underneath they feel bad (projection)	They may have been repeatedly criticised and their consequent bad self-image feels better when someone else is at fault not them
Difficulty asking for and accepting help	Only comfortable with being self-sufficient Learned need to be self-sufficient Asking for help brings up shame	Avoidant need to *not* engage or speak to others for fear of unavailability, rejection or being ignored Too much experience of criticism and humiliation No experience of significant adult being helpful

Screaming	Expression of unbearable frustration or hurt – Learned need to shout to be heard	There could have been lots of screaming and shouting at home. They could have learnt that the only way they can get their needs met is to shout or to manipulate adults through shouting, screaming, whining, etc. Repeated screaming may be related to repeated triggered fear of being ignored/blamed/ shouted at, again
They *have* to be the 'rescuer' and make things OK (Having to) rescue/ help struggling children in class or playground	Seeing others struggle without support is unbearable They have to calm or 'sort out' others' conflicts and stop others' anxiety – which they find unbearable to watch	Could be related to history of unsupported abuse, or observed abuse or domestic abuse, which they have coped with by becoming the rescuer in safer (school) situations
Picking on and attacking vulnerable/ younger children or girls	Inner vulnerability is feared and has to be annihilated immediately	Could be related to history of abuse, or scary observed abuse and the triggered unbearableness of observed vulnerability
Running away (not including a normal fun game of 'chase')	Wanting to be chased and found Or fear of being found and then told off and punished A way of escaping unbearable situations, anxiety or humiliation	Relating to not being held in mind enough – could be a way to keep an adult thinking of them – leading to an (unmet) need to be found again and again (Repeated?) frightening experiences at home/in the past
Bulimia	Unconscious acting out of neediness – followed by guilt Unbearableness of emptiness Full tummy means no space for thinking – followed by guilt	Comfort eating followed by guilt – self-punishment Influence of cultural slim figure Self-punishment is necessary because of conditioned guilt/ need for reparation
Anorexia	Self-punishment Habit or secondary addictive behaviour	Could be caused by severe unprocessed or early loss May be related to sexual abuse Influence of cultural body image
Biting	Primitive acting out of anger/ aggression/hatred Unbearableness of hurt projected on to others Triggered early years *fight* reaction	Expressing ambivalence or 'hatred' towards attachment figures because of their variable and unreliable emotional availability
Over-eating	Only way to feel comfortable is to eat, to feel full Pleasure of eating – comfort eating and always needing more	Unconscious replacement for negative self-esteem Displacement of need for love – because they don't feel loved

(continued)

(continued)

Behaviour	Possible meaning	Possible causes
Hoarding	May relate to the item being hoarded – the only way to get it A need to have lots of *things* to feel good – but its never enough Security blanket – things bring comfort	Attachment to objects rather than people has developed because of sparsity of relationships
Self-harm	Self-punishment because of guilt or shame Letting out the pain – physicalised release of tension or guilt – self-soothing	Because no one has comforted their pain Could link to sexual or other types of abuse Taking out anger, victimhood or hurt on themselves Internet/subculture
Trashing things when adults come too close	Avoidant response to unbearable closeness	They have learned to avoid closeness because of family pattern, or of closeness being associated with hurt Taking out anxiety on things rather than people – who they don't want to engage with because they may be rejected again
Trashing things, after praise	Praise is unbearable because it inadvertently triggers the opposite – its not good, its rubbish, I'm not good	Frequent humiliation has led to very low self-esteem, which is easily triggered
Lying	Fear of being found out and punished Dissociation – the experience is not in declarative memory Need to impress to feel good enough May relate to the specific content of the 'lie' – because the truth is unbearable	Could relate to unprocessed trauma Internalised critical parent forces the lie Automatic resistance to authority figures

Appendix 4

Possible unconscious meanings of learning difficulties and behaviours and what they might be communicating

Observed difficulty	Possible unconscious communication
Difficulty with remembering to bring required things/ materials/equipment	No capacity to hold things in mind/take in what they are told
	Relates to a child's and their family's chaotic/ disorganised inner world, in addition to lack of support from caregivers
Reluctant to engage with learning	Can't think – thinking is scary
	Fear of shame of getting it wrong
	Inertia relating to getting started – or with beginnings'
	Fear of needing help – 'switching off' is a defence against this
	Fear of losing the significant adults' direct attention when they look at the task
Difficulty finishing tasks	Way of not experiencing the ending
	Difficult experience/lack of support with endings in the past
	Way of prolonging attention. Need to 'cling' on to attention
	Not enough thoughtful attuned attention in the past
Frequently trashes work	Difficulty believing they can do something good
	Frustration with a mistake, or something they don't think is good enough, becomes unbearable and thus acted out
	Repeated history of good things turning bad and being criticised for being stupid, leading to very negative self-esteem/internalisation of critical parent
	Becoming aware that they are doing something good could also become unbearable, for fear that it may go wrong – better to trash it on purpose than bear the pain of making a mistake *again*

(continued)

(continued)

Observed difficulty	Possible unconscious communication
Frequently losing things	No internalised capacity to hold things in mind
	Can relate to not feeling held in mind enough themselves
	Muddled inner world
	Can't think
	Can't remember
Easily frustrated – no tolerance	Frustration is unbearable
Easily gives up when things go wrong	Can't ask for help
	Humiliation of mistakes is unbearable
	Not enough experience of their needs and struggles being supported
	Very low self-esteem easily triggered
Difficulty with/resistance to beginnings	Resistant/ambivalent anxieties
Inertia relating to getting started	Beginnings may evoke (unbearable) separation from mum, or with their teacher/TA in the transference
	Unconsciously repeated anxiety related to difficult/ traumatic beginnings, e.g. birth, early life or health difficulties
Difficulty being a learner/being taught	Can't bear not to be in control and not to know
	Need to be omniscient – can't bear being in the vulnerable, dependent position of not knowing
	Vulnerability has led to being hurt
	Vulnerability has been ridiculed or not supported
Can only do simple unaided tasks	Only way to feel OK is to manage simple tasks alone
	Too much experience of critical adults or adults who humiliate
	Avoidant behaviour because asking for help is impossible
Difficulty with asking for help	Having help makes them feel useless
Difficulty accepting help	No experience of significant adult being helpful
Only comfortable with being self-sufficient	Could be related to avoidant attachment pattern – making the closeness of asking for and receiving help unbearable
	Learned need to be self-sufficient to avoid the pain of being ignored, humiliated or attacked
Extra large full stops	Wanting an end to something
No capital letters for their own name	I am not important
Handwriting very small	Very low self-esteem
All letters in capitals	Expression of anger/shouting/fear
No gaps between words	Difficulty separating (from mum?)
	Difficulty with separations generally
	Enmeshed relationship with mum – because she needs it?
Muddled reading, which doesn't make sense	Fear of particular (threatened) meaning
Child not bothered or reacting to the lack of meaning	Chaotic inner world – means everything becomes chaotic at stressful times – chaotic/disorganised attachment pattern
	Resistance to meaning/need to destroy meaning
	No capacity/inhibited capacity to think
	Fear of terrifying thoughts that might come up – linked to trauma

Particular miscues	An unconscious anxiety may be being communicated ('Freudian slip')
Not keeping writing 'on the lines'	Difficulties with security or with feeling a secure base
Very muddled, messy handwriting	Chaos getting into handwriting or into coordination Chaotic/disorganised attachment pattern
Can't build up words – join letter sounds together meaningfully	Can't (or is resistant to) bring(ing) things together Relating to conflicted/broken relationships at home
Not remembering what has been read	Inability to contain information Relating to lack of adequate emotional containment No space inside to put information Inability to take things in, or to take things in from significant adult Not enough holding in mind at home
Difficulty with writing/reluctant to write	Spelling anxieties Dyslexic writing and spelling difficulties brings up fear of shame Fear of failure, fear of getting stuck Unconscious fear of being overwhelmed by what might come up in the writing Can't think – because any thinking is potentially scary Could be related to trauma in the past
Can't remember or gets in a muddle with time issues, e.g. telling the time, before/after, days/months, etc.	Can't think straight Reluctant to think Could relate to chaotic/disorganised, scary inner and outer worlds
Difficulty ordering, sequencing, etc.	One thing after another is overwhelming Anxiety about what might happen next (see above)
Difficulty with some aspects of history	Reluctant to 'come up close' to anything relating to the past (unconscious) fear of bringing up their own traumatic past
Difficulty with adding up	Muddling is more comfortable than adding on more Ambivalence/pain relating to uncomfortable family additions (e.g. new step-siblings/step-parent) may unconsciously inhibit addition
Difficulty taking away/subtraction	Muddling is more comfortable than taking away Experiences of loss/bereavement/separation anxieties may unconsciously inhibit taking away activities
Difficulty with multiplying	May unconsciously evoke fear of being overwhelmed
Difficulty with division	May unconsciously evoke fears of things being broken/split into bits, relating to painful 'splits' in their lives
Difficulty with geometry	Uncomfortable unconscious anxieties in relation to how things/people relate/join to each other or things/people having insides and outsides/edges, etc.

(continued)

(continued)

Observed difficulty	Possible unconscious communication
Difficulty with any work relating to self-image or with work relating to family members	Negative self-image easily triggered Child may have inner conflict/guilt in relation to self-image Shame/trauma/unbearable sadness, loss or hurt in relation to family members
Difficulty with place/aspects of geography	How places relate to each other in space, and relations of objects in space, are difficult to hold in mind. Chaotic inner and outer world means inner disorganisation prevents outer thinking about organisation and connection Muddle with question of, 'Where am I?'

Appendix 5

Safe to Learn

An eight-session PowerPoint training course

In 2013, two colleagues and I devised and ran a twilight course for teachers and school staff called Safe to Learn, which focused upon the value of attachment theory, psychodynamic thinking and the practice of nurture in their work.

The first component was a theoretical base, outlining some of the theories underpinning nurture: particularly Bowlby's attachment theory; emotional containment, drawing on the thinking of Bion and Winnicott; unconscious processes, including Freud's defence mechanisms; Dockar-Drysdale's integration; and appreciating transference and counter-transference as a tool for understanding, rather than a trigger for reactivity. We also included a session on neuroscience and the effects of trauma on the brain and on the inner world.

The second component introduced the nurture principles: children's learning needs can be understood developmentally, the classroom offers a safe base, nurture is important for the development of self-esteem, language is understood as a vital means of communication, all behaviour is communication and transitions are significant in the lives of children.

Then the third component linked the above with more practical strategies and ways of working with, relating to and nurturing children towards more secure ways of being and learning. We thought again about attachment, differentiating the three insecure categories and their features and causes, leading on to many (differentiated) suggestions for working with children in the different categories. We also emphasised using significant relationships in school as second-chance attachment experiences for the more damaged and deprived children. We addressed the effects of trauma on learning and behaviour, including how to alleviate and manage such relationships and triggered outbursts.

We looked at early developmental stages including how to fill in children's developmental gaps and safe ways to rework early unmet needs, introducing nurture groups, attachment-based play, the value and therapeutic use of play and the creative arts and stories in the school setting. We also looked at practical ways to contain children's powerful communications and projections, and calming and containing ways of *being* with children.

Throughout the course we addressed the links between inner and outer worlds – both within ourselves and within the students, within adult–child relationships in the classroom in a one-to-one setting and within the dynamics of the whole school. Towards the end of the course, having thought about the crucial importance of understanding and relationships for healing, nurturing, secure and restorative experiences and to facilitate openness to learning, we asked the participants to come up with their thoughts on what a secure nurturing school would look like.

The final strand of the course was for each participant to compile a 'pupil profile' on a pupil who puzzled or challenged them. Through observation of the pupil's behavioural communications, through reflecting on their own and other people's typical reactions to the pupil and the feelings the pupil evokes, they then came up with some helpful ways of relating to, understanding and nurturing them, in the light of the course material.

Sadly the course is no longer funded although it was very well received, but the local educational psychology service is continuing to deliver it on request. It is currently included in a local 'Healthy Schools' initiative.

A version of the Safe to Learn course is available via the eResources to the book at www.routledge.com/9780367025441.

Index

feelings 6, **149**, 189, 300; awareness of 11, 190; and the brain 10–11; in infancy 20; support with 27, 59; talking through 60, 75; unbearable 22, 32, 35; *see also* acting out; anger; defences; emotional containment; transference; wondering

fight/flight/freeze 9, 23, 29, 125

foetal experience 4, 9; and birth 222; and cortisol 15

frustration 34, 58, 63, 112, 167, 191, *235*

Geddes, H. 58

good enough 20, 229; mother 20, 130, 222, 249; in school 129–30, 190–91

growing stronger **142**, 208, 214, *215*, 317

guilt 25–27, 30; easing 116, 138, *235*; and shame 24, 27; transferred into staff 47; *see also* mediation; relationship breaks

hatred 33, 60, 91; bearing 147, 292, 309; *see also* closeness

help 5, 10, 11, 15, 27, 98; asking for 60, 65 27, 93; can't help it 16, 25; and girls 30, 35; helpful 56, 60, 103; helplessness 34, 36, *37*, 45; responding helpfully 38–41, 94; staff asking for 60, 244, 311; and transference 32, 50, 51, 53; *see also* avoidant attachment

holding in mind 101, *102*, 104, 136, 148, **149**, **188**, 313

hope 228; paradoxical signs of 91, 153, 157; underneath 231

humiliation 24, 25, 59, 111, 205, 214; fear of 27; and learning 117, 173; *see also* chaotic/disorganised attachment

hyperactivity 24, 48, 107

identification 33; with aggressor 37; with perpetrator 33, *35*, 37, 45, 230; as rescuer 23, 30, 149; swing between roles 24; as victim 23, 28, 33, 37, 46

inner growth 76, 112, *217*; acknowledging 214 *215*; moving them gently on 197, *198*; *see also* communication; growing stronger; inner directedness

inner directedness 213 *see also* inner growth

integration 138, 201; disintegration 248; *see also* unintegrated

internal working model 4, 53; hierarchy of 27

insecure attachment 90, 174, 299; *see also* avoidant attachment; chaotic/disorganised attachment; resistant/ambivalent attachment; second-chance attachment

joy 5–6, 9, 14, 58, 123, 124, 250, 275

key/attachment worker 148, 191, 197, 253; and behaviour 131; and learning 154, 175; and play 126; qualities of 147; and repair 130; role 138–43; selecting 147, 309–10; support for 139, 155, 302, **303**; and thoughtfulness **62**, **100**, 154; *see also* communication; curiosity; empathy; language

language 6; and the brain 11; dialogue 187; difficulties with 91, 100, 106, 108; **303**; and learning 261; listening skills 188–89; with staff **305**, 308, 312; story 262; swearing 168–69, 204; talking things through 188–92, 300; tentative 158, 195, 227; and thoughtfulness **62**, **100**, 154; and trauma 22; wondering 14, **51**, **60**, 148, 166; *see also* body language; communication; curiosity; empathy; nurture

leaking out **22**, *32*, *48*

learning 5, 11, 185; behaviours 173, 329–32; and the brain 11–12, 15, 16; and domestic abuse 34–5; early years 15; and emotional containment 58; from experience 20; and family changes **176**, **179**; inhibitions 6, 38, 45, 47, 49, 173–82; meanings of 173–76; and transference 68; ways of responding 176–81; writing *26 43, 44,* 268–69; *see also* avoidant suggestions; chaotic/disorganised suggestions; educational psychotherapy; resistant/ambivalent suggestions; secure base; stories

links between inner and outer worlds 180; anxieties around 48; and containment 58; and domestic abuse 29–31; help with 118; through play 96; and learning 34–35; and trauma 59, 108; transference effects 60; *see also* chaotic/disorganised tendencies; defences

localised provision 122, 125, 139; *see also* regression

looked-after children 26–28, adoptive/foster parents of 293–96; and attachment hierarchies 27; chaotic/disorganised 106; difficulty with excitement 114, 125; and home/school splits **46**; need for bonding 125, 152; and regression 122; and traumatic transitions 49, **106**, **152**, 301

looking after ourselves 273–81; *see also* mindfulness; self awareness

loss of significant adults 232, 233

mediation 211–12, 304

metaphor 25, 6, 7, 96, 118, 131, 238, 247–70; and absence 153; communication 180–81; in therapy *36, 37, 38,* 77–81, 178–81; *see also* play; stories; writing

mindfulness **17**, 54; creative relaxation 281–83; introductory course 275–81; mindfulness with children 284–85; other ways to practice 280

mother 157, 222; and attachment 4; avoidant mothers 90, 223; and baby 4–6; and baby in class 185–86; containing function of 58; chaotic/disorganised mothers 106; language 6, 14; mental health 97, 106; prenatal 4, 9, 14; primary maternal preoccupation 13; resistant/ambivalent mothers 97, 224; reverie 58, 60; supporting **289–92**, **292–93**; *see also* attachment-based play; attunement; good enough; parents; secure attachment